MY BEST GAMES OF CHESS
1924-1937

MY BEST GAMES
OF CHESS
1924-1937

BY

ALEXANDER ALEKHINE
late Chess Champion of the World

DAVID McKAY COMPANY, INC.

NEW YORK

First Published 1939
Reprinted 1943, 1945
Reprinted with Memoir, 1947
Reprinted 1949, 1955, 1960, 1962

First American Edition 1965
Published by arrangement with
G. Bell & Sons, Ltd., London

5 6 7 8 9 10

ISBN: 0-679-14024-7
Manufactured in the United States of America

CONTENTS

PART I (1924-1927)

TOURNAMENT GAMES
AND MATCH WITH CAPABLANCA

PART II (1929-1934)

TOURNAMENT GAMES
AND MATCHES WITH BOGOLJUBOW

PART III (1934-1937)

TOURNAMENT GAMES
AND MATCHES WITH DR. EUWE

PART IV (1924-1933)

SIMULTANEOUS AND BLINDFOLD PLAY
EXHIBITION AND CONSULTATION GAMES

MEMOIR OF ALEKHINE
By J. DU MONT

IN RECORDING the life of Alexander Alekhine, the annalist has the difficult task of remaining objective, of avoiding being carried away by his genius, by the glory of his achievements, or being led astray by a feeling of commiseration for the tragedy of his life.

Born of a wealthy and notable family in Czarist Russia, he enjoyed as a child and a youth all the advantages which this implies. He made use of his opportunities and made good progress in his early studies of the law. In his spare time he developed his marked talent for chess and was a recognised master at the age of 16.

Until the first world war broke out there was no cloud in his sky. He was then, at the age of 22, playing in and winning an important tournament at Mannheim. Then the storm burst and, together with other foreign masters, he was interned by the Germans. He managed to escape to Switzerland and returned home, via Siberia, to join the Russian Army. He was twice wounded and twice decorated. Then the second blow fell ! The Russian Revolution broke out and, as a member of the aristocracy, he had little hope of coming out unscathed. In fact, he and his family lost their all and he was lucky to escape with his life. It is said that chess saved him from the worst. Be that as it may, he had, for the next few years, to teach chess in schools and universities.

In 1921 he was allowed to take part in a tournament in Triberg, but he did not return to Russia and made his way to Paris. Here, starting life anew, he became a chess professional and began his long list of triumphs by taking part in all important tournaments, his great ambition being to establish his fame so securely that a match with Capablanca would have to follow.

In spite of the very exacting nature of these exertions, he managed, in his stride as it were, to renew his legal studies and to become a Doctor-at-Law of the French Faculty, a tribute indeed to his energy and his immense capacity for work.

By 1927 he had so established his superiority over all other contenders that his claim to be the rightful challenger for the world title could no longer be denied. How he won that match in 1927 is a matter of history. Thus he had built up for himself, by his own exertions, a new era of prosperity. In the years following upon his accession to the chess throne he conscientiously carried on his work, taking part in almost all masters' tournaments, and in these he even improved on all his previous achievements. He developed incidentally his gift for blindfold play, continually increasing the number of opponents he took on simultaneously until he reached the staggering number of thirty-two. In point of numbers this has been exceeded since ; in point of strength of the opposition and quality of the play it has never been equalled.

There is little doubt that these exhibitions undermine the stamina of the protagonists and cannot be good. In Russia, to-day the chess country *par excellence*, blindfold exhibitions are forbidden by law. These tremendous exertions left their mark on a highly sensitive temperament already shaken by the vicissitudes he had to fight against in early life, and periodically Dr. Alekhine gave way to drink, a circumstance not unprecedented in the life of many a genius.

Thus he was hardly at his best when he met Dr. Euwe for the Championship in 1935. Dr. Euwe, playing magnificent chess, won by a small margin. With a readiness unheard of in championship chess Dr. Euwe immediately agreed to a return match. This took place two years later. In the meantime Dr. Alekhine had had the strength of mind to give up entirely both drinking and smoking and he relentlessly carried out his determination to make himself fit. He won the match in decisive fashion and thus we had the unique spectacle of a Champion magnanimously granting his defeated opponent a return match almost at once and of the ex-Champion regaining his throne.

Nevertheless, there had been some falling off in Dr. Alekhine's powers, and several masters of the younger generation had legitimate claims to a match for the Championship. This aroused the Champion's natural combativeness and he accepted in 1939 the challenge of undoubtedly the strongest of the younger contenders, M. Botvinnik. This would probably have been the finest match ever played, for it is certain that Dr. Alekhine would not have come unprepared or unfit.

All the preliminaries had been arranged and settled, and the match was to be played in Russia, when the second World War broke out. Dr. Alekhine was at the time in Buenos Aires taking part in the international team match, where he captained the French players. He refused to allow his team to play the German team and returned to France by the first available boat to join the French Army. After the collapse of France he intended going to America for a return match with Capablanca ; he went as far as Lisbon. Here he waited in vain for the permit that was to enable him to leave Europe. Whether the reason was that permits were impossible to get immediately after "Pearl Harbour" or that Capablanca, after working hard for a return match, had lost interest, is difficult to say.

It was about that time that news reached Dr. Alekhine that his wife was in France in the hands of the Germans. He tried to get permission to join her. The German authorities, realising the

Champion's propaganda value, gave this permission on condition that he wrote two articles on Chess for the German *Pariser Zeitung*. It is a fact that he was able to return to France and that two articles appeared in the German-controlled press over his name.

These articles were received by all sections of the chess world with the greatest indignation. They were in fact a violent anti-Jewish and pro-Nazi diatribe. They were at the same time so utterly senseless that no unprejudiced person could believe in Dr. Alekhine's authorship. When years later he saw these articles he declared most solemnly that not a single word was from his pen.

In the meantime he and his wife were directed to take up residence in Prague from where, for the next two years, he attended various tournaments at Vienna, Munich and Salzburg, etc. His detractors claim that he was a willing tool in the hands of the Germans and had a prosperous time in their territory. This does not tally with the description given by the Portuguese Champion, Francisco Lupi, when he first met Dr. Alekhine after his return to Spain. Instead of the fine physical specimen of a man, such as he expected to meet, he found "a tall, very thin man waiting for me, whose words and gestures were those of an automaton. . . . It was Alekhine."

The effect of the condemnation by fellow chess players on a man who always had thrived on popularity can well be imagined. In addition, for the second time in his life, he had lost all he had. His fine home in France had been, as he put it, scientifically ransacked by the invader. Neither Spain nor Portugal could afford him the living to which he was accustomed or in fact, any living at all. The chances in France were even worse at the time.

And so we see him in 1945-6 living in a Lisbon boarding house, with his material circumstances gradually getting worse, suffering in addition from severe heart trouble. His only hope was England; the British chess world, be it said to its honour, was not prepared to condemn a man unheard. Indeed the first ray of light came when he was invited to take part in the London Tournament of 1946. The Champion's distress was overwhelming when the invitation was cancelled because of the objections of the Dutch and American Federations. Some of the masters had threatened to withdraw their entries !

It was about this time that Dr. Alekhine decided to return to France and to defend himself before the French Chess Federation. He applied for a visa, but the Spanish frontier had been closed and the visa never reached him.

Dr. Alekhine was still living in Lisbon and his affairs were at the lowest ebb when a telegram arrived from Mr. Derbyshire, the President of the British Chess Federation, transmitting a challenge to a match by the Russian champion, M. Botvinnik, on the terms that had been agreed in 1939. The Moscow Chess Club was providing 10,000 dollars for the match, which was to take place in England subject to the British Chess Federation's approval. Dr. Alekhine was to receive two-thirds of the amount.

This sudden change of fortune proved too much for the sick man and resulted in a heart attack. As soon as he recovered he accepted the challenge and started his preparations for the match. In the last letter to reach this country the Champion asked whether it would be possible to get a visa to England from where he would more easily reach France. He also enquired whether a practice match with Dr. Tartakower could be arranged.

Then came weeks of weary waiting until the meeting of the British Chess Federation had taken place at which it was to be decided whether the Federation would agree to sponsor the match. This meeting took place on March 23rd in the afternoon, and by a unanimous vote the Federation gave their agreement.

The same night Dr. Alekhine breathed his last. . . .

Alekhine's chess career can be divided into four periods. During the first, which ended with the advent of the first world war, his opportunities of playing in master-tournaments were infrequent. He entered the Military School at St. Petersburg in 1909 at the age of 17 (he was born in 1892) and could not take part in tournaments more than, on an average, once a year. His early development was in consequence comparatively slow, though even so he succeeded in gaining the first prize on three occasions.

Practically nothing was heard of Alekhine between the years 1914-1921, which covered the world war and the Russian Revolution, though he won the Russian Championship at Moscow in 1920.

The second period of his chess career began with his return to Western Europe in 1921, when, circumstances leaving him no choice, he devoted himself entirely to Chess. During the following six years he played in many great tournaments and his dazzling sequence of brilliant victories were the talk of the chess world. It is during this time that he scored perhaps the most astonishing of his many successes —he became a Doctor-at-Law of the French Faculty.

The match with Capablanca gave him the world's title and was the culmination of the second period. It can be said that he had reached the zenith of his powers, perhaps the zenith to which human endeavour can attain.

The third period of his career, which started with his winning the Championship, lasted until the advent of the second world war. Between 1927 and 1936 his successes in tournaments were unequalled by any master at any time in the history of Chess. In particular at

San Remo 1930 and Bled 1931, though many of the greatest masters of the day took part, he left the field so far behind that he was at that time indisputably in a class by himself.

The first signs of retrogression were his lost match to Euwe in 1935 and his comparative failure at Nottingham, a very strong Tournament in which he gained only the sixth prize, with Botvinnik and Capablanca equal first, by far his worst result for twenty-four years. Although he regained the Championship from Dr. Euwe in 1937, having seemingly regained his powers to the full, in the AVRO Tournament of 1938, younger players, in Keres, Fine and Botvinnik, were ahead of him. Whether he could have re-established himself in the match with Botvinnik which had been agreed in 1939 is an open question which no one can answer with any degree of certainty.

The fourth period of Dr. Alekhine's chess career is a tragedy, as was his life during that period. He still won tournaments in Germany and occupied territory during the war and after that in Spain and Portugal, but the opposition was comparatively weak on the whole and made no call on his combative instinct. The quality of his play showed a marked falling off, as can be expected, apart from other considerations, when the opposition is not of the first order. Whether the match with Botvinnik, finally arranged on the day of Dr. Alekhine's death, would have heralded for the Champion a fifth and glorious period in his career is doubtful, but I feel certain that with Dr. Alekhine's wonderful powers of recuperation and his iron determination, it would have been the match of the century.

Dr. Alekhine's achievements, tabulated for the period covered by this book, are given below. His results up to 1937 have appeared in the first volume of his games. It would take too much space to refer in detail to the various tournaments in which he took part. Let it suffice to state that he played in seventy tournaments apart from five team tournaments.

In these seventy tournaments he won the first prize forty-one times, sharing the first prize on nine occasions. He won or shared the second prize fourteen times. On no occasion since 1911 did he fail to win a prize when taking part in a tournament !

Alekhine contributed few works to the literature of Chess. Three important books are available in the English language : the New York Tournament and two volumes of his own games. The value of all three lies in the annotation. For objectivity, clarity and clear-cut finality, they stand alone. The reason why he wrote so little is that he would not have been interested in writing for the average player, even if he could, and the writing of "pot-boilers," no matter how remunerative, was foreign to his nature.

As to his style of play, it was that of the true artist ; it was art for art's sake. The inventing of a method, the playing according to set principles, were not for him. His play was neither classical nor hyper-modern. It combined the best of all known styles in one harmonious whole ; technique was to him a means to an end. He was truly a great artist.

In everyday life he was a striking personality, with a fine physique and excellent manners, at home in any company. In some ways his character was curiously contradictory. Although at the chessboard or in the tournament room he had the utmost self-possession, away from the Chess atmosphere he was very shy, so that many casual acquaintances thought him supercilious, even arrogant.

Yet, after a game with one of his weaker brethren, no great master has ever been more ready to spend his time going over the game, analysing the positions, explaining his motives and freely giving encouragement and advice. He had not a few detractors, but what great man has ever been without them ?

There is, however, one serious lapse which can be held up against him—his failure to allow Capablanca a return match. There was a deep antagonism between the two men, who had once been friends. How it arose, whether suddenly or gradually, is not known, nor will it ever be decided who was in the wrong. In my opinion, whatever may have been the circumstances of the case, it was Alekhine, as the "man in possession," who should have given way; it was he who should have shown a more generous spirit. Had he done so, who knows but that, after the fall of France, when he tried to go to America, a helping hand might not have been extended to him, and the whole tragic chapter which followed might never have been written.

But whatever his faults may have been, his sad end more than atoned for them. Among lovers of Chess his name will live for ever with those of Philidor, Morphy, Lasker and Capablanca.

TOURNAMENTS

DATE		PRIZE	P.	W.	D.	L
1927	Kecskemet	1	16	8	8	–
1929	Bradley Beach	1	9	8	1	–
1930	San Remo	1	15	13	2	–
1930	Hamburg—Team Tournament ..	–	9	9	–	–
1931	Nice—Consultation Games ..	1	8	4	4	–
1931	Prague—Team Tournament ..	–	18	10	7	1
1931	Bled	1	26	15	11	–
1932	London	1	11	7	4	–
1932	Berne	1	15	11	3	1
1932	Mexico City	1 & 2 eq.	9	8	1	–
1932	Pasadena	1	11	7	3	1
1933	Folkestone—Team Tournament	–	12	8	3	1
1933	Paris	1	9	7	2	–
1933-4	Hastings	2	9	4	5	–
1934	Zurich	1	15	12	2	1
1905	Warsaw—Team Tournament ..		17	7	10	–
1935	Orebro	1	9	8	1	–
1936	Bad Nauheim	1 & 2 eq.	9	4	5	–
1936	Dresden	1	9	5	3	1
1936	Podebrady	2	17	8	9	–
1936	Nottingham	0	14	0	0	2
1936	Amsterdam	3	7	3	3	1
1936-7	Hastings	1	9	7	2	–
1937	Margate	3	9	6	–	3
1937	Kemeri	4 & 5 eq.	17	7	9	1
1937	German Quadrangular Tourney	2 & 3 eq.	6	3	1	2
1938	Montevideo	1	17	9	8	–
1938	Margate	1	9	6	2	1
1938	Plymouth	1 & 2 eq.	7	5	2	–
1938	AVRO	4,5 & 6 eq.	14	3	8	3
1939	Caracas	1	10	10	–	–
1939	Buenos Aires—Team Tournament	–	10	5	5	–
1939	Montevideo	1	7	7	1	–

MATCHES

		PLAYED	WON	LOST	DRAWN
1927	Capablanca	34	6	3	25
1929	Bogoljubow	25	11	5	9
1934	Bogoljubow	26	8	3	15
1935	Euwe	20	8	9	13
1937	Euwe .. ,. ..	25	10	4	11

The following are the results of the tournaments during the war years and after :—

1941, Munich, 2nd and 3rd with Lundin ; 1941, Cracow, 1st and 2nd with Schmidt ; 1942, Salzburg, 1st ; 1942, Munich, 1st ; 1942, Cracow, 1st ; 1942, Prague, 1st and 2nd with Junge ; 1943, Prague, 1st ; 1943, Salzburg, 1st and 2nd with Keres ; 1944, Gijon, 1st ; 1945, Gijon, 2nd and 3rd with Medina ; 1945, Sabadell, 1st ; 1945, Almeria, 1st and 2nd with Lopez Nunez ; 1945, Melilla, 1st ; 1945, Caceres, 2nd.

In addition he played two short matches with Dr. Rey Ardid and Francisco Lupi, each of which he won by 4 wins, 1 loss, and 3 draws.

PART I (1924-1927)

TOURNAMENT GAMES AND MATCH WITH CAPABLANCA

GAME 1

KING'S INDIAN DEFENCE

New York Tournament, March, 1924.

Black : R. RETI

1. P—Q 4	Kt—K B 3
2. P—Q B 4	P—K Kt 3
3. P—K Kt 3	......

Nowadays 0. Kt—Q B 3, P—Q 4 ; 4. B—B 4 followed by P—K 3, etc., is considered a promising line.

3.	B—Kt 2
4. B—Kt 2	Castles
5. Kt—Q D 0	P—Q 3
6. Kt—B 3	Kt—B 3

If Black has nothing better (and this seems to be the case) than to induce the advance of White's Pawn to Q 5—where, to be sure, it shortens for the time being the diagonal of the Bishop, but, on the other hand, brings considerable pressure upon Black's position— then his plan of development surely is not to be recommended.

7. P—Q 5	Kt—Kt 1
8. Castles	B—Kt 5

The exchange of this Bishop is not reasonable and merely lessens the power of resistance in Black's position. Likewise unsatisfactory would be 8. .... P—K 4 on account of 9. P×P (*e.p.*), P×P ; 10. B— Kt 5, etc., as played in my game against Sir G. Thomas in Carlsbad, 1923. On the other hand, there comes into consideration the move 8. .... P—Q R 4 in order to secure the square Q B 4 for the Knight for a while ; but in this case also White would maintain his superior position, by means of P—K R 3, B— K 3, Q—B 2, P—Q Kt 3, P—Q R 3 and, finally, P—Q Kt 4.

9. P—K R 3	......

It was important to clear the situation before the opponent completed his development.

9.	B×Kt
10. P×B	......

Much better than to recapture with the Bishop, by which process either the K's Pawn would have remained inactive a long time or, if advanced, would have restricted the action of his own pieces. After the text-move, however, he takes over the guarding of the important square K 5, and, moreover, Black must reckon with an eventual hostile action on the K's file opened hereby.

10.	P—K 3

The K's Pawn had to be exchanged, but it would have been relatively better for Black to have done so through 10. ....P—K 4. White thereupon would have had only *one* good reply (11. P×P *e.p.*), inasmuch as 11. P—B 4, P×P ; 12. B×P, Q Kt—Q 2, etc., clearly would have been quite tolerable for Black. After the actual move, on the other hand, White has the pleasant choice between two good continuations.

11. P—B 4   ......

Even more favourable than 11. P×P, P×P ; 12. R—K 1, Q—Q 2, etc. ; whereupon it would have been by no means easy to profit from the weaknesses of Black's centre.

11. ......   P×P
12. P×P   ......

Now, however, Black has to make his choice between three distinct evils : (I) Weakness on Q B 2 if he should allow the Pawn position to remain intact. (II) Weakness on Q B 3 if after....P—B 4,P×P (*e.p.*) he should recapture with the Pawn and later on be forced to play .... P—Q 4. (III) And, finally, the line actually selected by him, through which he obtains an isolated Q's Pawn the protection of which, made difficult through the powerful co-operation of the hostile Bishops, will soon lead to a decisive weakening of his Q's side.

12. ......   P—B 4
13. P×P (*e.p.*)   Kt×P
14. B—K 3   Q—Q 2
15. Q—R 4   ......

A most effective square for the Queen, from which this piece will exert a troublesome pressure upon Black's Queen's wing.

15. ......   Q R—B 1
16. Q R—Q 1   ......

Both players follow out the same idea, that is, their Q Kt's Pawn must be removed beyond the reach of the hostile Bishops. Incidentally, 16. B×P would not do here, of course, on account of 16. ....R—R 1, etc.

16. ......   P—Kt 3
17. P—Kt 3   ......

This move has the additional purpose of further protecting the Queen in anticipation of the subsequent complications. How important this is will soon become apparent.

17. ......   K R—Q 1
18. R—Q 3   ......

It would have been premature to play Kt—Kt 5 at once, on account of 18. ....P—Q 4, etc. Now, however, White threatens to make this move after doubling the Rooks and therefore Black endeavours, through an exchange, to relieve the pressure exerted by the White Queen.

18. ......   Kt—K 2 ?

In this way, indeed, it cannot be done and Black immediately is at a material disadvantage. Somewhat better would have been 18. .... Kt—Q R 4 ; 19. Q—R 3, B—B 1 ; 20. K R—Q 1, etc., with a difficult game for Black, to be sure, but yet making defence possible.

19. Kt—Kt 5 !   P—Q 4

Clearly forced.

20. Kt×P   ......

This line was also made possible by White's 17th move.

20. ......   R—R 1
21. B×Kt P   Q×Q

Black has nothing better, because after 21. ....R (Q 1)—Kt 1 White would have continued simply with 22. Q×Q, Kt×Q ; 23. B—K 3, R—Kt 2 ; 24. B×P, Kt×B ; 25. R× Kt, R (R 1)×Kt; 26. B×R, R×B; 27. R (B 1)—Q 1, etc., with a decisive superiority.

22. P×Q   R—Q 2
23. Kt—Kt 5   R×P

Threatening also 24. ....R—

Kt 5 ; 25. R—Kt 3, R×R ; 26. P×R, R—Kt 2, etc.

24.	Kt—B 3	R—R 3
25.	R—Kt 1	R—Kt 2
26.	B—B 5	R×R ch
27.	Kt×R	Kt—B 3

The position is now cleared up, White having maintained his passed Pawn while Black's Queen's Pawn still remains weak.

28. Kt—B 3 !   ......

The quickest method of winning. While he relinquishes the Q R's Pawn, White in return is enabled to force an entrance for his Rook into the enemy camp, whereby the decisive Pawn attack is made possible. The tame 28. P—R 3 would have permitted the opponent a more stubborn resistance after 28. ....R—R 4 ; 29. B—K 8, R—Kt 4, etc.

28.	......	R—R 4
29.	B—K 8	Kt—Q Kt 5

After 29. ....P—Q 5 there would follow not 30. B×P, Kt×B ; 31. R×Kt, Kt—Q 4 ! etc., with drawing chances—but 30. B×Kt !, P× Kt ; 31. P—Q R 4, winning.

30. R—Q 2   P—R 3

If at once 30. ....Kt—K 5, then 31. Kt×Kt, P×Kt ; 32. R—Q 8 ch, B—B 1 ; 33. P—B 5 and wins.

31. P—Q R 4 !   ......

Threatening 32. B—Kt 6 and thereby forcing Black's next move.

31.	......	Kt—K 5
32.	Kt×Kt	P×Kt
33.	R—Q 8 ch	K—R 2
34.	B×P	R×P

If 34. ....P—B 4, then 35. R—Q 7 !, K—R 1 (or P×B ; 36. B—Q 4, R—Q 4 ; 37. R×B ch, K—R 1; 38. R—Q 7 disc. ch., followed by

the exchange of Rooks, and wins) ; 36. B—Q 4, B×B ; 37. R×B, P× B ; 38. R×Kt, and wins.

Position after Black's 34th move.

35. P—B 5 !   ......

The initiation of the deciding Pawn charge. For the present 36. P×P ch, P×P ; 37. R—Q 6, etc., is threatened.

35.	......	R—R 8
36.	P—R 4	P—R 4

Forced on account of the threat 37. P—R 5, etc.

37. P—Kt 4 !   R—R 4

Or 37. ....R P×P ; 38. P—R 5 and wins.

38.	P×P ch	P×P
39.	P×P	R×P
40.	B—Kt 5 !	......

Winning at least the exchange.

40.	......	B—B 6
41.	R—Q 7 ch	K—Kt 1
42.	B×P	......

Now, after 42. ....R—R 1, White wins immediately by the advance of the R's Pawn.

Resigns.

GAME 2

IRREGULAR DEFENCE

New York Tournament, March, 1924.

Black : D. JANOWSKI

1. P—Q 4	Kt—K B 3
2. P—Q B 4	P—Q 3
3. Kt—Q B 3	B—B 4 ?

This move would be reasonable if White had already developed his K's Knight, after which the control of his K 4 would temporarily remain in Black's hands. But in the actual situation the Bishop, after White's P—K 4, will have no future whatsoever. The late Janowski had certainly very fine feeling for handling the pair of Bishops—but was never the great openings connoisseur his contemporaries liked to represent him.

4. P—K Kt 3	......

Even 4. P—B 3 and P—K 4 would have strategically refuted Black's Bishop's move.

4.	P—B 3
5. B—Kt 2	Q Kt—Q 2
6. P—K 4	B—Kt 3
7. K Kt—K 2	P—K 4
8. P—K R 3	......

Preparing B—K 3. From now on Black has only the choice between more or less unsatisfactory moves.

8.	Q—Kt 3
9. Castles	Castles

This supplies the opponent with an objective for a direct attack, which, owing to the unfortunate position of the Black pieces, will have catastrophic consequences. Instead, 9. ....B—K 2 ; 10. B—K 3, Q—B 2, etc., would have permitted a steadier resistance.

10. P—Q 5 !	......

Demolishing all Black's hopes for eventual delivery by means of .... P—Q 4. The temporary release of the square Q B 5 is, in comparison with this main motive, altogether immaterial.

10.	Kt—B 4
11. B—K 3	P×P
12. B P×P	Q—R 3

Acceptance of the Pawn sacrifice would have led to a clearly losing position—for instance, 12. ....Q× P ; 13. B×Kt, P×B ; 14. Q—R 4, Q—Kt 3 ; 15. P—B 4 !, P×P ; 16. P×P, etc. ; but the continuation in text is likewise without prospects.

13. P—B 3	......

Simple and decisive—Black has no longer a defence against P—Q Kt 4. If, for instance, 13. .... Q—Q 6, then, of course, 14. Q—B 1, etc.

13.	K—Kt 1
14. P—Q Kt 4	Q Kt—Q 2
15. P—Q R 4	Q—B 5
16. Q—Q 2	......

Good enough ; but, considering White's tremendous positional advantage, there was no need for combining. The simple 16. R—Kt 1, followed by Q—Q 2 and K R—B 1, would have won without the slightest effort.

16.	Q×Kt P

In such a position one may "eat" anything !

17. B×P ch	K—R 1
18. K R—Kt 1	Q—R 4
19. B—K 3	Kt—B 4
20. R—Kt 5	Q—B 2
21. P—R 5	K Kt—Q 2

Black has weathered the first onset more or less successfully ; but inasmuch as White can attack the hostile King with all his seven pieces, while Black's King's side is still undeveloped and his Q's Bishop has long since forgotten that it is able to move, White's win is merely a matter of time.

| 22. Kt—B 1 | R—B 1 |
| 23. Kt—Kt 3 | Kt—R 3 |

If 23. ....Kt×Kt, then 24. P—R 6 ! forcing 24. ....P—Kt 3 (for after 24. .... Kt×Q or R ? 25. P×P ch would have forced mate).

| 24. Kt—R 4 | B—K 2 |

Black makes up his mind to give up the exchange, knowing that, if 24. ....K—Kt 1, White with 25. R Q B 1, Q—Q 1 ; 26. R—B 6 would have proceeded to institute a decisive attack.

Position after Black's 24th move.

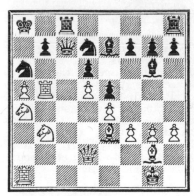

25. Kt—Kt 6 ch ......

The crisis. After 25. ....Kt × Kt ; 26. P × Kt, Q ad lib.; 27. R × Kt ch would win immediately.

25.	K—Kt 1
26. R—Q B 1	K Kt—B 4
27. Kt × Kt	P × Kt

28. Kt × R	R × Kt
29. B—B 1	Q—Q 2
30. R—Kt 6	P—B 5

Or 30. ....B—Q 1 ; 31. R—Kt 2, still winning the Pawn.

31. R × P	R × R
32. B × R	Q × R P
33. Q—K Kt 2	......

Technically simpler than 33. B × Kt, which would have won also.

33.	Q × Q ch
34. K × Q	B—Q 1
35. R—Kt 2	K—B 1
36. B × Kt	P × B
37. B—Kt 6	B—Kt 4
38. R—B 2 ch	K—Kt 2
39. P—Q 6	P—B 4
40. P—Q 7	Resigns.

GAME 3

QUEEN'S GAMBIT DECLINED (TCHIGORIN'S DEFENCE)

Paris Tournament, February, 1925.

Black : E. COLLE

1. P—Q 4	P—Q 4
2. P—Q B 4	Kt—Q B 3
3. Kt—K B 3	B—Kt 5
4. Q—R 4	......

A new move which I introduced here in order to avoid the usual variations deriving from 4. P × P, B × Kt, etc. I had the more reason to do so as the late Belgian Champion was a fine exponent of this particular defence and had obtained with it a number of notable successes.

| 4. ...... | B × Kt |
| 5. K P × B | P—K 3 |

After 5. ....P × P White can either play 6. B—K 3 or, even

better, sacrifice a Pawn for a big advantage in development by continuing 6. Kt—B 3, Q×P ; 7. B—K 3 followed by K B×P, etc.

6. Kt—B 3   B—Kt 5
7. P—Q R 3   ......

It is worth while to lose a *tempo* in order to be immediately informed as to the intentions of Black's Bishop.

7. ......   B×Kt ch
8. P×B   Kt—K 2
9. R—Q Kt 1   R—Q Kt 1
10. P×P   ......

In the Baden-Baden Tournament —which was played shortly after this one—I played against the same opponent 10. B—Q 3 and obtained a more convincing positional advantage. I reproduce here that game, because besides White's more accurate opening play it contains also a very instructive Q's and R's ending which probably induced Dr. Lasker to select it as one of the few games he included in his classic "Manual of Chess."

This was its continuation : 10. P×P ; 11. B×P, Castles ; 12. Castles, Kt—Q 4 ; 13. Q—B 2, Kt (B 3)—K 2 ; 14. B—Q 3, P—K R 3 ; 15. P—Q B 4, Kt—Q Kt 3 ; 16. R—Q 1, Kt (Kt 3)—B 1 ; 17. P—B 4, P—Q Kt 3 ; 18. B—Kt 2, P—Q B 3 ; 19. Q—K 2, Kt—Q 3 ; 20. Q—K 5, Kt—K 1 ; 21. P—Q R 4, R—Kt 2 ; 22. R—K 1, Kt—B 3 ; 23. R (Kt 1)—Q 1, R—Q 2 ; 24. B—B 2, P—R 3 ; 25. Q—K 2 !, Q—Kt 1 ; 26. P—Q 5 !, B P×P ; 27. B×Kt, P×B ; 28. Q—Kt 4 ch, K—R 1 ; 29. P—K B 5 !, Kt×P ; 30. B×Kt, P×B ; 31. Q×P, Q—Q 1 ; 32. P×P, R—Q 3 ; 33. Q—B 4 !, K—R 2 ; 34. Q—K 4 ch, K—R 1 ; 35. Q—K 3, K—Kt 2 ; 36. Q—Q 3 !, P—Q R 4 ; 37. R—K 3, R—Kt 1 ; 38. R—R 3, Q—Q 2 ; 39. Q—K 3, P—B 4 ; 40. R—Kt 3 ch, K—R 2 ;

41. R×R, K×R ; 42. Q—Kt 3 ch, K—R 2 ; 43. Q—Kt 3, K—Kt 2 ; 44. P—R 3, Q—Q 1 ; 45. Q—Kt 3 ch, K—R 2 ; 46. Q—K 5 !, Q—Q 2 ; 47. R—Q 3, P—B 3 ; 48. Q—Q 4, Q—Q 1 ; 49. Q—Q B 4 !, Q—Q 2 ; 50. R—Q 4, K—Kt 2 ; 51. Q—Q 3, K—B 2 ; 52. P—Kt 4 !, K—B 1 ; 53. P×P, Q—K 1 ; 54. R—K 4, Q—R 4 ; 55. R—K Kt 4, Q—B 2 ; 56. Q—K 3, Q—K R 2 ; 57. R—Kt 6, Black resigns.

10. ......   Q×P
11. B—Q 3   Castles
12. Castles   Q—Q 3 (!)

A good positional move freeing Q 4 for the Knight and preventing White's B—K B 4.

13. Q—B 2   Kt—Kt 3
14. P—K B 4   Q Kt—K 2

Preparing an action in the centre starting with P—Q B 4.

15. P—Kt 3   K R—Q 1
16. R—Q 1   P—Kt 3
17. P—Q R 4   ......

This weakens the square Q Kt 4 and thus allows Black to obtain a kind of initiative in the centre. Correct was 17. B—Kt 2, and if 17. ....P—Q B 4, then 18. P—B 4 !, P×P ; 19. B×P with some advantage, as neither 19. ....Q×B ; 20. B×Kt nor 19. ....Q×R P ; 20. R—R 1, Q—Kt 5 ; 21. R—R 4, Q—Q 3 ; 22. B—K 5 ! etc., would be favourable for Black.

17. ......   Kt—Q 4 !
18. B—Q 2   P—Q B 4
19. P—B 5   ......

Still trying to maintain a slight pressure. The variation 19. P—B 4, Kt—Kt 5 ; 20. B×Q Kt, P×B ; 21. P—Q B 5, P×P ; 22. P×P, Q—B 2 would have offered even less prospect of winning.

19.	K P×P
20. B×P	P×P
21. P×P	Q Kt—K 2
22. B—Q Kt 4	Q—K B 3
23. Q B×Kt	......

After 23. B—K R 3, Kt—Q 4 ! the pair of Bishops would be of little use. White therefore tries to take advantage of his passed Pawn in conjunction with the open Q B's file.

| 23. ...... | Q×QB |
| 24. Q R—B1 | ...... |

But the immediate 24. P—Q 5 was more consequent, for Black could now increase his prospects of a draw by answering 24. ....P—Kt 4 !

24.	R—Q 4
25. B—K 4	R—Q 2
26. P—Q 5	Q—B 3
27. R—K 1 !	......

The initial move of a rather hidden mating conception.

| 27. ...... | R (Kt 1)—Q 1 |
| 28. Q—B 6 ! | Q—Kt 4 |

Black is right in avoiding the exchange of Queens as both 28. .... Q×Q ; 29. P×Q and 28.....Kt—K 2 ; 29. Q×Q, P×Q ; 30. P—Q 6 ! would be decidedly in White's favour. But strange as it may seem, the square K Kt 4 for the Queen—which looks the most natural—will prove fatal. The right move was 28. ....Q—Q 5 after which there would not be anything decisive for White as yet.

| 29. B×Kt | R P×B |

As the answer shows, necessary was 29. ....B P×B (of course not Q×B ; 30. Q×R) ; 30. Q—K 6 ch, R—B 2 ; 31. R—B 8, R×R ; 32. Q×Q R ch, R—B 1 after which White would have had the pleasant choice between 33. R—K 8, Q—

B 3 ; 34. R × R ch, Q×R ; 35. Q—B 6 and 33. Q—K 6 ch, K—R 1 ; 34. P—Q 6, Q—Q 7 ; 35. R—K 2, Q—B 8 ch ; 36. K—Kt 2, Q—B 3 ch ; 37. K—R 3 most likely winning in either case.

Position after Black's 29th move.

| 30. Q×R ! | ...... |

This Queen's sacrifice is only possible because Black's K Kt 4 is occupied by the Queen, and the King, therefore, will have no escape after the Rook's doubling on the 8th rank.

30.	R×Q
31. R—K 8 ch	K—R 2
32. Q R—B 8	R—Q 1
33. R (K 8)×R ! Resigns.

GAME 4

QUEEN'S GAMBIT DECLINED (SLAV DEFENCE)

Paris Tournament, February, 1925.

Black : K. Opocensky

1. P—Q 4	P—Q 4
2. P—Q B 4	P—Q B 3
3. Kt—Q B 3	......

My second match with Dr. Euwe, in which the seemingly promising answer 3. ....P×P was refuted in a convincing manner, has proved that the text-move is at least as good as the fashionable 3. Kt—K B 3.

3.	Kt—B 3
4. P—K 3	B—B 4
5. P×P	Kt×P

If 5. ....P×P then, of course, 6. Q—Kt 3 with advantage.

6. B—B 4	P—K 3
7. K Kt—K 2	......

Introduced by Rubinstein against Bogoljubow at Hastings, 1922, and creating for Black a number of difficulties because of the inactive position of his Q's Bishop and his backward development.

7.	Kt—Q 2
8. P—K 4	Kt×Kt
9. Kt×Kt	B—Kt 3
10. Castles	Q—R 5

After the more natural 10. .... B—Kt 5 White would maintain his positional advantage by playing simply 11. P—B 3. The Queen's move prepares for castling on the Queen's side, and at the same time guarantees to the Bishop the square K R 4 in case of White P—K B 4—B 5.

11. P—Q 5 !   ......

This centre action afforded an exact calculation as Black will now force the weakening move P—K Kt 3. But White had practically no other way of keeping the initiative—after 11. P—B 3, Castles Black's prospects would have been excellent.

11.	K P×P
12. P—K Kt 3	Q—B 3
13. P×P	B—Q B 4 ?

Black's first and already decisive mistake. He now loses the possibility of castling and finally succumbs because of his inability to co-ordinate the action of the Rooks. Necessary was first 13. ....Kt—K 4 and only after 14. B—K 2, B—Q B 4 ; if in that case 15. K—Kt 2 renewing the threat P—B 4, etc., then 15. ....P—K R 4 ! after which White would have been practically forced to answer 16. P—K R 4 followed by B—K Kt 5, etc. The position in that case would remain full of dynamite, but by no means hopeless for the second player.

14. R—K 1 ch	K—B 1
15. B—B 4	Kt—Kt 3
16. B—Kt 3	P—K R 4
17. P—K R 4	......

From the 14th move onwards White has only one idea—to prevent the co-operation of Black's Rooks.

17.	K—Kt 1
18. P×P	P×P
19. R—Q B 1	......

After this Black cannot prevent the exchange of one of his Bishops against the Knight.

19.	B—Q 5
20. Kt—K 4	B×Kt
21. R×B	P—B 4

Or 21. ....B×P ; 22. R—B 5 !, Kt—Q 4 ; 23. B×Kt, P×B ; 24. R×P with a decisive advantage.

22. Q—K 2   ......

Starting the final attack against Black's K B 2.

22.	P—Kt 3
23. B—Kt 5	Q—Q 3

Attacking White's K Kt 3.

24. Q—B 3	Q—B 1

Position after Black's 24th move.

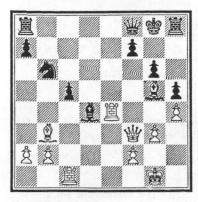

25. R×B !   . . . . . .

Eliminating the only active enemy's piece and thus practically breaking down any resistance.

25. . . . . . .   P×R
26 R—B 6 !   K—R 2

After 26. . . . . K—Kt 2 White would have sacrificed another Rook: 27. R×P ch !, K×R (or P×R ; 28. Q—Kt 7 ch followed by mate) ; 28. Q—B 6 ch, K—R 2 ; 29. B× P, R—K Kt 1 ; 30. Q—B 5 ch, K—Kt 2 ; 31. Q—Kt 6 ch, K—R 1 ; 32. B—B 6 ch and mate at the next move.

27. B×P   R—B 1
28. R× P   Resigns.

GAME 5

GIUOCO PIANO

Baden-Baden Tournament, May, 1925.

White : DR. S. TARRASCH

1. P—K 4   P—K 4
2. Kt—K B 3   Kt—Q B 3
3. B—B 4   B—B 4
4. P—B 3   B—Kt 3

5. P—Q 4   Q—K 2
6. Castles   Kt—B 3 (!)

This move, introduced by me instead of the usual 6. . . . . P—Q 3, leaves White less choice because his K's Pawn is now attacked.

7. R —K 1   P—Q 3
8. P—Q R 4   P—Q R 3
9. P—R 3   . . . . . .

A more or less necessary preparation for B—K 3.

9. . . . . . .   Castles
10. B—K Kt 5   . . . . . .

As White had no advantage to gain by provoking Black's next move he would have done better by playing 10. B—K 3 at once.

10. . . . . . .   P—R 3
11. B—K 3   . . . . . .

If 11. B—R 4 then of course 11. . . ., K—R 1 followed by R—K Kt 1 and P—Kt 4.

11. . . . . . .   Q—Q 1 !

This paradoxical move—the most difficult in the game—is very effective. The double idea is to prepare an eventual action in the middle— starting by . . . . P×P followed by . . . . P—Q 4 and, at the same time, free the K's file for the K's Rook.

12. B—Q 3   R—K 1
13. Q Kt—Q 2   B—R 2 (!)

Played in view of White's possible Kt—Q B 4.

14. Q —B 2   P×P

At the right time, as White cannot well retake with the Pawn because of 15. . . . . Kt—Q Kt 5.

15. Kt×P   Kt—K 4
16. B—B 1   P—Q 4 !

After this Black becomes at least as strong in the centre as his opponent. The tactical justification of the move is shown by the variation 17. P—K B 4, Kt—Kt 3 ; 18. P—K 5, Kt—R 4 ! etc. ∓

17. Q R—Q 1   P—B 4
18. Kt (Q 4)—Kt 3 Q—B 2
19. B—K B 4   ......

Also after 19. P×P, Kt×P ; 20. Kt—B 4, Kt×Kt ; 21. B×Kt, Kt × B ; 22. R×Kt, R×R ; 23. P×R, Q—K 2 Black would have kept the slightly better prospects.

19. ......   Kt—B 6 ch !
20. Kt×Kt   Q×B
21. P×P ?   ......

The decisive mistake, after which the game ends rapidly. I expected instead 21. P—K 5 and hoped after 21. ....B—B 4 ; 22. Q—Q 2, Q×Q ; 23. R×Q, Kt—K 5 ; 24. R (Q 2)—Q 1 ; (R×P ?, B—K 3) Q R—Q 1 to be able to exploit the advantage of the two Bishops.

Position after White's 21st move.

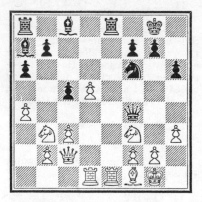

21. ......   B—B 4 !

An important intermediate move, after which there is not a sufficient defence. Much less convincing would be 21. ....B×P because of 22. P×B, Q×Kt ; 23. B—Kt 2, etc.

22. B—Q 3   ......

Or 22. Q—Q 2, Q×P ; 23. Kt—B 1, B—B 7 ! ; 24. R×R ch, R×R ; 25. R—K 1, Kt—K 5 ; 26. Q—B 4, P—B 5 ; 27. Kt—Q 4, B×Kt ; 28. P×Kt, Q—Kt 5 ! with a winning advantage for Black.

22. ......   B×P

And not 22. ....B×B ; 23. Q×B, P—B 5 because of 24. Q—Q 2.

23. P×B   Q×Kt
24. R×R ch   ......

After the immediate 24. B—B 1 and the following exchange of Rooks by Black he would, of course, have lost his only hope—the passed pawn. But after the text move Black forces the game by a mating attack.

24. ......   R×R
25. B—B 1   R—K 4
26. P—B 4   ......

26. P—Q 6 would not, obviously, alter matters.

26. ......   R—Kt 4 ch
27. K—R 2   Kt—Kt 5 ch
28. P×Kt   R×Kt P

Threatening an unavoidable mate.

Resigns.

GAME 6

KING'S FIANCHETTO

Baden-Baden Tournament, May, 1925.

White : R. Reti

1. P—K Kt 3   P—K 4
2. Kt—K B 3   ......

An experiment which Réti never repeated after the present game.

White intends to play the Alekhine's Defence with colours reversed, *i.e.*, with one *tempo* more. But the way he uses that *tempo* (P—K Kt 3) could have turned to his disadvantage (see next note).

  2. ......   P—K 5
  3. Kt—Q 4   P—Q 4

Black is satisfied with a free development of his pieces and about even middle game prospects. But he could obtain more by playing 3. ....P—Q B 4 !; 4. Kt—Kt 3, P—B 5 ; 5. Kt—Q 4, B—B 4 ; 6. P—Q B 3, Kt—Q B 3, thus bringing *ad absurdum* White's "development."

  4. P—Q 3   P×P
  5. Q×P   Kt—K B 3
  6. B—Kt 2   B—Kt 5 ch

Trying at all costs to bring as rapidly as possible all pieces into action. But nowadays I would probably have thought more about the security of the dark-coloured squares of my position and therefore have avoided the following exchange of Bishops.

  7. B—Q 2   B×B ch
  8. Kt×B   Castles
  9. P—Q B 4 !   ......

Apart from his eccentric first move, Réti plays the opening very well ; Black would not have any advantage by answering 9. ....P—B 4 because of 10. Kt—Kt 3 threatening both 11. Kt×P and 11. P×P.

  9. ......   Kt—R 3

Comparatively the best ; but it cannot be denied that White obtains now a sort of pressure on the half-open Q B's file.

10. P×P   Kt—Q Kt 5
11. Q—B 4   Q Kt×QP

12. Q Kt—Kt 3   P—B 3
13. Castles (K R)   R—K 1
14. K R—Q 1   B—Kt 5
15. R—Q 2   ......

After 15. P—K R 3 Black would have brought his Bishop to K 5 via R 4 and Kt 3.

15. ......   Q—B 1
16. Kt—Q B 5   B—R 6 !
17. B—B 3   ......

By his previous move Black had offered a Pawn, the acceptance of which would have been fatal for White, for instance : 17. B×B; Q×B ; 18. Kt× Kt P, Kt—K Kt 5 , 19. Kt—B 3, Kt (Q 4)—K 6 ! ; 20. P×Kt, Kt×K P ; 21. Q× P ch, K—R 1 !; 22. Kt—R 4, R—K B 1 and wins.

17. ......   B—Kt 5

Giving the opponent the choice between three possibilities : (1) to exchange his beloved "fianchetto" Bishop ; (2) to accept an immediate draw by repetition of moves (18. B—Kt 2, B—R 6 ; 19. B—B 3, etc.) which in such an early stage always means a moral defeat for the first player, and (3) to place the Bishop on a worse square (R 1). He finally decides to play "for the win" and thus permits Black to start a most interesting counter-attack.

18. B—Kt 2   B—R 6
19. B—B 3   B—Kt 5
20. B—R 1   ......

At last !

20. ......   P—K R 4 !

In order by the exchange of this Pawn to weaken White's K Kt 3.

21. P—Kt 4   P—R 3
22. R—Q B 1   P—R 5
23. P—R 4   P×P
24. R P×P   Q—B 2
25. P—Kt 5   ......

Consequent, but very risky to say the least. By playing 25. P—K 4, Kt—Kt 3 ; 26. Q—Kt 3, Q Kt—Q 2 etc. ! White could meet the immediate threats against his King, but the obstruction of the Bishop's diagonal would at the same time end his hopes on the other wing.

| 25. ...... | R P × P |
| 26. P × P | ...... |

Position after White's 26th move.

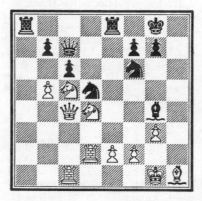

| 26. ...... | R—K 6 ! |

It seems almost incredible that this spectacular move not only stops White's attack but even brings him serious trouble. And yet it is so. It is obvious enough that the Rook cannot be taken because of 27. .... Q × P ch, followed by 28. .... Kt × P and wins ; and also that White has to do something in order to parry 27. ....R × P ch !, etc.

| 27. Kt—B 3 | ...... |

As the following shows, this natural move loses perforce. Also insufficient was 27. K—R 2 because of 27. ....Q R—R 6 ! ; 28. Kt (B 5)—Kt 3 (not 28. P × R, Kt × P followed by Kt—B 8 ch etc.), Q—K 4 ! ; 29. P × P, P × P with a powerful attack as 30. P × R would still be bad because of 30.

....Q—R 4 ch followed by 31. .... Q—R 6. The only chance of salvation was 27. B—B 3 !, B × B ; 28. P × B !, P × P ; 29. Kt × P (Kt 5), Q—R 4 ! still with advantage for Black, as 30. R × Kt ? would lose immediately after 30. ....R—K 8 ch ; 31. R × R, Q × R ch followed by 32. R—R 8.

27.	P × P
28. Q × P	Kt—B 6 !
29. Q × P	......

After 29. Q—B 4 the answer 29. ....P—Q Kt 4 ! would be decisive.

| 29. ...... | Q × Q |

And not 29. ....Kt × P ch because of 30. R × Kt !, Q × Q ; 31. R × R ! with some saving chances for White.

| 30. Kt × Q | Kt × P ch |
| 31. K—R 2 | ...... |

Or 31. K—B 1, Kt × P ch ; 32. P × Kt, B × Kt ; 33. B × B, R × B ch ; 34. K—Kt 2, R (R 1)—R 6 ; 35. R—Q 8 ch, K—R 2 ; 36. R—R 1 ch, K—Kt 3 ; 37. R—R 3, R (B 6)—Kt 6 ! and wins.

Position after White's 31st move.

| 31. ...... | Kt—K 5 ! |

The beginning of a new combination—which, however, is the absolutely logical consequence of the previous manœuvres—aiming, after a series of twelve practically forced moves, at the capture of White's exposed Knight at Q Kt 7. Black's Rook is still taboo as 32. P × R ?, Kt (K 5) × R ! would lose the exchange.

32. R—B 4 !   ......

Comparatively the best defence.

32. ......   Kt × B P

Insufficient would be 32. .... Kt × R because of 33. Kt × Kt ! or 32. ....B × Kt because of R × Kt (K 4)! etc. The situation is still very complicated.

33. B—Kt 2   B—K 3 !

One of the important links of the combination.

34. R (B 4)—B 2   ......

Here, and in the following, White, as it is easy to see, has no choice.

34. ......   Kt—Kt 5 ch
35. K—R 3   ......

Not 35. K—R 1 because of 35. .... R—R 8 ch.

35. ......   Kt—K 4 disc. ch
36. K—R 2   R × Kt !
37. R × Kt   Kt—Kt 5 ch
38. K—R 3   Kt—K 6 disc. ch
39. K—R 2   Kt × R
40. B × R   Kt—Q 5

If now 41. R—K 3 (K B 2) then 41. ....Kt × B ch ; 42. R × Kt, B—Q 4 ! (the final point !) winning a piece.

Resigns.

I consider this and the game against Bogoljubow at Hastings, 1922 (*cf. My Best Games* 1908–23) the most brilliant tournament games of my chess career. And by a peculiar coincidence they both remained undistinguished as there were no brilliancy prizes awarded in either of these contests !

GAME 7

QUEEN'S GAMBIT DECLINED (ORTHODOX DEFENCE)

Baden-Baden Tournament, May, 1925.

Black : Dr. K. Treybal

1.	P—Q 4	P—Q 4
2.	P—Q B 4	P—K 3
3.	Kt—Q B 3	Kt—K B 3
4.	B—Kt 5	Q Kt—Q 2
5.	P—K 3	B—K 2
6.	Kt—B 3	Castles
7.	R—B 1	P—B 3
8.	B—Q 3	P × P
9.	B × P	Kt—Q 4
10.	B × B	Q × B
11.	Kt—K 4	......

A very safe, but harmless move, for which I had a marked predilection during a certain period of my career, including the Capablanca Match. Now I have come to the conclusion that the old 11. Castles, although not extremely promising, still offers more fighting chances than the Knight's move.

11. ......   Q Kt—B 3

After this answer, however, Black will have difficulties in freeing his game by means of ....P—K 4, or ....P—Q B 4 and therefore White's position will soon become much preferable. Good methods in order to obtain equality are : 11. .... K Kt—B 3, and after 12. Kt—Kt 3 either 12. ....Q—Kt 5 ch (Capablanca) or even 12. ....P—K 4 (Dr. Lasker).

12. Kt—Kt 3	Q—Kt 5 ch
13. Q—Q 2	Q×Q ch
14. K×Q	R—Q 1
15. K R—Q 1	B—Q 2
16. Kt—K 5	B—K 1
17. K—K 2	K—B 1
18. P—B 4	P—K Kt 3

It is very seldom advisable in the end-game to place the Pawns on the squares of the colour of their own Bishop. A more logical plan was 18. ....Kt—Q 2, eventually followed by ....P—B 3.

19. K—B 3	Q R—B 1
20. B—Kt 3	R—B 2
21. Kt—K 2	Kt—K 2
22. P—Kt 4	K R—B 1
23. Kt—Kt 3 !	......

After this, Black's preparations for ....P—Q B 4 prove useless, as this move would now have fatal consequences after 24. P—Kt 5— for instance: I—24. ....Kt (B 3)—Q 4 ; 25. P×P, R×P ; 26. R×R, R×R ; 27. Kt—K 4, R—B 2 ; 28. Kt—Q 6, with a tremendous positional advantage for White.
II—24. .... Kt—Q 2 ; 25. Kt×Kt ch, B×Kt ; 26. R×P, R×R ; 27. P×R, K—K 1 ; 28. K—B 2 and White would retain the extra Pawn.

23.	Kt (B 3)—Q 4

Therefore this purely passive move, which permits White's following effective Knight's manœuvre.

~~24. Kt—K 4~~	R—Q 1

After 24. ....P—B 3 White would exchange two minor pieces for a Rook and two Pawns, thus obtaining a won position—for instance, 25 Kt—B 5 !, P×Kt ; 26. Kt×P ch, K—Kt 1 ; 27. Kt×R, P—K 5 ch (otherwise 28. P—K 4) ; 28. K×P, R×Kt ; 29. K—B 3 followed by P—K 4 ±.

25. Kt—B 5	P—Kt 3
26. Kt—R 6	R (B 2)—B 1
27. P—K 4	......

Position after White's 27th move.

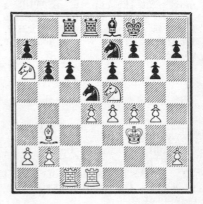

27.	P—B 3

A desperate attempt to get some freedom for his pieces. After 27. ....Kt—B 3 (or Kt—B 2 ; 28. Kt×Kt followed by 29. P—Q 5 ±) ; 28. P—Kt 5, Kt—Q 2 ; 29. Kt—K Kt 4, K—Kt 2 ; 30. P—K R 4, etc., he would rapidly perish from asphyxia.

28. P×Kt	P×Kt
29. P—Q 6 !	......

Forcing a decisive win of material; if now 29. ....P—K 5 ch, then 30. K×P, R×P ; 31. K—K 5 !, R (B 1)—Q 1 ; 32. Kt—B 7 and wins.

29.	R×P
30. B P×P	R—Q 4

30. ....R (Q 3)—Q 1 ; 31. B×P would be even more hopeless.

31. B×R	Kt×B
32. P—Q R 3	......

The beginning of the rather instructive technical part. First and foremost, White must force the exchange of the opponent's central Knight.

32.	P—K Kt 4
33. Kt—Kt 4	Kt—K 2
34. Kt—Q 3	Kt—Q 4
35. P—K R 4 !	P × P

If 35. ....P—K R 3, then 36. P × P, followed by Kt—B 2—K 4 (or R 3), etc.

36. Kt—B 4	Kt × Kt
37. K × Kt	......

White's next manœuvre will be the elimination of the K R 4 Pawn and the return of the King to the centre, in order to release the Rook from the protection of the Queen's Pawn.

37.	R—Q 1
38. K—Kt 3	K—Kt 2
39. K × P	R—Q 4
40. K—Kt 5	R—Q 1
41. K—B 4	R—Q 2
42. K—K 3	R—Kt 2
43. P—Kt 4	......

The beginning of the third phase —the blockade of Black's weak spots.

43.	P—Q R 3
44. R—B 1	R—R 2
45. R—B 6	R—K 2
46. P—R 4	K—Kt 1
47. P—R 5	P—Kt 4
48. P—Q 5 !	......

This Pawn sacrifice, in order to permit the victorious entrance of the King into the enemy's camp, is the absolutely logical conclusion of the whole procedure.

48.	K P × P

Or, 48 ... B P × P; 49. R—B 8, followed by R—R 8, etc.

49. P—K 6	K—Kt 2
50. P—Kt 5	P—R 4

51. K—Q 4	R—Q B 2
52. K—B 5	R—B 1
53. K—Kt 6	P—Q 5
54. P—K 7 !	Resigns.

Although this game, and the next one, do not exhibit any particularly thrilling points, I have included them in this collection because they illustrate in a convincing way the methods to follow in order to exploit an advantage in space obtained in the opening stage.

GAME 8

ALEKHINE'S DEFENCE

Baden-Baden Tournament, May, 1925.

White : SIR G. A. THOMAS

1. P—K 4	Kt—K B 3
2. P—Q 3	......

A very tame continuation, which does not offer prospects of any opening advantage.

2.	P—B 4
3. P—K B 4	Kt—B 3
4. Kt—K B 3	P—K Kt 3
5. B—K 2	B—Kt 2
6. Q Kt—Q 2 (?)	......

After this unnatural-looking move White's game remains very cramped. A much lesser evil was 6. P—B 4 ceding the square Q 4 but preventing the double advance of Black's Queen's Pawn.

6.	P—Q 4
7. Castles	Castles
8. K—R 1	P—Kt 3
9. P × P	Q × P

Even better than 9. ....Kt × P, which move would permit the answer 10. Kt—K 4.

10. Q—K 1	......

The Pawn sacrifice by 10. Kt—K. 5 would prove insufficient after 10. ....Kt × Kt ; 11. P × Kt, Q × K P ; 12. Kt—B 4 (or 12. B—B 3, R—Kt 1 ; 13. Kt—B 4, Q—B 2), Q—K 3 ! ; 13. B—B 3, Kt—Q 4, etc.

10.	B—Kt 2
11. Kt—B 4	Kt—Q 5
12. Kt—K 3	Q—B 3
13. B—Q 1	Kt—Q 4 !

Practically forcing the exchange of three minor pieces, and thus increasing by the simplest method the positional advantage already acquired. A similar procedure was adopted by me in a game against A. Evenssohn (see *My Best Games 1908–1923*).

14. K Kt × Kt	......

The consequences of an attempt to win a Pawn by 14. Kt (K 3) × Kt would be sad : 14. ....Q × Kt ; 15. Q × P, K R—K 1 ; 16. Q—Kt 5, Kt × Kt ; 17. B × Kt, Q × Q ; 18. P × Q, B × B ; 19. P × B, R—K 7 ∓.

14.	P × Kt
15. Kt × Kt	Q × Kt
16. B—B 3	Q—Q 2
17. B × B	Q × B
18. P—B 4	......

Otherwise he would remain with the awful weakness at Q B 2.

18.	P × P (*e.p.*)
19. P × P	Q R—B 1
20. B—Kt 2	......

Only slightly better would be 20. B—Q 2.

20.	K R—Q 1
21. R—B 3	B—B 3

Releases the Queen from the worry about K 2.

Position after Black's 21st move.

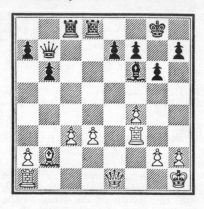

22. P—Q 4	......

The positional capitulation after which Black will have comparatively easy winning play, because of the full control of the light-coloured squares. But owing to the threat ....Q—R 3 in connection with the doubling of Rooks on the Q's file, White had already no real choice.

22.	Q—Q 4
23. Q—K 3	Q—Q Kt 4 !
24. Q—Q 2	R—Q 4
25. P—K R 3	P—K 3
26. R—K 1	Q—R 5
27. R—R 1	P—Q Kt 4
28. Q—Q 1	R—B 5

Also good was, of course, 28. .... Q × Q ; but Black is not in a hurry. The adversary will not be able to avoid the exchange.

29. Q—Kt 3	R—Q 3
30. K—R 2	R—R 3
31. K R—B 1	B—K 2
32. K—R 1	R (B 5)—B 3 !

Intending to force White to exchange Queens after ....Q—B 5 followed by ....R—R 5 and .... R (B 3)—R 3.

33. K R—K 1	B—R 5 !

Chasing the Rook from the K's file ; because if, for instance, 34. R—K 2, then 34. ....Q×Q ! 35. P×Q, R×R ch ; 36. B×R, R—R 3 ; 37. B—Kt 2, R—R 7 ; 38. P—Q Kt 4 (or 38. K—R 2, P—Q R 4 !), B—Kt 6 ; 39. P—Q 5, B×P (simpler than 39. ....P×P ; 40. P—B 4 !) etc., winning easily.

| 34. R—K B 1 | Q—B 5 |
| 35. Q×Q | ...... |

Otherwise Black would play, as mentioned, 35. ....R—R 5, etc.

35.	R×Q
36. P—R 3	B—K 2
37. K R—Q Kt 1	B—Q 3 !

Forcing also the K Kt's Pawn on to a dark-coloured square.

38. P—Kt 3	K—B 1
39. K—Kt 2	K—K 2
40. K—B 2	K—Q 2
41. K—K 2	K—B 3

After having protected the Q Kt's Pawn Black threatens ....R (B 5)—R 5.

42. R—R 2	R (B 5)—R 5
43. K R—Q R 1	K—Q 4
44. K—Q 3	R (R 3)—R 4
45. B—B 1	P—Q R 3
46. B—Kt 2	P—R 4

Threatening, of course, 47. .... P—R 5.

| 47. P—R 4 | P—B 3 ! |

After this White is without defence against ....P—K 4, etc.

48. B—B 1	P—K 4
49. B P×P	P×P
50. B—Kt 2	......

Or 50. P×P. B×K P ; 51. B—B 4, B×B ; 52. P×B, K—K 3 ! (the simplest), and wins.

| 50. ...... | P×P |
| 51. P×P | P—Kt 5 ! |

Resigns.

The late Nimzowitsch—who was rather reluctant to comment on the games of his colleagues—distinguished this one by including it as an example in his remarkable book, *My System*.

GAME 9

IRREGULAR DEFENCE

Baden-Baden Tournament, May, 1925.

Black : F. MARSHALL

| 1. P—Q 4 | Kt—K B 3 |
| 2. P—Q B 4 | P—Q 4 |

This move is very seldom adopted in Master play and in fact cannot be recommended. It partly succeeds, however, in the present game because of the not quite accurate opening play of White.

| 3. P×P | Kt×P |
| 4. P—K 4 | ...... |

As this advance could not be prevented by Black, it should have been delayed, and only executed after the development of the King's side pieces. A good plan here was 4. P—K Kt 3 followed by B—Kt 2, reserving P—K 4 for a more favourable moment.

| 4. ...... | Kt—K B 3 |
| 5. B—Q 3 | ...... |

Also after 5. Kt—Q B 3 Black could have obtained about an even game by answering 5. ....P—K 4.

5.	P—K 4 !
6. P×P	Kt—Kt 5
7. Kt—K B 3	Kt—Q B 3
8. B—K Kt 5 !	......

White realises that he cannot obtain any kind of advantage by trying to keep the extra-Pawn. If, for instance, 8. B—K B 4, then 8. ....Kt—Kt 5 ! ; 9. B—Kt 5 ch, B—Q 2 ; 10. B×B ch, Q×B ; 11. Q×Q ch, K×Q ; 12. Castles, Kt—B 7' ; 13. R—Q 1 ch, K—B 1 ; 14. P—K R 3 (or Kt—Kt 5), Kt—R 3 and White's positional advantage would not compensate the loss of the exchange.

8.	B—K 2
9. B×B	Q×B
10. Kt—B 3	Q Kt×P
11. Kt×Kt	Q×Kt

But here Black decidedly over-estimates his position. Instead of the text move which—as the following convincingly proves—only exposes his Queen to a Pawn attack, he could obtain a game with even prospects by continuing 11. .... Kt×Kt ; 12. Castles, Castles ; 13. B—K 2, B—K 3, etc.

| 12. P—K R 3 | Kt—B 3 |
| 13. Q—Q 2 ! | ...... |

It is certainly surprising to what extent the simple Queen's manœuvre — by which White strengthens the dark coloured squares of his position—improves his chances for the middle game. From now on Black will be gradually dragged into a lost position without having made a move which could be considered an actual mistake.

| 13. ...... | B—Q 2 |
| 14. Q—K 3 ! | ...... |

Not only taking control of the squares Q 4 and Q B 5 but, above all, preventing Black's castling (Q R).

| 14. ...... | B—B 3 |
| 15. Castles (Q R) | Castles (K R) |

As Black cannot bring his King in safety on the Queen's side (if 15. ....Q—Q R 4 then 16. B—B 4 ! ±) he has practically no choice.

| 16. P—B 4 | Q—K 3 |

After 16. ....Q—Q R 4 ; 17. P—K 5 Black would (as well as in the actual game) lose a Pawn by continuing 17. ....Kt—Q 4 ; 18. Kt×Kt, B×Kt ; 19. B×P ch followed by Q—Q 3 ch and Q×B.

| 17. P—K 5 | ...... |

With the main threat 18. P—B 5.

| 17. ...... | K R—K 1 |
| 18. K R—K 1 | Q R—Q 1 |

Better was 18. ....Kt—Q 2 after which White would have continued his attack by 19. P—K Kt 4, etc. The Rook's move permits him to obtain the win by a forced sequence of moves.

19. P—B 5	Q—K 2
20. Q—Kt 5	Kt—Q 4
21. P—B 6	Q—B 1

Position after Black's 21st move.

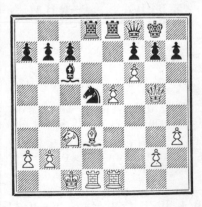

| 22. B—B 4 ! | ...... |

The action of this Bishop on the diagonal Q R 2—K Kt 8 proves immediately decisive. It is important to notice that Black does not dispose here of the intermediate move 22. ....P—K R 3 because of 23. P×P ! winning a piece.

22.	Kt×Kt
23. R×R	R×R
24. P×P !	......

Much more convincing than 24. P—K 6, R—Q 4 !

| 24. ...... | Kt×P ch |

Or 24. ....Q—K 1 ; 25. B×P ch !, K×B ; 26. R—B 1 ch, K—K 3 ; 27. R—B 6 ch, K—Q 4 ; 28. R—B 8 and wins.

| 25. K—Kt 1 ! | ...... |

And not 25. B×Kt, Q—B 4 ch.

| 25. ...... | Q—K 1 |
| 26. P—K 6 ! | ...... |

Now even stronger than 26. B× P ch.

| 26. ...... | B—K 5 ch |
| 27. K—R 1 | ...... |

Also possible was 27. R×B, R—Q 8 ch ; 28. K—B 2, Q—R 5 ch ; 29. P—Kt 3, Kt—Kt 5 ch ; 30. K×R, etc., but the text move is simpler.

| 27. ...... | P—K B 4 |

Despair ; as 27. ....P×P would lose after 28. B×P ch, Q×B ; 29. Q×R ch, K×P ; 30. Q—Q 4 ch, followed by 31. R×B.

28. P—K 7 disc. ch	R—Q4
29. Q—B 6 !	Q—B 2
30. P—K 8 (Q) ch	followed by

mate in two.

GAME 10

QUEEN'S GAMBIT DECLINED (SLAV DEFENCE)

Semmering Tournament, April, 1926.

White : J. Davidson

Brilliancy Prize

1. P—Q 4	P—Q 4
2. P—Q B 4	P—Q B 3
3. Kt—K B 3	Kt—B 3
4. P—K 3	P—K 3

The fashionable move nowadays is 4. ....B—B 4, as the so-called "Meran" system inaugurated by the text move is considered to be rather favourable for White.

| 5. Kt—B 3 | Q Kt—Q 2 |
| 6. Q—B 2 | ...... |

The natural—and best—move is 6. B—Q 3. But at that time the system mentioned was not yet elaborated in all its details.

6.	B—Q 3
7. B—Q 3	Castles
8. Castles	Q—K 2
9. P—K 4	P×B P
10. B×P	P—K 4

Thus Black has obtained a position similar to the one which Tchigorin considered as perfectly playable, but with the appreciable advantage that his Queen already occupies the natural developing square K 2, while the White Queen is not particularly well posted at Q B 2.

| 11. R—Q 1 | P×P |
| 12. Kt×P | Kt—Kt 3 ! |

Better than 12. ....Kt—K 4 ;

13. B—B 1, Kt—Kt 3 ; 14. Kt—
B 5, B×Kt ; 15. P×B, Kt—K 4 ;
16. B—K Kt 5 with a good game
for White.

13. B—B 1   R—Q 1

Threatening 14.... B×P ch ; 15.
K×B, R×Kt ; 16. R×R, Q—K 4
ch, etc., and thus inducing White to
weaken his King's position.

14. P—K R 3   B—B 2

Threatening to win a piece by
15. ....R×Kt followed by 16.
....Q—K 4.

15. B—K 3   R—K 1 !

As will be seen, both Bishops
are now badly posted for they
obstruct the action of some of the
other pieces and, besides, they
can be attacked by the enemy's
Knights.

16. B—Q 3   Kt—R 4
17. Q Kt—K 2   P—Kt 3

Chiefly in order to prepare, by
protecting the square K B 4, the
move Kt—Q 2.

18. R—K 1   Kt—Q 2
19. Kt—K B 3   ......

After this retreat Black gets a
definite pull. I expected here 19.
P—B 4 with the continuation 19....
Kt(Q 2)—B 3; 20. P—K 5, Kt—Q 4;
21. B—Q 2, B—Kt 3 after which,
although Black's game would still
remain preferable, White would not
be without some fighting chances.

19. ......   B—Kt 3 !

Expecting to increase the positional advantage already obtained
—after 20. P × B, P × B—on

account of the open Q R's file. In
order to avoid this unpleasant
variation White tries with his two
next moves to complicate matters,
but only succeeds in accelerating the
catastrophe.

20. B—K Kt 5   Q—B 4 !

If now 21. Q×Q, Kt×Q; 22.
Kt—B 1 (forced)—then 22. ....
P—B 3 ; 23. B—Q 2, Kt×B ; 24.
Kt×Kt, Kt—Kt 6 ; 25. P—K 5,
B—K B 4, with a winning positional
advantage.

21. Kt—B 3   Kt—K 4 !

Forcing the following exchange
and thus renewing the attack on
the diagonal Q Kt 1—K R 7, which
will prove decisive.

22. Kt×Kt   Q×Kt (K 4)
23. B—K 3   B—B 2
24. Kt—K 2   ......

Also 24. P—K Kt 3, B×P, etc.
would have lost in the long run.

24. ......   Q—R 7 ch
25. K—B 1   ......

Position after White's 25th move.

25. ......   B×P !

This sacrificing combination is neither particularly complicated nor unusual. But its value is considerably increased by the fact that it forms the logical conclusion of the previous positional play.

26. P×B	Q×R P ch
27. K—Kt 1	B—R 7 ch
28. K—R 1	Kt—B 5 !

Doubtless the shortest way to a win.

| 29. Kt×Kt | ...... |

If 29. B×Kt then 29. ....B—Kt 6 disc. ch followed by mate in two moves.

29.	B×Kt disc. ch
30. K—Kt 1	B—R 7 ch
31. K—R 1	Q—B 6 ch !

The point of the whole combination which forces the win of the Queen for a Rook and a Bishop.

| 32. K×B | R—K 4 |
| 33. Q—B 5 | ...... |

The only move.

33.	R×Q
34. B×R	Q—R 4 ch
35. K—Kt 2	Q×B

The rest is merely a matter of routine. 36. R—K 3, R—K 1 ; 37. Q R—K 1, Q—K 4 ; 38. Q R —K 2, R—K 3 ; 39. P—Kt 3, R—B 3 ; 40. R—Kt 3, K—Kt 2 ; 41. B—Kt 1, R—B 5 ; 42. B—Q 3, R—R 5 ; 43. K—B 3, Q—B 5 ch ; 44. K—Kt 2, Q—B 8 ; 45. K—B 3, P—K R 4 ; 46. R—B 2, Q—Q 8 ch ; 47. K—K 3, R—R 8 ; 48. K— Q 4, P—R 5 ; 49. R—K 3, R—K 8 ; 50. R×R, Q×R (K 8); 51. R—K 2, Q—R 8 ch ; 52. K—B 4, P—Kt 4 ch. White resigns.

GAME 11

QUEEN'S INDIAN DEFENCE

Semmering Tournament, April, 1926.

White : A. RUBINSTEIN

Brilliancy Prize

1. P—Q 4	Kt—K B 3
2. P—Q B 4	P—K 3
3. Kt—K B 3	P—Q Kt 3
4. P—K Kt 3	B—Kt 2
5. B—Kt 2	B—Kt 5 ch

This simplification is hardly advisable, as White's Queen's Bishop should develop less activity in the future than Black's King's Bishop. More promising, therefore, is 5. .... D—K 2.

| 6. Q Kt—Q 2 | ...... |

For reasons just mentioned 6. B—Q 2 seems to be the logical answer.

| 6. ...... | Castles |
| 7. Castles | P—Q 4 |

As the following shows, this is good enough to equalise. A good manœuvre was also 7. ....R—K 1 followed by ....B—K B 1.

| 8. P—Q R 3 | B—K 2 |
| 9. P—Q Kt 4 | P—B 4 |

The right way to keep the balance in the centre. Unsatisfactory in the positional sense would be 9. .... P—Q R 4 ; 10. P—Kt 5.

| 10. Kt P×P | Kt P×P |
| 11. P×P | ...... |

Also 11. R—Kt 1, Q—B 1 ; 12. Q—Kt 3, B—R 3, etc., would be satisfactory for Black.

| 11. ...... | B×P |

12. B—Kt 2   Q Kt—Q 2
13. Kt—K 5   Kt × Kt
14. B × Kt   Kt—Kt 5 !

This diversion is by no means as harmless as it looks. White loses the game chiefly because he under-estimates its importance.

15. B—Q B 3   ......

And not 15. B—Kt 2, Q—Kt 3, etc.

15. ......   R—Kt 1

At this moment 15. ....Q—Kt 3 would have been answered by 16. P—K 3. The text move prepares an eventual advance of the Q's Pawn.

16. R—Kt 1   ......

Although this move cannot be considered a decisive mistake, it certainly facilitates the opponent's plans. Unsatisfactory would be also 16. P—R 3, Kt × P !; 17. R × Kt, Q—Kt 4 !; 18. Kt—B 1, B × R ch ; 19. K × B, P × P, etc. to Black's advantage. But by continuing 16. P × P, B × Q P !; 17. Kt—K 4 ! (and not 17. P—K 4, Kt × B P !; 18. R × Kt, B × R ch ; 19. K × B, Q—Kt 3 ch ; 20. K—B 1, B—Kt 2, etc.∓), with the subsequent dislodging of the threatening Black Knight, White could still obtain an even game.

16. ......   P—Q 5 !
17. R × B (?)   ......

Rubinstein does not foresee the surprising 18th move of Black and consequently will find himself at a material disadvantage. The only possibility here was, 17. B—Kt 4, Q B × B ; 18. K × B, Q—B 2 reaching a position which would be in

Black's favour, too, but hardly in a decisive way.

17. ......   R × R
18. B × R   ......

Position after White's 18th move.

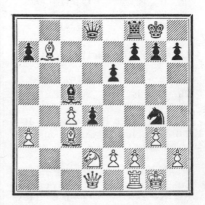

18. ......   Kt × B P !

By this pseudo sacrifice Black forces the win of at least a Pawn with an overwhelming position. Of course, ineffective would be the immediate 18. ....P × B because of 19. Kt—K 4, etc.

19. K × Kt   ......

Other moves were no better, to say the least. For instance :
I—19. Q—R 1 (19. R × Kt ? P × B and wins), P × B ; 20. Kt—Kt 3, Kt—Kt 5, disc. ch ; 21. Kt × B, Q—Q 5 ch.
II—19. B—R 5, Kt × Q ; 20. B × Q, P—Q 6 disc. ch ; 21. P—K 3, Kt × P ! with an easy win for Black in both cases.

19. ......   P × B disc. ch
20. P—K 3   ......

Or 20. K—K 1, P × Kt ch ; 21. Q × P, Q—Kt 3, with a rapidly winning attack.

20.	......	P × Kt
21.	K—K 2	Q—Kt 1
22.	B—B 3	R—Q 1
23.	Q—Kt 1	Q—Q 3

Gaining the square Q Kt 5 for the Bishop.

24.	P—Q R 4	P—B 4
25.	R—Q 1	B—Kt 5
26.	Q—B 2	Q—B 4
27.	K—B 2	P—Q R 4
28.	B—K 2	P—Kt 4
29.	B—Q 3	P—B 5 !

If now 30. B × P ch, K—R 1; 31. Q—K 4, then 31. ....Q × P ch ; 32. K—Kt 2, P—B 6 ch ; 33. K—R 3, Q—K 7 ! ; 34. Q—Kt 6, P—Kt 5 ch ; 35. K—R 4, B—K 2 ch ; 36. K—R 5, Q × P ch, and wins.

Resigns.

GAME 12

QUEEN'S GAMBIT ACCEPTED

Semmering Tournament, April, 1926.

Black : F. GRUENFELD

1.	P—Q 4	P—Q 4
2.	P—Q B 4	P × P
3.	Kt—K B 3	B—Kt 5

This move, recommended in the last edition of Collijn's Swedish Manual, was introduced in Master play by Bogoljubow in his game against Vukovic at the Vienna Tournament, 1922. The present game shows the danger connected with the early development of the Bishop in case of the slightest inexactitude on Black's part.

| 4. | Kt—K 5 | B—R 4 |
| 5. | Kt—Q B 3 | P—K 3 ? |

Already at the 5th move Black

commits the decisive positional mistake ! Necessary was 5. .... Kt—Q 2, after which I intended to play 6. Q—R 4, P—Q B 3 ; 7. Kt × Kt, Q × Kt (not P—Q Kt 4 ; 8. Kt × Kt P, P × Kt ; 9. Q × Kt P, Q × Kt ; 10. Q × B) ; 8. Q × P (B 4) followed by P—K 4 and B—K 3 with a good game.

| 6. | P—K Kt 4 ! | B—Kt 3 |
| 7. | P—K R 4 | P—K B 3 |

A sad necessity !

| 8. | Q—R 4 ch | ...... |

Also 8. Kt × B, P × Kt ; 9. P—K 3, etc., was good enough.

8.	......	P—B 3
9.	Kt × B	P × Kt
10.	Q × P	K—B 2
11.	P—K 4	Kt—Q 2
12.	B—K 3	Q—R 4
13.	P—R 3	......

It was important to prevent .... Q—Kt 5.

13.	......	R—K 1
14.	P—B 4	Kt—K 2
15.	Castles	......

Instead 15. P—B 5, Kt—B 1, etc., would hardly prove more convincing than the simple text move.

15.	......	Kt—B 1
16.	P—B 5	Kt—Q 3
17.	Q—R 2.	......

After 17. Q—Kt 3 Black could play 17. P—B 4, which move now would lose a piece because of 18. QP × P followed by P—Kt 4.

| 17. | ...... | P—K Kt 4 |
| 18. | P—R 5 | P—Q Kt 4 |

Black has no longer even more or less satisfactory moves.

Position after Black's 18th move.

19. P—K 5 !   ......

In conjunction with the next move this advance is absolutely decisive. Not quite so good would be the immediate 19. B—Q 3 because of 19. ....P—Kt 5.

19. ......   B P×P

If instead 19. ....P—Kt 5 then 20. P×Kt, P×Kt ; 21. P×P ch, R×P ; 22. B—Q B 4 and wins.

20. B—Q 3 !   P—K 5

Or 20. ....Kt—B 5 ; 21. B×Kt, P×B ; 22. Q×P, etc., with an easily won game.

21. Kt×K P	Kt×Kt
22. B×Kt	Kt—B 3
23. P×P ch	R×P
24. B—Kt 6 ch !	......

Stronger than the win of the exchange by 24. B—B 5.

24.	K—K 2
25. B×P	P—Kt 5
26. B—B 5	R—K 7
27. K R—K 1	......

If now 27. ....Q—Kt 4, then 28. P—R 4 !, Q—R 3 ; 29. B—Q 3, etc.;

and if 27. ....R×R then 28. R×R ch, K—Q 1 ; 29. Q—B 7 ! followed by mate.

Resigns.

GAME 13

QUEEN'S INDIAN DEFENCE

Dresden Tournament, May, 1926.

White : F. SAEMISCH

| 1. P—Q 4 | Kt—K B 3 |
| 2. Kt—K B 3 | ...... |

The opinion that 2. P—Q B 4 is a better move here, is nowadays almost unanimous. But at the time this actual game was played some of the Masters still "feared" the so-called Budapest Gambit (2. ....P—K 4 as answer to 2. P—Q B 4).

| 2. ...... | P—Q Kt 3 |
| 3. P—B 4 | ...... |

If 3. P—K Kt 3, then 3. ....B—Kt 2 ; 4. B—Kt 2, P—B 4 !

3.	B—Kt 2
4. P—K 3	P—K 3
5. B—Q 3	B—Kt 5 ch
6. B—Q 2	B×B ch
7. Q Kt×B	P—Q 3
8. Castles	Q Kt—Q 2
9. Q—B 2	......

White has obtained a fairly good position which he could still improve by continuing 9. Kt—Kt 5, and if 9. .... P—K R 3 then 10. K Kt —K 4, Castles ; 11. P—B 4, P—Q 4 (or 11. Kt×Kt ; 12. B×Kt !) ; 12. Kt—K Kt 3, P—B 4 ; 13. Q—K 2 followed by Q R—Q 1, etc. The text move, although not actually bad, is still rather aimless and allows Black to preserve his well-posted Bishop.

9. ......   Castles

| 10. Q R—Q 1 | Q—K 2 |
| 11. Kt—Kt 5 | ...... |

Two moves too late !

| 11. ...... | P—K R 3 |
| 12. Kt—R 7 | ...... |

Or 12. K Kt—K 4, K R—Q 1, etc., analogous to the text continuation.

12.	K R—Q 1
13. Kt×Kt ch	Kt×Kt
14. Kt—K 4	P—B 4
15. Kt×Kt ch	Q×Kt
16. P×P	......

White has succeeded in exchanging almost all the minor pieces, but he is still very far from obtaining the draw he was obviously playing for, as Black's Pawn's position is much more elastic. The exchange in text has the evident disadvantage of opening to the opponent the Q Kt's file, but on the other hand the alternative 16. B—K 4 would also be not quite satisfactory because of 16. ....P—Q 4 ! ; 17. B—B 3 (or 17. P×Q P, K P×P followed by ....P—B 5 ∓), B—R 3 ; 18. P—Q Kt 3, Q R—B 1, etc. to Black's advantage.

| 16. ...... | Kt P×P ! |

After 16. ....Q P×P Black on account of the symmetrical Pawn position could hardly have avoided a draw.

17. R—Q 2	Q R—Kt 1
18. K R—Q 1	B—B 3 !
19. P—Q Kt 3	......

Of course not 19. B—R 7 ch, K—R 1 ; 20. R×Q P ?, R×R ; 21. R×R, R×P and wins. But now White threatens both the gain of a Pawn and 20. B—K 4 which would lead to a further simplification.

Position after White's 19th move.

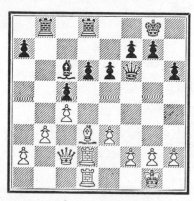

| 19. ...... | Q—K 4 ! |

A very important move, which not only parries the threats mentioned but also prepares a further improvement of Black's position by means of ....P—B 4. White has therefore nothing better than to offer the exchange of Queens, thus producing an ending which proves (because of the typical Pawn constellation) very instructive in spite of the apparent simplicity.

20. Q—Kt 2	Q×Q
21. R×Q	P—Q R 4
22. R (Kt 2)—Q 2	K—B 1
23. B—B 2	K—K 2

The first result of Black's middle-game strategy. The so-called weakness at Q 3 is purely illusory, and White's troubles on the Q R and Q Kt files are on the contrary very real.

24. P—B 3	P—R 5 !
25. K—B 2	P×P
26. B×P	......

After 26. P×P Black would of course get the full control of the Q R file.

| 26. ...... | P—B 4 |

It might be useful to prevent P—K 4.

| 27. K—K 2 | R—Kt 5 |
| 28. K—Q 3 | B—R 5 |

The only, but effective, method to prove the weakness of White's Q R 2 and Q B 4.

| 29. B × B | ...... |

Or 29. K—B 3, K R—Q Kt 1 !; 30. R—Kt 2 (R × P ?, R × B ch ! and wins), P—Q 4 ! etc. ±

| 29. ...... | R × B |
| 30. R—Q Kt 1 | ...... |

Costs a Pawn which in this kind of position is generally decisive. But also 30. R—Q B 1, R—R 6 ch ; 31. K—K 2, K R—Q R 1 ; 32. R (B 1)—B 2, K—Q 2 followed by K—B 3 and P—Q 4 would prove, in the long run, hopeless.

| 30. ...... | R—R 6 ch |
| 31. K—K 2 | ...... |

After 31. R—Kt 3, K R—Q R 1 Black's win would have been even simpler.

| 31. ...... | R—B 6 |
| 32. P—Q R 4 | R—R 6 ! |

Much better than 32. ....R × P ; 33. R—R 2, after which White's passed Pawn would create some trouble for Black.

33. R—Kt 7 ch	R—Q 2
34. R(Q2)—Kt2	R × P
35. R × R ch	K × R
36. R—Kt 7 ch	K—B 3
37. R × P	R × P
38. R—Kt 6	......

White wins the Pawn back, but this proves to be without any effect as Black's Rook will occupy the 7th rank and his King is able to support the free Q B Pawn. The rest is merely routine.

38.	K—Q 4
39. R × R P	R—B 7 ch
40. K—B 1	P—B 5
41. R—R 8	P—B 6
42. P—R 4	......

Or 42. R—Q B 8, P—B 5 !; 43. P × P, K—Q 5 ; 44. P—R 4, K—K 6 ; 45. K—Kt 1, K × P; 46. P—R 5, K—Kt 4 ; 47. P—Kt 4, P—Q 4, etc., winning easily.

42.	R—Q 7
43. K—K 1	R × P
44. R—Q B 8	P—B 7
45. P—R 5	R—R 7
46. P—R 6	R × P
47. R × P	R—R 8 ch
48. K—Q 2	R—R 7 ch
49. K—Q 3	R × R
Resigns.	

GAME 14

QUEEN'S INDIAN DEFENCE

Dresden Tournament, May, 1926.

White : A. RUBINSTEIN

Brilliancy Prize

1. P—Q 4	Kt—K B 3
2. Kt—K B 3	P—K 3
3. B—B 4	P—Q Kt 3
4. P—K R 3	......

It was certainly not necessary to prevent Black's Kt—K R 4 at this moment. The weakening of the square K Kt 3 gave me the idea of a quite unusual but, as the following proves, very effective system of development.

| 4. ...... | B—Kt 2 |
| 5. Q Kt—Q 2 | B—Q 3 ! |

After this, White has the unpleasant choice between (1) the exchange, which strengthens Black's position in the middle ; (2) 6. P—

K 3, which would spoil, after 6.
....B×B, his Pawn position ; and
(3) 6. B—Kt 5 after which Black
would secure the advantage of the
pair of Bishops by means of ....
P—K R 3.

6. B×B	P×B
7. P—K 3	Castles
8. B—K 2	......

And not 8. B—Q 3 as he intends
to play Kt×Kt after Black's P—
Q 4, followed by Kt—K 5.

8.	P—Q 4
9. Castles	Kt—B 3
10. P—B 3	......

If 10. Kt—K 5 then 10. ....
Kt—K 2 followed by ....P—Q 3, etc.

| 10. ...... | Kt—K 5 ! |

Black has already obtained the
initiative.

11. Kt×Kt	P×Kt
12. Kt—Q 2	P—B 4
13. P—K B 4	......

Otherwise Black would play ....
Q—Kt 4 preventing the text-move
for a long time.

| 13. ...... | P—K Kt 4 ! |

Black must play most energetically before the opponent finds time
to co-ordinate the activity of his
pieces.

| 14. Kt—B 4 | P—Q 4 |
| 15. Kt—K 5 | Kt×Kt |

Much better than 15. ....P×P ;
16. Kt×Kt ! followed by 17. R×P,
etc.

| 16. Q P×Kt | ...... |

In case of 16. B P×Kt Black

would eventually break through by
means of ....P—B 5.

| 16. ...... | K—R 1 |
| 17. P—Q R 4 (?) | ...... |

White has no time for this
counter attack. His only chance of
a successful defence was 17. P—
K Kt 3 followed by 18. K—R 2,
etc. After he has missed this
opportunity Black gradually exerts
an overwhelming pressure.

| 17. ...... | R—K Kt 1 |
| 18. Q—Q 2 | P×P ! |

At the right time, as White
cannot retake with the Pawn on
account of 19. ....Q—R 5 with the
double threat 20. ....Q×P or
20. ....R×P ch !

| 19. R×P | Q—Kt 4 |
| 20. B—B 1 | Q—Kt 6 ! |

Forcing White's next King's
move and thus preparing the win
of a *tempo* at the 23rd move.

21. K—R 1	Q—Kt 2
22. Q—Q 4	B—R 3 !
23. R—B 2	......

White has most obviously no
choice.

| 23. ...... | Q—Kt 6 ! |

Compare the note to Black's 20th
move.

| 24. R—B 2 | B×B |
| 25. R×B | Q R—Q B 1 |

Still working with gains of *tempi*
as he threatens now 26. ....R—B 5.

26. P—Q Kt 3	R—B 2
27. R—K 2	Q R—K Kt 2
28. R—B 4	......

Position after White's 28th move.

28. ......   R—Kt 3 !

After this move a highly original position is obtained, the outstanding particulars of which are the following : Black's immediate threat is 29. ....R—R 3 ; 30. Q—Q 1, Q—Kt 2 winning the King's Pawn, as 31. Q—Q 4 would be answered by 31. ....R×P ch. If White tries to parry this by playing 29. Q—Q 1, Black still answers with 29. ....R—R 3 !, thus putting the opponent in a position of a complete Zugzwang.

As a matter of fact (1) R at K B 4 could not move because of 30. .... Q×K P. (2) R at K 2 is tied by the defence of the squares K 3 and K Kt 2. (3) The King could not move because of 30. ....R (or Q)× R P. (4) The Queen could not move either on the first rank—because of 30. ....Q—Kt 2 ! etc., nor on the Q's file—because of 30. ....R×P ch ! etc. (5) Finally in the event of 30. P—B 4 Black would win by 30. ....P—Q 5 ! etc., and in the event of 30. P—Kt 4— by 30. ....Q—Kt 2 ; 31. Q—Q 4, R—Q B 1 ! followed by 32. .... R—B 5.

Therefore White offers a Pawn in the hope of exchanging a pair of Rooks and thus weakening the enemy's attack.

29. Q—Kt 4   R—R 3
30. P—R 4   ......

Now absolutely forced.

30. ......   Q—Kt 2 !

Much better than the rather prosaic 30. .... R×P ch. If now 31. Q—Q 6, then 31. ....R—Kt 3 ; 32. R (B 4)—B 2, P—B 5 ! ; 33. P×P, P—K 6 ! and wins.

31. P—B 4   R—Kt 3
32. Q—Q 2   R—Kt 6 !

Threatening 33. ....R—R 6 ch ; 34. K—Kt 1, Q—Kt 6 ; and, if immediately 33. K—Kt 1, then 33. ....P—Q 5 ! ; 34. P×P, P—K 6 ! ; 35. Q—B 2 (Kt 2), R—R 6 followed by Q—Kt 6 and wins. White is helpless.

33. Q—K 1   R×Kt P
Resigns.

GAME 15

NIMZOWITSCH'S DEFENCE

New York Tournament, March, 1927.

Black : A. NIMZOWITSCH

1. P—Q 4	Kt—K B 3
2. P—Q B 4	P—K 3
3. Kt—Q B 3	B—Kt 5
4. Q—B 2	P—Q 3

The only fashionable move nowadays (see, for instance, my second match with Dr. Euwe) is 4. .... P—Q 4.

5. B—Kt 5	Q Kt—Q 2
6. P—K 3	P—Q Kt 3
7. B—Q 3	B—Kt 2
8. P—B 3	......

By retaining control on his K 4 White makes it very difficult for the opponent to form a suitable plan of further development.

8.	B × Kt ch
9. Q × B	P—B 4
10. Kt—R 3 !	......

Black expected here either 10. Kt—K 2 or 10. R—Q 1, both permitting him to simplify matters by means of 10. ....Kt—Q 4 !. The move selected permits White to make an effective use of his Bishops.

| 10. ...... | P—K R 3 |
| 11. B—B 4 | ...... |

And not 11. B—R 4 because of the possibility of ....P—K Kt 4— Kt 5, etc.

| 11. ...... | Q—K 2 |
| 12. B—Kt 3 ! | ...... |

Black threatened 12. ....P—K 4 eventually followed by .... P—K 5.

| 12. ...... | P—K 4 ? |

This not too unnatural attempt to clear the situation in the middle is most likely already the decisive error. After the simple 12. .... Castles K R White would not have found it very easy to exploit the unmistakable weakness of the dark-coloured squares of Black's position.

| 13. P × K P | P × P |
| 14. Castles (Q R) | P—Kt 3 |

14. ....P—K 5 ; 15. B—K 2, etc. would be useless, and the immediate 14. Castles (Q R) would have been met by 15. B—B 5, P—Kt 3 ; 16. B × K P !, P × B ; 17. R × Kt followed by 18. B × Kt or 18. B × R, etc., with a decisive advantage.

| 15. B—Q B 2 | ...... |

This Bishop will prove very useful on the diagonal Q R 4—K 8.

15.	Castles (Q R)
16. B—Q R 4	K R—K 1
17. Kt—B 2	Q—K 3

Black wants to dislodge the ominous White King's Bishop, but this plan costs a lot of time which White will utilise to strengthen his pressure on the Queen's file in a decisive manner. A slightly better chance of salvation was offered by 17. ....Kt—R 4, and if 18. R—Q 2 then 18. ....Kt × B ; 19. P × Kt, R—R 1 ! ; 20. K R—Q 1, Kt—Kt 1, etc.

18. Kt—Q 3	R—K 2
19. R—Q 2	Q R—K 1
20. K R—Q 1	......

If now 20. ....Kt—R 4 then simply 21. B × Kt ch, R × B ; 22. Kt × B P and wins.

| 20. ...... | B—B 3 |
| 21. B—Q B 2 ! | ...... |

Position after White's 21st move.

| 21. ...... | Kt—R 4 |

In this rather harmless-looking position—with only one pawn exchanged and none of White's pieces posted further than his third rank !—Black is already completely helpless against the threats of 22. Kt × B P followed by 23. R—Q 6, or alternatively 22. P—Kt 4. If, for instance, 21. ....K—B 2 (in order to protect his Q 3), then 22. P—Kt 4 !, P × P ; 23. Kt × Kt P, Kt

—B 4 ; 24. Kt—Q 5 ch, B × Kt ; 25. P × B, Q—Q 3 ; 26. P—B 4 ! and wins. And after the text move Black loses the Queen and a Pawn for a Rook and Knight, after which the rest is merely a matter of technique.

Although this game is one of my happiest achievements in the domain of the openings strategy, it has passed almost unnoticed, merely because of its length and the predilection of most of the chess journalists for short "brilliancies." Yet it was certainly not my fault that Nimzowitsch (whose hopes for the second prize were more than strongly compromised by this loss) decided to fight a desperate struggle to the bitter end.

22. Kt × B P !	Kt × Kt
23. R—Q 6	Kt × B
24. P × Kt	Q × R
25. R × Q	R—B 2
26. P—Q Kt 4	Kt—Kt 2
27. R × B	......

It is obvious that every reduction of material will from now on be in White's favour.

27.	R × R
28. B—R 4	R (K 1)—K 3
29. B × R	R × B
30. Q × P	......

This particular exchange opens new fields of action for both White's Queen and King.

30.	R × P ch
31. K—Q 2	P—K R 4
32. P—R 3	......

White's next object will be to tie up Black's Rook and Knight. He succeeds, by bringing his Queen into a very strong position in the middle of the board (see 43rd move).

32.	R—B 2
33. Q—K 8 ch	Kt—Q 1
34. P—K 4	R—Q 2 ch

35. K—K 3	R—B 2
36. K—B 4	......

Also good was 36. K—B 2 followed by K—Kt 1—R 2 and eventually P—B 4—B 5, etc. But White wants his King to participate in the final battle.

36.	R—B 6
37. P—R 4	R—B 7
38. Q—K 7	R—B 2
39. Q—B 6	R—B 7
40. Q—K 7	R—B 2
41. Q—Q 6	Kt—K 3 ch
42. K—K 5	......

Or 42. K—K 3—B 2—Kt 1, etc., as mentioned in the previous note.

42.	Kt—Q 1
43. Q—Q 5 !	R—B 3
44. K—B 4	......

From now on White decides to provoke the move ....P—Q R 4 which will create a new weakness at Black's Q Kt 3.

44.	Kt—K 3 ch
45. K—K 3	R—B 6 ch
46. K—K 2	R—B 2
47. P—B 4	Kt—Q 1
48. K—K 3	R—B 6 ch
49. K—Q 4	R—B 2
50. K—K 5 !	P—R 4

Now practically forced, as after 50. ....R—B 3 ; 51. P—B 5 !, etc., there would not be a satisfactory move left.

51. Q—R 8 ch	K—Q 2
52. P—Kt 5	K—K 2

Instead 52. ....R—Kt 2 ; 53. K—B 6, etc., would have been perfectly useless.

53. P—B 5 !	......

And not 53. Q—Kt 8 ? because of 53. ....Kt—K 3 ! winning the Queen because of the mating threat at Q B 4.

53.	......	P—B 3 ch
54.	K—Q 4	R—Q 2 ch
55.	K—K 3	P×P
56.	P×P	......

After this Black's K R's Pawn is bound to fall rapidly.

| 56. | ...... | Kt—B 2 |
| 57. | Q—B 3 | Kt—K 4 |

This Knight's position, though good, is not a sufficient compensation for the further material loss.

58.	Q×P	R—Q 6 ch
59.	K—B 2	R—Q 7 ch
60.	K—B 1	R—Q 5
61.	Q—R 7 ch	K—Q 3

If 61. ....Kt—B 2 then 62. Q—Kt 8, followed by Q—Kt 8 with the win of the Q Kt Pawn.

62.	Q—Q Kt 7	Kt—Q 2
63.	Q—B 6 ch	K—K 2
64.	Q—K 6 ch	K—Q 1
65.	Q—Kt 3	R—Q Kt 5
66.	Q—Q 1	K—K 2
67.	Q—K 2 ch	K—Q 1
68.	Q—R 2	K—K 2
69.	K—K 2 !	R—K 5 ch

Or 69. ....K—Q 1 ; 70. Q—Kt 8 ch, followed by 71. P—Kt 4, etc.

70.	K—B 3	R—Q Kt 5
71.	K—K 3	Kt—B 4
72.	Q—Kt 8	Kt—Q 2
73.	P—Kt 4 !	......

This brings now a prompt decision.

73.	......	R×R P
74.	P—Kt 5	P×P
75.	Q×P ch	K—Q 3
76.	Q—Kt 6 ch	K—B 2
77.	Q—B 6 ch	K—Q 1
78.	P—B 6	R—R 8
79.	P—Kt 4	R—K B 8
80.	P—Kt 5	R—B 4
81.	Q—R 8 ch	K—B 2
82.	Q—B 6 ch	K—Q 1
83.	P—Kt 6 !	......

If now 83. ....R×B P then 84. P—Kt 7 and if 83. Kt×P then 84. Q—Q 6 ch followed by 85. P—Kt 7, etc.

Resigns.

GAME 16

QUEEN'S PAWN'S OPENING

New York Tournament, March, 1927.

Black : F. MARSHALL

Brilliancy Prize

1.	P—Q 4	Kt—K B 3
2.	P—Q B 4	P—K 3
3.	Kt—K B 3	Kt—K 5

This unnatural and time-wasting move can be successfully answered in different ways. One of the simplest is 4. Q—B 2 and in the event of 4. ....P—Q 4 or 4. ....P—K B 4 ; 5. Kt—B 3, etc.

| 4. | K Kt—Q 2 | ...... |

With the obvious idea of exchanging at K 4 and developing the other Knight at Q B 3. The present game proves rather convincingly the soundness of this scheme.

| 4. | ...... | B—Kt 5 |

A typical Marshall trap : if now 5. P—Q R 3 then 5. ....Q—B 3 ! with an immediate win !

| 5. | Q—B 2 | P—Q 4 |

Or 5. ....P—K B 4 ; 6. P—Q R 3 forcing the exchange of both Black's developed pieces.

| 6. | Kt—B 3 | P—K B 4 |
| 7. | K Kt×Kt | ...... |

After this White will easily force the opening of the central files, by means of P—K B 3 and eventually

P—K 4. And as he is better developed, this opening must secure him a substantial positional advantage.

| 7. ...... | B P×Kt |
| 8. B—B 4 | ...... |

This Bishop will protect the King's position against any sudden attack.

| 8. ...... | Castles |
| 9. P—K 3 | P—B 3 |

White was threatening, by means of 10. P—Q R 3, to force the exchange of the Bishop at Kt 5 for his Knight (10. P—Q R 3, B—Q 3 ?; 11. B×B followed by 12. P×P, K P×P ; 13. Kt×Q P !, etc.),

| 10. B—K 2 | Kt—Q 2 |
| 11. P—Q R 3 | ...... |

I considered this as being sounder play than 11. Castles K R, Kt—B 3 ; 12. P—B 3, Kt—R 4 !; 13. P × K P, Kt × B ; 14. R × Kt, R × R ; 15. P × R, P × B P, etc.

| 11. ...... | B—K 2 |

After the exchange at B 6 his dark-coloured squares would have remained helplessly weak.

| 12. Castles K R | B—Kt 4 |

There is hardly anything better.

| 13. P—B 3 ! | B × B |
| 14. P × B | R × P |

Instead, 14. ....P×K B P; 15. R × P, Kt—B 3; 16. P—Q B 5! would be a sad enough alternative because of the weakness at K 3. By the text move, in conjunction with the three following moves, Marshall tries to save his compromised game through combinative play.

| 15. P × K P | R × R ch |

| 16. R × R | P—K 4 |

Or 16. ....P × B P ; 17. B × P, Kt—Kt 3 ; 18. Q—B 2 !, etc., with a clear advantage.

| 17. Q—Q 2 ! | ...... |

The initial move of the decisive manœuvre. If now 17. ....Q—Kt 3 then 18. P—B 5, Q—R 4 ; 19. P × Q P, K P×P ; 20. P—Q Kt 4 !, P × Kt ; 21. Q—Kt 5, Q—B 2 ; 22. P—Q 6, P—K R 3 ; 23. Q—K 7 and wins.

| 17. ...... | P—B 4 |

Trying to increase the tension at any cost, as the Pawn exchanges would have proved rapidly disastrous.

Position after Black's 17th move.

| 18. P × K P ! | ...... |

Erroneous would have been instead 18. Kt × P, B P × P ; 19. Q—Kt 4 because of 19. ....Kt—B 3.

| 18. ...... | P—Q 5 |
| 19. Q—B 4 ! | ...... |

This sacrifice in connection with the "quiet" 21st move is doubtless the safest and quickest method to force a victory.

Not 19. Kt—Q 5 because of 19.
....Kt×P followed by 20. ....
Q—Q 3 etc.

19. ......   P×Kt

Forced.

20. Q—B 7 ch   K—R 1
21. P×P !   ......

This alone proves the correctness
of the sacrifice. Tempting, but
premature, would have been instead
21. P—K 6 because of 21. ....Kt—
B 3 ; 22. P—K 7, Q—Kt 1 ; 23.
R×Kt, B—Kt 5 ! ; 24. Q×Q ch,
K×Q ; 25. R—Q 6, R—K 1 !, etc.∓

21. ......   Q—Kt 1
22. Q—K 7   P—K R 3
23. B—R 5 !   ......

And not 23. P—K 6, Kt—B 3 ;
24. P—K 5, Kt—R 2 !, etc.

23. ......   P—R 4

If 23. ....Q×P then of course
24. B—B 7.

24. P—K 6   P—K Kt 3
25. P×Kt   B×P
26. R—B 7   Resigns.

GAME 17

QUEEN'S GAMBIT DECLINED
(ORTHODOX DEFENCE)

Kecskemet Tournament, July,
1927.
Black : Dr. L. Asztalos.

Brilliancy Prize

1. P—Q 4   P—Q 4
2. P—Q B 4   P—K 3
3. Kt—K B 3   Kt—K B 3
4. B—Kt 5   P—K R 3

This is, rightly, considered not
satisfactory because Black's pair
of Bishops will not quite compensate for White's advantage in
space. The modern line 4. ....B—
Kt 5 ch in connection with 5. ....
P×P (forming the so-called Vienna
variation) has not yet been analysed
to its ultimate end, but offers anyhow more fighting chances than the
one chosen here.

5. B×Kt   Q×B
6. Kt—B 3   P—B 3
7. Q—Kt 3   ......

The right preparation for P—K 4.

7. ......   Kt—Q 2
8. P—K 4   P×K P
9. Kt×P   Q—B 5
10. B—Q 3   B—K 2
11. Castles   Castles
12. K R—K 1   R—Q 1
13. Q R—Q 1   Q—B 2

In consequence of the variation
selected, Black has a lot of difficulties in developing his pieces, especially the Queen's Bishop. The
Queen's retreat is practically forced,
as 13. ....Kt—B 1, for instance,
would have been answered by 14.
Q—R 8 with the threat of 15.
Kt—K 5,

14. Kt—Kt 3   Kt—B 1
15. Q—B 3 !   ......

White intends to continue with
Kt—R 5 followed by P—Q 5
which would force a fatal weakening
of Black's King's position. Black's
next manœuvre parries that danger,
but at the cost of the disorganisa-
tion of the Queen-side Pawns.

15. ......   P—Q R 4
16. P—Q R 3   P—R 5
17. Kt—K 5   ......

After 17. Kt—R 5 the answer 17.
....Q—R 4 would force the exchange of Queens.

17. ......   Q—R

4

| 18. Q—B 1 | B—Q 2 |
| 19. P—B 5 ! | ...... |

The logical reply to the advance of Black's Q R's Pawn. White threatens now to install his Knight at Q Kt 6 and thus forces the following Pawn's move which deprives the Q B 3 Pawn of its natural protection.

19.	P—Q Kt 4
20. B—K 4	Q—B 2
21. Q—B 3	......

Threatening 22. Q—K B 3, etc.

| 21. ...... | B—K 1 |
| 22. Kt—K 2 ! | ...... |

The beginning of a series of manœuvres against which Black has no adequate defence. In the first place White threatens to bring his Knight via Q B 1 to Q Kt 4 and in order to prevent this Black is forced to exchange his valuable Knight, thus leaving his K R 2 defenceless.

22.	R—R 3
23. Kt—B 1	Kt—Q 2
24. Kt×Kt	R×Kt
25. Kt—Q 3	R—Q 1
26. Kt—K 5	B—B 1

Hoping to build a new defensive position by means of ....P—Kt 3 followed by ....B—Kt 2; but White's next move does not leave him the time to do it.

| 27. P—R 4 ! | R (R 3)—R 1 |

If 27. ....P—K Kt 3 then 28. P—R 5, P—Kt 4 ; 29. P—B 4 ! with a speedy demolition of Black's last ramparts.

| 28. B—Kt 1 | ...... |

Threatening 29. Q—B 2, P—K Kt 3. 30. P—R 5, etc.

28.	P—R 4
29. Q—B 3	P—Kt 3
30. P—K Kt 4	P×P

| 31. Q×Kt P | B—Kt 2 |
| 32. B—R 2 ! | ...... |

An important move which prevents the advance of Black's K B's Pawn. Black cannot prepare this advance by playing 32.....Q—K 2, as the answer 33. Kt×Kt P ! would win immediately.

| 32. ...... | P—Kt 5 ! |

An ingenious, but insufficient resource : if 33. P×P then 33. .... P—R 6; 34. P×P, R×R P, etc., with some counter-play.

33. B—B 4 !	P×P
34. P×P	Q—R 4
35. Q—K 4	......

Best. Premature would be 35. Kt×Kt P, R×P !; or 35. P—R 5, P×P; 36. Q×R P, R×P !, etc.

| 35. ...... | Q—B 2 |
| 36. Q—B 4 | ...... |

Preparing the following Pawn's move, against which no defence exists.

36.	Q R—Kt 1
37. P—R 5 !	P×P
38. K—R 1	R—Kt 2
39. R—K Kt 1	Q—K 2

Position after Black's 39th move.

40. R×B ch !   ......

Black hoped that he had defended himself against this possibility by his last move. Yet the combination still works because of the unexpected point at the 42nd move.

40. ......   K×R
41. R—Kt 1 ch   K—R 2
42. Kt×K B P ! ! ......

Only so ! If now 42. .... Q×Kt, then 43. B—Q 3 ch, Q—Kt 3 ; 44. B×Q ch, B×B ; 45. R×B ! K×R ; 46. Q—K 4 ch, K—Kt 2 ; 47. Q—K 5 ch ! and Black, after a few further checks, would inevitably lose one of his Rooks.

Resigns.

GAME 18

CARO-KANN DEFENCE

Kecskemet Tournament, July, 1927.

Black : DR. S. TARTAKOWER

1. P—K 4   P—Q B 3
2. P—Q 4   P—Q 4
3. Kt—Q B 3   P×P
4. Kt×P   Kt—B 3
5. Kt—Kt 3   ......

In the Hastings Tournament of 1936-37 I successfully tried against W. Winter the Pawn's sacrifice 5. B—Q 3, recommended by Dr. Tarrasch shortly before his death. This game continued 5. .... Q×P ; 6. Kt—K B 3, Q—Q 1 ; 7. Q—K 2, Kt×Kt (slightly premature would be here 7. .... Q Kt—Q 2 as four (!) amateurs in consultation played against me in Majorca, January, 1935—because of the unpleasant answer 8. Kt—Q 6 mate ....) 8. B×Kt, Kt—Q 2 ; 9. Castles, Kt—B 4 ; 10. R—Q 1, Q—B 2 ; 11. Kt—K 5 ! Kt×B ; 12. Q×Kt, B—K 3 ; 13. B—B 4, Q—B 1 ; 14. Kt—B 4 !

P—K Kt 4 !? ; 15. B×P, R—K Kt 1 ; 16. B—B 4, B×Kt ; 17. Q×B, Q—Kt 5 ; 18. P—K Kt 3, P—K 4 ; 19. R—K 1 (a more elegant solution was 19. Q—Kt 3 ! as 19. .... Q or P×B would have led to an immediate disaster after 20. Q×P), Castles ; 20. R×P and Black resigned after a few moves.

5. ......   P—K 4

Most probably sufficient to equalise. But in order to achieve this Black must play the next moves with care.

6. Kt—B 3   P×P
7. Kt×P   ......

Also 7. Q×P, Q×Q ; 8. Kt×Q, B—Q B 4 ; 9. Kt Q 4—B 5, Castles ; 10. B—K 3 played by me against Capablanca in New York, 1927, does not give any serious chances of favourable complications.

7. ......   B—Q B 4

Already a rather serious loss of time. Indicated was the immediate 7. .... B—K 2 followed by castling with a satisfactory position.

8. Q—K 2 ch !   B—K 2

Or 8. .... Q—K 2 ; 9. Q×Q ch, B×Q ; 10. Kt (Q 4)—B 5 with some advantage for White.

9. B—K 3   P—B 4 (?)

This attempt to prevent White's Q R castling fails completely. A much lesser evil was 9. .... Castles ; 10. Castles, Q—R 4 ; 11. K—Kt 1, Kt—Q 4 ; 12. Q—B 3 with no immediate danger for Black.

10. Kt (Q 4)—B 5 Castles
11. Q—B 4 !   ......

An important move which prepares with tempo (attacking Black's

Q B 4) the development of the K's Bishop.

11. ......   R—K 1

Also after the immediate 11. .... P—Q Kt 3 White would gradually obtain a winning attack by continuing 12. R—Q 1 followed by Q—K R 4, etc.

12. B—Q 3   P—Q Kt 3
13. Castles (Q R) B—R 3

It is obvious that other moves would also lead to a more or less rapid catastrophe.

Position after Black's 13th move.

14. Kt—R 6 ch ! ......

By making this forcing combination White calculated that his opponent cannot obtain three pieces for the Queen, but—as a consequence of the weakness of his Q R 1—K R 8 diagonal—only two ; the remainder is compulsory for Black.

14. ......   P×Kt
15. B×P ch !   Kt×B

If 15. ....K—R 1 then 16. Q×K B P followed by 17. Kt—B 5 with a mating attack.

16. Q—Kt 4 ch   K—R 1

17. R×Q   R×R

Or 17. B×R ; 18. Q—B 3, etc.

18. Q—K 4   Kt—Q B 3
19. Q×Kt   B—K B 1
20. Kt—B 5   B—B 5
21. B×R P   B—Q 4
22. Q—B 7   Q R—B 1
23. Q—B 4   R—B 3
24. B×B   R×B
25. Q—K 5 ch   Kt—B 3
26. Kt—Q 6 !   Resigns.

GAME 19

QUEEN'S PAWN OPENING

Kecskemet Tournament, July, 1927.

White : H. KMOCH

1. P—Q 4   P—Q 4
2. Kt—K B 3   P—Q B 3
3. P—K 3   ......

After this tame move Black has no difficulty with his Queen's Bishop. More usual and better is 3. P—B 4, leading to the Slav Defence of the Queen's Gambit Declined.

3. ......   B—B 4
4. B—Q 3   P—K 3
5. Castles   ......

The exchange here or at the next move certainly cannot be recommended.

5. ......   Q Kt—Q 2
6. P—B 4   K Kt—B 3
7. Q—B 2   ......

It is easily comprehensible that White wants to clear the situation in the middle as soon as possible. 7. Kt—B 3 would have been simply answered by 7. ....B—K 2.

7. ......   B×B
8. Q×B   Kt—K 5

In order to eliminate as many light pieces as possible, because White will sooner or later obtain some more space by playing P—K 4.

9. K Kt—Q 2   Q Kt—B 3
10. Kt—Q B 3   ......

After 10. Kt × Kt, Kt × Kt ; 11. P—B 3, Kt—B 3 ; 12. P—K 4, P × B P ; 13. Q × P, Q—Kt 3 ; 14. Kt—B 3, R—Q 1 ; 15. R—Q 1, B—K 2 followed by ....Castles, etc., White's position would have remained rather shaky.

10. ......   Kt × K Kt
11. B × Kt   B—K 2
12. P—K 4   ......

The surplus freedom which White obtains by this move will be neutralised by the necessity for him to protect permanently his Queen's Pawn. But he hardly had another plan at his disposal as blocking attempts would fail, e.g. : 12. P—B 5, P—K 4 ! ; or 12. P—B 4, P—B 4 !—both rather in Black's favour.

12. ......   P × K P
13. Kt × P   Castles
14. B—B 3   Q—B 2

Q Kt 3 was also a good square for the Queen.

15. Q R—Q 1   Q R—Q 1
16. R—Q 2 ?   ......

White loses this game not because of the opening, which was more or less satisfactory, but chiefly because of his altogether passive and conventional play. Here, for instance, he could quite safely play 16. P—B 4, preventing the Black Queen from occupying that square. From now on the chances of the second player can be considered as decidedly the better ones.

16. ......   Q—B 5 !
17. Kt × Kt ch   B × Kt

18. K R—Q 1   R—Q 2
19. Q—Kt 3   ......

The exchange of Queens would doubtless increase White's drawing prospects. But Black can easily avoid it.

19. ......   Q—B 4
20. P—B 4   ......

The main object of this move seems to be the prevention of the eventual replies ....B—Kt 4 or ....P—K 4.

20. ......   K R—Q 1
21. Q—K 3   P—K R 4 !

Not only giving a loophole for the King but also blocking White's King's side (22. P—K R 3, P—R 5, etc.).

22. P—Q Kt 4   ......

This facilitates the job of Black, who will immediately eliminate the opponent's Q B 4, and thus obtain full control over his Q 4.

22. ......   P—Q Kt 4 !
23. Q—B 3   ......

This attempt to save by tactical means a strategically very sick position leads to a rapid debacle. But also after the quieter 23. P—B 5, R—Q 4 followed by ....P—K Kt 4 !, etc., the game could hardly last very long.

23. ......   P × P
24. Q × B P   Q × P
25. Q × B P   P—K 4 !

Obtaining a decisive material advantage.

26. Q—K 2   P × P
27. R—Q 3   ......

If this blockade would be possible Black would have had to face some technical difficulties. But as it is, he succeeds in forcing an immediate win by a keenly calculated combination.

Position after White's 27th move.

27. ......   P×B !

The chief variation of this transaction is both pretty and convincing : 28. R×R, R×R ; 29. Q—K 8 ch, K—R 2 ; 30. Q×R, Q—K 5 ! ! ; 31. Q×B P (or Q—Q 5, Q×Q ; 32. R×Q, P—B 7 and wins, as 33. R—Q B 5 is refuted by 33. ....B—Q 5 ch), P—B 7 ; 32. Q×R P ch, K—Kt 1 and wins.

28. R×R   R×R
29. R×R   ......

Loses instantly.

29. ......   B—Q 5 ch
30. K—R 1   ......

Or, 30. R×B, Q×R ch ; 31. K—B 1, Q—B 5 ch ; 32. K—K 1, Q×Kt P etc.

30. ......   Q—Q B 8 ch

Resigns.

GAME 20

FRENCH DEFENCE

First Match-Game, Buenos Aires, September, 1927.

White : J. R. CAPABLANCA

1.	P—K 4	P—K 3
2.	P—Q 4	P—Q 4
3.	Kt—Q B 3	B—Kt 5
4.	P×P	P×P
5.	B—Q 3	Kt—Q B 3
6.	Kt—K 2	K Kt—K 2
7.	Castles	B—K B 4
8.	B×B	......

Other moves like 8. P—Q R 3 or 8. Kt—Kt 3 would also prove perfectly harmless. This game shows once more that, if White has any fighting ambitions, he must avoid in this variation the Pawn exchange at the 4th move.

8.	......	Kt×B
9.	Q—Q 3	Q—Q 2
10.	Kt—Q 1	......

The beginning of a long series of slightly inferior moves. The natural development move, 10. B—B 4, which Black intended to answer by 10. ....Castles Q R would have led to a more lively struggle.

10.	......	Castles K R
11.	Kt—K 3	Kt×Kt
12.	B×Kt	......

White's minor pieces are now obstructing the vital K's file. This is a convincing proof of the inexactitude of his opening strategy.

12.	......	K R—K 1
13.	Kt—B 4	......

As the answer proves, the Knight has no future on this square.

Natural and good enough for a draw was 13. B—B 4 followed by P—Q B 3, etc.

| 13. ...... | B—Q 3 ! |

Thus Black proposes a transaction whose results would be very satisfactory for himself. If, namely, 14. Kt×P, B×P ch ; 15. K× B, Q×Kt ; 16. P—Q B 4 then 16. ....Q—R 4 ch ; 17. K—Kt 1, Q R—Q 1 ; 18. P—Q 5, R—Q 3 and White's King position would be in danger.

| 14. K R—K 1 | ...... |

White continues to play superficially. Indicated was first 14. P—Q B 3.

| 14. ...... | Kt—Kt 5 |
| 15. Q—Kt 3 ? | ...... |

After this he will be obliged at least to spoil his Pawn position in rather an ugly way. The lesser evil was 15. Q—Q 2, Q—B 4 ; 16. K R—Q B 1, P—K R 4 ! (threatening R—K 5 followed by P—R 5) with some positional advantage for Black.

| 15. ...... | Q—B 4 |
| 16. Q R—B 1 ? | ...... |

After this further mistake, the game can hardly be saved as Black now wins a Pawn, with a fairly good position. Necessary was 16. Kt—Q 3 after which Black, it is true, would have obtained a far superior end game by continuing 16. ....Kt×Kt ; 17. Q×Kt, Q× Q ; 18. P×Q, B—Kt 5 ; 19. K R—Q B 1, P—Q B 3, eventually followed by ....P—Q R 4 !, etc.

Position after White's 16th move.

| 16. ...... | Kt×B P ! |
| 17. R×Kt | Q×Kt |

This is the possibility overlooked by Capablanca at his 16th move. He expected only 17. ....B×Kt after which he would have re-established the balance by 18. R—B 5, etc.

| 18. P—Kt 3 | ...... |

It is merely a matter of taste whether this or 18. Q×Q P, Q× R P ch.; 19. K—B 1, P—Q B 3, etc., is preferable.

| 18. ...... | Q—B 4 |

Tempting was also 18. ....Q— B 6 ; 19. Q×Kt P, P—K R 4 ; 20. Q—Kt 5, P—R 5 ; 21. Q—K 2, Q—B 4, etc., with a good attack. But the decision to keep the material advantage obtained can certainly not be blamed.

19. Q R—K 2	P—Q Kt 3
20. Q—Kt 5	P—K R 4
21. P—K R 4	R—K 5

Threatening 22. ....R×R P !, etc.

| 22. B—Q 2 (!) | ...... |

This temporary sacrifice of a second Pawn offers comparatively the best saving chances—in case Black accepts it. Perfectly hopeless would have been 22. Q—Q 3, QR—K 1 ; 23. B—Q 2, Q—K 3, etc.

22. ......   R×Q P

This acceptance—which had to be calculated very carefully—was by no means necessary. Simple and convincing was instead 22. .... Q R—K 1, as after the exchange of the White Queen for two Rooks by 23. Q×R ch, R×R ; 24. R×R ch, K—R 2, etc. Black, because of his considerable positional advantage, would have but little difficulty in forcing the win.

23. B—B 3   R—Q 6

Also after 23. ....R—K Kt 5 (23. ....R—Q B 5 ? ; 24. R—K 5 ! etc.) ; 24. B—K 5 White would have finally won back one of his minus Pawns.

24. B—K 5   R—Q 1
25. B×B   R×B

Technically simpler than the unaesthetic 25. .... P×B ; 26. Q—B 6 !, etc.

26. R—K 5   Q—B 6

Of course not 26. ....Q—Kt 3 ; 27. R—Kt 5, etc.

27. R×R P   Q×R

And here 27. ....R—K 3 would be another way of suicide (28. Q—K 8 ch !, etc.).

28. R—K 8 ch   K—R 2
29. Q×R ch   Q—Kt 3
30. Q—Q 1   R—K 3 !

An interesting conception. Black gives back his plus Pawn in order to combine the advance of the free Q's Pawn with a mating attack.

Much less convincing would be 30. ....P—Q 5 because of the answer 31. Q—B 3 threatening both 32. Q—R 8 and 32. P—R 5.

31. R—R 8   R—K 4 !

Intending to place the Queen behind the Rook and at the same time preparing the formation of the Pawn chain Q Kt 3—Q B 4— Q 5.

32. R×P   P—Q B 4
33. R—Q 7 (?)   ......

Shortens the agony. I expected, instead, 33. K—Kt 2, P—Q 5 ; 34. R—R 3, Q—K 3 ! ; 35. Q—B 3, P— B 5 followed by the decisive advance of the Q's Pawn.

33. ......   Q—K 3
34. Q—Q 3 ch   P—Kt 3
35. R—Q 8   P—Q 5
36. P—R 4   ......

Despair !

36. ......   R—K 8 ch

This direct attack is convincing enough. But Black could also take immediate advantage of the exposed position of the adventurous Rook—for instance, 36. ....Q— K 2 ! ; 37. R—Q Kt 8, Q—B 2 ; 38. Q—Kt 3, R—K 3 ; 39. R—R 8, Q—Kt 2 and the Rook would be lost because of the threat 40. .... R—K 8 ch, etc.

37. K—Kt 2   Q—B 3 ch
38. P—B 3   R—K 6
39. Q—Q 1   Q—K 3
40. P—K Kt 4   R—K 7 ch
41. K—R 3   Q—K 6
42. Q—K R 1   Q—B 5 !

After this there is no way of preventing the next Rook move.

43. P—K R 5   R—K B 7

Resigns.

GAME 21

QUEEN'S GAMBIT DECLINED (CAMBRIDGE SPRINGS DEFENCE)

Eleventh Match-Game, Buenos Aires, October, 1927.

White : J. R. CAPABLANCA

1. P—Q 4	P—Q 4
2. P—Q B 4	P—K 3
3. Kt—Q B 3	Kt—K B 3
4. B—Kt 5	Q Kt—Q 2
5. P—K 3	P—B 3
6. Kt—B 3	Q—R 4
7. Kt—Q 2	B—Kt 5
8. Q—B 2	P×P
9. B×Kt	Kt×B
10. Kt×P	Q—B 2
11. P—Q R 3	B—K 2
12. B—K 2	......

White does not need to hurry to prevent ....P—Q B 4 by playing 12. P—Q Kt 4, as that advance would be still premature because of 13. Kt—Kt 5, Q—Kt 1 ; 14. P×P, B×P ; 15. P—Q Kt 4, B—K 2 ; 16. Kt—R 5, etc.±

12.	Castles
13. Castles K R	B—Q 2

And here also 13. ....P—B 4 would not have been advisable for analogous reasons.

14. P—Q Kt 4	P—Q Kt 3

Safer would be first 14. ....K R —Q 1 followed by ....B—K 1. Black's plan to continue by 15. ....P—Q R 4 ; 16. P×P, P—Q Kt 4 will be parried by the following answer.

15. B—B 3 !	......

If now 15. ....P—Q R 4 then 16. Kt—K 5 !, P×P ; 17. Kt—Kt 5, etc., with the advantage.

15.	Q R—B 1
16. K R—Q 1	K R—Q 1
17. Q R—B 1	B—K 1
18. P—Kt 3	......

A good positional move, the immediate object of which is to prevent the answer ....Q—B 5 in case of P—K 4.

18.	Kt—Q 4
19. Kt—Kt 2	Q—Kt 1

More exact was the immediate 19. ....Q—Kt 2 keeping in mind the possibility of ....Q—R 3.

20. Kt—Q 3	B—Kt 4

With the eventual threat ....Kt ×K P, etc.

21. R—Kt 1	Q—Kt 2
22. P—K 4	Kt×Kt
23. Q×Kt	Q—K 2 (?)

Disadvantageous, as his King's Bishop will now be put temporarily out of play. Correct was 23. ....R —B 2 and if 24. B—Kt 2 then 24. ....B—B 3 ; 25. P—K 5, B—K 2 ; 26. Q R—B 1, Q—B 1, after which Black could quietly wait for further developments.

24. P—K R 4 !	B—R 3
25. Kt—K 5	......

Threatening 26. Kt—Kt 4

25.	P—Kt 3
26. Kt—Kt 4 (?)	......

Now it is White's turn to miss the best move ! After 26. Kt—B 4 !, B—Kt 2 ; 27. P—K 5, P—K R 4 ; 28. Kt—Q 6, Black would have nothing better than to start to fight for a draw by sacrificing the exchange for a Pawn ; 28. ....R × Kt ; 29. P×R, Q×Q P ; 30. Q—B 4 ! etc.±

26.	B—Kt 2
27. P—K 5	P—K R 4
28. Kt—K 3	P—Q B 4 !

Black profits by the great opportunity to free at last his Q's Bishop, correctly realising that White will be unable to take real advantage of the open Q Kt's file.

| 29. Kt P×P | ...:... |

If 29. Q P×P then 29. ....P×P; 30. R×R, Q×R ; 31. P×P, Q—B 2, etc.

| 29. ...... | P×P |
| 30. P—Q 5 | ...... |

This attempt to complicate matters—most unusual for Capablanca—turns decidedly to Black's advantage. An easy draw was obtainable by 30. R—Kt 7, R—Q 2 ; 31. R×R, B×R ; 32. P—Q 5 (or 32. P×P, B—K 1 ; 33. P—B 6, Q—B 2, etc.), P×P ; 33. Kt×P, Q—K 3 ; 34. Kt —B 4, B×P, followed by a general liquidation and Bishops of different colours.

| 30. ...... | P×P |
| 31. Kt×P | Q—K 3 |

Of course not 31. ....Q×K P ; 32. Q×Q, B×Q ; 33. Kt—K 7 ch, etc.

Position after Black's 31st move.

| 32. Kt—B 6 ch(?) ...... |

As the following shows, the exchange thus forced only facilitates Black's task, as his passed Pawn will from now on largely compensate him for the troubles connected with the appearance of a White Pawn at his K B 3. Comparatively better was 32. R—Kt 7, B×P ; 33. Q—R 5, K—Kt 2 ; 34. R×P and Black's advantage—the pair of Bishops—would not yet have been decisive.

32.	B×Kt
33. P×B	R×R ch
34. R×R	B—B 3 !

White cannot exchange the Bishops, as in that case he would lose his only pride—the Pawn at B 6.

35. R—K 1	Q—B 4
36. R—K 3	P—B 5 !
37. P—R 4	......

Realising the inferiority of his position, White begins to "swindle." If now 37. ....B×P, then 38. B—K 4, Q—Kt 5 (Q—Q 2 ; 39. R—B 3, K—R 2 ; 40. Q—K 5, etc., would even lose) ; 39. B—B 3, Q—Q 2 ; 40. R—K 7, Q—Q 6 ; 41. Q×Q, P×Q ? ; 42. R×R P etc., with a draw in view. But after the following simpler answer Black's position is even better than before, as he obtains the full control upon his Q Kt 5.

37.	P—R 4
38. B—Kt 2	B×B
39. K×B	Q—Q 4 ch
40. K—R 2	Q—K B 4
41. R—B 3	Q—B 4
42. R—B 4	......

After 42. R—K 3, Q—Kt 3, White would not have any useful move at his disposal (43. R—B 3, Q—B 3 ! etc.).

42. . ....   K—R 2

This was not necessary here : it was much more important to prevent White's next move by 42. ....Q—Kt 3. But insufficient would be the tempting 42. .... Q—Kt 5 ; 43. Q—K 3, Q×P because of 44. R—B 5 !, Q—Kt 5 ; 45. R×K R P, P×R ; 46. Q—R 6, Q—B 1 ; 47. Q—Kt 5 ch etc., with a perpetual check.

43. R—Q 4   Q—B 3 ?

A miscalculation, after which White could have saved the game. Correct was still 43. ....Q—Kt 3 ! and if 44. R—B 4 then 44. .... K—Kt 1 obtaining the same position as he could have had two moves earlier.

44. Q×R P   ......

Forced, but good enough.

44. ......   P—B 6

If instead 44. ....Q×B P then 45. R—B 4 with the following possibilities : (a) 45. ...., Q—Kt 2 ; 46. Q—Q 5 ; (b) 45. ....Q—K 3 ; 46. Q—B 3 followed by P—B 5, with no danger for White in either case.

45. Q—R 7 !   K—Kt 1

Other moves, also, cannot force the win against correct replies—for instance :

I. 45. .... Q×B P ? ; 46. R—K B 4, Q×R ; 47. P×Q, P—B 7 ; 48. Q×P ch., K—R 3, 49. P—B 5 ! etc.

II. 45. ....Q—B 2 ; 46. Q×Q followed by 47. R—Q 1, etc.

III. 45.....R—B 2 ; 46. Q—Kt 8, P—B 7 ; 47. R—Q 8, Q× B P ! ; 48. R—R 8 ch ! ! (That was the move I had overlooked when I started the

combination by playing 43. ....Q—B 3), Q×R ; 49. Q× R, etc., with salvation in all cases.

46. Q—K 7   ......

If now 46. ....P—B 7 then 47. R—Q 8 ch, R×R ; 48. Q×R ch. K—R 2 ; 49. Q—K 7, Q—K 3 ; 50. Q—B 7, etc., forcing a draw.

46. ......   Q—Kt 3

Position after Black's 46th move.

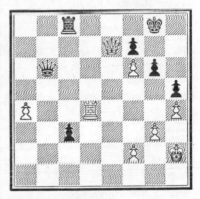

47. Q—Q 7 ?   ......

Capablanca does not take full advantage of the opportunity given to him by my 43rd move, and the game again takes its natural course. By playing 47. R—Q 7 ! he could have obtained a draw, as after 47. ....Q×P ch (if 47. ....R—B 1 then 48. P—R 5, Q×P ; 49. R—R 7, Q—Q 4 ; 50. R—Q 7, Q—R 4 and the White Rook, because of the threat Q×R ch ! would eternally persecute the Queen) ; 48. K—R 1 ! (48. K—R 3 would lose, as in the main variation the Black Queen would reach the square K 3 *with check*), Q—R 7 ; 49. R—Q 8 ch, R×R ; 50. Q×R ch, K—R 2 ; 51. Q—K B 8 and there would not be anything better than perpetual check, White's K B 6

Pawn remaining invulnerable. A most unusual escape !

47. ......   Q—B 4 !
48. R—K 4   ......

Now the only way to parry 48. ....P—B 7.

48. ......   Q × P ch
49. K—R 3   Q—B 8 ch
50. K—R 2   Q—B 7 ch
51. K—R 3   R—B 1
52. Q—B 6   ......

Again the only move.

52. ......   Q—B 8 ch
53. K—R 2   Q—B 7 ch
54. K—R 3   Q—B 8 ch
55. K—R 2   K—R 2 !
56. Q—B 4   ......

If 56. Q × P, then 56. .... Q—B 7 ch ; 57. K—R 1, R—Q 1 ; 58. Q—K 1, Q—B 6 ch ; 59. K—R 2, R—Q 8 and wins.

56. ......   Q—B 7 ch
57. K—R 3   Q—Kt 8 !

The decisive manœuvre. As an alternative 57. ....P—B 7 would be insufficient because of 58. R—B 4 ! followed by R—B 1.

58. R—K 2   ......

Instead, 58. P—Kt 4 would have led to a pretty finish : 58. ....P—B 7 !, 59. Q × P, R—K 1 !!, etc.

58. ......   Q—B 8 ch ?

For the second time Black misses an easy win !
The right sequence of moves (which I actually intended by playing 57. ....Q—Kt 8 !) was 58. Q—R 8 ch ; 59. R—R 2, Q—B 6 !, after which White could not play 60. R—Q B 2 because of 60. .... Q—B 4 ch ; and he would be

helpless against the threat 61..... Q × B P, etc. (If 60. Q—B 4, then 60. ....Q—Q 8 ! etc.).

59. K—R 2   Q × P
60. P—R 5 ?   ......

Instead of securing the draw by 60. R—Q B 2, R—K 1 ; 61. K—Kt 2 ! (threatening either 62. R × P or 62. R—B 2) Capablanca commits another error and should now lose instantly.

60. ......   R—Q 1 ?

An immediate decision could be obtained by 60. ....Q—B 8 ! ; 61. Q—K 4, R—Q 1 or Q Kt 1. After the text move the win should become again quite a problem.

61. P—R 6 ?   ......

After 61. K—Kt 2 Black could only obtain a Queen's ending with three Pawns against two, which, with the right defence, should most probably end in a draw. Now at last, it is the end !

61. ......   Q—B 8 !
62. Q—K 4   R—Q 7
63. R × R   P × R
64. P—R 7   P—Q 8 Queens
65. P—R8 Queens Q—Kt 8 ch
66. K—R 3   Q (Q8)—B 8 ch

If now 67. Q—Kt 2 then 67. .... Q—R 8 mate.

Resigns.

In my opinion this game has been praised too much, the whole world over. It was doubtless very exciting both for the players—who were continuously short of time—and the public. But its final part represents a true comedy of errors in which my opponent several times missed a draw and I missed about the same number of winning opportunities. In short, but for its outstanding sporting importance (it became, in fact, the crucial point of the match) I would hardly have included it in this collection.

GAME 22

QUEEN'S GAMBIT DECLINED (ORTHODOX DEFENCE)

Twenty-first Match-Game, Buenos Aires, October, 1927.

White : J. R. CAPABLANCA

1. P—Q 4	P—Q 4
2. P—Q B 4	P K 3
3. Kt—Q B 3	Kt—K B 3
4. B—Kt 5	Q Kt—Q 2
5. P—K 3	B—K 2
6. Kt—B 3	Castles
7. R—B 1	P—Q R 3

Although with this less usual defence I obtained quite a success in this match ($+1, =7-0$), I consider it now as not being satisfactory because of the possible answer 8. P×P, adopted by Capablanca in the 23rd, 25th and 27th games.

8. P—Q R 3 (?) ......

This tame rejoinder will be convincingly refuted (as a winning attempt, of course) in the present game. It has since completely disappeared from the master's practice.

8.	P—R 3
9. B—R 4	P×P
10. B×P	P—Q Kt 4 !

More natural and better than 10. ....P—Q Kt 3 which, however, in the 13th, 15th, 17th, and 19th games proved sufficient for maintaining the balance of the position.

11. B—K 2	B—Kt 2
12. Castles	......

In the event of 12. P—Q Kt 4

Black would have obtained the initiative by 12. ....P—Q R 4 !; 13. Q—Kt 3, P×P ; 14. P×P, P—Kt 4 ; 15. B—Kt 3, Kt—Q 4, etc.

12.	P—B 4
13. P×P	Kt×P
14. Kt—Q 4	

As White has not an atom of advantage the logical course for him was to simplify matters by means of 14. Q×Q, K R×Q ; 15. K R—Q 1, etc. Entirely wrong would be, instead of the text move, 14. B×Kt, B×B ; 15. Kt×P, because of 15. ....Q×Q ; 16. K R ×Q, Kt—Kt 6 ; 17. R—B 7, B× Kt ; 18. B×B, P×Kt ; 19. B×R, R×B∓.

14. ......   R—B 1

Preventing once and for all Kt × Kt P.

15. P—Q Kt 4 ......

Weakening, without necessity, the square Q B 4. Simpler was 15. B—B 3, Q—Kt 3 ; 16. Q—K 2, etc.

15.	Q Kt—Q 2 !
16. B—Kt 3	......

In the event of 16. B—B 3 I intended to play 16. ....Q—Kt 3 ; 17. Kt—K 4, R×R ; 18. Q×R, R—B 1, after which the White Queen would have had no good square at her disposal, for instance : (I) 19. Q—Kt 1 ? or Q 2 ?, Kt×Kt, etc., (II) 19. Q—Kt 2, P—Kt 4 ; 20. Kt×Kt ch, B×Kt∓, (III) 19. Q—Q 1 or K 1, P—Kt 4—also to Black's advantage. The text move is therefore comparatively the best.

16.	Kt—Kt 3
17. Q—Kt 3	......

In order to answer 17. ....Kt— B 5 by 18. K R—Q 1, Q—Kt 3, 19. P—Q R 4, etc.

17. ......   K Kt—Q 4

A good move connected with the positional threat 18. ....Kt×Kt; 19. R×Kt, B—Q 4 ; 20. Q—Kt 2, R×R ; 21. Q×R, Q—R 1, followed by R—B 1 with advantage. White's answer is practically forced.

18. B—B 3   R—B 5 !
19. Kt—K 4   Q—B 1
20. R×R   ......

I am inclined to consider this exchange as the decisive positional error, as from now on Black, taking advantage of the formidable position of his Knight at Q B 5, will be able gradually to concentrate all his pieces for a forcing action in the centre. White's correct move was 20. Q—Kt 1, threatening both 21. Kt—Q 6 or B—Q 6 ; if in that case 20. ....R—Q 1, then 21. Kt—Q 2, R×R ; 22. R×R, Q—R 1 ; 23. B—B 7, and White would succeed in exchanging some further material without compromising his position.

Still, the text move can by no means be considered as an actual blunder ; and Capablanca lost this game only because he did not realise in time the dangers of his position and was, in the issue, regularly outplayed.

20. ......   Kt×R
21. R—B 1   Q—R 1 !

Threatening 22. ....Kt×Kt P or K P, and thus forcing White to abandon control of the light-coloured squares in the middle.

22. Kt—B 3   ......

If 22. Kt—Q B 5, then 22. .... B×Kt ; 23. P×B, R—B 1 ; 24. B—K 2, R×P ; 25. B×Kt, Q— Q B 1, etc., winning a Pawn.

22. ......   R—B 1

Threatening 23. ....Kt—Q 7, etc.

23. Kt×Kt   B×Kt
24. B×B   Q×B
25. P—Q R 4   ......

The wish to reduce the Pawn material on the Q's side is natural, but White's position still remains compromised, inasmuch as his Q Kt's Pawn will become a welcome object of attack in the end game.

25. ......   B—B 3
26. Kt—B 3   ......

Of course not 26. R—Q 1 because of 26. ....P×P ; 27. Q×P, Kt— Kt 7 ; 28. Q×P, R—R 1 and wins.

Position after White's 26th move.

26. ......   B—Kt 7 !

In order to play ....P—K 4 without restricting the activity of the Bishop. The tactical justification of this move is shown by the following variations :

I 27. R—Q 1, P×P ! ; 28. Q×P, Kt—Kt 3 ; 29. R×Q, Kt×Q ; 30. R—Q 1, Kt—B 6 ; 31. R—K 1, R—B 5 ; 32. B—Q 6, Kt—K 5 ; 33. B—K 7, P—B 3 ; 34. R—Kt 1, K—B 2 ; 35. K—B 1, B—B 6, etc., with an easy win in the end game.

II 27. R—Kt 1, Kt—R 6 ! ; 28. Q×B, Kt×R ; 29. Q×Kt, Q—Kt 6; 30. Q—K B 1, P×P ; 31. P—R 3, P—R 6 and wins.

27. R—K 1   R—Q 1
28. P×P   P×P
29. P—R 3   ......

This emergency exit is absolutely necessary.

29. ......   P—K 4
30. R—Kt 1   P—K 5 !

The beginning of the end.

31. Kt—Q 4   ......

Or *A*. 31. Kt—K 1, Q—Q 7 ; 32. Q—B 2 (32. K—B 1, R—R 1 ; 33. R—Q 1, R—R 6 and wins), Q×Q ; 33. Kt×Q, R—Q 7 ; 34. Kt—K 1, Kt—R 6 and wins. *B*. 31. Kt—R 2, Q—Q 6 ! ; 32. R×B !, Q×Q ; 33. R×Q, R—Q 8 ch ; 34. Kt—B 1, Kt—Q 7 ; 35. R—R 3, Kt×Kt and White would be helpless.

31. ......   B×Kt
32. R—Q 1   ......

Loses immediately. But also after 32. P×B, Q×P, etc., the game could not have lasted long.

32. ......   Kt×P !
Resigns.

This and the 34th game are, in my opinion, the most valuable of the match.

GAME 23

QUEEN'S GAMBIT DECLINED (ORTHODOX DEFENCE)

Thirty - second   Match - Game, Buenos Aires, November, 1927.

Black : J. R. CAPABLANCA

1. P—Q 4   P—Q 4
2. P—Q B 4   P—K 3
3. Kt—Q B 3   Kt—K B 3
4. B—Kt 5   Q Kt—Q 2

5. P—K 3   P—B 3
6. P×P   K P×P
7. B—Q 3   B—K 2
8. K Kt—K 2   ......

This Knight's development was played here for the first time. Because of White's success in the present game, it became fashionable in the following years. In my opinion it is neither better nor worse than the usual Kt—K B 3 ; only, if he elects to castle on the Queen's side White has to be particularly careful, as Black's counter-attack on this wing may easily become more dangerous than his own initiative on the King's side.

8. ......   Castles

In this kind of position ....P—K R 3 is generally played before castling, in order not to allow White to answer this Pawn's move by P—K R 4. If Black had done this, my answer would have not been 9. B—R 4, but 9. B—K B 4.

9. Kt—Kt 3   Kt—K 1

There is hardly another way of emancipation, as 9. ....R—K 1 would have been very strongly answered by 10. Kt—B 5.

10. P—K R 4   ......

The natural consequence of the whole opening plan.

10. ......   Q Kt—B 3
11. Q—B 2   B—K 3
12. Kt—B 5   B×Kt
13. B×B   Kt—Q 3
14. B—Q 3   ......

Of course not 14. B×Kt, Kt×B, etc., with equality. This text move forces Black to weaken his King's position.

14. ......   P—K R 3
15. B—K B 4   ......

In case of 15. Castles (Q R) Black would have been able to try a counter-attack starting by 15. .... P—Q Kt 4, etc.

15. ......   R—B 1

Black intends to start an action on the Q B's file, as soon as his opponent castles Queen's side, and hereby overlooks the combinative reply. A more logical course was 15. ....R—K 1, intending ....K Kt—K 5.

16. P—K Kt 4 ! ......

This advance, made possible through the fact that 16. ....Kt× P ? ; 17. B×Kt followed by 18. B—B 5, etc., would lose the exchange for Black, considerably strengthens White's position and leaves Black but little choice.

16. ......   K Kt—K 5
17. P—Kt 5   P—K R 4
18. K B×Kt   ......

White decides to accept the (forced) Pawn sacrifice, although he realises that the ensuing ending will be extremely difficult to win— if possible at all—owing to the very effective position of the black Rook on White's second rank. A promising alternative was 18. Q B×Kt. Kt×B ; 19. Castles (Q R) (not 19. P—Kt 6 immediately, because of 19. ....B×P with counterplay), Kt—Kt 4 ; 20. K—Kt 1, Kt×Kt ch ; 21. Q×Kt and, in spite of the different-coloured Bishops, Black would not have found it easy to obtain a draw.

18. ......   Kt×B
19. Kt×Kt   P×Kt
20. Q×K P   Q—R 4 ch
21. K—B 1   ......

White cannot risk the variation 21. K—K 2, Q—Kt 4 ch ; 22. K—B 3, K R—K 1, etc.

21. ......   Q—Q 4 !

The point of Black's counterplay : after the forced exchange of Queens the only open file will become a very important factor in his favour.

22. Q×Q   P×Q
23. K—Kt 2   R—B 7
24. K R—Q B 1 ......

It is obviously of importance to eliminate one pair of Rooks. If now 24. ....R × P, White would secure a strong end-game advantage by means of 25. K R—Q Kt 1 !, etc.

24. ......   K R—B 1
25. R×R   R×R
26. R—Q Kt 1   K—R 2

Black prepares to take advantage of the fact that the light-coloured squares of White's position are insufficiently protected. White's next moves show the only appropriate defence against this plan.

27. K—Kt 3   K—Kt 3
28. P—B 3   P—B 3 !

And not 28. ....K—B 4 ? because of 29. P—K 4 ch, etc. Both sides, so far, are treating the difficult end-game in the right manner.

29. P×P   B×P
30. P—R 4   ......

Preparing to relieve the Rook from the defence of the Queen's side Pawns.

30. ......   K—B 4
31. P—R 5   R—K 7

Black is threatening now (in the event of 32. P—Kt 4, for instance) 32. ....P—K Kt 4 ! ; 33. P×P, B× Kt P ; 34. B×B, K×B, after which 35. P—B 4 ch, K—B 4 ; 36. K—B 3, R—K R 7 ; 37. R—Kt 1, R—R 6 ch ; 38. R—Kt 3, R×R ch !

etc., would only lead to a drawn Pawn ending.

Position after Black's 31st move.

32. R—Q B 1   ......

If White wants to play for a win he is compelled to give back (at least temporarily) the extra-Pawn. But a more efficient and, taking into consideration his two last moves, logical, method of doing it, was 32. P—R 6! After 32. .... P×P (32. ....P—Q Kt 3; 33. B—Kt 8, etc.) the answer 33. R—Q R 1! would have prevented 33. ....P—Kt 4, because of 34. P×P, B×Kt P; 35. P—K 4 ch! etc.; while after 33. ....R×Kt P; 34. R×P, R—Kt 2; 35. R—R 5, etc., White's positional advantage would become decisive. After the move selected, Black will be able to put up a long and not altogether hopeless resistance.

32.	R×Kt P
33. R—B 5	K—K 3
34. P—K 4	B×P

Here, as on several future occasions in this game, Black could have played differently, but it is doubtful if it would have altered the final result. If, for instance, 34. .... P×P, then 35. P—Q 5 ch, K—B 4; 36. P—Q 6 disc. ch, K—K 3;

37. P×P, R—Kt 6 ch; 38. K—Kt 2, B×P; 39. R×P, followed by 40. R—R 7 and the fight against the central passed Pawns would prove extremely difficult.

| 35. R×P | B—B 6 |

By playing 35. ....B—B 7 ch; 36. K—R 3, R—Kt 6; 37. R—K 5 ch, K—B 2, he could temporarily save the Pawn, but his position after 38. B—Kt 5! would still look very compromised.

| 36. R×P | P—R 3 |

If 36. ....B—K 8 ch; 37. K—R 3, R—K B 7, then 38. R—K 5 ch! followed by 39. R—B 5 ch, or 39. R—Q 5 ch—Q 3, etc., still keeping the plus Pawn.

| 37. B—B 7 | B—K 8 ch |

Or 37. ....R—Kt 4; 38. R—Kt 5! etc.

| 38. K—Kt 4 | R—Kt 7 ch |
| 39. K—R 3 | ...... |

Of course not 39. K—B 4, B—Q 7 mate!

39.	R—K B 7
40. K—Kt 4	R—Kt 7 ch
41. K—R 3	R—K B 7
42. P—B 4!	R—B 6 ch
43. K—Kt 2	......

Another method of suicide occurred here: 43. K—Kt 4, R—Kt 6 mate.

43.	R—B 7 ch
44. K—R 3	R—B 6 ch
45. K—Kt 2	R—B 7 ch
46. K—Kt 1	R—B 7
47. B—Kt 6	R—B 5

This facilitates White's task, as it enables his King to give effective support to the central Pawns. Better was 47. ....B—Kt 6, after which White would have tried to obtain the victory by means of 48. R—K 5 ch (K—Q 3 ; 49. R—K Kt 5 or K—B 2 ; 49. P—R 5 ! etc.).

Position after Black's 47th move.

48. K—Kt 2 ! ......

By this move White obtains at last a clearly won position. It is obvious that after 48. ....R × P ? ; 49. K—B 3 Black would immediately lose.

48.	P—Kt 3
49. R—K 5 ch	K—Q 2
50. P—R 5 !	P × P
51. K—B 3	P—R 5

51. ....R—B 6 ch ; 52. K—K 2, B—Kt 6 ; 53. B—K 3, P—R 5 ; 54. R—R 5, etc., would not help any better.

52. R—R 5	R—B 6 ch
53. K—Kt 4	R—B 5
54. K—B 5 !	......

Apparently falling into the trap, but in reality selecting the surest and quickest way to make use of the passed Pawns.

| 54. ...... | B × P |
| 55. R—R 7 ch | ...... |

Of course not 55. B × B, R—B 4 ch ; 56. K—Kt 4 ? because of 56.

....R × R followed by 57. ....P— R 6 winning.

55.	K—B 3
56. B × B	R—B 4 ch
57. K—K 6 !	R × B
58. P—B 5	R—R 6
59. P—B 6	R—K B 6
60. P—B 7	P—Kt 4
61. R—R 5 !	......

The neat final point of this colourful ending.

61.	P—R 6
62. R—B 5	R × R
63. P × R	......

If now 63. ....P—R 7 ; 64. P— B 8 (Q), P—R 8 (Q), then 65. Q—R 8 ch, etc., wins.

Resigns.

GAME 24

QUEEN'S GAMBIT DECLINED

Thirty-fourth—and last—Match-Game, Buenos Aires, November, 1927.

Black : J. R. CAPABLANCA

1. P—Q 4	P—Q 4
2. P—Q B 4	P—K 3
3. Kt—Q B 3	Kt—K B 3
4. B—Kt 5	Q Kt—Q 2
5. P—K 3	P—B 3
6. P—Q R 3	......

This quiet move, whose main object is to avoid the Cambridge-Springs Defence, should hardly promise White more than a comfortable equality. I selected it here merely in order to come out of the book variations as rapidly as possible.

6.	B—K 2
7. Kt—B 3	Castles
8. B—Q 3	P × P

A sound alternative was 8. ....
P—K R 3 ; 9. B—R 4, P—B 4,
etc.

9. B×P   Kt—Q 4
10. B×B   Q×B

Also possible was 10. .... Kt×
Kt.

11. Kt—K 4   K Kt—B 3
12. Kt—Kt 3   P—B 4

12. .... P—Q Kt 3, followed
by .... B—Kt 2—as played by
Maroczy against me at San Remo
in 1930—is worth consideration.
The text manœuvre has the slight
drawback of not yet solving the
problem of the development of the
Queen's Bishop.

13. Castles   Kt—Kt 3
14. B—R 2   P×P
15. Kt×P   P—Kt 3

In order to be able to answer
P—K 4 by .... P—K 4 without
ceding the square K B 4 to the
White Knights.

16. R—B 1   ......

Threatening eventually Kt—
Q Kt 5.

16. ......   B—Q 2
17. Q—K 2   Q R—B 1
18. P—K 4   P—K 4
19. Kt—B 3   K—Kt 2

Black should here exchange both
Rooks, as after 19. .... R×B ; 20.
R×R, R—B 1; 21. R×R ch,
Kt×R, the move 22. Kt—Kt 5
could have been sufficiently met by
22. .... B—K 1, etc. The text
move, and especially the next one,
brings his position suddenly into
danger.

20. P—R 3   P—K R 3 ?

Position after Black's 20th move.

21. Q—Q 2 !   ......

This harmless-looking move is in
reality very hard to meet. White's
main threat is 22. Q—R 5, and if
Black should try to parry this by
the counter-attack, 21. .... B—B 3
(or Kt 4), then an unexpected diversion on the King's side would make
a rapid end : 22. Kt—R 4 !, Kt×
P (or 22. .... B×P ; 23. Q—K 3 !
or 22. .... B—Q 2 ; 23. Q—R 5,
etc.) ; 23. Kt (R 4)—B 5 ch, P×Kt ;
24. Kt×P ch, K—B 3 ; 25. Q×
P ch, K×Kt ; 26. P—Kt 4, mate !

The only move which offers some
prospects of a successful defence is
that suggested by Dr. Lasker, 21.
.... Kt—R 5 ! In that case, White
would simply continue to strengthen
his position—for instance, by means
of 22. K R—Q 1.

21. ......   B—K 3 ?

The position has proved too difficult for Black ; he now loses a Pawn
and, after a desperate struggle, the
game and the match. The following
sharp combinations, as well as the
subsequent Queen-and-Rook ending,
are both exciting and instructive.

22. B×B   Q×B
23. Q—R 5   Kt—B 5

Or 23. ....Q—Kt 6 ; 24. Q×
K P, Kt—B 5 ; 25. Q—Q 4, etc. ±

24. Q × R P	Kt × Kt P
25. R × R	R × R
26. Q × P	Kt—B 5
27. Q—Kt 4	R—Q R 1
28. R—R 1	Q—B 3 !

Threatening to blockade the
Q R's Pawn by 29. ....R—R 5, and
also (at least apparently) to win the
King's Pawn. But White's two
next moves put the situation in the
true light.

29. P—Q R 4 !	Kt × P
30. Kt × P	......

Thus avoiding the pitfall 30.
Kt × Kt, Q × Kt ; 31. R—Q B 1,
R—Q B 1 ; 32. Kt × P (?), Kt—K 6!;
33. Q × Q, R × R ch ; 34. K—R 2,
Kt—B 8 ch, followed by Kt—Kt 6
disc. ch, and Kt × Q, after which
Black could even win.

30.	Q—Q 3 !

In the circumstances comparatively the best, as both pairs of
Knights will now soon disappear
from the board.

31. Q × Kt	Q × Kt
32. R—K 1	Kt—Q 3
33. Q—Q B 1 !	Q—B 3
34. Kt—K 4	Kt × Kt
35. R × Kt	......

The winning procedure which
follows is a rather elaborate one,
and consists in combining the
threats connected with the passed
Pawn and an attack against the
somewhat exposed Black King.
First and foremost, White will succeed in controlling the important
diagonal, Q R 1—K R 8.

35.	R—Q Kt 1
36. R—K 2	R—Q R 1
37. R—R 2	R—R 4
38. Q—B 7 !	Q—R 3

Obviously, the only way to prevent the advance of the passed
Pawn.

39. Q—B 3 ch	K—R 2
40. R—Q 2	......

With the deadly threat 41. R—
Q 8,

40.	Q—Kt 3
41. R—Q 7	......

The sealed move. Black's next
manœuvres offer the only chance,
if not to save the game, at least to
permit a longer resistance.

41.	Q—Kt 8 ch
42. K—R 2	Q—Kt 1 ch
43. P—Kt 3	R—K B 4
44. Q—Q 4	......

Threatening 45. P—R 5 ! followed by R—Q 8.

44.	Q—K 1
45. R—Q 5	R—B 6

The Queen's ending would be, of
course, tantamount to resignation.

46. P—R 4	......

White does not need to prevent
the Black Queen's following manœuvre, which finally leads to an
easily won Rook's ending for him.

46.	Q—K R 1
47. Q—Kt 6 !	......

At this moment the exchange
would be premature, as it would
allow Black to bring his Rook
behind the passed Pawn.

47.	Q—R 8
48. K—Kt 2	R—B 3

If 48. ....R—R 6 White wins as
follows : 49. R—Q 7, K—Kt 1 (or
K—Kt 2 ; 50. Q—K 6 ! or Q—R 7 ;
50. Q—K B 6, etc.) ; 50. Q—Q 8 ch,

K—Kt 2 ; 51. Q—K 7, Q—R 7 ;
52. Q—K 5 ch, K—R 2 ; 53. Q—
B 6, etc.

49. Q—Q 4 ......

Now the right moment to exchange has come, as it is the *White*
Rook that will get behind the
passed Pawn.

49. ...... Q×Q
50. R×Q K—Kt 2

Instead 50. ....R—R 3 would
have immediately lost after 51. K—
B 3, followed by K—K 4—Q 5, etc.

51. P—Q R 5 R—R 3
52. R—Q 5 R—K B 3
53. R—Q 4 R—R 3
54. R—R 4 K—B 3
55. K—B 3 K—K 4
56. K—K 3 P—R 4
57. K—Q 3 K—Q 4
58. K—B 3 K—B 4
59. R—R 2 K—Kt 4
60. K—Kt 3 ......

White makes use of every opportunity, by repetition of moves, to
gain time with the clock, so as to
avoid a slip just before the capture
of the title.

60. ...... K—B 4
61. K—B 3 K—Kt 4
62. K—Q 4 ......

If now 62. ....K—Kt 5, then
63. R—R 1 ! etc.

62. ...... R—Q 3 ch
63. K—K 5 R—K 3 ch
64. K—B 4 K—R 3

65. K—Kt 5 R—K 4 ch
66. K—R 6 R—K B 4
67. P—B 4 ......

The simplest method to force the
capitulation was 67. K—Kt 7, R—
B 6 ; 68. K—Kt 8, R—B 3 ; 69.
K—B 8 !, R—B 6 (or R—B 4 ; 70.
P—B 4) ; 70. K—Kt 7, R—B 4 ;
71. P—B 4, etc.

67. ...... R—B 4 !
68. R—R 3 R—B 2
69. K—Kt 7 R—Q 2
70. P—B 5 ......

Another inexact move. A more
direct way was first 70. K—B 6,
and only after 70. ....R—B 2 ; 71.
P—B 5, P×P ; 72. K×P, R—B 4
ch ; 73. K—B 6, R—B 2 ; 74. R—
K B 3, K×P ; 75. R—B 5 ch, and
wins ;

70. ...... P×P
71. K—R 6 P—B 5
72. P×P R—Q 4
73. K—Kt 7 R—K B 4
74. R—R 4 K—Kt 4
75. R—K 4 ! K—R 3
76. K—R 6 R×R P

Or 76. ....K—Kt 2 ; 77. R—K 5,
R×P ; 78. K—Kt 5 !, R—B 8 ;
79. K×P, P—B 4 ; 80. K—Kt 5,
P—B 5 ; 81. R—K B 5, P—B 6 ;
82. K—Kt 4 and wins.

77. R—K 5 R—R 8
78. K×P R—K Kt 8
79. R—K Kt 5 R—K R 8
80. R—K B 5 K—Kt 3
81. R×P K—B 3
82. R—K 7 Resigns.

GAME 25

QUEEN'S GAMBIT ACCEPTED

Bradley-Beach Tournament, June 1929.

Black : H. STEINER

Brilliancy Prize

1. P—Q 4	P—Q 4
2. P—Q B 4	P×P
3. Kt—K B 3	Kt—K B 3
4. P—K 3	P—K 3
5. B×P	P—B 4
6. Castles	P—Q R 3
7. Q—K 2	Q Kt—Q 2

If 7. .... Kt—B 3, the best answer according to the latest practice (Euwe-Alekhine, fifth match-game, 1937, and Alekhine-Böök, Margate, 1938) would still be 8. Kt—B 3 !

8. Kt—B 3	Q—B 2

If Black did not want to risk the "fianchetto" development which, in fact, is hardly recommendable (for instance, 8. ....P—Q Kt 4 ; 9. B—Kt 3, B—Kt 2 ; 10. R—Q 1, B—K 2 ; 11. P—K 4 !, P—Kt 5 ; 12. P—K 5, P×Kt ; 13. P×Kt, etc.±, as in the game Alekhine-Letelier, Montevideo, 1938) · he should simply play 8. ....B—K 2 ; for the square Q B 2 for the Queen, in case of the following Q's Pawn advance, will prove a very unfortunate one.

9. P—Q 5 !	P×P
10. B×Q P	......

One of Black's troubles from now on will consist in the fact that in case of the exchange of this Bishop, White would always recapture *with tempo*.

10.	B—Q 3
11. P—K 4	Castles
12. B—Kt 5	Kt—Kt 5

In order to develop his Q's side pieces Black is forced to lose time with this Knight, and, moreover, facilitate the dangerous advance of White's K B's Pawn.

13. P—K R 3	K Kt—K4
14. Kt—K R 4 !	......

In view of Black's cramped position the right policy is to avoid exchanges. Besides, Black is now forced to prevent the move Kt—B 5, and consequently has even less choice than before.

14.	Kt—Q Kt 3
15. P—B 4	Kt—B 3
16. P—B 5 !	......

A paradoxical, but most effective, continuation of the attack, by which White "sacrifices" the central square K 5. The "natural" advance 16. P—K 5 instead would have left White—strange as it may seem—after 16. ....B—K 2 with but an insignificant positional advantage.

16.	Kt—K 4
17. Q—R 5	R—K 1

Parrying the threat 18. P—B 6 which now would be met by 18. .... P—Kt 3 ; 19. Q—R 6, B—B 1.

18. R—B 4   B—K 2

This will be refuted by a pretty combination, but, as Black still could not take the powerful Bishop —after 18. .... Kt × B ? follows 19. Kt × Kt, Q—B 3 ; 20. Kt—B 6 ch !, P × Kt ; 21. B × P, etc.—there was no longer a sufficient defence.

Position after Black's 18th move.

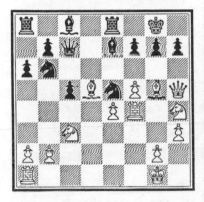

19. P—B 6 !   ......

Because of Black's last move White is enabled to effect this advance *in spite of the possible defence* 19. .... *P—Kt* 3 ; 20. *Q—R* 6, *B —B* 1—and this because of the following combination : 19. .... P—Kt 3 ; 20. Kt × P ! !, P × Kt (or A) ; 21. B × P ch !, K × B ; 22, P × B disc. ch, K—K 3 (or K—Kt 1 ; 23. R—B 8 ch, R × R ; 24. P × R= Q ch, K × Q ; 25. Q—R 8 ch, K—B 2 ; 26. Q—R 7 ch, winning the Queen) ; 23. R—B 6 ch, K × P (or K—Q 2 ; 24. R—Q 1 ch, etc.) ; 24. Q—R 7 ch, K—Q 1 ; 25. R— Q 6, mate.

(A) 20. .... Kt × Kt ; 21. B × P ch !, K × B ; 22. Q × P ch, K—K 3 ; 23. Q × Kt and wins.   After the following retreat which permits the opening of the K B's file, the game is also practically over.

19. ......   B—B 1

20. P × P   B × Kt P
21. Q R—K B 1   B—K 3
22. Kt—B 5   ......

Threatening also R—R 4, etc.

22. ......   B × B
23. Kt × K B !   Kt—Kt 3
24. Kt × R   R × Kt
25. Kt × B   Resigns.

GAME 26

QUEEN'S GAMBIT DECLINED (SLAV DEFENCE)

First Match-Game, Wiesbaden, September, 1929.

Black : E. BOGOLJUBOW

1. P—Q 4   P—Q 4
2. P—Q B 4   P—Q B 3
3. Kt—K B 3   Kt—B 3
4. Kt—B 3   P × P
5. P—Q R 4   P—K 3

It has been my peculiar luck that this illogical move (instead of the natural 5. .... B— R 4) has been adopted against me, with a disastrous effect, no less than four times, namely (besides the present game) by Bogoljubow again (Nottingham, 1936), by Dr. Euwe (19th Match-Game, 1935), and by the late German master, Helling, in Dresden, 1936.

6. P—K 4   B—Kt 5
7. P—K 5   Kt—Q 4

In the three other games mentioned the reply was 7. .... Kt— K 5, which is at least as bad as the text move.

8. B—Q 2   B × Kt

If, instead, 8. .... P—Q Kt 4, then 9. Kt—K 4, B—K 2 ; 10. P—

Q Kt 3 !, etc., winning back the Pawn with decidedly the better position.

9. P×B   P—Q Kt 4
10. Kt—Kt 5 !   ......

An important move with many objects, one of which, and not the least important, is to prevent Black's 10. Castles, because of the answer 11. Q—Kt 1 ! followed by 12. P×P, etc. ±

10. ......   P—B 3

Prevents the manœuvre Kt—K 4 —Q 6 ch, but at the cost of a serious compromising of the central position.

11. P×B P   Kt×K B P

Or 11. Q×P; 12. P×P, P×P; 13. Kt—K 4, Q—K 2; 14. B—Kt 5, followed by Q—R 5 ch, etc. ±

12. B—K 2   P—Q R 3

12. ....Castles ; 13. P×P, P—K R 3 (if 13. ....P×P then 14. B—B 3, Kt—Q 4; 15. Q—Kt 1, etc.); 14. P—Kt 6 !, Q×P; 15. Kt—B 3, etc., would prove in the long run positionally hopeless.

13. B—B 3 !   ......

With the threat 14. P×P, etc., which is by no means easy to parry. If, for instance, 13. ....Kt—Q 4, then 14. Q—Kt 1 !, P—Kt 3; 15. Kt×R P, R×Kt; 16. Q×P ch, R—B 2; 17. B—R 5 followed by 18. Q—Kt 8 ch and wins. Or 13. ....R—R 2; 14. B—B 4, R—Kt 2; 15. P×P, R P×P; 16. R—R 8, etc., also with a winning attack.

13. ......   P—R 3

Already mere desperation.

14. B—R 5 ch   Kt×B
15. Q×Kt ch   K—Q 2
16. Kt—B 7   Q—K 1
17. Q—Kt 6   R—Kt 1
18. B—B 4   B—Kt 2

Or 18. ....R—B 1; 19. Kt—K 5 ch, K—Q 1; 20. Q—K 4, etc.

19. B—Kt 3   K—K 2
20. B—Q 6 ch   ......

A bit of cat-and-mouse play.

20. ......   K—Q 2
21. Castles K R   P—B 4
22. P×B P   B—Q 4
23. P×P   P×P
24. R×R   B×R
25. R—R 1   Kt—B 3

Position after Black's 25th move.

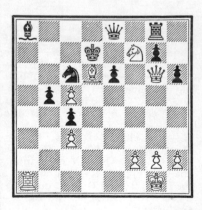

26. Kt—K 5 ch !   ......

If now 26. ....Kt×Kt; 27. R—R 7 ch, K—B 3, then 28. Q—K 4 mate.

Resigns.

GAME 27

QUEEN'S GAMBIT DECLINED (SLAV DEFENCE)

Fifth Match-Game, Wiesbaden, September, 1929.

Black : E. BOGOLJUBOW

1. P—Q 4	P—Q 4
2. P—Q B 4	P—Q B 3
3. Kt—K B 3	Kt—B 3
4. Kt—B 3	P×P
5. P—Q R 4	B—B 4
6. Kt—K 5	P—K 3

A simple and good move ; but by making it here (and in the third match game, in which I adopted the less logical answer 7. P—B 3), Bogoljubow, as the following shows, did not fully understand its real value.

7. B—Kt 5   B—K 2

Decidedly too passive : the right continuation is 7. ....B—Q Kt 5 (introduced by me in a consultation game, played against Bogoljubow and Dr. Seitz immediately after the match) ; 8. P—B 3, P—K R 3 ! (as in my eleventh match game against Dr. Euwe, Groningen, 1937) obtaining at least an even game.

8. P—B 3	P—K R 3
9. P—K 4 !	......

This move, which by the position of Black's King's Bishop at Kt 5 would have been answered by 9. ....P×B ; 10. P×B, P—Kt 4 ! ; 11. P×K P, P×K P ; 12. Q—B 2, Castles ! etc.∓, in the actual position practically shuts out the opponent's Queen's Bishop for the rest of the game.

9. ......   B—R 2

Or 9. ....P×B ; 10. P×B, P×

P ; 11. B×P, Castles ; 12. P—R 4 ! etc. to White's advantage.

10. B—K 3	Q Kt—Q 2
11. Kt×P (B 4)	Castles
12. B—K 2	P—B 4

The following exchanges are decidedly in White's favour as they do not eliminate the main defect of Black's position—the awkward situation of his Queen's Bishop.

13. P×P	B×B P
14. B×B	Kt×B
15. P—Q Kt 4	Kt—R 3

Also unsatisfactory was 15. .... Q×Q ch ; 16. R×Q, Kt×R P ; 17. Kt×Kt, P—Q Kt 4 ; 18. Kt (B 4)— Kt 6 !, R P×Kt ; 19. B×P, etc. ⊥

16. Q×Q	K R×Q
17. Kt—R 2 !	......

The only way to keep the positional advantage, as 17. P—Kt 5 would have cede the important square Q B 5, and 17. R—Q Kt 1 would have permitted a promising counter-attack starting by 17. ....Kt— Q 4 !

17. ......   Kt—Kt 1

White threatened 18. Kt—R 5, Q R—Kt 1 ; 19. Kt×P, etc.

18. K—B 2	Kt—B 3
19. K R—Q 1	Kt—Q 5

Instead, 19. ....R×R ; 20. R× R, R—Q 1, would have been rapidly fatal : 21. P—Kt 5, R×R ; 22. B×R, Kt—Q 1 ; 23. Kt—Q 6, followed by 24. Kt—Kt 4 and 25. Kt—B 8 ! etc.

20. Q R—B 1   K—B 1

The first step towards the emancipation of the Bishop at R 2 by means of B—Kt 1, Kt—K 1, P—

B 3, etc. But this plan will obviously take a long time, which White will use for a decisive strengthening of the pressure on the Q's side. From now on the game develops in a perfectly logical manner.

| 21. B—B 1 | Kt—K 1 |
| 22. Kt—B 3 | ...... |

A strong alternative here was 22. Kt—R 5 ; for instance :
I. 22. .... Q R—Kt 1 ; 23. Kt—B 3, P—Q Kt 3 ; 24. R × Kt !, R × R ; 25. Kt—B 6, Q R—Q 1 ; 26. K—K 3, R (Q 5)—Q 3 ; 27. Kt × R, R × Kt ; 28. Kt—Kt 5.
II. 22. ....P—Q Kt 3 ; 23. Kt—Kt 7, R—Q 2 ; 24. B—Kt 5 !, R × Kt ; 25. R × Kt, with a tremendous positional advantage in both cases.

| 22. ...... | P—B 3 |
| 23. Kt—R 5 | Q R—Kt 1 |

This natural-looking answer gives White the opportunity for the following combination, which wins a Pawn per force. Better was 23. ....P—Q Kt 3 ; 24. Kt—Kt 7, R—Q 2 ; 25. B—Kt 5, R × Kt ; 26. R × Kt, R—B 2 ; 27. Kt—K 2, R × R ; 28. Kt × R, R—B 1 ; 29. Kt—Q 3, etc. ; with some possibilities of defence in spite of the indisputable advantage of White.

Position after Black's 23rd move.

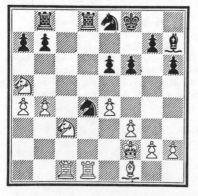

24. Kt—Kt 5 !   ......

Eliminating the enemy's central Knight just at the right moment : if Black could have found time for a further consolidation by means of ....P—K 4 there would be a very little left of White's pressure on the Q's side.

24. ......   Kt × Kt

Obviously forced.

| 25. R × R | R × R |
| 26. Kt × P ! | R—Kt 1 |

Or 26. ....R—Q 7 ch ; 27. K—K 3, Kt (Kt 4)—Q 3 ; 28. K × R, Kt × Kt ; 29. R—B 8, followed by 30. R—R 8 and R × Q R P, etc., winning.

27. Kt—B 5   K—K 2

Because of the threat 28. Kt—Q 7 ch the Knight had still to keep quiet. The following end-game, with an extra-Pawn and a far better position, is actually a walk-over for White.

28. P × Kt !   ......

Much more effective than 28. B × Kt, because now Black's Q R Pawn becomes extremely weak.

28.	Kt—Q 3
29. R—R 1	Kt—B 1
30. B—B 4	B—Kt 1

After 30. .... P—K 4 White would win immediately by 31. B—K 6, etc.

| 31. P—B 4 | B—B 2 |
| 32. P—K 5 | ...... |

All Black's pieces will be gradually stalemated, and the White King will soon be in a position to pay a significant visit to the adversary's Knight in its very residence.

32.	P×P
33. P×P	R—Kt 3
34. K—K 3	B—K 1
35. R—R 3	B—Q 2
36. K—Q 4	B—K 1

Black has nothing left but patiently to wait for the execution.

37. P—R 4	B—Q 2
38. B—K 2	R—Kt 1
39. Kt×B	K×Kt
40. B—B 3 !	......

Preventing the manœuvre .... R—Kt 2—B 2 which would allow Black to prolong the agony.

40.	R—Kt 3
41. K—B 5	R—Kt 1
42. P—R 5	K—Q 1
43. B—B 6	K—K 2
44. R—R 3	K—B 2
45. B—K 4	K—K 2
46. K—B 6 !	......

Now the Knight must perish.

46.	K—Q 1
47. R—Q 3 ch	K—K 2
48. K—B 7	Resigns.

GAME 28

QUEEN'S INDIAN DEFENCE

Eighth Match-Game, Wiesbaden, September, 1929.

White : E. BOGOLJUBOW

| 1. P—Q 4 | Kt—K B 3 |
| 2. P—Q B 4 | P—Q Kt 3 |

Although this system of development is by no means easy to refute, it can hardly be considered absolutely correct as it allows White in such an early stage of the game to get full control upon the central squares ; and the fact that Black can attack the Pawn's centre by means of ....P—Q B 4 should not offer him full compensation for the lack of space he will have to suffer from after the next 10-15 moves. Undoubtedly sounder is therefore 2. ....P—K 3,

3. Kt—Q B 3	B—Kt 2
4. P—B 3	P—Q 4
5. P×P	Kt×P
6. P—K 4	Kt×Kt
7. P×Kt	......

White's position looks now rather promising ; but he spoils it in a very few moves by adopting a totally wrong middle game plan.

| 7. ...... | P—K 3 |
| 8. B—Kt 5 ch | ...... |

Neither better nor worse than the immediate 8. B—Q 3, as Black's ....P—Q R 3 will not prove weakening to his position in the course of the game.

8.	Kt—Q 2
9. Kt—K 2	B—K 2
10. Castles	P—Q R 3
11. B—Q 3	P—Q B 4
12. B—Kt 2 ?	......

A really bad move which shows an entire misconception of the needs of the present situation. White had instead the choice between at least two good Bishop moves— 12. B—K 3, and 12. B—K B 4. Also 12. P—Q R 4 (in order to fix Black's slight weakness at Q Kt 3) came into consideration. From now on Black gradually gets the initiative.

| 12. ...... | Q—B 2 |
| 13. P—K B 4 | ...... |

This allows Black to win a couple of *tempi* by attacking the insufficiently protected central Pawns. A lesser evil was 13. P—K 5, temporarily restricting the field of activity of Black's Knight.

| 13. ...... | Kt—B 3 |
| 14. Kt—Kt 3 | P—K R 4 ! |

By his last aimless moves White has provoked an immediate King's attack.

15. Q—K 2	P—R 5
16. Kt—R 1	Kt—R 4
17. Q—Kt 4	......

In spite of his previous indifferent play White probably could still have held the game if he had recognised his mistake at the 12th move and had removed his Bishop to Q B 1. The seemingly more aggressive move here made by him instead, in reality relieves Black from the worry about his Q's R Pawn, and thus permits him to castle Q's side with an overpowering position.

| 17. ...... | Castles (Q R) |
| 18. Q R—K 1 | ...... |

If 18. P—B 5 then 18. ....Kt—B 3 (19. Q×Kt P ?, R—R 2), followed by 19. .... P—K 4 with advantage.

| 18. ...... | K—Kt 1 |
| 19. P—B 5 | ...... |

This attempt to blockade the centre proves unsuccessful as Black can secure strong diagonals for both his Bishops. But the game already was strategically lost.

| 19. ...... | P—K 4 |
| 20. P—Q 5 | P—B 5 ! |

Securing the future of the K's Bishop.

| 21. B—B 2 | B—B 4 ch |

| 22. Kt—B 2 | P—Kt 3 ! |

And after this the Q's Bishop will also develop a deadly activity on the diagonal Q B 1—K R 6.

| 23. P×P | Q R—Kt 1 |
| 24. B—B 1 | ...... |

A much too belated sign of remorse !

| 24. ...... | B—Q B 1 |
| 25. Q—B 3 | R×P |

Position after Black's 25th move.

| 26. K—R 1 | ...... |

White is anxious to save his Queen (which Black threatened to win by 26. ....B—K Kt 5) and overlooks the following mating combination. However, his position was hopeless anyhow—if, for instance, 26. B—K 3, then 26. .... B×B ; 27. R×B, Kt—B 5 ; 28. P—Kt 3, P×P ; 29. P×P, P—B 4 followed by 30. .... Q—K R 2 and mate.

26.	Kt—Kt 6 ch !
27. P×Kt	P×P disc. ch.
28. Kt—R 3	B×Kt
29. P×B	R×P ch
30. K—Kt 2	R—R 7 mate

GAME 29

KING'S INDIAN DEFENCE

Seventeenth Match-Game, Berlin, October, 1929.

Black : E. BOGOLJUBOW.

1. P—Q 4	Kt—K B 3
2. P—Q B 4	P—K Kt 3
3. P—B 3	P—Q 4

Although this system is not quite sound, it is by no means as easy to meet as it looks at first sight, because White's central position may eventually become weak. Care is therefore required from the first player.

4. P × P	Kt × P
5. P—K 4	Kt—Kt 3
6. Kt—B 3	B—Kt 2
7. B K 3	Kt—D 3 ?

But Black, also, must make the correct opening moves, which he does not on this occasion. Necessary was 7. ....Castles, as played by Bogoljubow against me in Bled, 1931. The right answer for White would have been in that case 8. P—B 4 !

The text-move is most likely already a decisive positional error.

| 8. P—Q 5 | Kt—K 4 |
| 9. B—Q 4 | P—K B 3 |

Practically forced, as after 9. ....Castles; 10. P—B 4, Kt (K 4)—Q 2 ; 11. B × B followed by 12. Q—Q 4 ch, Castles, P—K R 4, etc., White would have obtained a winning King's attack.

10. P—B 4 (?) ......

This is sufficient in order to keep some opening advantage—but much more unpleasant for Black would have been first 10. P—Q R 4 ! as in that case he would not have had the possibility of playing ....

P—K 4 which in the actual game somewhat relieved his cramped position.

| 10. ...... | Kt—B 2 |
| 11. P—Q R 4 | P—K 4 |

Otherwise the "hole" at his K 3 would rapidly prove fatal.

12. P × P (*e.p.*)	B × P
13. P—R 5	Kt—Q 2
14. P—R 6	......

By an analogous manœuvre on the K's side I obtained a winning position in the decisive game against Rubinstein in The Hague, 1921. In the present position it is certainly not so forcible, but still strong enough.

| 14. ...... | P—Kt 3 |
| 15. B—Kt 5 | ...... |

Threatening 16. B—B 6 followed by 17. Kt—Kt 5, etc.

15. ...... Q—K 2

In order to answer 16. B—B 6 by 16. ....Castles (Q R).

| 16. K Kt—K 2 | P—Q B 4 |
| 17. B—B 2 | Castles (Q R) |

In making this risky move Bogoljubow probably already planned the sacrifice at K 4 which, doubtless, gave him some fighting chances. He can hardly be blamed for that decision, inasmuch as the alternative 17. ....Castles (K R); 18. Kt—Q 5, B × Kt (or 18. ....Q—Q 3; 19. K Kt—B 3, etc.±); 19. Q × B, K R—Q 1 ; 20. Castles (Q R), Kt—B 1 ; 21. Q—Kt 7, etc., would have left him but very few chances of salvation.

| 18. Q—R 4 | P—B 4 |
| 19. P—K 5 | ...... |

At this moment the move 19. B—B 4 would not have led to anything particular after 19. ....Kt—Kt 1 ;

20. B×B ch, Q×B; 21. Kt—Kt 5, Kt—B 3 (or R—Q 2), etc.

19. ......   P—Kt 4

Forcing White to show his hand, as after 20. P—K Kt 3, P×P; 21. P×P the sacrifice 20 ....Kt (Q 2) × P! etc., would have been more than disagreeable.

20. B—B 4!   Q Kt× P!

A passive resistance commencing by 20. ....Kt—Kt 1 would soon prove hopeless after 21. B×B ch, Q×B; 22. Castles K R with the strong threat 23. P—Q Kt 4, etc. But now White will be obliged to play very exactly in order to keep an advantage.

21. B×B ch   Q×B
22. P×Kt   Kt×P
23. Castles   Q—B 5!

The point of the sacrifice: after 24. Q×Q, Kt×Q; 25. Kt—Kt 5, K—Kt 1, etc., Black hopes to get some further material for his piece, after which the end game would have offered him not too bad prospects; and if 24. Q—B 2, then Q—Q 6 with about the same result. White's following move, therefore, came quite unexpectedly for him.

Position after Black's 23rd move.

24. P—Q Kt 4!   ......

White sacrifices another Pawn—thus re-establishing the equilibrium of forces—only in order to avoid the exchange of Queens. If now 24. ....P×P, then 25. Kt—Kt 5!, Q×Kt (K 7); 26. K R—K 1, Q—Q 7; 27. Kt×P ch, K—Kt 1; 28. Kt—B 6 ch! etc., winning.

24. ......   Q×Kt P
25. Q—B 2   Kt—Q 6

The only defence against the double threat 26. R—R 4 and 26. Q×B P ch.

26. K R—Kt 1   Q—B 5
27. R—R 4   Q—K 3

If instead 27. ....Q—B 2 then 28. B—Q 4!, P×B (or B×B ch; 29. Kt×B, R×Kt; 30. R×R, P×R; 31. Q×Kt, P×Kt; 32. Q×Q B P ch and wins); 29. Kt—Q 5 disc. ch!, Kt—B 4; 30. Kt×P ch!, P×Kt; 31. R×Kt P followed by 32. P—R 7 and wins.

28. Kt—Kt 5   K—Kt 1

A longer resistance was possible after 28. ....Kt×B; 29. K×Kt (and not 29. Kt×P ch, K—Kt 1; 30. Q×Q B P?, R—Q 8 ch! etc.), K—Kt 1; but by continuing 30. Kt—Kt 3, K R—B 1; 31. R—R 3! (followed by 32. R—K 3 or Q 3, etc.)—White would still increase his pressure in a decisive manner.

29. Kt (K 2)—Q 4!   Q—K 5

Or 29. ....B×Kt; 30. B×B, R×B; 31. R×R, Q—K 6 ch; 32. K—B 1 and the Rook is taboo because of a mate in two in case of its capture.

30. Kt—Q B 3   Q—K 1
31. Q×Kt   P×Kt
32. B×P   Q—K 3
33. Q—B 3!   Q—B 2

34. B × P   ......

If now 34. ....P × B ; 35. R × P ch, K—B 1, then 36. Q—B 6 ch Q—B 2 ; 37. R—Kt 8 ch !, K × R , 38. P—R 7 ch, and mate in two. ;

Resigns.

GAME 30

RUY LOPEZ

Twenty - second Match - Game, Amsterdam, November, 1929.

White : E. BOGOLJUBOW.

1. P—K 4	P—K 4
2. Kt—K B 3	Kt—Q B 3
3. B—Kt 5	P—Q R 3
4. B—R 4	P—Q 3
5. P—B 3	......

The fashionable move here—especially after Keres' win against me in Margate, 1937—is 5. P—Q R 4. But for how long ? Black seems to be able to obtain quite a satisfactory position by continuing 5. ....B—Q 2 ; 6. Kt—B 3, Kt—B 3 ; 7. P—Q 4, Kt × Q P ; 8. B × B ch, Q × B ; 9. Kt × Kt, P × Kt ; 10. Q × P, B—K 2 followed by .... Castles etc.

5.	B—Q 2
6. P—Q 4	P—K Kt 3
7. B—K Kt 5	......

As the following shows, White has no means of exploiting the diagonal Q Kt 3—K Kt 8, and, on the other hand, K B 2 will prove a suitable square for Black's King's Knight. It looks as though after 5. P—B 3 White's opening advantage is bound to vanish within a few moves and that, therefore, the usual 5. B × Kt ch followed by 6. P—Q 4 offers him more fighting chances.

7.	P—B 3
8. B—K 3	Kt—R 3
9. Castles	B—Kt 2
10. P—K R 3	......

In order to prevent ....Kt—K Kt 5 in case of Q Kt—Q 2.

10.	Kt—B 2
11. Q Kt—Q 2	Castles
12. P × P	......

White—rightly—recognises that a further maintaining of the tension in the centre would be rather to Black's advantage and aims at simplification. The problem of the defence has been solved in this game in quite a satisfactory way.

12.	Q P × P

Also 12. ....B P × P—in the hope of exploiting the K B's file—could be played. White would in that case probably try to bring a Knight to Q 5 after the moves 13. B—Kt 3, P—R 3 ; 14. P—Q R 4, followed by Kt—B 4, B—Q 2, Kt—K 3, etc. I preferred the text-move because of the tempting possibility of attacking shortly White's central position by means of ....P—K B 4.

13. B—B 5	......

In order to provoke the move ....P—Kt 3, which slightly weakens Black's Queen's side position.

13.	R—K 1
14. B—Kt 3	P—Kt 3
15. B—K 3	Q—K 2
16. Q—K 2	......

Or 16. B—Q 5, Q R—Q 1 ; 17. Q—K 2, Kt—Kt 1 followed by .... B—K 3, etc.

16.	Q Kt—Q 1
17. B—Q 5	......

Still playing for simplification which Black cannot well avoid as 17. ....P—B 3 would lose a Pawn after 18. B × Kt ch following by 19. B × P.

17. ......   B—B 3
18. P—B 4 ?   ......

But this is certainly not in accordance with the requirements of the position, as the Pawn at Q 5 after ....P—K B 4 will become very weak. Necessary was 18. B × B, Kt × B ; 19. K R—Q 1, etc., with only a slight advantage for Black because of the possibility (after a due preparation) of the K B's Pawn's advance.

18. ......   B × B
19. B P × B   ......

Even worse would be 19. K P × B, P—K B 4, etc.

19. ......   P—K B 4
20. Kt—B 4   Kt—Kt 2

Black is by no means in a hurry to play ....P—B 5 as the combined threat of this advance and an eventual ....P × K P will limit White's choice of moves much more than any direct action.

21. Q R—B 1   Q R—Q 1 !

Deliberately permitting the following transaction which only apparently relieves White from his troubles in the centre. Instead, 21. ....K R—Q 1 would have left the Queen unprotected and thus have allowed the counter-action 22. P × P, P × P ; 23. B—Q 4 ! (R × P, 24. K R—K 1, P—K 5 ; 25. B × B, K × B ; 26. Kt—K 3 ! ±) etc.

22. P—Q 6   Q Kt × P
23. Kt × Kt   R × Kt
24. Q × P   Q—Q 2 !

An important intermediate move

securing with *tempo* (the threat ....P—B 5) the control of the open file.

25. R—B 2   P—B 4
26. P—Q R 4   P—K B 5 !

Now the time has come, as the following advance of the K Kt's Pawn will be connected with the formidable threat 28. ....P—Kt 5 ; 29. P × P, Q × Kt P, etc., with a mating attack.

27. B—Q 2   P—K Kt 4
28. Q—Kt 5   ......

Although practically forced, this move actually brings but little help, as, after the Queen's exchange proposed here, Black not only obtains a far superior end game, but also—a very rare case considering the reduced material—a direct attack against the enemy's King.

28. ......   Q × Q
29. P × Q   R—Q 6 !

Freeing the important square Q 3 for the Knight.

30. R—R 1   Kt—Q 3
31. R—R 6   R—Kt 1

If now 32. Kt × Kt P, then simply 32. ....B—B 3 ; 33. Kt—B 3, Kt × K P, etc., with a sufficient positional advantage. And if 32. R—B 3, then 32. ....P—B 5 ! ; 33. R × R, P × R; 34. R—R 3, Kt × K P ; 35. R × P, R—R 1 ! ; 36. R—R 3, R—Q 1, etc., winning.

32. B—B 3   ......

As inoperative as the rest.

32. ......   Kt × K P
33. B × P   B × B
34. Kt × B   R—Q 8 ch
35. K—R 2   ......

Position after White's 35th move.

35. ......   Kt—Q 7 !

This sudden stroke—threatening mate in three by 36. ....Kt—B 8 ch, etc.—should have won at least the exchange. But Bogoljubow, as so often, prefers suicide to a long agony.

36. P—K R 4   R—K 1 !
37. Kt—B 3   ......

Or 37. Kt—Kt 4, R (K 1)—K 8 ; 38. K—R 3, R—R 8 ch ; 39. Kt—R 2, P—R 4 ! ; 40. P×P, Kt—B 8 followed by mate.

37. ......   Kt×Kt ch
38. P×Kt   R (K 1)—K 8
39. K R 3   P—R 4 !
Resigns.

GAME 31

RUY LOPEZ

San Remo Tournament, January 1930.

White : F. D. Yates

1. P—K 4   P—K 4
2. Kt—K B 3   Kt—Q B 3
3. B—Kt 5   P—Q R 3
4. B—R 4   P—Q 3
5. Kt—B 3   ......

An unusual way to fight against the Steinitz Defence delayed.

White's idea was probably to play P—Q B 3 after having brought the Q's Knight to Q 5 ; but in the meantime Black succeeds in exchanging the "Spanish" Bishop, and thus obtains the advantage of the pair of Bishops with a more elastic Pawn skeleton.

5. ......   B—Q 2
6. P—Q 3   ......

Logical—but more promising was still 6. B×Kt followed by 7. P—Q 4.

6. ......   P—K Kt 3
7. Kt—Q 5   P—Q Kt 4 !

Necessary because if White could have succeeded in fulfilling his plan (8. P—B 3) he would have in fact obtained a superiority in space.

8. B—Kt 3   Kt—R 4
9. B Kt 5 !   ......

The weakening of the diagonal Q R 2—K Kt 8, thus provoked, could eventually become of some importance—especially if White should decide to retain the corresponding Bishop.

9. ......   P—K B 3
10. B—Q 2   P—B 3

Necessary, as after the immediate 10. ....Kt×B White, after 11. R P×Kt, would have threatened 12. B—R 5, etc. with advantage.

11. Kt—K 3 (?)   ......

Comparatively better was 11. B× Kt, Q×B ch ; 12. Kt—B 3, after which Black would be compelled, before undertaking any action in the centre, to finish his development by means of ....Kt—R 3— B 2, followed by ....B—Kt 2 and Castles K R. After the text-move his task in increasing his advantage in space will be, on the contrary, a comparatively easy one.

11. ......   Kt×B

12. R P×Kt   Kt—R 3
13. P—Q Kt 4   ......

The real trouble for White consists in the fact that he has no secure squares for his Knights, and, on the other hand, if he tries to open the position the Black Bishops will become over-powerful.

13. ......   P—K B 4

If White's previous move had been 13. P—Q 4, this answer would prove even more effective.

14. Q—K 2   Kt—B 2
15. Kt—B 1   Q—K 2

Quiet positional play : Black is in no particular hurry to play .... P—B 5 as White has nothing else to do but try to stabilise the situation in the centre—even at the cost of a few *tempi*.

16. Kt—Kt 3   P—B 5
17. Kt—B 1   P—Kt 4
18. B—B 3   P—K R 4 !

Planning 19. ....P—R 5 and only after 20. P—R 3, P—Kt 5; 21. P×P, B×P followed by .... Kt—Kt 4, P—R 6, etc. In order to prevent this pinning, White decides to weaken his dark-coloured squares by playing P—K B 3.

19. Kt (B 3)—Q 2   B—Kt 5
20. P—B 3   B—K 3
21. P—Q 4   ......

If 21. Kt—Q Kt 3 Black would not have exchanged his valuable Q's Bishop for the Knight, but would have played 21......P—B 4 followed by ....Kt—Q 1—B 3—Q 5.

21. ......   B—Kt 2
22. Q—Q 3   ......

The "combination" 22. P—Q 5, P×P ; 23. R×P, R×R ; 24. Q×P

ch, Q—Q 2 ; 25. Q×R, P—Q 5, etc. would lose a piece.

22. ......   P×P
23. B×P   Kt—K 4

The occupation of this powerful central square signifies the strategical decision.

24. Q—K 2   Castles (K R)

As the position from now on will become still more open, the co-operation of the Rooks will be vital.

25. P—R 3   P—B 4 !

The beginning of the decisive action.

26. B—B 3   ......

Instead 26. P×P, P×P ; 27. B× Kt, B×B, etc., would be perfectly hopeless.

26. ......   P×P
27. B×P   Kt—B 3
28. B—B 3   B×B

The advantage is already so definite that the combined action of the two Bishops is no longer needed.

29. P×B   ......

Position after White's 29th move.

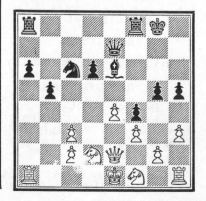

29. ......   Q—B 3

This move cannot actually be severely criticised as it wins a Pawn and allows Black after a few moves to simplify matters, and to obtain a technically rather easily won end-game. Still, Black did not need to give his opponent, even temporarily, the square White's K 4 for the Knight. Logical was therefore 29. ....Q—K Kt 2 ! (30. P—K 5, P—Q 4 ! etc.) after which all the tenacity of Yates would not have succeeded in prolonging the game much longer. I did not play my Queen to K Kt 2 in order to prevent the possibility of 30. Q—Q 3, Kt—Kt 5 ; 31. Q × Q P attacking the Bishop ; but 31. ....Kt × P ch ; 32. K—Q 1, Kt × R (or even 32. ....R—B 3) would in that case be decidedly favourable for Black. White's play from now on is an example of a patient and ingenious defence in a theoretically lost position.

30. P—K 5 !   Kt × P
31. Kt—K 4   Q—K 2
32. Kt (B 1)—Q 2 B—B 5
33. Kt × B   Kt × Kt

Threatening 34. ....P—Q 4 as well as 34. ....Kt—K 6. One would think that the game can last only a couple of moves more.

34. R—Q 1 !   ......

Threatening 35. R—Q 5.

34. ......   Q—K 4
35. Q—Q 3 !   ......

Again preventing 35. ....Kt—K 6 because of 36. Q × Q P etc. Besides, White threatens now 36. Q—Q 5 ch, etc.

35. ......   R—B 4
36. Castles !   ......

Thus White definitely saves himself

from a debacle in the middle-game, as—strange as it may seem—Black would hardly obtain a sufficient advantage by playing 36. .... Kt—K 6. The continuation would be 37. Kt × Q P !, R—Q 1 (or R—B 3 ; 38. K R—K 1, R—Q 1) ; 38. K R—K 1, R—B 3 ; 39. Q—K 4 ! (the point of the defence) after which 30. ....Q × P would be a mistake because of 40. Kt × P ! etc. ; and also 39. ....Q × Q ; 40. Kt × Q, R × R ; 41. Kt × R ch, K—B 2 ; 42. R × R, Kt × R ; 43. Kt—K 4 would not be yet quite convincing (43. ....P—R 4 ; 44. Kt—Q 6 ch or 43. ....K—K 3 ; 44. Kt—B 5 ch). Black's next move is therefore the simplest method of obtaining a winning end-game advantage.

36. ......   P—Q 4 !

Not only the extra-pawn is given back, but even the passed Q R's Pawn will be sacrificed in order to establish the Rook on the 7th rank. The following ending is sharp and full of tactical points.

37. Q × P ch   ......

There is, obviously, no choice left.

37. ......   Q × Q
38. R × Q   R × R
39. Kt—B 6 ch   K—B 2
40. Kt × R   R—Q 1

Instead 40. ....P—R 4 ; 41 Kt—B 7, R—Q Kt 1 ; 42. R—Kt 1, etc., would not have been convincing.

41. Kt—Kt 4   R—Q 7 !
42. R—R 1   ......

The main variation I expected was 42. Kt × P, Kt—K 6 ; 43. R—Kt 1, R × P ch ; 44. K—R 1, R × P ; 45. R × P, P—Kt 5 ! ; 46. R P × P, P × P ; 47. P × P, P—B 6 and wins.

42.	P—R 4
43. Kt—B 6	R × P
44. Kt × P	Kt—K 6
45. R—Kt 1	R × P ch
46. K—R 1	R—Kt 6

Not as simple as it looks would be instead 46. .... P—K Kt 5 because of 47. R P × P, P × P; 48. Kt—B 6!, etc.·

47. Kt—B 6 !	R × P ch
48. K—Kt 1	R—Kt 6 ch
49. K—R 2	K—B 3
50. Kt—Q 4	P—K Kt 5 !

This exactly-timed advance in fact saves the Q Kt's Pawn because of the strong threats it involves.

| 51. P × P | Kt × P ch |
| 52. K—R 1 | P—B 6 |

Threatening mate in two, and thus forcing the rejoinder.

53. R—K B 1	R—R 6 ch
54. K—Kt 1	P—B 7 ch
55. K—Kt 2	R × P
56: R—K R 1	......

Yates is still fighting ! Instead 56. Kt × P would lose rapidly after 56. .... R—Kt 6 ; 57. Kt—Q 4, R—Q 6 ; 58. Kt—B 2, R—Q 7 etc.

| 56. ...... | R—Q 6 ! |
| 57. Kt—K 2 | ...... |

Or 57. Kt × P, R—Q 7 ; 58. R—R 3, R—Q 8, etc.

| 57. ...... | R—Q 7 |
| 58. Kt—Kt 3 | R—Kt 7 ! |

Starting the final combination. 58. .... Kt—R 7 at once would be of course wrong because of 59. Kt—K 4 ch.

| 59. Kt × P ch | K—K 4 |
| 60. Kt—Kt 3 | Kt—R 7 ! |

An elegant stroke by which Black forces the exchange of Knights and keeps his two extra Pawns.

61. Kt—B 1	Kt × Kt
62. R—R 5 ch	K—Q 5
63. K × Kt	P—Kt 5
64. R—R 8	R—B 7
65. R—Q Kt 8	K—B 6
66. R—Kt 7	P—Kt 6
Resigns.	

GAME 32

FRENCH DEFENCE

San Remo Tournament, January, 1930.

Black : A. NIMZOWITSCH

1. P—K 4	P—K 3
2. P—Q 4	P—Q 4
3. Kt—Q B 3	B—Kt 5
4. P—K 5	P—Q B 4
5. B—Q 2	......

This rather tame move in connection with the following Knight's manœuvre should not cause Black much trouble. More promising—perhaps only because less explored—seems 5. Q—Kt 4 or even 5. P × P.

5.	Kt—K 2
6. Kt—Kt 5	B × B ch
7. Q × B	Castles
8. P—Q B 3	P—Q Kt 3

The wish to solve the Queen's Bishop's problem as rapidly as possible is, by the second player in the French Defence, quite legitimate, —but in this particular position the attempt will prove a failure *as Black cannot succeed in exchanging that piece against White's King's Bishop.* Good—and natural enough —was, instead of this, 8. .... Kt—B 4 ! (preventing Kt—Q 6) as played with success by the same Nimzowitsch against Dr. Lasker in Zurich, 1934.

9. P—K B 4   B—R 3

Trying to force White's P—Q R 4 in order to play afterwards Q Kt—B 3—R 4, etc. But, as will be seen, the second part of this plan cannot be executed.

10. Kt—B 3   Q—Q 2
11. P—Q R 4   Q Kt—B 3
12. P—Q Kt 4 ! ......

Strangely enough, this more or less conventional move (by which White prevents ....Kt—R 4 and at the same time forces a clearing of the situation in the centre) created at the time a kind of small sensation ; the late Dr. Tarrasch, for instance, called it in his comments "highly original." To my mind more surprising than the move is the fact that a player of Nimzowitsch's class, when adopting the plan started by 8. ....P—Q Kt 3, did not take this possibility into serious consideration.

12. ......   P × Kt P

Comparatively better than 12. ....P—B 5, after which White would not have much technical difficulty in exploiting, in a decisive manner, his advantage in space on the King's side.

13. P × P   B—Kt 2
14. Kt—Q 6   P—B 4 ?

The decisive strategical error in an already compromised situation. In view of the threatening advance of White's Q R's Pawn the only chance of obtaining some more space lay in 14. ....P—Q R 4 ; 15. B—Kt 5 (better than 15. P—Kt 5, Kt—Kt 5), P × P ; 16. Castles, after which the initiative of White—who would have to spend some time in regaining the Q Kt's Pawn—would not develop so rapidly. By moving his K B's Pawn, Nimzowitsch was obviously afraid of an attack against his King—and that was the one thing in the present game he did not have to worry about !

15. P—R 5 !   ......

As 15. ....P × P ; 16. P—Kt 5 ! followed by 17. R × P, etc., is now obviously bad for Black, this advance secures for the white Bishop the most important square Q Kt 5.

15. ......   Kt—B 1

The elimination of the terrible Knight at Q 6—which under other circumstances would signify the beginning of a complete emancipation—does not in fact bring Black any relief.

16. Kt × B   Q × Kt
17. P—R 6   Q—K B 2

To his misfortune 17. ....Q—K 2 does not work, because of 18. B—Kt 5 !, Kt × Kt P ? ; 19. R—Q Kt 1, etc.

18. B—Kt 5   ......

From now on Black may play what he likes—he will be unable to protect sufficiently his squares Q B 3 and Q B 2. The following hopeless tie-up is only the unavoidable consequence of that organic evil.

18. ......   Kt (B 1)—K 2
19. Castles (K R) P—R 3

Although Kt—Kt 5 was not yet a threat it could become one in the near future. Besides, the immediate 19. ....K R—B 1 would not change the situation a bit : Black loses not because of lack of time, but because of lack of space.

20. K R—B 1   K R—B 1
21. R—B 2   ......

If now 21. ....Kt—Q 1 then simply 22. R (R 1)—Q B 1, R × R ;

23. R×R, R—Q B 1 ; 24. R×R, Kt×R ; 25. Q—B 3 followed by Q—B 7, and wins.

21. ......   Q—K 1
22. Q R—Q B 1   ......

This and the next move are not the most exact ones, as the winning formation : Q at B 1, R s at Q B 2 and B 3, was to be reached in three moves instead of five, as occurred in the actual game : 22. R—R 3 ! followed by Q R—B 3 and Q—B 1.

22. ......   Q R—Kt 1
23. Q—K 3   R—B 2
24. R—B 3 !   ......

From now on, White wins in the shortest number of moves.

24. ......   Q—Q 2

In order to give the King the possibility of protecting the Rook at Q B 2—a desperate idea in a desperate position !

25. R (B 1)—B 2   K—B 1
26. Q—B 1   R (Kt 1)—B 1

Position after Black's 26th move.

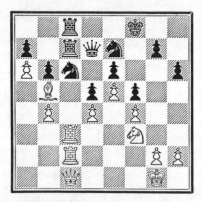

27. B—R 4 !   ......

The last link of the positional attack started by 15. P—Q R 5.

In order to save the piece threatened by 28. P—Kt 5 Black must sacrifice the Q Kt's Pawn. After this he succeeds in protecting the important squares with the King, but must still resign as a consequence of a complete *Zugzwang*. An instructive finish !

27. ......   P—Q Kt 4
28. B×P   K—K 1
29. B—R 4   K—Q 1
30. P—R 4 !   ......

After a couple of irrelevant Pawn moves Black will be obliged to play Q—K 1 after which P—Kt 5 wins immediately.

Resigns.

GAME 33

NIMZOWITSCH'S DEFENCE

San Remo Tournament, January, 1930.

White : Dr. M. Vidmar

1. P—Q 4   Kt—K B 3
2. P—Q B 4   P—K 3
3. Kt—Q B 3   B—Kt 5
4. Q—B 2   P—Q 4
5. P—Q R 3   B×Kt ch
6. Q×B   Kt—K 5
7. Q—B 2   Kt—Q B 3

According to the actual views of the theory, 7. ....P—Q B 4 ; 8. P×B P, Kt—Q B 3, etc., is sufficient for equalising. The text-move —in connection with the following pawn-sacrifice—was introduced by me in the present game, and was considered, for quite a long time, a kind of refutation of 5. P—Q R 3. Only recently have a few tournament games and subsequent analysis cast doubt on the efficiency of Black's counter-play. As the idea occurred to me only during this game and as I have never tested it since, I would not be at all surprised if a further, detailed analysis will definitely prove its insufficiency.

8. P—K 3 ......

After 8. Kt—B 3, P—K 4 ; 9. P×KP, B—B 4 ; 10. Q—Kt 3, Kt—R 4 ; 11. Q—R 4 ch, P—B 3 ; 12. P×P, Q×P, etc., Black should obtain a good positional compensation for the minus pawn.

8. ...... P—K 4
9. P—B 3 ? ......

Very harmless, to say the least ; White should have entered into the main variation starting with 9. P× Q P, which would have brought him, after a rather venturesome King's trip, it is true, two minor pieces for a Rook, and a safe enough position. The play might be : 9. ....Q×P ; 10. B—B 4, Q—R 4 ch; 11. P—Kt 4 !, Kt×Kt P ; 12. Q× Kt, Kt—B 7 doub. ch, ; 13. K—K 2, Q—K 8 ch ; 14. K—B 3, Kt×R ; 15. B—Kt 2, B—K 3 ! (Finc's move) ; 16. P—Q 5, Castles (Q side) ; 17. P×B, P×P ; 18. K—Kt 3 ! after which the few threats Black would still possess would hardly compensate for his material loss. After the text-move, Black gets an advantage in development without having sacrificed anything in exchange.

9. ...... Kt—B 3

A premature attack would be 9. ....Q—R 5 ch ; 10. P—Kt 3, Kt× Kt P ; 11. Q—B 2, Kt—B 4 ; 12. P×Q P, etc.±

10. P×Q P Q×P
11. B—B 4 ......

This gain of a *tempo* is not enough compensation for all the time wasted previously.

11. ...... Q—Q 3

12. P×P Kt×P
13. B—Q 2 ......

Not satisfied with the results of the opening play, White begins to set little traps, which, however, will prove quite ineffective. Comparatively better than this artificial development was 13. Kt—K 2 followed by O—O.

13. ...... Castles !

Rightly ignoring White's combination.

14. B—Kt 4 ......

Also, 14. R—Q 1, Q—Kt 3, etc., would be in Black's favour.

14. ...... P—B 4
15. R—Q 1 ......

Of course not 15. B × P, Q×B; 16. B×P ch, R×B ; 17. Q×Q, Kt—Q 6 ch, etc. But also the intermediate move in the text, on which White obviously relied, is of little help.

15. ...... Q—B 3 !

The point of Black's active defence : if now 16. B×P, then 16. ....Kt×B ; 17. Q×Kt (or 17. B × R, K × B, etc.), P—Q Kt 3, etc., winning a piece. White must therefore remove his Bishop.

16. B—Q 2 B—B 4 ! ?

From now on Black's trouble will be that he will have too many promising continuations at his disposal, and therefore it will be extremely difficult to decide each time which is actually the best. As the game goes, he succeeds in winning, by interesting tactical play, first a Pawn and finally the exchange—but White still preserves, almost to the end, excellent drawing chances ! Consequently, something *must* have been out of order in Black's method of exploiting his considerable positional advantage. Most likely, the rational way consisted not in trying to profit by the insufficient protection of White's King's Pawn, but in increasing two already existing advantages: (1) the Pawn majority on the Queen's side, and, especially, (2) the weakness of the light coloured squares in White's camp. Therefore, the tempting Bishop-move should have been replaced by the simple variation, 16. ....Kt × B ; 17. Q × Kt, B—B 3 ; 18. Q—B 2, Q—Kt 4 ! etc.∓, after which White would hardly succeed in bringing his King into safety.

17.	Q × B	Kt × B
18.	B—B 1	K R—K 1

By no means convincing was here 18. ....Q R—Q 1 ; 19. R × R, R × R ; 20. Kt—K 2, Kt—Q 4 ; 21. Q—Q 3 ! threatening 22. P—K 4, etc.

19.	K—B 2	R—K 3

Planning the following intermezzo, which wins a pawn perforce.

20.	Kt—R 3 !	......

Comparatively better than 20. Kt—K 2, since the Knight can eventually be useful at K Kt 5. After the unlucky opening, Dr. Vidmar defends his compromised position with extreme care and determination.

20.	......	Kt—K 5 ch !
21.	K—K 1	......

Of course, the Knight was taboo because of 21. ....R—B 3.

21.	......	K Kt—Q 3
22.	Q—Q 3 !	......

If 22. Q—Q 5, Black would

naturally have avoided exchange of Queens with 22. ....Q—Kt 4.

Position after White's 22nd move.

22.	......	Kt × K P !

The point of the previous moves of Black, whose aim is *not* to exchange the two Rooks for the Queen, but simply to win back the Bishop, remaining with an extra Pawn. However, as White will now be able to force the exchange of Queens, the fight is by no means near its end.

23.	B × Kt	P—B 5 !
24.	Q—Q 5	......

Otherwise Black plays 24. .... Kt—B 4.

24.	......	R × B ch
25.	K—B 2	Q × Q

After this, Black will have almost no choice for the next 10-12 moves, when an extremely difficult ending of R+2 Ps v. Kt+3 Ps will be reached. Possibly a somewhat more promising alternative was, therefore, 25. ....R—K 3 ; 26. Q × Q (else Black will avoid this exchange) P × Q ; 27. K R—K 1, R × R ; 28. K × R, Kt—B 4 ! eventually followed by ....Kt—K 6. But at this stage it was not at all easy to decide which line would leave White less drawing chances.

26. R×Q   R—Q 6

This was, of course, planned on the previous move. After 26. ....
R—K 3 ; 27. K R—Q 1, etc., White would easily obtain a draw.

27. R×R	P×R
28. R—Q 1	Kt—B 5
29. R×P	Kt×Kt P
30. R—Kt 3	Kt—B 5
31. R×P	Kt×P
32. Kt—Kt 5	......

At last White succeeds in justifying the move 20. Kt—R 3. Obviously enough, Black has no time for protecting his K B P, since, after 32. ....P—B 3, the manœuvre Kt—K 6—B 7 would immediately force a draw.

32.	P—Q R 4
33. Kt×B P	P—R 5

33. ....Kt—B 5 would be useless, because of 34. R—B 7.

34. Kt—Q 6	Kt—B 7
35. R—Kt 2	......

Otherwise the passed Pawn goes through.

35.	P—R 6 !
36. R×Kt	P—R 7
37. R×P ?	......

It is difficult to explain why White takes the Pawn at once instead of playing 37. R—B 1, P=Q ; 38. R×Q, etc., which would give him the option of playing the King to Kt 3 (as in the actual game) or making another move. Actually, after 38. ....R×R ; 39. P—Kt 4 ! Black's win, if possible at all, would be even more remote than in the line selected.

37.	R×R ch

38. K—Kt 3   K—B 1

Black's plan evidently consists in gradually restricting the activity of both White's pieces and in trying to create Pawn-weaknesses in the enemy's structure. Whether this can be carried out against an impeccable defence is another question. Not having seen an end-game like this in the literature devoted to that branch of chess, I confess I was rather expecting my opponent to succeed in finding an impregnable defensive position for both his Knight and King.

Position after Black's 38th move.

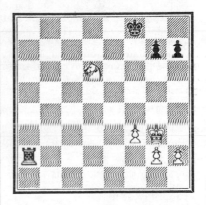

39. P—R 4   ......

It is difficult to suggest exactly what White's manœuvres must be in order to prevent the gradual advance of Black's King, but one positional consideration is beyond dispute : *White's Pawns should not be touched without necessity or without real prospects of being exchanged.* Although the move in the text can hardly be considered a decisive mistake, it certainly helps the execution of the first part of Black's plan, for from now on the White King will have to take care not only of K Kt 2 but also, eventually, of K R 4.

| 39. ...... | K—K 2 |
| 40. Kt—K 4 | P—R 3 |

Necessary, in order to permit the King's advance.

41. Kt—B 2	K—K 3
42. Kt—Q 3	K—B 4
43. Kt—B 4	R—R 5
44. Kt—Q 3	R—Q B 5
45. Kt—B 2	R—B 3
46. Kt—R 3	K—K 4

Black now threatens to bring his King to K B 8, for instance : 47. Kt—B 4, K—Q 5 ; 48. K—B 2, R—B 7 ch ; 49. K—Kt 3, K—K 6 ; 50. Kt—Q 5 ch, K—K 7 ; 51. Kt—B 4 ch, K—B 8 ; after this, the next step would be to secure square K B 7 for the King by using *zugzwang* and even that would not yet be the end of the winning procedure ! One may therefore imagine how welcome was White's next Pawn-move, which afforded me a number of new attacking possibilities.

| 47. P—R 5 ? | ...... |

Depriving Black of square K Kt 3 —but, as will be seen, the control of K Kt 4 was far more important.

47.	R—B 7
48. Kt—B 4	R—Q 7 !
49. Kt—R 3	......

Already he has no choice.

49.	K—Q 5
50. Kt—B 4	K—K 6
51. Kt—K 6	......

Impatience or despair ? If the latter, it was already justified, because the retreat 51. Kt—R 3 would mean sure defeat : 51. .... R—R 7 ! ; 52. Kt—B 4, R—R 4 ; winning, to begin with, the adventurous R P.

| 51. ...... | R—Q 4 |

The beginning of the end, since 52. K—R 4 no longer helps because of ....R—K 4 ! ; 53. Kt×P, R—

K Kt 4 followed by R × Kt P, etc.

| 52. P—B 4 | R—K B 4 ! |

The K B P is much more important than the K R P, which, anyhow, is bound to be captured sooner or later.

| 53. K—Kt 4 | R—B 3 ! |

Preventing White from protecting the B P by 54. P—Kt 3, which would be played against 53. .... K—K 5.

| 54. P—B 5 | R—B 2 |

Not the shortest way, which was : 54. ....K—K 5 ; 55. Kt×P, R—B 2 ; 56. Kt—K 6 (or Kt—K 8, K—K 4 !), R×P ; 57. P—Kt 3, R—K 4 ; 58. Kt—B 4, R—Kt 4 ch ; 59. K—R 4, K—B 6 and wins.

| 55. P—Kt 3 | ...... |

Hastening the end. After 55. Kt—Q 8 !, R—B 3 ; 56. Kt—K 6, Black would have adopted the variation given above starting with 56. ....K—K 5 !

55.	K—K 5
56. Kt—B 5 ch	K—Q 5 !
57. Kt—Kt 3 ch	K—K 4

Resigns.

My games with Dr. Vidmar have generally been full of life and struggle.

GAME 34

QUEEN'S GAMBIT DECLINED

San Remo Tournament, January, 1930.

Black : G. Maroczy

1. P—Q 4	P—Q 4
2. P—Q B 4	P—K 3
3. Kt—Q B 3	Kt—K B 3
4. B—Kt 5	B—K 2
5. P—K 3	Q Kt—Q 2
6. Kt—B 3	Castles
7. R—B 1	P—B 3

The recent praxis seems to show that the intermediate move 7. .... P—K R 3 gives Black more opportunities of solving the centre-problem in a satisfactory way than this old-fashioned so-called "Capablanca's freeing manœuvre" (although it had already been played, for instance, by Mason in Hanover, in 1902).

8.	B—Q 3	P×P
9.	B×P	Kt—Q 4
10.	B×B	Q×B
11.	Kt—K 4	P—Q Kt 3

An attempt to solve immediately the problem of the Q's Bishop. Although it is rewarded in the present game by a partial success (at least in the opening stage) it can hardly be recommended, as White could play the following moves more energetically. Instead, Dr. Lasker's idea 11. ....K Kt—B 3; 12. Kt—Kt 3, P—K 4 ! (*see* Game No. 70) seems to be sufficient for equalising.

12.	Castles	B—Kt 2
13.	Kt—Kt 3	P—Q B 4
14.	P—K 4	......

An interesting alternative here was 14. B—Kt 5 in order to answer 14. ....P×P ? by 15. P—K 4 ! followed by R—B 7. Black would have in that case to deal with the usual troubles caused in this variation by an insufficiently prepared advance of the Q B Pawn.

| 14. | ...... | K Kt—B 3 |
| 15. | R—K 1 | ...... |

White's previous move would have found its logical justification if he had continued here with 15. P—Q 5; for instance, 15. .... P×P, 16. P×P, Q—Q 3; 17. Kt—B 5, Q—B 5; 18. Kt—K 7 ch, K—R 1; 19. B—Kt 5 ! after which the Queen's Pawn would remain an important factor in White's favour.

By the selected quiet continuation (due chiefly to the fact that having started the tournament by five straight wins I did not want, in the sixth round, to take any chances), White still keeps a slight positional advantage—but against an end-game specialist like Maroczy White's winning prospects become rather problematical.

| 15. | ...... | P×P |
| 16. | B—Kt 5 ! | ...... |

If instead 16. P—K 5, then 16. ....Kt—Kt 5 !; 17. Q×P, B×Kt ; 18. P×B, K Kt×K P !; 19. R×Kt, Kt×R ; 20. Q×K Kt, Q R—B 1, etc., to Black's advantage.

16.	......	K R—B 1
17.	Q×P	R—B 4
18.	B×Kt	Kt×B
19.	P—Kt 4	R×R
20.	R×R	R—Q B 1
21.	R×R ch	B×R
22.	Q—B 3	......

The position is not quite as dead a draw as one may think at the first glance. For the moment, for instance, Black will have to lose time in order to parry White's threats on the Q B's file.

22.	......	Q—Q 1
23.	Kt—Q 4	B—Kt 2
24.	P—B 3	......

One of White's advantages consists in the fact that Black's Bishop, owing to the general Pawn structure, has but very poor prospects.

| 24. | ...... | Kt—B 3 |

In order to be able to oppose the Queen at B 2—doubtless the right scheme.

| 25. | Kt—B 1 | ...... |

This Knight had obviously nothing more to do at K Kt 3.

| 25. ...... | Kt—K 1 |
| 26. Kt—K 3 | P—Q R 3 |

Maroczy seems not to be in a mood to play the purely passive end-game which he could obtain by the—otherwise logical—26. .... Q—B 2; 27. Q×Q, Kt×Q; 28. Kt—B 4, Kt—K 1 ! White's advantage in space in this variation would be evident, but as the direct threat 29. Kt—Kt 5 could be sufficiently parried by 29. ....B—R 3 the draw-conclusion would be still probable. After the move made, Black on the other hand will hardly be able to offer the exchange of Queens because of the weakness of his Q Kt 3.

27. P—Q R 4 !   ......

The intended P—R 5 will fulfil a double object : (i) fix Black's weakness at Q R 3 ; (ii) secure the strong Q B 5 square for a Knight.

| 27. ...... | P—R 3 |
| 28. P—R 3 | ...... |

Not in order to give the King a—here unnecessary—loophole, but simply planning to move that piece, eventually, to the centre, and therefore putting the K R's Pawn on a protected square.

28. ......   P—K R 4 ?

Black's 26th move, although not very logical (avoiding the exchange of Queens and creating a weakness on the Q's side), was hardly sufficient to compromise the situation seriously. But this peculiar Pawn's move—the significance of which will not be explained by Black's further play—by creating a new (although, one must admit, for the moment hardly perceptible) weak spot at Black's K Kt 4, procures White unmistakable winning chances.

29. P—R 5   P×P

| 30. P×P | Q—Q 3 |
| 31. Kt—Kt 3 | B—B 3 |

The desire to bring the Bishop on to a more active square (Q Kt 4) is reasonable ; but White seizes at once the opportunity to bring his central Pawns forward, and thus limits the action of the hostile Knight.

32. P—K 5 !	Q—B 2
33. Kt—Q B 5	B—Kt 4
34. P—B 4	......

The slight weakening of the light-coloured squares occasioned by this advance does not matter any longer, as the Bishop is already pinned to the Q R's Pawn.

| 34. ...... | Q—Q 1 |
| 35. P—B 5 | ...... |

The only winning possibility for White consists in combining the pressure on the Q's side with direct threats against the Black King.

35.	P×P
36. Kt×B P	Q—Kt 4
37. Kt—Q 4 !	......

An important tactical detail (37. ....Q×P ; 38. Kt×B, etc.).

| 37. ...... | Kt—B 2 |
| 38. Kt—B 3 | ...... |

From now on Black will realise that he erred by playing ....P—K R 4.

| 38. ...... | Q—B 5 |
| 39. K—B 2 | ...... |

Thus showing that he is already willing to exchange Queens. As a matter of fact the end-game after 39. ....Kt—Q 4 ; 40. Q—Q 4, Q×Q ch; 41. Kt×Q, B—B 5 ; 42. Kt—B 5 ! followed by Kt—Q 6 would be extremely critical, if not hopeless, for Black.

| 39. ...... | Q—B 4 |
| 40. Q—Q 2 | K—R 2 |

Instead, 40. ....Kt—K 3; 41. Kt—Kt 7 ! followed by Kt—Q 6± would have enabled him to resist longer. The following winning procedure is instructive.

Position after Black's 40th move.

41. Kt—K 4 !   ......

If now 41. ....Kt—K 1 then 42. Kt—Kt 3, Q—Kt 3; 43. Q—Q 8, etc., with gradual strangulation. Black prefers, therefore, to sacrifice a Pawn in order to get rid of at least one of the tedious Knights.

| 41. ...... | Kt—K 3 |
| 42. Kt—Q 6 | Q—Kt 8 |

If 42. .... Q—Kt 3 White wins by 43. Kt×B, P×Kt ; 44. P—R 6, since 44. ....Kt—B 4 does not work because of 45. Kt—Kt 5 ch, Q×Kt ; 46. Q×Q, Kt—K 5 ch ; 47. K—K 3, Kt×Q ; 48. P—R 7.

43. Kt×P	B—B 3
44. Kt (B 7)—Kt 5 ch	Kt×Kt
45. Kt×Kt ch	K—Kt 3
46. P—R 4	......

Thus White has taken the maximum of advantage from the weakness of Black's K Kt 4 !

| 46. ...... | K—B 4 |

The threat was 47. Q—Q 6 ch, K—B 4 ; 48. Q—K 6 ch, K—B 5 ; 49. P—Kt 3 mate.

| 47. P—K 6 | Q—Kt 4 |
| 48. Q—B 2 ch | ...... |

The object of the following checks is to prevent *with tempo* Black's ....Q—Q B 4 ch and thus make possible the further advance of the passed Pawn.

48.	K—K 4
49. Q—B 3 ch	K—Q 3
50. Q—Kt 3 ch	K—Q 4
51. Q—B 3 ch	K—K 4
52. Q—K 3 ch	K—B 3

Or 52. ....K—Q 3 ; 53. Q—B 4 ch ! etc.

53. Q—Q B 3 ch	K—Kt 3
54. P—K 7	Q—K B 4 ch
55. K—K 3	......

The King is here—for once—even safer than on the wing (55. K—Kt 1, Q—Kt 8 ch, etc.).

55.	B—K 1
56. Q—Q 4	B—Kt 4
57. Q—Q 6 ch	Q—B 3
58. Kt—K 4 !	Resigns.

GAME 35

DUTCH DEFENCE

San Remo Tournament, January, 1930.

Black : Dr. S. Tartakower

1. P—Q 4	P—K 3
2. P—Q B 4	P—K B 4
3. P—K Kt 3	Kt—K B 3
4. B—Kt 2	B—Kt 5 ch
5. Kt—Q 2	Kt—K 5

Black is aiming to exchange the pieces he has just developed—a doubtful strategy, to say the least. More in the spirit of the opening chosen would be 5. ....Castles ; 6. P—Q R 3, B—K 2, etc.

6. P—Q R 3	Kt × Kt
7. B × Kt	B × B ch
8. Q × B	Castles
9. Kt—R 3	......

Chiefly in order to enforce the control of Q 5 in case Black selects the development ....P—Q 3 and ....P—K 4.

| 9. ...... | P—Q 4 |

After this the dark squares of Black's position may sooner or later become very weak ; and White, in order to exploit that weakness, decides to free the centre from Pawns as rapidly as possible. Although it was very difficult to foresee at this moment that Black, after the transaction projected, would have at his disposal adequate defence against the many threats, a slower policy—like 10. R—Q B 1 (instead of 10. P × P), P—B 3 ; 11. Castles, Q—K 2 ; 12. Q—K 3 ! followed by Kt—B 4, etc.—would have been more appropriate in order to take advantage of Black's manœuvre of the 5th-7th moves.

10. P × P	P × P
11. Kt—B 4	P—B 3
12. Castles (KR)	Q—K 2
13. P—Q Kt 4 !	......

The real object of this move—besides a "minority" attack which by means of the continuation P—Q R 4 was also quite possible—is to open for the Queen the way to Q R 2. The following will prove the importance of that diversion.

| 13. ...... | P—Q R 3 |
| 14. P—B 3 | ...... |

All in accordance with the plan inaugurated by his 10th move. But Black, by keeping a cool head, succeeds in emerging from the skirmish without much damage.

14.	Kt—Q 2
15. P—K 4	B P × P
16. P × P	P × P
17. Q—R 2 ch	......

Sadly enough, the tempting 17. B × P does not work—for instance, 17. ....Q × B ; 18. Q R—K 1, Q—B 4 ; 19. Q—R 2 ch (or 19. Kt—K 6, Q—Kt 3 ; 20. Kt × R, Kt × Kt, etc. ∓), R—B 2 ! ; 20. R—K 8 ch (or K 7), Kt—B 1—and Black escapes.

| 17. ...... | K—R 1 |
| 18. Kt—K 6 | ...... |

Unconvincing is 18. Q—K 6, R—K 1 ! etc.

18.	R × R ch
19. R × R	Kt—B 3
20. Kt—Kt 5	P—R 3
21. Q—B 7 !	......

This strong move, which forces the exchange of Queens because of the threat 22. R × Kt !, etc., had to be foreseen when the centre-action was started ; otherwise Black would have obtained even the better game.

21.	Q × Q
22. Kt × Q ch	K—R 2
23. Kt—Q 6	......

This menacing Knight position secures White the recapture of the sacrificed Pawn ; but on the other hand, Black should, in the meantime, find the opportunity to finish his development and obtain equality.

| 23. ...... | B—K 3 ? |

Obviously over-estimating the value of the central Pawn. The right way was 23. ....P—Q R 4 ! ; 24. Kt × K P (if 24. P—Kt 5 then simply 24. ....P × P), P × P ; 25.

Kt × Kt ch (or 25. P × P, Kt—Q 4), P × Kt ; 26. P × P, K—Kt 2 with a probable draw in view.

    24. Kt × Kt P   B—Q 4
    25. R—K 1 !   ......

Otherwise Black, in many cases, could play ....P—K 6.

    25. ......   R—R 2
    26. Kt—B 5   P—Q R 4

Giving White a passed Pawn ; but the Rook, naturally, cannot always remain pinned to the Q R Pawn.

    27. P × P   R × P
    28. P—Q R 4   R—R 1

With the object of occupying the Q Kt's file, or (as actually happens) of diminishing somewhat White's pressure against the K's Pawn.

    29. R—R 1   R—R 4
    30. R—R 3 !   ......

Still with the object of preventing ....P—K 6.

    30. ......   K—Kt 3

Black hopes to have just time to execute the important manœuvre Kt—K 1—Q 3, but is prevented from this by what Dr. Tartakower himself calls " the combinative wonder."

    31. P—R 3   K—B 4
    32. K—B 2   Kt—K 1

Everything according to the pre-conceived plan. Instead, 32. .... P—R 4 would have prevented the following surprise, but after 33. K—K 3, etc., the tying of all Black pieces would in any case have led to material loss.

Position after Black's 32nd move.

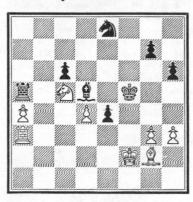

33. B × P ch !   ......

At first sight, having in view the (very poor) transaction 33. .... B × B ; 34. Kt × B, K × Kt ; 35. R—K 3 ch, K × P ; 36. R × Kt, R × P, etc. ; but in reality forcing a tech-nically rather easily won Rook end-game with an extra Pawn.

    33. ......   B × B
    34. P—Kt 4 ch   ......

The simple but very unkind point: 34. ...., K—B 5 ; 35. Kt—K 6 mate !

    34. ......   K—B 3
    35. Kt × B ch   K—K 3
    36. K—K 3   Kt—Q 3
    37. K—Q 3   Kt × Kt
    38. K × Kt   P—R 4

Black realises that "quiet" play would not leave him any chances—for instance, 38. ....K—Q 3 ; 39. K—Q 3, K—Q 4 ; 40. R—R 1, P—B 4 ; 41. P × P, K × P ; 42. K—B 3, etc.—cf. my last match-game with Capablanca. He tries, therefore, to create attacking objects on the King's side, but only hastens the end by accepting the following Pawn sacrifice.

    39. P—Kt 5 !   R × P

After 39. .... K—Q 3 ; 40. P—
R 4 his situation would be even
worse than before.

40.	P—R 5	R—Kt 4
41.	P—R 6	R—Kt 1
42.	P—R 7	R—Q R 1
43.	P—R 4 !	P—Kt 4
44.	P×P	P—R 5
45.	R—R 6	K—B 2
46.	K—B 4	P—R 6
47.	K—Kt 3	K—Kt 3
48.	P—Q 5 !	K×P
49.	P×P	K—B 4
50.	P—B 7	Resigns.

GAME 36

QUEEN'S INDIAN DEFENCE

San Remo Tournament, January,
1930.

White : K. AHUES

1.	P—Q 4	Kt—K B 3
2.	Kt—K B 3	P—Q Kt 3
3.	P—K 3	B—Kt 2
4.	Q Kt—Q 2	......

This system of development has
been favoured by Rubinstein and
the late Belgian Champion, Colle.
It is not particularly aggressive but
not without sting—especially if
White succeeds in time in opening
for his Q's Bishop a suitable
diagonal.

4.	......	P—B 4
5.	B—Q 3	P—K 3
6.	P—B 3	B—K 2
7.	Q—K 2	......

White is over-cautious. More in
the spirit of the variation selected
would have been 7. P—K 4, and
only after 7. .... P—Q 3 ; 8. Q—
K 2, as after the move made Black
succeeds by the following original
answer in preventing the advance
of the King's Pawn.

| 7. | ...... | Kt—Q 4 ! |

With by no means hidden inten-
tions : if P—K 4, then .... Kt—
B 5 ; if P—B 4, then .... Kt—
Kt 5, etc. !

| 8. | P×P | ...... |

With this exchange White starts
an elaborate manœuvre the ultimate object of which is to bring
the Q's Bishop on the diagonal
Q R 1—K R 8. As a matter of
fact there is hardly a more promising line to be recommended for
him.

| 8. | ...... | P×P |
| 9. | Kt—B 1 | ...... |

He does not play this Knight to
Q B 4 as he intends to dislodge
Black's central Knight by P—Q B 4.

9.	......	Q—B 2
10.	Kt—Kt 3	Kt—Q B 3
11.	B—Q 2	P—Kt 4 !

A bold idea, connected in one
variation with the offer of a Pawn
and based on the following general
considerations : Black possesses on
the King's side an elastic Pawn
mass, not obstructed by his own
pieces ; the natural thing for him
to do is therefore to try to gain
space by gradually advancing these
Pawns. But which Pawn shall he
start with ? The move 11. .... P—
K R 4 would be met by 12. P—
K R 4 ! stopping any further action
on that side ; on the other hand 11.
.... P—B 4 would also have been
premature as it would allow White
to open the position by 12. P—K 4,
P×P ; 13. Q×P ! etc. There remains the text move, which, by
the way, is more effective than the
preparatory 11. .... Castles K R,
permitting White to answer 12. P—
Q R 3 ! followed by P—Q B 4, etc.

| 12. | P—B 4 | K Kt—Kt 5 |
| 13. | B—B 3 | ...... |

One must admit that White plays at least logically—the diagonal Q R 1—K R 8 is for the time being his only counter-chance.

13.	Kt × B ch
14. Q × Kt	Kt—Kt 5
15. Q—K 2	......

The main variation considered by Black when playing 11. ....P—Kt 4 was 15. Q—Kt 1, P—B 3; 16. Kt × P (or 16. P—Q R 3, Kt—B 3; 17. Kt × P, Kt—K 4 ! ∓), B × P; 17. R—Kt 1, B—Kt 2; 18. Kt × R P, Castles !, etc., with a more than sufficient positional compensation for the material sacrificed.

15.	R—K Kt 1
16. P—Q R 3	Kt—B 3
17. Kt—Q 2	Kt—K 4
18. Q—R 5	......

White, obviously not satisfied with his position, is looking for complications. Of course Black's chances would also have remained superior (chiefly because of the possibilities offered by the pair of Bishops) after the quiet 18. P—B 3.

| 18. ...... | Castles |

Even more forcible would have been 18. ......B × P; 19. R—K Kt 1, B—Q B 3; 20. Q × R P, Castles, etc. ∓. After the text-move White decides to renounce—at the cost of two *tempi* !—making that compromising transaction.

19. Castles (KR) P—B 4

Threatening 20. ....P—Kt 5.

20. Q—K 2 P—K R 4 !

No reason to give the opponent even one moment's relief !

21. Kt × R P ......

White is forced to take this Pawn, as otherwise its advance would be too painful.

21. ...... R—Kt 3

Threatening 22. ....R—R 3 followed by Q R—R 1, etc., with a deadly effect.

22. P—B 4 ......

The exchange thus proposed will bring the Knight into an excellent defensive position—but, unfortunately for White, only for a very short time. However, as White did not have even a shade of counter-play, his King's position was in the long run indefensible anyhow.

22.	P × P
23. Kt × P	R—R 3
24. P—R 3	R—Kt 1

With the strong threat 25. .... Kt—Kt 3, etc.

| 25. B × Kt | Q × B |
| 26. Kt—B 3 | Q—Kt 2 |

Position after Black's 26th move.

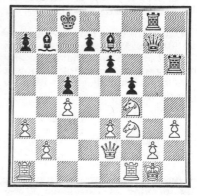

27. Q R—Q 1 ......

After this Black wins the Pawn back and at the same time demolishes the last fortifications protecting the enemy's King. But also the protection of the K R's Pawn by 27. K—R 1 would have led to an untenable position after 27. ....B—Q 3; 28. Q—K B 2, Q—Kt 5 ! (threatening 29. K B × Kt ; 30. P×B, R×P ch ! etc.) ; 29. K—Kt 1, R×P !; 30. Kt×R, Q×Kt (R 6), etc.

27.	......	P—K 4 !
28.	Kt—Q 5	R×P
29.	Q—Q 2	B×Kt
30.	P×B	P—K 5
31.	P—Q 6	P×Kt
32.	R×P	R×R
33.	P×B	Q×K P

Resigns.

GAME 37

NIMZOWITSCH'S DEFENCE

San Remo Tournament, January, 1930.

Black : H. Kmoch

1.	P—Q 4	Kt—K B 3
2.	P—Q B 4	P—K 3
3.	Kt—Q B 3	B—Kt 5
4.	B—Q 2	......

One of the most harmless answers to Black's 3rd move. Also the present game shows that Black, by making even the simplest moves, can obtain a middle-game with even prospects.

4.	......	Castles
5.	P—K 3	P—Q 4
6.	Kt—B 3	P—B 4
7.	P—Q R 3	......

Again a passive move. In playing the opening of this game I was decidedly not in my happiest mood ! First 7. Q—B 2, and only after 7. .... Kt—B 3; 8. P—Q R 3, B×Kt ; 9. B×B, etc., which leads to a more colourful position.

7.	......	B×Kt
8.	B×B	Kt—K 5

Perfectly logical as a further simplification, is here only in favour of the second player.

| 9. | R—B 1 | ...... |

Even now 9. Q—B 2 was more promising.

9.	......	Kt×B
10.	R×Kt	P×Q P
11.	K P×P	Kt—B 3 !

Black does not hurry with 11. ....P×P, since after 12. P—B 5 he would be able to start a successful battle in the centre by answering 12. ....P—K 4 !

12.	B—K 2	P×P
13.	B×P	......

It is not difficult to see that the opening play has resulted rather in Black's favour, as White's isolated Pawn is decidedly not an ornament to his position and, on the other hand, the advantage in space which he still possesses has for the moment not much importance, because of the absence of vulnerable spots in the enemy's position. White's only chance, therefore, is to try to create a King's side attack —and the reader will see how difficult this task proved to be against the author of *Die Kunst der Verteidigung.*

13.	......	Q—B 3
14.	Castles	R—Q 1
15.	R—Q 3	B—Q 2
16.	R—K 1	......

In spite of his scarcely brilliant prospects White still decides to play for a win, and does not try therefore to exchange the isolated Pawn. Otherwise he would have played here 16. Q—Q 2, preparing P—Q 5, which move at this moment was

not good because of the answer 16.
....Kt—R 4 !

| 16. ...... | B—K 1 |
| 17. Q—Q 2 | Kt—K 2 |

Now Black becomes ambitious
also and prevents for a while P—
Q 5.

| 18. Kt—Kt 5 ! | Kt—Q 4 |

But not 18. ....Kt—B 4 because
19. Kt×K P !, P×Kt ; 20. R×P
and wins.

| 19. R—K B 3 | Q—K 2 |
| 20. R—K Kt 3 | ...... |

White is anxious to provoke a
weakening Pawn-move on Black's
King's side, and therefore protects
the Knight in order to be able to
play Q—Q 0.

| 20. ...... | P—K R 3 |
| 21. Kt—B 3 | ...... |

It was difficult to decide which
Knight's retreat was best. I finally
rejected 21. Kt—K 4 because of the
possible answer 21. ....Q—R 5 ;
however, also in that case White,
after 22. P—R 3 ! Q—B 5 ; 23.
Q—K 2, etc., would have kept
fairly good attacking chances.

| 21. ...... | Q—B 3 |
| 22. R—K 4 | ...... |

Defending Q 4 and K B 4 and
threatening eventually K R—Kt 4.
But Black's next Knight's manœuvre again protects everything.

22.	Kt—K 2
23. Kt—K 5	Kt—B 4
24. R—Q 3	......

A mistake would have been 24.
R—K B 3 because of 24. ....B—
B 3 ; 25. Kt×B, P×Kt, etc.∓

| 24. ...... | Q R—B 1 |

| 25. P—R 3 ! | ...... |

White profits by the fact that
the opponent does not threaten
anything of importance, to secure
an escape for his King. The following part of the game will clearly
show the significance of this
quiet preparatory move.

| 25. ...... | Kt—Q 3 ? |

Seizing the first opportunity for
a further simplification which, however, will this time prove perfectly
welcome to White. As a matter of
fact the Knight at this stage was
too important a defensive piece to
be eliminated. Instead, 25. ....
B—B 3 ! offered—temporarily at
least—a quite sufficient defence ;
for instance, 26. Kt×B, P×Kt (not
R×Kt because of 27. P—Q 5 !) or
26. R—K 1, B—Q 4, etc.=

| 26. R—B 4 | Kt×B |
| 27. Kt×Kt | Q—Kt 4 |

This move has been generally
criticized as time-wasting, but also
after 27. ....Q—K 2 ; 28. Kt—K 5
White would obtain the better
fighting chances. If in that case
28. ....P—B 3 then 29. Kt—Kt 4
threatening eventually sacrifices at
K B 6 or K R 6.   Speaking in
general, the Black King is from now
on quite insufficiently protected.

| 28. R—K Kt 3 | Q—Q 4 |
| 29. Kt—K 3 | Q—B 3 |

Exchange of Queens would be
here, of course, paradise for him !

| 30. K—R 2 | ...... |

The pleasant consequence of
White's 25th move.

| 30. ...... | Q—B 8 |

Hoping for 31. Q—R 5, Q—B 2,
etc. But White selects the right
square for his Queen.

31. Q—Kt 4 !   Q—B 2

Position after Black's 31st move.

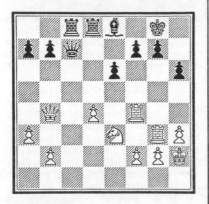

32. P—Q 5 !   ......

Such an effective advance of the would-be weakling must certainly have pleased the greatest friend of the isolated Queen's Pawns, the late Dr. Tarrasch ! It is obvious enough that in case of ....P × P (here or on the next move) the answer Q—Q 4 would have led to a rapid debacle for Black. But also by the defence selected he will be forced to give up at least the exchange.

32. ......   P—Q R 4
33. Q—K 4   ......

Of course not 33. Q—Q 4, P—K 4.

33. ......   R—Q 3 !
34. Q—K 5   P—K Kt 3
35. Q—R 5 !   ......

Instead the tempting 35. R—B 4 would have led to nothing after 35. ....R—B 3 ! and also 35. Kt—Kt 4 would have brought after 35. .... P × P, etc., *only* the exchange for a Pawn.

35. ......   R × P

Instead of resigning. I should have preferred 35. .... K—R 2, 36. Kt—Kt 4 ! !, P × Q; 37. Kt—B 6 ch. followed by mate.

36. Kt × R   P × Kt
37. Q × R P   Resigns.

GAME 38

NIMZOWITSCH'S DEFENCE

Hamburg Team Tournament, July, 1930.

White : G. STAHLBERG

Brilliancy Prize

1. P—Q 4   Kt—K B 3
2. P—Q B 4   P—K 3
3. Kt—Q B 3   B—Kt 5
4. Q—Kt 3   P—B 4
5. P × P   Kt—B 3
6. Kt—B 3   Kt—K 5
7. B—Q 2   Kt × Q B P

This move became a fashion after the game Bogoljubow-Nimzowitsch, in the San Remo Tournament, brilliantly won by Black. It is doubtless more logical than the former 7. ....Kt × B ; 8. Kt × Kt after which White by castling Q side will soon obtain a strong pressure on the open file.

8. Q—B 2   P—B 4
9. P—Q R 3   ......

Thus White obtains—at least temporarily—the pair of Bishops. Strangely enough, Bogoljubow, in the game above-mentioned, delayed this move until it became actually a mistake and by making it at that moment gave his opponent the game out of hand ! It came about this way: 9. P—K 3, Castles ; 10. B—K 2, P—Q Kt 3 ; 11. Castles (Q R), P—Q R 4 !; 12. P—Q R 3, P—R 5 ! ! etc.∓.

9.	B × Kt
10. B × B	Castles
11. P—Q Kt 4	Kt—K 5
12. P—K 3	P—Q Kt 3
13. B—Q 3	......

He could play also 13. B—Kt 2 but would not have obtained by doing this any real advantage : for instance, 13. ....B—Kt 2 ; 14. B—Q 3, Q—K 2 ! and 15. B × Kt, P × B ; 16. Q × P would turn to Black's advantage after 16. .... Kt × P ; 17. Q × B, Kt—Q 6 ch, etc.

13.	Kt × B
14. Q × Kt	B—Kt 2
15. Castles (K R)	Kt—K 2

It certainly looks risky to leave the central dark squares without adequate defence—but I estimated that something had to be done in order to prevent White increasing his pressure in the middle by means of P—Q B 5.

16. B—K 2   ......

Threatening to bring a Rook and the Queen on the open file with unpleasant consequences for Black.

16.	Q—K 1
17. K R—Q 1	R—Q 1

Not yet 17. ....P—B 5 because of 18. P × P, R × P ; 19. Q—Q 2, etc.

18. P—Q R 4   ......

The serious defect of this otherwise strategically justified advance is that it takes decidedly too much time and thus permits Black to build the ensuing instructive attack. Undoubtedly better was therefore 18. Q—K 5 with the strong threat 19. Q—B 7. The game would have continued in that case 18. ....P—B 5 ! ; 19. Q—B 7 ! (and not 19. P × P, Kt—Kt 3 ; 20. Q—B 7, Kt × P∓), B × Kt ; 20. B × B, P × P ; 21. P × P, Kt—B 4 with the double

tendency 22. ....Kt × P and 22. ....Kt—R 5. Although White would not find time in this variation to exploit the weakness of Black's Queen's side he would still have been perfectly able to protect his King—and this was for the moment the most important problem !

18. ......   P—B 5 !

From now on, and until the end, all Black's moves are very exactly timed. It is hardly possible to replace any one of them by a better one.

19. P—R 5	P × K P
20. Q × P	Kt—B 4
21. Q—B 3	P—Q 3 !

A simple but very effective defence against White's R—Q R 7.

22. P × P	P × P
23. Kt—K 1	......

If 23. R—R 7, then of course 23. ....R—Q 2, threatening to win a piece by 24. ....B × Kt, etc.

23. ......   P—K 4

Securing the square Q 5 for the Knight. As may be noticed, the weakness of the dark squares has been, without apparent effort, transformed into strength.

24. R—R 7   ......

Hoping to complicate matters after 24. ....R—Q 2 ; 25. P—B 5 with the threat 26. B—Kt 5. But Black has at his disposal an important intermediate move.

24.	Kt—Q 5 !
25. Q—K 3	R—Q 2

Threatening 26. ....B—B 6, etc.

26. R—R 2	R (Q 2)—KB 2
27. P—B 3	......

One would suppose that this Pawn, besides being protected by its neighbour, and easily supported by 3—4 Pieces, cannot possibly form a welcome object for Black's attack. And yet White's K B 3 will be captured, almost inevitably. It was certainly the unusualness of Black's winning stratagem which induced the judges to award to this game the Brilliancy Prize.

27. ......   R—B 5
28. B—Q 3   Q—R 4

Threatening 29. ....P—K 5 !, etc.

29. B—B 1   Q—Kt 4 !

With the main threat 30. .... R×P ! forcing the win of the Queen.

White's answer is forced.

30. R—K B 2   ......

Position after White's 30th move.

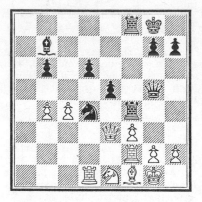

30. ......   P—R 3 !

A terrible move in its simplicity. Black threatens 31. ....R×P ! ; 32. Q×Q, R×R, etc., and in case of 31. Q—Q 2 (comparatively the best) he would play 31. ....B×P ; 32. Kt×B, Kt×Kt ch ; 33. R×Kt,

R×R ; 34. Q×Q, R×B ch ; 35. R×R, R×R ch ; 36. K×R, P×Q ; 37. K—K 2, K—B 2 ; 38. K—B 3, K—K 3 ; 39. K—K 4, P—Kt 4 !, etc., with a won Pawn end-game. White's next move practically does not change anything.

31. K—R 1   R×P !

With the same point as mentioned above.

Resigns.

GAME 39

QUEEN'S INDIAN DEFENCE

Prague Team Tournament, July, 1931.

Black : E. ANDERSEN

1. P—Q 4   Kt—K B 3
2. P—Q B 4   P—Q Kt 3

I have tried this fianchetto development (before ....P—K 3) on several occasions at the beginning of my professional career in the early twenties—and also played it with success in a match-game in 1929 against Bogoljubow (*cf.* No. 28). Its disadvantage consists in allowing White considerable freedom in the centre ; its merit in forcing the opponent to select a definite opening plan possibly earlier than he would like to.

3. Kt—Q B 3   B—Kt 2
4. Q—B 2   ......

About 4. P—B 3 see the game above-mentioned.

4. ......   P—K 3 ?

But this is not in accordance with 2. ....P—Q Kt 3. The only logical continuation consists in 4. ....P—Q 4 ; 5. P×P, Kt×P ; 6.

Kt—B 3 (in case of 6. P—K 4 Black can play 6. ....Kt × Kt; 7. P × Kt, P—K 4), P—K 3; 7. P—K 4, Kt × Kt; 8. P × Kt, B—K 2 followed by ....Kt—Q 2 and, eventually, ... P—Q B 4, etc., with fighting chances.

| 5. P—K 4 | B—Kt 5 |
| 6. P—B 3 ! | ...... |

Avoiding the doubling of Pawns on the Q B's file. Black has now not the slightest compensation for White's predominance in the centre.

| 6. ...... | Castles |
| 7. B—Q 3 | ...... |

Threatening 8. P—K 5, etc.

| 7. ...... | P—K R 3 |
| 8. Kt—K 2 | P—Q 4 |

Something had to be undertaken in order to increase the activity of the minor pieces—and the way selected is probably not worse than any other; at least Black will now have, for a short time, the illusion of a "counter-attack" starting by ....P—Q B 4.

9. B P × P	P × P
10. P—K 5	K Kt—Q 2
11. Castles	P—Q B 4

If instead 11. ....B—K 2, then 12. Kt—B 4±.

| 12. P—Q R 3 | B × Kt |

After 12. ....B—R 4 the Pawn-sacrifice 13. P—Q Kt 4 ! P × Kt P; 14. Kt—Kt 5, etc., would bring Black into a hopeless position.

| 13. P × B | Kt—Q B 3 |
| 14. B—K 3 | ...... |

Also the combination starting by 14. P—K 6 in connection with Kt—B 4, etc., was strong enough; but the simple concentration of the

forces by keeping the Pawn-structure in the centre intact brings a more rapid decision.

14.	P × P
15. P × P	R—B 1
16. Q—Q 2 !	......

As Black's answer was obvious, this move must be considered as the beginning of the final combination. Another, purely positional, and much slower, method of keeping some advantage consisted in 16. Q—Kt 1, Kt—R 4; 17. P—B 4, Kt—B 5; 18. B—B 1, etc.

| 16. ...... | Kt—R 4 |

Intending, if nothing special happens, to force the exchange of one of White's Bishops by 17. ....Kt—B 5.

Position after Black's 16th move.

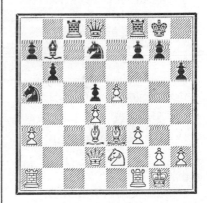

| 17. B × P ! | ...... |

Of course the offer cannot be accepted : this is by far the easiest part of the combination. But the complications issuing from the best defence, actually selected by Black, demanded a thorough examination.

| 17. ...... | Kt—Kt 6 |
| 18. Q—B 4 | R—B 3 ! |

If instead 18. .... Kt×R, then
19. Q—Kt 3, P—Kt 3 ; 20. B×P,
K—R 1 ; 21. B—B 5, R—K Kt 1 ;
22. Q—R 3, and wins.

19. B—K Kt 5   P—B 3

White was also threatening 20.
Q—R 4.

20. P×P   Kt×R

His last chance, which will be
annihilated by the following intermediate check.

21. B—R 7 ch !   K—R 1

The alternative was 21. ....
K×B ; 22. Q—R 4 ch, K—Kt 3
(or K—Kt 1 ; 23. P—B 7 ch) ; 23.
Kt—B 4 ch, K—B 4 ; 24. P—Kt 4
mate.

22. Q—R 4 !   Kt×P
23. Kt—B 4   ......

If now 23. .... P—Kt 3, then
24. Q—R 6 ! with debâcle.

Resigns.

GAME 40

QUEEN'S GAMBIT DECLINED
(SLAV DEFENCE)

Prague Team Tournament, July,
1931.

Black : H. WEENINK

1. P—Q 4	P—Q 4
2. P—Q B 4	P—Q B 3
3. Kt—K B 3	Kt—B 3
4. P—K 3	B—B 4

As my first championship match
with Dr. Euwe has proved, this
move happens to be sufficient for
equality, and therefore White does
better by playing 4. Kt—B 3
instead of 4. P—K 3.

5. P×P   B×Kt ?

But the exchange of the Bishop
just developed is completely out of
place.   Strangely enough, it has
been warmly recommended by the
great openings specialist, Dr. Tarrasch, although its defects (the
cession of the centre and of the
pair of Bishops to White) are obvious at a first glance. Good enough
is, instead, the simple 5. .... P×P ;
6. Q—Kt 3, Q—B 2, etc.

| 6. R×B | Q×P |
| 7. P—Q R 3 | ...... |

Also tempting was the Pawn
sacrifice 7. Q—B 2, Q×R P (or
P—K 3 ; 8. P—Q Kt 4 !) ; 8. B—
B 4, Q—R 4 ch ; 9. B—Q 2, Q—
B 2 ; 10. P—K 4, etc. But why
take chances when the simple continuation assures an unquestionable
positional advantage ?

| 7. ...... | P—K 3 |
| 8. Q—B 2 | B—K 2 |

A mistake would be 8. .... P—
B 4 because of 9. P—Q Kt 4 ! etc.

9. B—Q 3   P—K R 3

The immediate 9. .... Castles
would be refuted by 10. P—K 4
followed by P—K 5.

10. P—K 4	Q—Q 1
11. Castles	Q Kt—Q 2
12. P—Q Kt 4 !	......

Not only preventing for a long
time .... P—Q B 4, but also preparing the following further development of the Queen's Rook.

| 12. ...... | Castles |
| 13. Q—K 2 | R—K 1 |

In order to have the defence ....
Kt—B 1 in case White should play
14. P—K 5 followed by Q—K 4.

14. R—Kt 3 ! ......

Although this Rook will not move until the end of the game, it will play an important part in the following attack. But the text-move has also another purpose—to free the square Q Kt 1 for the Bishop.

14. ......   Q—B 2
15. B—Kt 1   Kt—R 2

This induces White to clear, at last, the situation in the centre, as from now on there will be no time to install a black Knight at Q 4. But also the demonstration on the Queen's side by means of 15. .... P—Q R 4 would end in White's favour : 16. Q—B 2 (threatening P—K 5), Kt—B 1 ; 17. P—Kt 5, etc.+

16. P—K 5   P—K B 4

Black prefers to execute this sooner or later unavoidable advance immediately, because after 16. .... Kt (R 2)—B 1, for instance, it could be prevented by 17. P—Kt 4 ! The following exchange gives his pieces some more freedom —at least temporarily ; but on the other hand K 3, and also the other light-coloured squares of his position, remain weaker than ever.

17. P×P (*e.p.*)   B×P
18. Q—K 4   ......

By this and the two following moves the Queen will be brought without loss of time into a very strong attacking position.

18. ......   Kt (R 2)—B 1
19. Q—Kt 4   ......

Threatening, of course, 20. B × P.

19. ......   K—R 1
20. Q—R 5   Kt—R 2

White was threatening now 21. B × P !, P × B ; 22. Q × P ch, K— Kt 1 ; 23. Kt—Kt 5 etc., with a speedy win.

21. R—K 1   ......

Bringing the only inactive piece into play and preventing at the same time 21. ....P—K 4 because of the possible answer 22. B— B 4 !

21. ......   Q R—Q 1

There is not much use in such a "development"—however, the position was hopeless, anyhow.

Position after Black's 21st move.

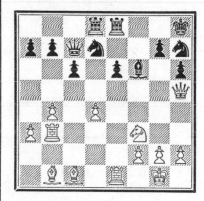

22. P—Kt 4 ! ......

This little Pawn threatens by its further advance to set on fire the black King's residence—and cannot possibly be stopped from that dark design.

22. ......   Q—Q 3

Hoping to parry 23. P—K Kt 5 by 23. ....Q—Q 4. But White has in reserve an intermediate move.

23. B—Kt 6 !   R—K B 1
24. P—K Kt 5   B×Q P

There is no choice.

25. P×P   Kt (Q 2)—B 3

White threatened mate in three moves.

26. P×P ch   K×P
27. Q—R 6 ch   K—R 1

Or 27. ....K—Kt 1 ; 28. Kt×B, Q×Kt ; 29. R—Kt 3, and wins.

28. Kt×B   Q×Kt
29. B—Kt 2 !   ......

If now 29. ....Q—Q 2 (the only possible defence), then 30. R—Q 3 !, Q—Kt 2 ; 31. Q B×Kt ! followed by mate in three moves.

Resigns.

GAME 41

RETI'S OPENING

Prague Team Tournament, July, 1931.

Black : E. STEINER

1. Kt—K B 3   Kt—K B 3
2. P—B 4   P—B 4
3. P—Q 4   ......

Somewhat premature. As White does not have to worry about the answer 3. ....P—Q 4 in case of 3. Kt—B 3 (because of 4. P×P, Kt×P ; 5. P—K 4, Kt—Kt 5 ; 6. B—B 4±), he should select that move in order to be able to answer 3. ....Kt—B 3 by 4. P—Q 4 and 3. ....P—K 3 by 4. P—K 4.

3. ......   P×P
4. Kt×P   P—K 3
5. P—Q R 3   ......

I did not like after 5. Q Kt—B 3 the possibility of 5. ....B—Kt 5 ;

6. Q—Kt 3, B—B 4—and decided simply not to allow the unpleasant Bishop move. But even playing with White one cannot afford to lose such an important *tempo* in the opening stage without the risk of giving the opponent the initiative. Therefore—although the move P—Q R 3 proved in the actual game to be a distinct success —I must most emphatically recommend the reader *not to make it*, but to try instead, for instance, 5. Q Kt —B 3, B—Kt 5 ; 6. B—Q 2.

5. ......   Kt—K 5

To an eccentricity Black answers by another, bigger one, which allows White again to take the lead in the fight for the central squares. Correct was the natural 5. ....P—Q 4, and if 6. P×P, then 6. .... B—B 4 ! ; 7. Kt—Kt 3, B—Kt 3, followed by ....P×P and ..... Castles with a splendid development.

6. P—K 3   P—B 4
7. Kt—Q 2   Kt—K B 3
8. P—Q Kt 3   B—K 2
9. B—Kt 2   Castles
10. B—Q 3   ......

In spite of the delaying 5th move White has already acquired an appreciable advantage in development. It becomes evident that something was not in order with 5. ....Kt—K 5.

10. ......   Kt—B 3
11. Castles   Kt—K 4

A complicated manœuvre in order to prevent White from playing P—K 4—which would occur, for instance, after 11. ....P—Q Kt 3 ; 12. Kt×Kt, P×Kt ; 13. Q—K 2, P—B 4 ; 14. P—K 4, etc. ±.

12. B—B 2   Kt—Kt 3

Hoping to get counter-chances in

case of 13. P—K 4, P×P; 14. Q Kt×P, P—Q 4; 15. Kt×Kt ch, B×Kt, etc. But White is in the fortunate position of being able to increase his pressure without opening prematurely the central files.

13. P—B 4 !   Kt—Kt 5

After 13. ....P—Kt 9 the advance 14. P—K 4 would become much more effective than previously—for instance 14. ....P×P; 15. Q Kt×P, R—Kt 2 ; 16. Kt—K Kt 5, etc.±

| 14. Q—K 2 | Q—B 2 |
| 15. P—R 3 | Kt—R 3 |

Black has succeeded in prohibiting P—K 4—but at what price ! Both his Knights are out of play and his Queen's side is still undeveloped. No wonder that White will have plenty of time to gain more and more space and gradually bring the opponent to despair. The reader may compare this game with some other specimens of entanglement-policy in this collection—as, for instance, those against Nimzowitsch and Yates (San Remo), Mikenas (Folkestone), Winter (Nottingham). In all of them the losers became victims of their passivity and lack of a definite plan in the opening stages.

16. P—K Kt 4	P—Kt 3
17. P—Kt 5	Kt—B 2
18. Q Kt—B 3	B—Kt 2
19. P—K R 4	B—B 4

An attempt to create complications in case of the immediate 20. P—R 5, which would be answered by 20. ....Kt×B P !; 21. P×Kt, Q×P, etc.∓. But White does not need to hurry !

20. Q—R 2 !	Q R—K 1
21. P—R 5	Kt—K 2
22. Q R—K 1	......

Preparing Kt—Kt 5 followed by P—Kt 4 :

22. ......   Kt—B 3

If 22. ....P—Q R 3 then 23. P—Kt 4, B×Kt (Q 5) ; 24. B×B, Q×B P ; 25. B×Q Kt P, etc.±

23. Kt—Kt 5	Q—Q 1
24. P—Kt 4	B—K 2
25. Q—Q 2 !	......

All of a sudden Black's K Kt 2 has become deadly weak—a not unusual phenomenon in overcramped positions !

Position after White's 25th move.

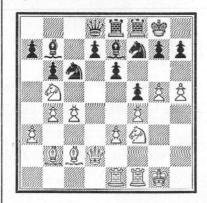

25. ......   B × K Kt P

This kind of desperate sacrifice must be met as a rule with the greatest care as it *may* contain more poison than appears at first. In view of the threat 26. Q—B 3, Black, as a matter of fact, had practically no choice : 25. ....P—Q 3 ; 26. Kt (Kt 5)—Q 4, Kt×Kt ; 27. Kt×Kt, Q—Q 2 ; 28. Q—B 3 would be, if possible, even more welcome for White.

| 26. P×B | Kt×K Kt P |
| 27. Q—Kt 2 ! | ...... |

The most convincing refutation of the "offer."

27.	......	Kt × Kt ch
28.	R × Kt	R—K 2
29.	Kt—Q 6	B—R 1
30.	P—K 4	......

Putting an end to all kinds of "swindles" on the diagonal K R 1—Q R 8.

30.	......	Q—Kt 1
31.	R—K Kt 3	P—K 4
32.	Kt × P	R × Kt
33.	P × R	Kt—Q 5
34.	B—K 4	Kt × P
35.	B × B	Kt × R
36.	B—Q 5 ch	Resigns.

GAME 42

QUEEN'S GAMBIT DECLINED
(SLAV DEFENCE)

Bled Tournament, August, 1931.

Black : J. STOLTZ

1.	P—Q 4	P—Q 4
2.	P—Q B 4	P—Q B 3
3.	Kt—K B 3	Kt—B 3
4.	Kt—B 3	P × P
5.	P—Q R 4	B—B 4
6.	Kt—R 4	......

The main objection which can be made against this move is that White wastes time in order to exchange a piece he has already developed. However, the idea (of Dr. Krause) of eliminating at all costs the ominous black Queen's Bishop is not as anti-positional as generally thought, and, at least, has not been refuted in the few games where it was tried.

| 6. | ...... | P—K 3 |

Natural and good enough. White, it is true, will enjoy a pair of Bishops, but as long as Black is able to control the central squares he should not have much to fear. Less satisfactory for him, on the contrary, would be 6. ....B—B 1 (as played for instance by Dr. Euwe in the 15th game of our 1935 Match). In that case White (besides, of course, the draw-opportunity 7. Kt—B 3) would have the choice between 7. P—K 3, P—K 4 ; 8. B × P (of course not 8. P × P ?, Q × Q ch ; 9. Kt × Q, B—Kt 5 ch∓ played—to my sorrow—in the game mentioned), P × P ; 9. P × P, with slightly the better prospects—or 7. P—K 4, P—K 4 ; 8. B × P ! P × P ; 9. P—K 5, etc., leading to complicated situations like those of the 6th game of the 1937 Match. Anyhow, an interesting field for investigation.

7.	Kt × B	P × Kt
8.	P—K 3	Q Kt—Q 2
9.	B × P	Kt—Kt 3

The Knight has little to do here —but something had to be done to prevent 10. Q—Kt 3.

| 10. | B—Kt 3 | B—Q 3 |
| 11. | Q—B 3 | Q—Q 2 |

Black will lose this game chiefly because from now on he decides to avoid the "weakening" move .... P—K Kt 3 and tries to protect his K B 4-Pawn by artificial methods. As a matter of fact there was not much to say against 11. ....P—Kt 3, as 12. P—K 4 ? would have been refuted by 12. ....Kt × K P ; 13. Kt × Kt, Q—K 2 !—and 12. P—R 5 answered by 12. ....Kt (Kt. 3)—Q 4 ; 13. Kt × Kt, Kt × Kt, etc.

| 12. P—R 3 ! | ...... |

Threatening 13. B—B 2, P—Kt 3 ; 14. P—K Kt 4, etc.±. Black's next move parries the danger.

| 12. ...... | Kt—B 1 |
| 13. P—R 5 | ...... |

Playing simultaneously on both sides of the board—my favourite strategy. The threat is now 14. P—R 6, P—Q Kt 3 ; 15. P—Q 5 ! etc.

| 13. ...... | Kt—K 2 |
| 14. B—Q 2 | ...... |

Instead, White could at once try 14. P—Kt 4, but to do so would be to miss the developing Bishop's move which he makes now. Besides, it was not without importance to prepare, against certain eventualities, the possibility of castling on the Queen's side.

| 14. ...... | R—Q Kt 1 |

This plausible move—made in order to weaken the effect of the possible advance P—R 6—will prove an important, if not decisive, loss of time. The only possibility of offering a serious resistance consisted in 14. ....P—R 4 !

Position after Black's 14th move.

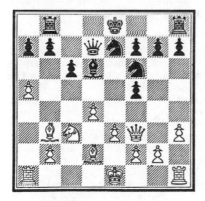

15. P—Kt 4 !   ......

Through this transaction White at least obtains the extremely important square K 4.

| 15. ...... | P—Q Kt 4 |

According to his aggressive style, Stoltz tries to solve the difficult problem in a purely tactical way—with the result that his Queen's side soon becomes lamentably weak. Also 15. ....P×P ; 16. P×P, Q×P ; 17. Q×Q, Kt×Q ; 18. R—K Kt 1, P—K B 4 ; 19. P—B 3, Kt—B 3 (after 19. ....Kt—R 7 ; 20. K—K 2, etc., the Knight would not come out alive) ; 20. R×P, etc., would have been quite unsatisfactory for Black ; but the quiet 15. ....Castles (to which White's best answer would be 16. R—K Kt 1) would still leave him some possibilities of defence.

16. P×P   ......

16. P—Kt 5 would be answered by 16. ....P—Kt 5 ! by which Black would have obtained the central squares for his Knights.

16.	Q×P
17. Q×Q	Kt×Q
18. B—B 2 !	......

White will succeed in exploiting the Queen's side weakness before the opponent finds time to concentrate his forces for the defence. The following part of the game is convincing and easy to understand.

18.	Kt—R 5
19. K—K 2	Castles
20. Kt—K 4	Kt × Kt
21. B × Kt	P—Q B 4

The exchange of this Pawn brings him but a slight relief as the fatal weakness of the Queen's side squares still remains.

| 22. P×P | B×P |
| 23. Q R—Q B 1 | B—Q 3 |

Or 23. ....Q R—B 1 ; 24. P—R 6 threatening 25. B—Kt 7 followed by 26. B—R 5, etc.

24. R—B 6   Q R—Q 1
25. R—R 6   K R—K 1
26. B—B 6   R—K 2

For the moment everything is more or less in order as 27. B×P, R—Kt 2, etc., would not be convincing. But White's following move—by which the lack of coordination of Black's pieces is underlined in a most drastic way—brings the fight to a rapid end.

27. R—Q 1 !   Kt—B 4

The Bishop did not have any suitable square of retreat. If for instance 27. .....B—Kt 1, then 28. B—Kt 4, R×R ; 29. B×R ! and wins.

28. B—Kt 4   P—Kt 3
29. B—B 5 !   ......

Threatening to confiscate the Q R's as well as the Q Kt's Pawn. Black, in his despair, sacrifices the exchange.

29. ......   B×B
30. R×R ch   K—Kt 2
31. R—Q 5 !   ......

Faulty would be 31. R—Q 7 or 31. B×P because of 31. .....Kt—Q 5 ch, etc.

31. ......   B—Q 5
32. R—Q 7   ......

Now, after the square Q 4 has been taken by the Bishop, this move is strong.

32. ......   R—K 4
33. K—Q 3   B×Kt P
34. R (R 6)×P   R—B 4
35. R×P ch   K—R 3
36. R×P ch   K—Kt 4
37. R (Q R 7)—K B 7 !   ......

With the most unpleasant threat 38. P—B 4 ch, etc.

Resigns.

GAME 43

FRENCH DEFENCE

Bled Tournament, September, 1931.

Black : A. Nimzowitsch

1. P—K 4   P—K 3
2. P—Q 4   P—Q 4
3. Kt—Q B 3   B—Kt 5
4. Kt—K 2   ......

This move, which is quite satisfactory in the MacCutcheon Variation (1. P—K 4, P—K 3 ; 2. P—Q 4, P—Q 4 ; 3. Kt—Q B 3, Kt—K B 3 ; 4. B—Kt 5, B—Kt 5 ; 5. *Kt—K 2*), is perfectly harmless at this moment. I selected it, however, in the present game because I knew that already on one occasion (against Sir G. Thomas at Marien bad, 1925) Nimzowitsch had shown an exaggerated voracity (6. ..... P—K B 4) without having been duly punished for it.

4. ......   P×P
5. P—Q R 3   B×Kt ch

Also 5. .....B—K 2 is good enough for equality.

6. Kt×B   P—K B 4

Played against all the principles of a sound opening strategy, as the dark-coloured squares of Black's position will become very weak, especially because of the exchange of his King's Bishop. The correct reply which secures Black at least an even game is 6. .....Kt—Q B 3 ! and if 7. B—Q Kt 5 then 7. ..... Kt—K 2 followed by Castles, etc.

7. P—B 3   ......

The sacrifice of the second Pawn is tempting, most probably correct —and yet unnecessary, as White could obtain an excellent game without taking any chances, by playing first 7. B—K B 4, and if 7. ....Kt—K B 3 then 8. P—B 3, P×P; 9. Q×P, after which 9. ....Q×P would be refuted by 10. Kt—Kt 5.

| 7. ...... | P×P |
| 8. Q×P | Q×P |

Contrary to the opinion of the theorists, this move is as good—or as bad—as 8. ....Q—R 5 ch; 9. P—Kt 3, Q×Q P: in that case White would play 10. Kt—Kt 5 and Black would not have had—as in the actual game—the defence .... Q—R 5 ch, P—K Kt 3; Q—K 2, etc.

9. Q—Kt 3 ! ......

A by no means obvious continuation of the attack. White's main threats are 10. Kt—Kt 5 (.... Q—K 5 ch; 11. B—K 2) and 10. B—K B 4, or K 3.

9. ...... Kt—K B 3

This bold move is Black's comparatively best chance. Insufficient would be 9. ....Kt—K 2 because of 10. B—K 3 !, Q—B 3; 11. Castles, etc. ±

10. Q×Kt P Q—K 4 ch ?

Inconsequent and therefore fatal. Black—in order to keep a fighting game—should give up also the Q B's Pawn, as after 10. ....R—Kt 1; 11. Q×B P, Kt—B 3 there would not be a win for White by means of 12. Kt—Kt 5, because of 12. ....Q—R 5 ch !; 13. P—Kt 3, Q—K 5 ch; 14. K—B 2, Q×P ch, followed by ....Kt—K 5, etc. The check in the text allows White to win a development *tempo*—and time in such a tense position *is* a decisive factor.

| 11. B—K 2 | R—Kt 1 |
| 12. Q—R 6 | R—Kt 3 |

13. Q—R 4 ......

White does not need to protect his K Kt's Pawn by 13. Q—R 3, as after 13. ....R × P the answer 14. B—B 4 would have been decisive.

13.	B—Q 2
14. R—Kt 5	B—B 3
15. Castles (Q R)	B × P

Under normal circumstances this capture should be considered as another mistake, but as—owing to White's tremendous advance in development — Black's game is hopeless (if, for instance, 15. Q Kt—Q 2 then also 16. K R—K 1 followed by a move with the K's Bishop) his morbid appetite cannot spoil anything more.

16. K R—K 1	B—K 5
17. B—R 5	Kt × B
18. R—Q 8 ch	K—B 2
19. Q × Kt	......

Final Position.

Nimzowitsch quite rightly resigned here, as there are no more decent moves for Black—even 19. ....K—Kt 2 would lose the Queen after 20. Kt × B, P × Kt; 21. B—R 6 ch, etc. ! This was, I believe, the shortest defeat in his career.

GAME 44

QUEEN'S GAMBIT DECLINED
(LASKER'S DEFENCE)

Bled Tournament, September, 1931.

Black : Dr. M. Vidmar

1. P—Q 4	P—Q 4
2. Kt—K B 3	Kt—K B 3
3. P—B 4	P—B 3
4. Kt—B 3	P—K 3

This is not exact, since in the orthodox defence the move .... P—Q B 3 is not always of use. Until now (summer, 1939) no clear way has been found for White to gain an advantage after 4. .... P×P.

5. B—Kt 5   ......

Also, 5. P—K 3 is thought to be good for White.

5.	B—K 2
6. P—K 3	Castles
7. Q—B 2	Kt—K 5
8. B×B	......

Has anybody ever tried in this kind of position P—K R 4 ? The move might be taken into consideration.

8.	Q×B
9. B—Q 3	Kt×Kt

After 9. .... P—K B 4 ; 10. Kt—K 5, Kt—Q 2 ; 11. Castles, the exchanges in the centre should profit White, since he would have a minor piece more in play than the opponent.

10. P×Kt   ......

In this particular case, more promising than 10. Q×Kt, because Black will be forced to lose a *tempo* for the protection of his K R P.

10. ......   K—R 1

As the sequence will prove, this is only a temporary defence (11. B×R P ?, P—K Kt 3), and that permits White, from now on, to build up his plan of attack. Less binding was, anyhow, 10. ....P—K R 3.

11. P×P !   ......

Both logical and psychological chess. The object of this exchange is, first and foremost, to prevent Black's obtaining, by means of .... P×P followed by ....P—Q B 4 and ....P—Q Kt 3, the diagonal Q R 1—K R 8 for his Bishop ; but, independently of this consideration, White was entitled to suppose that, *after having avoided weakening his K Kt 3 by not playing ....P K R 3, Black would now profit by this and try to bring his Bishop to K Kt 3 via Kt 5 and R 4.* By provoking this last manœuvre, White rightly considered that the opening of files on the King's side—ensuing from the eventual capture of Black's K R P—could only be favourable to the better developed party.

11.	K P×P
12. Castles K R	B—Kt 5

If 12. .... Kt—Q 2, White would have started a promising play in the middle with 13. Q R—K 1, Kt—B 3 ; 14. Kt—K 5 followed by P—K B 4, etc. The text-move is the start of an adventure.

13. Kt—K 5	B—R 4
14. B×P !	......

This Bishop will now be in no more danger than his black colleague.

14.	P—K Kt 3
15. P—Kt 4	B×P

Thus Black, for the time, avoids material loss—but his horse still remains in the stable and White's defensive moves serve at the same time for attacking purposes.

16. Kt×B	Q—Kt 4
17. P—K R 3	K×B
18. P—K B 4	Q—R 5
19. K—R 2	Kt—Q 2

At last.

20. Q R—Kt 1 !   ......

Provoking the answer, which weakens Black's Q B P. How important this detail is will appear half-a-dozen moves later on.

20.	P—Kt 3
21. R—Kt 1	Kt—B 3
22. Kt—K 5	......

Threatening 23. Kt×Kt P, the K B P, and also the Q B P.

22. ......   Kt—K 5

Not only parrying all the threats (23. Kt×Q B P, Q R—B 1) but also intending to simplify by 23. ....Q—B 7 ch.

23. Q R—K B 1   K—Kt 2

Black's possible threats on the K R-file are insignificant in comparison with White's attack along the K B and K Kt-files.

24. R—Kt 4   Q—R 3

Position after Black's 24th move.

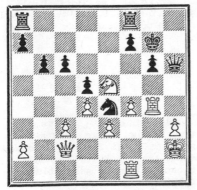

25. P—B 5 !   ......

The tactical justification of this energetic advance is based on two variations—that played in the actual game, and the other starting with 25. ....P—K Kt 4. In that case I intended *not* to exchange two Rooks for the Queen by continuing with 26. P—B 6 ch, Kt×P ; 27. R×P ch, Q×R ; 28. R—K Kt 1, Q×R ch ; 29. K×R, Kt—K 5 (which also would be good but, still, not quite decisive)—but to sacrifice the exchange : 26. R×Kt !, P×R ; 27. P—B 6 ch, K—R 1 (or Kt 1); 28. Q×P, etc., with a winning positional advantage. Dr. Vidmar selected, therefore, the by far more promising line of resistance.

25. ......   Q×P !

This finally loses *only* the exchange for a Pawn and leads to a difficult end-game. It is easy to see that, apart from 25. ....P—K Kt 4, there was nothing else to do.

26. Q—K Kt 2   Q—Q 7

Or, 26. ....P—K Kt 4 ; 27. P—B 6 ch, K—R 2 ; 28. R—R 4 ch !, K—Kt 1 ; 29. Kt× Q B P, etc., with even more tragical consequences.

27. P—B 6 ch	K—Kt 1
28. Kt×Q B P	......

The deserved reward for the well-timed 20th move.

28.	Q×Q ch
29. K×Q	K R—K 1

There was no other reasonable defence against the threatened mate in two.

30. Kt—K 7 ch   R×Kt

And now 30. ....K—B 1 would have been victoriously answered by

31. Kt×P (not 31. R—R 4 ?, Kt×
K B P) threatening both 32. R—
R 4 and 32. Kt—B 7.

    31. P×R   R—K 1

Again forced, since 31. ....Kt×
P would lose rapidly after 32. R—
B 1 followed by R—B 7 or even-
tually R—B 6.

    32. P—B 4 !   ......

Without this possibility, whereby
White secures a passed Pawn, the
win would be still rather doubtful.

    32. ......   R×P
    33. P×P   Kt—B 6
    34. P—Q 6   R—Q 2
    35. R—B 1   Kt—Kt 4

If 35. ....Kt × P, White, in
order to force the win, would select
the following sharp continuation :
36. R—B 8 ch, K—Kt 2 ; 37. P—
Q 5 ! (threatening to win the
Knight), P—R 4 ; 38. R—B 7,
R×P ; 39. R—K B 4, R—K B 3
(otherwise White gets a mating
attack) ; 40. K—B 3, Kt—Kt 5 ;
41. R×R, K×R ; 42. K—K 4—
and in spite of equal material
Black would lose, as his two Queen-
side Pawns would have but a short
life.

    36. R—Kt 5 !   Kt×P (Q 3)

After 36. ....Kt×P (Q 5) the
win would be technically easier :
37. R—Q 5, Kt—B 4 ; 38. R—B 7 !,
R×P (or R—Q 1 ; 39. P—Q 7) ; 39.
R×R, Kt×R ; 40. R×R P, etc.

    37. R—Q 5 !   ......

From now on, the purely technical part of the end-game begins.
Through combined play of his two
Rooks and King, White must make
the utmost of the pinning of the
hostile Knight.

    37. ......   K—B 1
    38. R—K 1 !   ......

The black King must not be
allowed to approach the centre
before all White's units are brought
to the most effective squares.

    38. ......   R—Q 1
    39. K—B 3   R—Q 2

It is obvious enough that the
exchange of Rooks, after 39. ....
Kt—Kt 2, would not make any
serious resistance possible.

    40. K—B 4   K—Kt 2
    41. R—K 8 !   ......

A further restriction of Black's
moving capacities.

    41. ......   K—B 3
    42. P—K R 4   K—Kt 2
    43. P—R 4   K—B 3
    44. R—Q B 8 !   ......

Intending to substitute for the
vertical pinning an even more
effective horizontal one.

    44. ......   K—K 3
    45. R—K 5 ch   K—B 3
    46. R—B 6   R—Q 1
    47. P—Q R 5 !   P—Kt 4

Black must lose a Pawn and
prefers to do it this way, since, after
47. ....P×P ; 48. R×P, R—Q 2 ;
49. R (B 6)—R 6, etc., White would
also force the exchange of Rooks.

    48. R×P   K—K 3
    49. R—K 5 ch   K—B 3
    50. R—R 6   R—Q 2
    51. K—Kt 4   R—Q 1
    52. K—B 3 !   ......

A little finesse : it is more advantageous for White to make the
advance P—R 5 at the moment
when the Black Rook is at Q 1,
because then he will capture the
Q R P, having the other Rook at K 5.

52.	......	R—Q 2
53.	K—B 4	R—Q 1
54.	P—R 5	P×P
55.	R×K R P	R—Q 2
56.	R—K 5	R—Q 1
57.	R×P	......

Now White takes this Pawn without permitting the reply ....Kt—B 4, which would have been possible before the exchange of the K Kt P.

57.	......	Kt—B 5
58.	R—R 6 ch	K—Kt 2
59.	R—Kt 5 ch	K—B 1
60.	K—K 4	......

The rest is easy.

60.	......	K—K 2
61.	R—Q B 5	Kt—Q 3 ch
62.	K—Q 3	K—K 3
63.	R (B 5)—B 6	K—Q 4
64.	R×Kt ch	R×R
65.	R×R ch	K×R
66.	P—R 6	Resigns.

APPENDIX TO THE GAME ALEKHINE-VIDMAR (44)

Two Rooks v. Rook and Knight

End-games with two Rooks against Rook and Knight are comparatively uncommon, and the manuals devoted to the end-game —even the most up-to-date, such as the recent edition of E. Rabinovitsch's excellent work—do not give any convincing examples. The materially stronger party should win in the majority of cases, but not without serious technical difficulties.

According to the general opinion, I succeeded, against Vidmar, in finding the shortest and most instructive winning method, and I owe, in a great part, this achievement to a practical lesson that I received in the beginning of my career (in St. Petersburg, 1914) from the great end-game artist, Dr. Lasker. That lesson cost me a full point, for I happened to be the man with the Knight! Dr. Lasker, to the general surprise, demonstrated that even with one Pawn on each side (and *not* a passed Pawn) the stronger party is able to force the decisive exchange of Rooks.

Since the game with Dr. Vidmar I have had the opportunity of playing the same kind of ending twice, and both times the winning procedure had the same characteristics: (1) Restriction of the Knight by binding and, eventually, pinning it. (2) Gradual undermining of the strong points, which, as a rule, happen to be in the middle. (3) Threats to exchange Rooks, which always means a step forward—especially if the Knight party does not possess passed pawns. Other tactics, such as centralization of the King, freeing of Pawns, etc., are, of course, common with those of all types of end-games.

I have not fully commented on the two following games for this collection, because, although they are interesting, I do not count either among my best achievements. Kashdan, to his bad luck and without knowing it, repeated, up to the 15th move, a variation known as lost for Black since the Carlsbad Tournament, 1929 ; and against Dr. Bernstein, instead of winning the exchange, I could have forced the gain of a full piece and, consequently, his resignation. Nevertheless, I believe both these end-games—in connexion with the previous one—may be of use to the student.

With *Kashdan (Black), Pasadena,* 1932, the characteristic end-game began after the moves : 1. P—Q 4, Kt—K B 3 ; 2. P—Q B 4, P—K 3 ; 3. Kt—Q B 3, P—Q 4 ; 4. B—Kt 5, Q Kt—Q 2 ; 5. P×P, P×P ; 6. P—K 3, P—B 3 ; 7. B—Q 3, B—

K 2 ; 8. Q—B 2, O—O ; 9. K Kt—
K 2, R—K 1 ; 10. O—O—O, Kt—
K 5 ? (the same mistake was made
by Spielmann against Nimzowitsch,
Kissingen, 1928, and by Sir G. A.
Thomas against Spielmann, Carls-
bad, 1929) ; 11. B×Kt, P×B ; 12.
P—K R 4 !, P—K B 4 ; 13. Q—
Kt 3 ch, K—R 1 ; 14. Kt—B 4,
Kt—B 3 ; 15. P—R 5, P—K R 3 ; 16
Q—B 7 !, Kt—Kt 1 ; 17. Kt—Kt 6
ch, K—R 2 ; 18. Kt×B, R×Kt
(forced) ; 19. B×R, Q×B ; 20. Q×
Q, Kt×Q ; 21. P—Q 5 !, B—Q 2 ;
22. P×P, B×P ; 23. R—Q 6, R—
Q B 1 ; 24. K R—Q 1, Kt—Kt 1 ;
25. R—Q 8, R—B 2 ; 26. R—K B 8,
Kt—B 3 ; 27. R (Q 1)—Q 8, Kt×P ;
28. R×P, Kt—B 3 ; 29. K—Q 2,
K—Kt 3 ; 30. R—B 5, R—B 2 ;
31. R—Q 6, K—R 2 ; 32. R—
B 5, K—Kt 3 ; 33. R—Q R 5,
P—R 3 ; 34. Kt—Q 5, B×Kt ;
35. Q R×B, K—R 2—when the
following position was reached :—

Position after Black's 35th move.

36. R—K B 5   ......

The combined vertical and horizontal pinning is similar to what
happened in the Vidmar-game.

36.	K—Kt 3
37. R—B 5	K—R 2
38. K—K 2	......

In order to parry the move ....
Kt—Kt 5, by P—B 3. If Black
should now remain passive, White
would advance his Pawn to Q Kt 6,
after the exchange at Kt 5, and then
play R—Q B 7.

38.	P—K Kt 4
39. P—Q Kt 4	K—Kt 2
40. P—R 4	Kt—Kt 5

The only possible attempt.

41. P—B 3	P×P ch
42. P×P	Kt—R 7
43. P—B 4 !	P×P
44. P×P	Kt—Kt 5

The old story ! 44. ....R×P
would be fatal since 45. R—B 7 ch,
etc., would force the exchange of
Rooks.

45. K—B 3	Kt—B 3
46. P—Kt 5	Kt—Q 2
47. R (B 5)—Q 5	Kt—B 3
48. R—K B 5 !	......

Again the pinning as a method
for gaining an important *tempo*.

48.	K—Kt 3
49. R—B 5	P×P
50. R×P	......

Here even more effective than
50. P×P.

50.	R—B 2
51. R (Kt 5)—Kt 6	R—B 2
52. P—R 5	K—Kt 2
53. R—Kt 5	R—B 2
54. R (Q 6)—Kt 6	R—B 6 ch
55. K—K 2	R—B 5
56. R×P ch	K—Kt 3
57. P—B 5 ch	K—Kt 4
58. P—R 6	R—Q R 5
59. P—R 7	Kt—K 5
60. K—K 3 !	......

If now 60. ....Kt—Q 3, then
61. P—B 6 disc. ch !, Kt×R ; 62.
P—B 7, etc.

Resigns.

Against Dr. Bernstein the task was even more difficult because his Knight was strongly posted at Q 4, protected by a Pawn. The previous moves, before the end-game position under discussion was reached, were :

Black, Dr. O. Bernstein, Zurich, 1934.
1. P—Q 4, P—Q 4 ; 2. P—Q B 4, P —K 3 ; 3. Kt—Q B 3, Kt—K B 3 ; 4. B—Kt 5, B—K 2 ; 5. P—K 3, P—K R 3 ; 6. B—B 4, P—B 3 ; 7. Kt—B 3, Q Kt—Q 2 ; 8. P×P, Kt×P ; 9. B—Kt 3, Q—R 4 ; 10. Q—Kt 3, O—O ; 11. R—K 2, Q Kt —B 3 ; 12. Kt—Q 2 !, P—B 4 ; 13. Kt—B 4, Q—Q 1 ; 14. P×P, B×P ; 15. B—B 3 !, P—Q Kt 3 ; 16. O—O, Q—K 2 ; 17. Kt—Kt 5, P—R 3 ; 18. Q Kt—Q 6, B—Q 2 ; 19. P— K 4 !, P—Q Kt 4 ; 20. P×Kt, P×Kt ; 21. Kt×Q B P, Kt×P ; 22. K R—K 1, Q—Q 1 ; 23. Q R— Q 1, Q—B 1 ; 24. R—Q B 1 !, R— R 2 ? (a mistake in an already very compromised position) ; 25. Kt— Q 6, Q—B 3 ; 26. Kt—K 4, R— Kt 2 ; 27. R×B ? (instead, 27. Q— Q 1 !, R—Kt 4 ; 28. P—Kt 4, etc. would have won immediately), R×Q ; 28. R×Q, R×B ; 29. R— Q 6, R×B ; 30. R P×R, B—Kt 4 ; 31. Kt—B 5, R—B 1 ; 32. R—Q B 1, P—Kt 4 ; 33. Kt—Kt 3, R—Kt 1 ; 34. Kt—Q 4, K—Kt 2 ; 35. Kt×B, P×Kt.

Position after Black's 35th move.

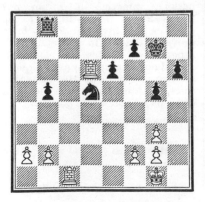

White's first object is to prevent Black's King from approaching the centre, which is achieved by the move :—

36. R—B 5 ! ......

—which, for the moment, also ties up the black Rook. But after the answer

36. ...... P—Q Kt 5

White must also parry the threat 37. ....R—Q R 1 by playing.

37. R—R 6 ......

and now everything is ready for the centralization of the King, which will permit the exploitation of the Queen's side advantage.

37. ...... Kt—B 3

An attempt to stop the normal course of events by means of tactical threats.

38. K—B 1 Kt—K 5
39. R—B 7 K—Kt 3
40. K—K 2 R—Kt 4
41. K—K 3 ......

This dissolves the counter-attack started with Black's 37th move. If now, 41. ....R—K 4 ?, then 42. P—B 4, etc.

41. ...... Kt—B 3
42. R—B 4 ......

Preventing also 42. ....Kt— Kt 5 ch.

42. ...... P—R 4
43. P—B 3 K—B 4

Now this King's advance has not much importance as his White opponent is also in the centre.

44. K—Q 3 Kt—Q 4
45. R—R 7 P—B 3

46. R—K 4   . . . . .

Making room for the King.

46. . . . . . .   R—Kt 3
47. P—Kt 4 ch !. . . . . .

The beginning of the decisive part of this end-game. In order to have a free hand on the Queen's side, White must eliminate any danger on the other wing and the text-move answers that purpose, since it puts an end to Black's possible threat . . . . P—R 5 ; P × P, P × P followed by . . . . Kt—B 5, etc.

47. . . . . . .   K—Kt 3
48. P × P ch   K × P
49. P—K Kt 3   K—Kt 3
50. K—B 4   P—B 4

Something must be done against the threat 51. K—B 5.

51. R—K 2   K—B 3
52. K—B 5   . . . . . .

Intending R—Q 7—Q 6, etc.

52. . . . . . .   R—Kt 1
53. R—R 6   R—K 1
54. R—Q 6 !   . . . . . .

Threatening 55. R (K 2) × P ch, R × R ; 56. K × Kt, etc., and thus forcing at last the Knight to leave the central square.

54. . . . . . .   P—B 5
55. P × P   Kt × P
56. R (K 2)—Q 2   . . . . . .

Forcing the exchange of Rooks —or the win of the Q Kt P.

56. . . . . . .   R—Q R 1
57. P—Kt 3   K—K 4
58. R—Q 8   R—R 2
59. K × P   Kt—Q 4 ch
60. K—B 5   R—B 2 ch
61. K—Kt 5   R—B 6
62. R—K 2 ch   K—B 5

63. R—B 8 ch   K—Kt 6
64. R—K 5 !   . . . . . .

But not 64. R × P ? since . . . . Kt—B 2 ch and Black will take two Rooks for one.

64. . . . . . .   Kt—B 5
65. R × P ch   K × P
66. R—K 5   R—K 6
67. R × Kt ch !   Resigns.

I believe that these three examples taken as a whole represent a rather important contribution to the chapter "Two Rooks against Rook and Knight (with Pawns)."

GAME 45

QUEEN'S GAMBIT DECLINED (TARRASCH'S DEFENCE)

Bled Tournament, August, 1931.

White : V. PIRC

1. P—Q 4   P—Q 4
2. P—Q B 4   P—K 3
3. Kt—Q B 3   P—Q B 4
4. P × Q P   B P × P

This interesting Pawn-offer (instead of the usual 4. . . . . K P × P) has been analysed by some German amateurs, and introduced in international practice—if I am not mistaken—by Dr. Tartakower. As subsequent investigations have proved, Black, in spite of the superiority of his development, should not be able, against adequate defence, to prevent the opponent emerging from the opening with an extra-pawn and a safe position.

5. Q—R 4 ch   . . . . . .

Better than 5. Q × P, Kt— Q B 3.

5. . . . . . .   B—Q 2

An error would be here 5. ....
Q—Q 2 because of 6. Kt—Q Kt 5!±

6. Q×Q P   P×P
7. Q×Q P   Kt—Q B 3

Black could also play 7. .... Kt—
K B 3 after which 8. Q×P,
Kt—Q B 3, etc., would have been
decidedly too risky for White ; but
8. Q—Q 1 followed by P—K 3, etc.,
would have led to the same variations as could easily occur after
the move in text.

8. B—Kt 5   ......

On account of White's backward
development it would be safer for
him to use this Bishop for defensive
purposes on the Queen's side, and
to play instead 8. P—K 3 (....Kt—
B 3 ; 9. Q—Q 1). However, the
text-move cannot be considered as
an actual mistake.

8. ......   Kt—B 3
9. Q—Q 2   P—K R 3

This rather harmless attempt to
create (in case of the natural answer
10. B—R 4) new threats in connection with .....B—Q Kt 5, followed
by ....P—K Kt 4 and ....Kt—
K 5, has unexpected and pleasant
consequences.

10. B×Kt   ......

This certainly gives Black more
attacking chances than the retreat
mentioned, but would not have
proved too bad if White had taken
full advantage of the square Q 5
which he gains by this exchange.

10. ......   Q×B
11. P—K 3   Castles
12. Castles ?   ......

The decisive error, permitting
Black to regain the gambit-pawn

with a persisting pressure. Necessary was 12. Kt—Q 5 ! and if
12. ....Q—Kt 3 (best) then 13.
Kt—K 2 followed by K Kt—B 4
or B 3 with possibilities of defence. Black has now the opportunity to carry on a King's attack
in the "good old style."

12. ......   B—K Kt 5
13. Kt—Q 5   ......

Too late !

13. ......   R×Kt !
14. Q×R   ......

Position after White's 14th move.

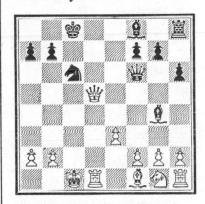

14. ......   B—Q R 6 !

After 14. ....B×R ; 15. Q×B,
Q×P ; 16. Q—Kt 4 ch, P—B 4 ;
17. Q—K 2, Q×Q followed by ....
B—B 4, Black would probably
have won after a long end-game.
The move chosen by him shows the
decision, plainly justified under the
circumstances, to find a winning
solution in the middle-game.

15. Q—Kt 3   ......

There is nothing better ; if, for
instance, I. 15. P×B, then 15. ....
Q—B 6 ch ; 16. K—Kt 1, R—Q 1 ! ;

17. Q×R ch, Kt×Q with the double threat 18. ....B×R and 18. ....B—B 4 ch. II. 15. R—Q 2, then 15. ....B×P ch ! ; 16. R×B, Q—B 6 ch ; 17. K—Kt 1 (or 17. R—B 2, Q—R 8 ch followed by ....R—Q 1 ch), Q—K 8 ch ; 18. K—B 2, R—Q 1 and wins.

15.	......	B×R
16.	Q×K B	Q×P
17.	Q—Q 3	B—Kt 5 !

And not 17. ....R—Q 1 because of 18. Kt—R 3 !, Q—B 3 ; 19. Q—B 3, etc., with chances of salvation.

| 18. Kt—B 3 | B×Kt |

Also here 18. ....R—Q 1 would have been out of place because of 19. Q—K 2, etc.

19. Q—B 5 ch	K—Kt 1
20. Q×B	Q—K 8 ch
21. K—B 2	......

If he had given up the Pawn the agony would not have lasted long : 21. Q—Q 1, Q×P ch ; 22. Q—Q 2, Q—K 3 ! ; 23. K—Kt 1, R—Q 1 ; 24. Q—B 4 ch, K—R 1, etc., with quite a few deadly threats.

21.	......	R—Q B 1
22.	Q—Kt 3 ch	Kt—K 4
		disc. ch. !
23.	K—Kt 3	Q—Q 8 ch
24.	K—R 3	R—B 4 !

Quick death is now unavoidable —for instance A. 25. P—Kt 4, R—B 6 ch ; 26. K—Kt 2, Q—B 8 mate.   B. 25. P—Kt 3, R—R 4 ch ; 26. K—Kt 4, Q—Q 7 mate ; and the prettiest. C. 25. K—Kt 4, Q—Q 7 ch ! 26. K×R, P—Kt 3 ch; 27. K—Kt 5, Q—R 4 mate.

Resigns.

GAME 46

QUEEN'S GAMBIT ACCEPTED

Bled Tournament, August, 1931.

Black : S. FLOHR

1. P—Q 4	P—Q 4
2. P—Q B 4	P×P
3. Kt—K B 3	Kt—K B 3
4. P—K 3	P—K 3
5. B×P	P—B 4
6. Castles	Kt—B 3
7. Q—K 2	P—Q R 3
8. R—Q 1	......

Peculiarly enough, this move—which does not contain any real threat and is therefore at this particular moment, to say the least, inexact—was almost unanimously adopted at the time the actual game was played. After Euwe's win against me, in the 5th Match-game, 1937, and my win against Böök at Margate, 1938, "theory" will probably recognise the natural development move 8. Kt—B 3 ! as the best.

| 8. ...... | P—Q Kt 4 |
| 9. P×P | ...... |

The positional refutation of 9. P—Q 5 ! ? consists in 9. ....P×P ; 10. B×Q P, Kt×B ; 11. P—K 4, Q—K 2 ! 12. R×Kt, B—K 3, etc.∓.

9.	Q—B 2
10. B—Q 3	B×P
11. P—Q R 4	......

Hoping to disorganise Black's position on the Queen's side, and succeeding in doing so because of the following inferior rejoinder.

| 11. ...... | P—Kt 5 ? |

After this a number of squares on this sector will remain insufficiently protected and, what is more,

Black will remain without any hope of a counter-attack as White's position is practically without weaknesses. A quite different situation would have been produced by the right answer 11. ....P×P! which would give Black, as a compensation for the weak Q R's Pawn, a counter - attack against White's Q Kt's Pawn.

12. Q Kt—Q 2   Castles

Slightly better, although not entirely satisfactory, was 12. .... Kt—Q R 4, as played, for instance, by Flohr in a Match-game against Dr. Euwe in 1932.

13. Kt—Kt 3   B—K 2
14. P—K 4   Kt—Q 2

The possibility of 15. P—K 5 in connection with Q—K 4 was certainly unpleasant.

15. B—K 3   Kt (Q 2)—K 4

The intended exchange of Knights does not bring relief as it does not help to solve the important problem of the co-ordination of Black's Rooks. Slightly preferable was therefore 15. ....B—Kt 2; 16. Q R—B 1, Q—Kt 1.

16. Kt×Kt   Kt×Kt
17. Q R—B 1   Q—Kt 1
18. B—B 5!   ......

From now on every exchange will facilitate the exploitation of the organic Pawn weaknesses created by Black's 11th move.

18. ......   B×B
19. Kt×B   Q—Kt 3
20. Q—R 5!   Kt—Q 2

As the Knight was the only active piece of Black's, it would have been advisable not to remove it unless necessary. By playing 20. ....P—B 3 he could offer some more resistance, although White's advantage after 21. B—B 1, R—Q 1; 22. R—Q 4! followed by Q—Q 1, etc., would still remain considerable.

21. B—K 2   P—Kt 3

In order to open, without loss of time, a "hole" for the King; but, as the following shows, this move weakens the King's side, *especially as White is by no means in a hurry to exchange Queens*. Black should rather take the Knight immediately.

22. Q—Kt 5   Kt×Kt
23. R×Kt   P—Q R 4

One of White's positional threats was also 24. P—R 5.

24. P—R 4   ......

The punishment for 21. ....P—Kt 3.

24. ......   B—R 3
25. B—B 3!   ......

White's Bishop is here stronger than Black's. White threatens now everywhere and everything (26. P—R 5; 26. R×P; 26. R—Q 7, etc.).

25. ......   P—B 3
26. Q—K 3   ......

And from now on he begins to speculate on the unprotected position of the enemy's Queen !

26. ......   Q R—Q 1
27. R×R   R×R

Or 27. ....Q×R; 28. P—K 5, P—B 4; 29. R—B 6, B—B 1; 30. Q—B 5, etc., with a winning position.

Position after Black's 27th move.

28. P—K 5 !   ......

Forcing either the win of a Pawn by an overwhelming position after 28. ....P×P; 29. Q×P (even stronger is perhaps first 29. P—R 5!), or the catastrophe which occurs in the actual game.

The immediate 28. R—B 8 was not convincing because of 28. .... Q—Q 3.

28. ......   P—B 4
29. R—B 8 !   ......

Winning at least a Rook.

Resigns.

GAME 47

RUY LOPEZ

Bled Tournament, September, 1931.

White : G. STOLTZ

1. P—K 4	P—K 4
2. Kt—K B 3	Kt—Q B 3
3. B—Kt 5	P—Q R 3
4. B—R 4	P—Q 3
5. P—Q 4	P—Q Kt 4
6. B—Kt 3	Kt×P

| 7. Kt×Kt | P×Kt |
| 8. B—Q 5 | ...... |

If the unusual 5th move of White has a point at all, it can be only the Pawn-offer 8. P—Q B 3, after which acceptance Black would have some difficulties of development. The Bishop-move in the text in connection with the ensuing exchange finally gives Black, on the contrary, an advantage in space.

| 8. ...... | R—Kt 1 |
| 9. B—B 6 ch | ...... |

White is obviously in a hurry to "simplify" matters. If he was told that this is the easiest way to obtain a draw, he was certainly ill-advised.

9.	B—Q 2
10. B×B ch	Q×B
11. Q×P	Kt—B 3
12. Kt—B 3	......

12. Q—R 7 does not lead to anything after 12. ....Q—B 1.

12.	B—K 2
13. Castles	Castles
14. B—Q 2	......

This Bishop has no good squares of development. In a training-game with clocks played in Paris, 1933, Dr. Bernstein tried against me 14. B—Kt 5, but after 14. .... P—Kt 5; 15. Kt—Q 5 (15. Kt—K 2, Kt×P loses a Pawn), Kt× Kt, had to resign as 16. Q×Kt would have been answered by 16. ....R—Kt 4.

14.	K R—K 1
15. Q—Q 3	P—Kt 5
16. Kt—K 2	......

Inconsequent, as he had here more reasons than before to pursue his policy of exchanges. After 16. Kt—Q 5, Kt×Kt; 17. Q (or P)×Kt, Q—Kt 4, etc., Black would have only a slightly more comfortable end-game, which by right play by White could, however, eventually end in a draw. After the text-move White's task will become much more complicated.

16. ......   Q—B 3
17. P—K B 3   ......

In the event of 17. Kt—Kt 3 the answer 17. .....Kt—Kt 5—followed by ....Kt—K 4 or ....B—B 3— would be strong. The Pawn's move, however, weakens the dark-coloured squares (especially K 3) and thus gives to Black's initiative a concrete object.

17. ......   P—Q 4 !
18. P×P   ......

Otherwise he would lose this Pawn with practically no compensation.

18. ......   Kt×P
19. Q R—K 1   B—B 3
20. P—Q B 4   ......

Also 20. P—B 3, which was slightly preferable, would not prove quite satisfactory after 20. .... Q—B 4 ch ; 21. Kt—Q 4, K R— Q 1, etc.∓

20. ......   Q—B 4 ch
21. R—B 2   Kt—K 6
22. P—Q Kt 3   Q R—Q 1
23. B×Kt   R×B
24. Q—B 2   ......

As is easy to see, the last 3-4 moves were practically forced. Black has not only obtained the full control of the board, but is even in a position to obtain a material advantage. The final part of the fight does not lack, however, some sort of piquancy.

24. ......   B—R 5 !
25. P—Kt 3   R×B P
26. R—K B 1   B—Kt 4
27. K—Kt 2   R×R ch

28. R×R   Q—B 3 ch
29. K—R 3   ......

Forced, because of Black's threats 29. ....R—Q 7 or 29. ....B—K 6.

29. ......   B—K 6
30. R—B 1   ......

Position after White's 30th move.

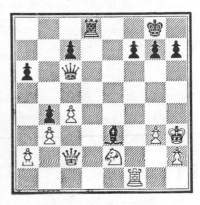

30. ......   R—Q 4 !

Not yet decisive was 30. .... R—Q 3 (or Q 7) because of 31. Q—B 5 with counter-attack ; but after the text-move the co-operation of the Rook will leave White without defence.

31. Kt—B 4   Q—Q 2 ch
32. P—Kt 4   R—Q 5
33. Q—K Kt 2   ......

He still succeeds in finding defensive moves—but it obviously cannot long go that way.

33. ......   P—Q B 3
34. Kt—R 5   B—Kt 4 !

After this there is no remedy against 35. ....P—Kt 3, etc.

35. Q—K 2   P—Kt 3
36. Kt—Kt 3   P—K R 4
37. Kt—K 4   Q×P ch !

Only *apparently* allowing White to reach a Rook-ending with only one Pawn less: in reality it will be only Black who will keep a Rook.

38. Q×Q	P×Q ch
39. K×P	R×Kt ch
40. K×B	K—Kt 2

Black's next move would be now 41. ....P—B 3 ch ! followed by 42. ....R—K 4 ch, winning the Rook. Therefore—

Resigns.

GAME 48

QUEEN'S GAMBIT DECLINED (ORTHODOX DEFENCE)

Bled Tournament, September, 1931.

Black : G. MAROCZY

1. P—Q 4	P—Q 4
2. P—Q B 4	P—K 3
3. Kt—Q B 3	Kt—K B 3
4. B—Kt 5	B—K 2
5. P—K 3	Q Kt—Q 2
6. Kt—B 3	Castles
7. R—B 1	P—K R 3
8. B—R 4	P—B 3
9. B—Q 3	P—R 3

The fashionable continuation, by which in fact Black has but little to fear is 9. ....P×P ; 10. B×P, P—Q Kt 4 ; 11. B—Q 3, P—R 3 and if 12. P—R 4 (12. P—K 4 ?, Kt × P∓ : Euwe-Alekhine, 28th game, 1935), then simply 12. .... P×P.

| 10. Castles | P×P |
| 11. B×P | P—B 4 |

It is rather risky to delay the development of the Queen's side. Instead, 11. ....P—Q Kt 4, fol-

lowed by ....B—Kt 2 and .... P—B 4 was still a fairly good alternative.

12. P—R 4 !   ......

This move, in connection with the following isolation of the central Pawn, gives the game its character. After 12. B—Q 3 or 12. Q—K 2, P—Q Kt 4, etc., it would develop on conventional lines—and probably end by an honourable draw.

12. ......   Q—R 4

Maroczy from now on plays very enterprising chess, combining defensive moves with counter-attacks against White's weaknesses at Q R 4 and Q 4.

13. Q—K 2   P×P !

At the right moment as 14. Kt × P, Kt—K 4 ; 15. B—Q Kt 3, Kt—Kt 3 ; 16. B—Kt 3, P—K 4 etc., would be in Black's favour.

| 14. P×P | Kt—Kt 3 |
| 15. B—Q 3 ! | ...... |

Practically leaving the Q R's Pawn to its fate. For the moment, it is true, it cannot well be taken because of 16. Kt—K 4 ! with a very strong attack ; but it remains weak almost until the—dramatic— end.

| 15. ...... | B—Q 2 |
| 16. Kt—K 5 | ...... |

Threatening 17. B × Kt followed by 18. Q—K 4, etc.

| 16. ...... | K R—Q 1 |
| 17. P—B 4 | ...... |

White had decided already, by 12. P—Q R 4, to conduct the whole game in a fortissimo style. Although the result justified this method, I am by no means sure that it was the most logical way to exploit the—unquestionable—advantage in space. Here, for instance, the simple move 17. Q—B 3 was to be seriously taken into consideration as (1) 17. ....Kt×P would still be answered by 18. Kt—K 4 !± (2) 17. ....B×P would be obviously unsatisfactory because of 18. Q×P, and (3) after 17. .... B—B 3 ; 18. Kt×B, P×Kt ; 19. K R—Q 1, etc., Black's Pawn weaknesses would be at least as vulnerable as White's.

17. ......   B—K 1
18. Kt—Kt 4   ......

The logical consequence of the previous move. White offers the Queen's Pawn, as its defence by 18. K R—Q 1 or 18. B—K B 2 would permit Black to parry the important threats by means of Q (or K) Kt—Q 4.

18. ......   R×P

Black, on the other hand, has nothing better than to accept the offer, as by other moves White's attack would remain—with even material—at least as strong as in the actual game.

19. B×Kt   B×B
20. Kt×B ch   P×Kt
21. Kt—K 4   ......

Black's King's position is now dangerously compromised, especially as he cannot well protect the *square* K B 3 (if 21. Kt—Q 2, then 22. P—B 5 ! with a strong attack).

21. ......   Q R—Q 1 ?

But he could—and should—save the *Pawn* K B 3 by playing 21. .... P—B 4, to which White would reply 22. Kt—B 6 ch, K—B 1 (or K—Kt 2 ; 23. Kt—R 5 ch followed by P—Q Kt 3) ; 23. P—Q Kt 3 ! and try afterwards to exploit the weakness of the opponent's darkcoloured squares—with an uncertain result.   The counter-attack initiated by the text-move will be refuted chiefly because White will succeed in protecting his Bishop *indirectly*, without any loss of time.

22. Kt×P ch   K—B 1
23. Kt—R 7 ch !   ......

Perhaps Maroczy had underestimated this check. If now 23. ....K—Kt 1, then 24. Q—Kt 4 ch, K—R 1 ; 25. Q—R 4 !, R×B ; 26. Q×P and wins.

23. ......   K—K 2
24. P—B 5 !   ......

The first indirect defence ; if 24. ....R×B ? then 25. P—B 6 ch followed by 26. Q×R ch, etc.

24. ......   R(Q 1)—Q 3

But after this everything seems to be again in order, as the King has got a comfortable escape at Q 1. The following reply, which was by no means easy to find, however, turns the tables :—

Position after Black's 24th move.

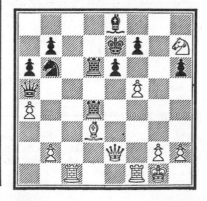

25. P—Q Kt 4 ! ! ......

A surprising solution of the attacking problem, the idea of which is as follows : White *succeeds* either (in case of 25. ....R × P) *by playing* 26. Q—R 5 ! *without permitting the strong answer* 26. .... Q—Q 7 ! or (as in the actual game) *by entering with the Queen into Black's position via K 5.*

25. ......   Q × Kt P

An interesting finish would have occurred after 25. ....R × P—26. Q—R 5 !, P—K 4 ! ; 27. P—B 6 ch, K—Q 1 ; 28. Q × R P !, R × B ; 29. Q—B 8, R—Q 2 ; 30. R—Q B 5, Q × P ; 31. R × P and wins.

26. Q—K 5 !   ......

Threatening 27. Q—B 6 ch, K—Q 2 ; 28. Kt—B 8, mate.

26. ......   Kt—Q 2

Protects both critical squares and —apparently—at last wins the Bishop.

27. Q—R 8 !   R × B

Losing one move earlier than he should. The best reply 27. .... Q—Kt 3 would have forced White to disclose the last point of the combination started by his 25th move—28. P—R 5 ! (the triumph of the neglected Pawn !) with two variations : (a) 28. ....Q × P ; 29. R—B 8, or (b) 28. ....Q—R 2 ; 29. P—B 6 ch, etc., as in the actual game.

28. P—B 6 ch!   ......

If 28. .... Kt × P, then 29. Q × Kt ch and 30. Kt—B 8 mate ; if 28. ....K—Q 1, then 29. Q × B ch ! and 30. R—B 8 mate.
Resigns.

GAME 49

CARO-KANN DEFENCE

London Tournament, February, 1932.

Black : W. WINTER

1. P—K 4	P—Q B 3
2. P—Q 4	P—Q 4
3. P × P	P × P
4. P—Q B 4	......

One of the best ways to meet the Caro-Kann. Nowadays it is slightly out of fashion, in my opinion without much reason and probably only temporarily.

4.	Kt—K B 3
5. Kt—Q B 3	Kt—B 3
6. Kt—B 3	......

If 6. B—Kt 5 (Botvinnik's move), then 6. ....P—K 3 ; 7. Kt—B 3, B—K 2, etc., with a slightly cramped but solid enough defensive game.

6.	B—Kt 5
7. P × P	K Kt × P
8. B—Q Kt 5	Q—R 4

Introduced by me in a game against Nimzowitsch (Bled, 1931), in which my opponent, after 9. Q—Kt 3 !, B × Kt ; 10. P × B, Kt × Kt made the curious miscalculation 11. B × Kt ch, P × B ; 12. Q—Kt 7 ? —and after 12. ....Kt—Q 4 disc. ch ; 13. B—Q 2, Q—Kt 3 ! ; 14. Q × R ch, K—Q 2 ; 15. Castles K R, Kt—B 2, was forced to give up a piece by 16. B—R 5, making further resistance practically hopeless. However, the Queen's move is—as the present game shows—decidedly too risky. The correct line is 8. .... R—B 1 ; 9. P—K R 3, B × Kt ; 10. Q × B, P—K 3, etc., with about even prospects.

9. Q—Kt 3 !   B × Kt

10. P×B	Kt×Kt
11. P×Kt	P—K 3

Black has obtained, it is true, the better Pawn position, but as the following efficient Pawn sacrifice of White will show, his King's position is by no means safe. The next part of the game is highly instructive, as White's attack needed, in order to succeed, a particularly exact calculation.

12. P—Q 5 !	......

It is necessary to sacrifice the Pawn at once, as after 12. Castles, R—Q 1 Black would obtain a satisfactory position.

12.	P×P
13. Castles	Castles

The only move. After 13. .... B—K 2 ; 14. R—K 1, the pin on the King's file would be deadly.

14. B×Kt	P×B
15. R—Kt 1	Q—B 2

Or 15. ....K—Q 2; 16. P—QB4!, etc., with a tremendous attack.

16. Q—R 4	R—Q 2
17. B—Q 2 !	......

A difficult move, much more effective than 17.B—B 4 or K 3. In spite of his accurate defence Black will be unable to prevent a gradual further demolition of his King's residence.

17.	B—B 4
18. P—Q B 4	K—Q 1

Again comparatively the best, as 18. ....B—Kt 3 would fail because of 19. P—B 5 !, B×P ; 20. Q—R 6 ch, K—Q 1 ; 21. B—R 5, B—Kt 3 ; 22. R×B, etc.

19. B—R 5	B—Kt 3
20. B×B	P×B

21. Q—R 8 ch !	......

The objects of this rather profound Queen's manœuvre are the following :—

(1) If White plays at once 21. P×P, Black can answer 21. .... R×P ; 22. K R—Q 1, K—K 2 ; 23. R×R, P×R ; 24. R—K 1 ch, K—B 3 ; 25. Q—R 4 ch, K.—Kt 3, and White would have no more than perpetual check. Therefore he has to prevent the Black King escaping via K 2.

(2) In some important variations a White Rook has to be posted at Q R 4—so the Queen frees that square in view of that eventuality.

21.	Q—B 1
22. Q—R 3	Q—Kt 1
23. P×P	P×P

After 23. ....R×P ; 24. K R—Q 1, R—K 1 ; 25. R×R ch, P×R ; 26. R—Q 1, Q or R—K 4 ; 27. P—B 4 Black would have no adequate defence.

Position after Black's 23rd move.

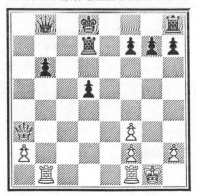

24. R—Kt 4 !	......

The winning move, as Black has no time to play 24. ....R—K 1 on account of 24. R—Q R 4, etc.

24.	Q—Q 3

25. R—K 1 !   R—B 2

Or 25. ....R—K 2 ; 26. R—Q 1, etc., with a winning attack.

26. Q—Kt 3   R—K 1
27. R—Q 1   R—K 4

Obviously, Black cannot protect both his Pawns.

28. R × Kt P   R—B 3
29. R × R   R—Kt 4 ch

Forced (29. ....Q × R ; 30. Q—Kt 8 ch, etc.).

30. K—R 1   Q × R
31. R—K 1 !   ......

Initiating the final attack.

31. ......   Q—B 3
32. Q—Kt 8 ch   K—Q 2
33. P—B 4   R—Kt 3

I expected here 33. ....R—R 4; 34. Q—K 8 ch, K—Q 3 ; 35. R—Q B 1 !, R × P ch; 36. K—Kt 1 ! forcing the win.

34. Q—K 8 ch   K—B 2
35. R—B 1 ch   K—Kt 3
36. R—Kt 1 ch   K—B 4
37. Q—Kt 5 ch   Resigns.

GAME 50

QUEEN'S INDIAN DEFENCE

London Tournament, February, 1932.

White : Miss Vera Menchik

1. P—Q 4   Kt—K B 3
2. P—Q B 4   P—K 3
3. Kt—K B 3   P—Q Kt 3
4. P—K 3   ......

A tame developing system but by no means a bad one. Black has thereby no opening difficulties, providing he does not over-estimate his position, and realises that although he has sufficient forces to *control* White's K 4, he is not yet developed enough for *occupying* it.

4. ......   B—Kt 2
5. B—Q 3   B—Kt 5 ch
6. B—Q 2   B × B ch
7. Q Kt × B   ......

This Knight is not very happily placed at Q 2. More promising would be, therefore, 7. Q × B, followed by Kt—B 3.

7. ......   P—Q 3
8. Castles   Q Kt—Q 2
9. Q—B 2   Q—K 2
10. K R—Q 1   Castles (K R)
11. Kt—K 4   P—Kt 3

A good move, the object of which is, as the continuation shows, to avoid exchange of the Q's Bishop. It is to Black's interest to keep as many pieces as possible on the board, his Pawn position being much more elastic than his opponent's.

12. R—Q 2   Kt × Kt
13. B × Kt   P—Q B 3 !
14. Q—R 4   ......

Probably hoping to provoke the answer 14. ....P—Q Kt 4 which move would be advantageously answered by 15. Q—Kt 3 !

14. ......   K R—B 1
15. B—Q 3   P—Q B 4
16. Q—Q 1   ......

None of the White pieces has a suitable square. But it will still be some time before Black will be able to obtain a serious initiative.

16. ......   Kt—B 3
17. P × P   Kt P × P

The right way to recapture, as

the backward Queen's Pawn is very easy to protect in this kind of position.

18. Q—K 2   Kt—R 4
19. Q R—Q 1   R—B 1 !

Preparing the advance of the K B's and the K's Pawns.

20. P—K 4   Kt—B 5
21. Q—K 3   P—K 4
22. B—B 1   Q R—Q 1

Up to this point Black's tactics have been irreproachable, but here 22. ....K R—Q 1; followed by Kt —K 3—Q 5 would be more convincing as it would prevent White's next attempt.

23. P—Q Kt 4 !   ......

An interesting Pawn sacrifice in a difficult position. If now 23. .... P×P; 24. Q×P, R—R 1; 25. Q—Kt 6, B×P, then 26. Q× Q P, Q×Q ; 27. R×Q, B×Kt ; 28. P×B, R×P ; 29. R—Kt 6, with good drawing chances for White.

23. ......   Kt—K 3
24. R—Kt 2   B—R 1
25. P×P   Kt×P
26. Kt—Q 2   P—B 4
27. P×P   P×P

With the opening of the K Kt's file, Black gets at last the basis for a powerful King's attack.

28. P—B 3   Q—K Kt 2

Threatening 29. ....P—B 5, followed by .... P—K 5.

29. R (Q 1)—Kt 1 K—R 1
30. Kt—Kt 3   Kt—K 3
31. R—Q 2   Kt—Kt 4
32. K—R 1   R—K Kt 1
33. R—K B 2   ......

The only defence against 33. .... Kt×P,

33. ......   Q R—K 1 !
34. R—Q 1   R—K 3

Position after Black's 34th move.

35. P—B 4   ......

Desperation, as Black was threatening 35. ....R—R 3 followed by 36. ....R×P ch ; 37. ....Q—R 3 ch ; 38. ....Kt—R 6 ch, etc. And after 35. P—B 5, P—Q 4, etc., he would win by the simple advance of his centre Pawns.

35. ......   P×P
36. Q—Q 4   R—K 4 !
37. P—B 5   P×P
38. Kt×P   Kt—R 6
39. R—Kt 2   P—B 6 !
40. P—Kt 3   P—B 7 disc. ch

This is the longest Bishop's check I ever gave in my life !

Resigns.

GAME 51

RUY LOPEZ

London Tournament, February, 1932.

Black : G. KOLTANOWSKI

Brilliancy Prize

1. P—K 4   P—K 4
2. Kt—K B 3   Kt—Q B 3
3. B—Kt 5   P—Q R 3

4. B—R 4   P—Q 3
5. B × Kt ch   P × B
6. P—Q 4   P × P

The usual defensive scheme is here 6. ....P—B 3, followed by Kt—K 2—Kt 3, etc. But Black in this game obviously wants a free diagonal for his K's Bishop.

7. Kt × P   B—Q 2
8. Castles   P—Kt 3
9. Kt—Q B 3 ......

White has nothing better than this calm development of forces—in the hope that the slight weakness of the dark-coloured squares in Black's camp sooner or later will give him real chances.

9. ......   B—Kt 2
10. R—K 1   Kt—K 2
11. B—B 4   Castles
12. Q—Q 2   P—Q B 4
13. Kt—Kt 3 ......

Not 13. Kt—B 3 because of 13. ....B—Kt 5. But 13. K Kt—K 2 came seriously into consideration.

13. ......   Kt—B 3
14. B—R 6   B—K 3
15. B × B   K × B
16. Kt—Q 5   P—B 3
17. Q R—Q 1 R—Q Kt 1
18. Q—B 3   Q—B 1
19. P—Q R 3 R—B 2
20. P—R 3 !   ......

This and the following moves were by no means easy to find as, in preparing the decisive combination, I had to keep in mind at the same time the possibility of the simplifying variation beginning by ....B × Kt.

20. ......   Q—Kt 2
21. R—K 3   Q—Kt 4

As the sequel shows, Black should here play 21. ....B × Kt—but after 22. P × B, Kt—Q 5 ; 23. Kt × Kt,

P × Kt ; 24. R × P, Q × P ; 25. Q—Q 2, White would still keep a real, if not easily realisable, positional advantage.

Position after Black's 21st move.

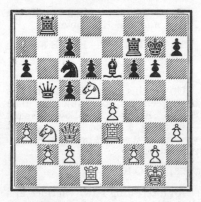

22. Kt × P (B 7) ! ......

As a rule, so-called "positional" sacrifices are considered more difficult, and therefore more praiseworthy, than those which are based exclusively on an exact calculation of tactical possibilities. The present position offers, I believe, an exception, as the multitude and complexity of the variations following the Knight's sacrifice demanded much more intensive mental work than any general evaluation of mutual possibilities.

22. ......   R × Kt
23. R × P   B—B 5

Black had several other answers, but all of them would finally lose, as shown below : (I.) 23. ....B × Kt ? ; 24. Q × P ch, followed by 25. R × B, etc. (II.) 23. ..... Kt—Q 5 ?; 24. Kt × Kt, etc. (III.) 23. .... Q—B 5 ; 24. Kt × P ! etc. (IV.) 23. ....Kt—Q 1 ; 24. R—B 3, R—B 2 ; 25. Kt × P, etc. (V.) 23. ....B—B 2 ; 24. R × P !. Kt—Q 5 ; 25. Kt × Kt, P × Kt ; 26. Q × R, K × R ; 27. R—B 3 ch, etc.

(VI.) 23. ....R—K 1 ; 24. Kt×P, Kt—Q 1 ; 25. P—Q Kt 4, Kt—B 2 ; 26. R×B, etc.   (VII.) 23. ....K—B 2 ; 24. R—B 3, K—K2 ; 25. P—Q R 4, Q—Kt 3 (best) ; 26. R × B ch, K×R ; 27. Kt×P ch, K—Q 3 (or K—B 2 ; 28. Q×P ch, K—Kt 1 ; 29. Kt—K 6 ! etc.) ; 28. Q×P ch, K×Kt ; 29. R—B 3 ch, K—Kt 5 ; 30. Q—Q 6 ch and wins.

24. P—Q R 4 !	Q×P
25. Kt×P	Q—Kt 4
26. Q×P ch	K—Kt 1
27. Kt—Q 7 !	R—Q 1

Or 27. ....R—K 1 ; 28. Q—Q B 3 and wins.

28. R—K B 3	Q—Kt 5
29. P—B 3	Q—Kt 4
30. Kt—K 5 !	R (Q 1)—Q B 1
31. Kt×Kt	

If now 31. ....R×Kt, then 32. R—Q 8 ch winning.

Resigns.

GAME 52

BUDAPEST DEFENCE

London Tournament, February, 1932.

Black : Dr. S. Tartakower

1. P—Q 4	Kt—K B 3
2. P—Q B 4	P—K 4
3. P×P	Kt—K 5

Less usual, but not better than 3. ....Kt—Kt 5 against which move I have had (excepting the Gilg-game, Semmering, 1926) rather pleasant experiences, too. Here, for instance, two typical short "Budapest" stories.

I. *Black*, E. Rabinowitsch, Baden-Baden, 1925. 1. P—Q 4, Kt—K B 3 ; 2. P—Q B 4, P—K 4 ; 3. P×P, Kt—Kt 5 ; 4. P—K 4, Kt× K P ; 5. P—B 4, Kt—Kt 3 ; 6. Kt—K B 3, B—B 4 ; 7. P—B 5 !, Kt—R 5 ; 8. Kt—Kt 5 !, Q—K 2 ; 9. Q—Kt 4, P—K B 3 ;

10. Q—R 5 ch !, P—Kt 3 ; 11. Q×Kt, P×Kt ; 12. B×P, Q—B 2 ; 13. B—K 2, Castles ; 14. R—B 1, Kt—B 3 ; 15. Kt—B 3, Kt—Q 5 ; 16. P×P, Q×Kt P ; 17. R×R ch, B×R ; 18. B—R 5, Q—Kt 3 ; 19. Castles, B—Kt 2 ; 20. R—B 1, Kt—K 3 ; 21. B—B 7 ch, K—R 1 ; 22. B×Kt, P×B ; 23. B—R 6 ! Resigns.

II. *Black :* Dr. Seitz, Hastings, 1925-1926. 1. P—Q 4, Kt—K B 3 ; 2. P—Q B 4, P—K 4 ; 3. P×P, Kt —Kt 5 ; 4. P—K 4, Kt×K P ; 5. P—B 4, Kt (K 4)—B 3 ; 6. B—K 3, B—Kt 5 ch ; 7. Kt—B 3, Q—K 2 ; 8. B—Q 3, P—B 4 ; 9. Q—R 5 ch, P—Kt 3 ; 10. Q—B 3, B×Kt ch ; 11. P×B, P×P ; 12. B×K P, Castles ; 13. B—Q 5 ch !, K—R 1 ; 14. Kt—R 3, P—Q 3 ; 15. Castles (K R), B×Kt ; 16. Q×B, Q—Q 2 ; 17. P—K B 5 !, P×P ; 18. Q R—Kt 1 !, P—B 5 ; 19. B× B P, Q×Q; 20. B—K 5 ch. Resigns.

| 4. Kt—Q 2 | Kt—B 4 |

If 4. ....B—Kt 5, then 5. Kt—B 3 followed by P—Q R 3, in order to obtain the advantage of the two Bishops.

5. K Kt—B 3	Kt—B 3
6. P—K Kt 3	Q—K 2
7. B—Kt 2	P—K Kt 3
8. Q Kt—Kt 1 !	......

This at first sight surprising move is in reality perfectly logical. After Black has clearly shown his intention to develop the King's Bishop at K Kt 2, White has no longer to reckon with any action on the diagonal K 1—Q R 5. There is no reason, therefore, for delay in placing his Knight on the dominating square Q 5.

8.	Kt×P
9. Castles	Kt×Kt ch
10. P×Kt	B—Kt 2
11. R—K 1	Kt—K 3
12. Kt—B 3	Castles
13. Kt—Q 5	Q—Q 1
14. P—B 4	P—Q B 3

He has willy-nilly to dislodge the White Knight—thus creating a dangerous weakness at Q 3—because after the immediate 14. .... P—Q 3 the temporary sacrifice 15. P—K B 5, etc., would be too dangerous for him.

15.	Kt—B 3	P—Q 3
16.	B—K 3	Q—B 2
17.	R—Q B 1	B—Q 2
18.	Q—Q 2	Q R—Q 1
19.	K R—Q 1	B—B 1
20.	Kt—K 4	Kt—B 4

This will be finally refuted by the combination starting with White's 24th move—but owing to the weakness mentioned above Black's position was already very difficult. Unsatisfactory would be, for instance, 20. ....P—Q 4 ; 21. P×P, R×P ; 22. Kt—B 6 ch, followed by 23. B×R, etc., winning the exchange ; or 20. ....P—Q B 4 ; 21. P—B 5 !, P×P ; 22. Kt—B 3, Kt—Q 5 ; 23. Kt—Q 5, Q—Kt 1 ; 24. B—Kt 5, etc.± ; and after the comparatively safest 20. ....P—Kt 3, White could also easily increase his advantage in space by continuing 21. P—Q Kt 4, etc.,

21.	Kt×P !	Kt—R 5
22.	P—Q B 5	Kt×Kt P
23.	R—K 1	......

Position after White's 23rd move.

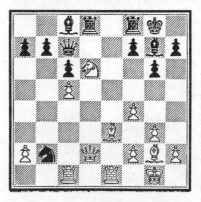

23. ......   P—Q Kt 4

This rejoinder—the logical consequence of the three previous moves—will prove insufficient ; but Black did not have any saving course : for instance, 23. ....B—K 3 ; 24. B—Q 4 ! or 23. ....B—B 4 ; 24. P—Kt 4 !, B×P ; 25. B—Q 4, in each case with a decisive advantage for White.

24. P×P (*e.p.*) !   ......

A surprising but not very complicated combination. The only difficulty consisted in the necessity of foreseeing this possibility several moves before, when making the capture 21. Kt×P.

24.	......	Q×Kt
25.	Q×Q	R×Q
26.	P×P	B—Kt 2
27.	B—B 5	R (Q 3)—Q 1
28.	B×R	K×B
29.	B×P	B×B
30.	R×B	R—R 1

The last moves of Black were practically forced and, his position being absolutely hopeless, he prefers a quick end. If, instead of this, 30. ....B—Q 5, then 31. R—Q 6, also winning immediately.

31.	R—Kt 6	R×P
32.	R—Kt 8 mate	

GAME 53

CARO-KANN DEFENCE

Berne Tournament, July, 1932.

Black : Sultan Khan

1.	P—K 4	P—Q B 3
2.	P—Q 4	P—Q 4
3.	P×P	P×P
4.	P—Q B 4	Kt—K B 3
5.	Kt—Q B 3	Kt—B 3
6.	Kt—B 3	B—Kt 5

7. P×P   K Kt×P
8. B—Q Kt 5   P—Q R 3

About 8. ....Q—R 4 see the
game against Winter (No. 49). The
point of the text-move is a positional Pawn-offer, by no means easy
to refute over the board.

9. B×Kt ch   P×B
10. Q—R 4 !   Kt×Kt

The logical consequence of his
8th move, as 10. ....B—Q 2 ; 11.
Kt—K 5, etc., would be obviously
to White's advantage.

11. Q×P ch   B—Q 2
12. Q×Kt   R—B 1
13. Q—K 3   B—Kt 4

It becomes evident that Black is
not without compensation for the
minus Pawn : White's Q's Pawn is
isolated and—what is more important—he will be forced, in order to
be able to castle, to weaken by the
following moves his Q's side.

14. P—Q R 4   B—B 5
15. P—Q Kt 3   B—Q 4
16. Castles   Q—Kt 3
17. B—Q 2 !   ......

A poor strategy would be to
protect the Knight Pawn by 17. R—
Q Kt 1, after which Black would
have found time to finish his
development by 17. ....P—K 3,
B—Q 3 (K 2) and Castles.

17. ......   P—K 3

If, instead, 17· ....Q×Kt P,
then 18, K R—B 1 ! R×R ch ;
19. R×R, Q×Q ; 20. P×Q, P—K 3
(or B×Kt ; 21. P×B, K—Q 2 ;
22. B—R 5, etc.) ; 21. R—B 7
followed by R—R 7±.

18. K R—B 1   R—Q Kt 1

Comparatively better than the
exchange of Rooks.

19. Kt—K 5   P—B 3

Probably under-estimating the
strength of the reply ; but also 19.
....B—K 2 was not satisfactory :
for instance, 20. Kt—B 4, Q×Kt P;
21. Q×Q, R×Q; 22. Kt—Q 6 ch!
etc.±

20. Kt—B 6 !   ......

The object of this Knight manœu-
vre is to make a definite end to
Black's attacks against the Q Kt's
Pawn.

20. ......   R—R 1

The only move, as 20. ....R—B 1
would be inferior because of 21.
Kt—Kt 4 !

21. Kt—R 5   ......

Intending eventually 22. R—B 6 !
etc.

21. ......   K—B 2

This King's position in an early
stage of the game is more familiar
to Sultan Khan than to European
or American players, as in Indian
Chess castling is effected in three
movements : (1) K—K 2, Q 2 or B 2;
(2) a Rook move from its original
square ; (3) a Knight's move, with
the King back on the first rank and
on the side of the Rook's movement
—this provided the King has not
been under check in the meantime.
Returning to the present game, one
must admit that Black, owing to
the threat above mentioned, did not
have, in reality, anything better
than the King's move.

22. Kt—B 4   Q—Kt 2
23. Q—Kt 3   B—K 2
24. P—R 5   ......

The initial move of the decisive
scheme : the establishment of the
Knight at Q Kt 6 will permit White

to take full advantage of the Q B's file.

```
24. ......        Q R—Q 1
25. Kt—Kt 6      B—B 3
26. R—B 4 !      ......
```

This had to be exactly calculated, because of the possible answer 26. ....P—K 4, in which case White had decided to give back the extra Pawn, in order to obtain a strong direct attack. The continuation would be 27. Q R—Q B 1 !, R × P ; 28. R × B, R × B ; 29. Q—Kt 4 !, K R—Q 1 ; 30. Q—K 6 ch, K—B 1 ; 31. P—R 3, R—Q 8 ch ; 32. R × R, R × R ch ; 33. K—R 2, etc.±

```
26. ......        K R—K 1
27. Q R—Q B 1    B—Kt 4
28. R—B 7        Q—K 5
```

Position after Black's 28th move.

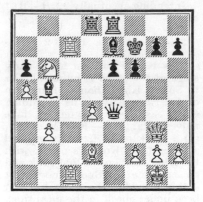

```
29. P—Q 5 !      ......
```

Instead of the simple 29. B—B 3 —which in the long run would probably also prove sufficient—White decides to force the game by a sharply calculated combination. If Black had tried now his best practical chance by 29. .... P × P the following variation would have occurred : 30. R—K 1, B— K 7 ; 31. Kt—R 4 ! (one of the important links of White's com-

bination), P—Q 5 ; 32. Kt—B 5, Q—B 7 ; 33. R × B, Q—Q 8 ch ; 34. R—K 1, Q × B ; 35. K—B 1! and Black would be defenceless against the many threats. The remaining moves would probably be 35. .... K—Kt 1 ; 36. Kt—K 6, P—Kt 3 ; 37. Kt × R, Q × R ch ; 38. K × Q, B—Q 3 disc. ch. ; 39. K—Q 2, B × Q ; 40. R P × B, R × Kt ; 41. R— B 6, R—Q 4 ; 42. P—Q Kt 4, after which Black would have to resign.

```
29. ......        K—Kt 1
```

Leads to an even more rapid debacle because of White's 31st move.

```
30. R—K 1        Q—B 4
31. B—Kt 4 !     R—Q 2
```

As useless as anything else.

```
32. R × R        B × R
33. B × B        P × P
```

Or 33. ....R × B ; 34. Q—Q 6 and wins.

```
34. Q—Q 6        Resigns.
```

GAME 54

RUY LOPEZ

Berne Tournament, July, 1932.

Black : H. GROB

```
1. P—K 4         P—K 4
2. Kt—K B 3      Kt—Q B 3
3. B—Kt 5        P—Q R 3
4. B—R 4         Kt—B 3
5. Castles       P—Q 3
6. P—B 3         ......
```

Also good is here 6. B × Kt ch, P × B ; 7. P—Q 4, Kt × P ; 8. Q— K 2, P—K B 4 ; 9. Q Kt—Q 2, Kt × Kt ; 10. Kt × Kt ! and White will regain the Pawn with advantage ; for instance, 10. ....P—K 5 ;

11. P—K B 3, P—Q 4 ; 12. P×P,
Q P×P ; 13. Kt×P !, etc. ±

6.	......	B—Kt 5
7.	P—Q 4	P—Q Kt 4
8.	B—Kt 3	B—K 2
9.	B—K 3	......

Instead, the wing-demonstration
9. P—Q R 4 was quite in order.
The continuation selected leads to
a very complicated game in the
centre.

| 9. | ...... | Castles |
| 10. | Q Kt—Q 2 | P—Q 4 ! |

At this moment I felt that I had
been "lured" into a variation prepared beforehand by my opponent.
This is what happened : A few years
before the Berne Tournament—to be
exact in 1925—I gave in Basle a
time - handicap exhibition, with
clocks, against 10 first-class amateurs, where the following game,
*identical with the present one until
the 10th move of White inclusive*, was
played and published (because of
the instructive attack and the
pretty finish) in the Swiss Press as
well as in one of my German books :
Black : K. Meck. 10. ....Kt—
Q R 4 ; 11. B—B 2, P—B 4 ; 12.
P—K R 3, B×Kt ; 13. Q×B, Kt—
Q 2 ; 14. Q R—Q 1, Q—B 2 ; 15.
B—Kt 1, Q R—Q 1 ; 16. Q—Kt 3,
K R—K 1 ; 17. P—K B 4, Kt—
Q B 3 ; 18. B P×P, Q P×P ; 19. P—
Q 5, Kt—Q R 4 ; 20. Kt—B 3, Kt—
B 5 ; 21. B—R 6, P—Kt 3 ; 22. R—
B 2, B—B 1 ; 23. Q—R 4, B—K 2 ;
24. Kt—Kt 5 !, Kt—Q 3 ; 25. Q R—
K B 1, B×Kt ; 26. B×B, R—Q B 1;
27. R×P !, Kt×R ; 28. R×Kt,
P—K R 4 ; 29. R—B 3, R—
B 1 ; 30. R—Kt 3, R—B 2 ; 31.
B—K 7, K—R 2 ; 32. B—Q 3, P—
B 5 ; 33. B—K 2, Q—Kt 3 ch ; 34.
K—R 2, Kt—B 3 ; 35. P—Q 6,
R×B ; 36. Q×Kt !, R—K Kt 2 ;
37. B×R P, R (B 1)—K Kt 1 ; 38.

Q—R 4 !, P—Kt 4 ; 39. B—Kt 6
double ch, followed by mate in two.
It is certainly to the credit of the
talented Swiss master to have found
the exact spot where his country-
man went wrong, and to have
substituted for the harmless 10. ....
Kt—Q R 4 the promising central
action in the text ; and it can be considered as his bad luck that the
whole variation (as the present game
seems to prove) is still not quite
satisfactory in spite of the improvement. Anyhow, I had quite a few
minutes of anxiety before discover-
ing the way which finally assured
me the advantage.

| 11. | P×Q P | P×P |
| 12. | P×P | K Kt×P |

White has now to solve a double
problem : to free his K's Knight
from the unpleasant pin, and at the
same time to undertake necessary
measures in order to meet effec-
tively the threatening advance of
Black's K B's Pawn.

13. Q—Kt 1 !   ......

This is the hidden solution :
White intends to protect his Q's
Bishop through a counter-attack
against Black's central Knight.

13. ......   P—B 4

Not only an attack, but also a
defence against the possibility of
Q—K 4.

14. P—Q R 3 !   ......

Freeing the square Q R 2 (1) for
the Bishop in case of 14. ....Kt—
R 4 (2) for the Queen—if played
as in the actual game.

| 14. | ...... | K—R 1 |
| 15. | Q—R 2 | ...... |

Position after White's 15th move.

15. ......   K Kt—Kt 5 ! ?

Black continues to speculate, but will soon be forced to recognise that he has been outplayed in the battle for the central squares. Also after 15. ....Kt—Kt 3 ; 16. B—K 6 ! followed by P—Q 5, etc., White would easily have obtained the best of it.

16. P × Kt   Kt × Kt P
17. Q—Kt 1   P—B 5

The material equilibrium will be thus re-established, but not for long, as White's Knight at K 5 will exert a tremendous pressure.

18. Kt—K 5   B—K B 4

Or 18. .... B—R 4 ; 19. Q—K 4 ! P × B ; 20. P × P, B—B 3 ; 21. R—B 5 ! etc., with an overwhelming position.

19. Q—Q 1   P × B
20. P × P   Kt—Q 4
21. Kt—B 6 !   ......

The simplest, as it wins two minor pieces for a Rook by avoiding the middle-game complications. Not convincing would have been instead 21. R × B, R × R ; 22. P—K 4, because of 22. ....R × Kt, etc.—

but 21. Q—R 5, P—Kt 3 (not 21. ....Kt × P ? ; 22. R × B and wins) ; 22. Kt × P ch, B × Kt ; 23. Q × Kt, etc., was an equally pleasant alternative.

21. ......   Kt × P
22. Kt × Q   Kt × Q
23. Kt—B 6   B—Kt 4
24. K R × Kt !   ......

Instead, 24. Q R × Kt would—strangely enough—permit Black a convincing escape by means of 24. ....B—K 6 ch ! , 25. K—R 1 ; B × Kt ; 26. R × B, B—K 5 !, etc.

24. ......   B—K 6 ch
25. K—R 1   B—Kt 5
26. Kt—B 1   ......

Of course not 26. Kt—B 3, R × Kt ! etc.

26. ......   B × R
27. R × B   B—B 5
28. B—Q 5 !   ......

This Bishop's manœuvre prevents ....Q R—K 1—K 7.

28. ......   Q R—K 1
29. B—B 3   R—B 3
30. K—Kt 1   P—Kt 3

Obviously a loss of time if one compares this with the next move ; but in this position a *tempo* more or less cannot have any influence on the final outcome. If, for instance, 30. ....P—Kt 4, then 31. P—R 3, B—K 6 ch ; 32. Kt × B, R × Kt (K 6) ; 33. P—Q 5, R—Kt 6 ; 34. R—Q 2 with an easy technical job for White.

31. R—R 1   P—Kt 4
32. P—R 3   B—K 6 ch
33. Kt × B   ......

Of course not 33. K—R 1, P—K Kt 5 ! etc.

33. ......   R × Kt (K 6)

| 34. R × P | R—Kt 6 |
| 35. B—Q 5 ! | ...... |

The beginning of a successful mating attack.

35.	R × Kt P
36. R—R 8 ch	K—Kt 2
37. R—Kt 8 ch	K—R 3
38. Kt—K 5	K—R 4
39. R—Kt 7	K—R 5
40. K—R 2	P—R 3
41. B—B 3	R—Q 7
42. R—Kt 6 !	P—K Kt 5

Obviously forgetting to resign.

43. R × Kt P ch	K—R 4
44. R—Kt 3 disc. ch	K—R 5
45. Kt—Kt 6 ch	R × Kt
46. R × R	P—Kt 5
47. R—Kt 4 ch	K—R 4
48. K—Kt 3	R—Q 6
49. R—Kt 7 disc. ch	R × R ch
50. K × R	Resigns.

GAME 55

COLLE'S SYSTEM

Berne Tournament, July, 1932.

Black : S. FLOHR

1. P—Q 4	P—Q 4
2. Kt—K B 3	Kt—K B 3
3. P—K 3	......

This quiet move—the idea of which is to postpone the fight for the centre until White has brought his King into safety—procured the regretted Belgian champion a long series of brilliant victories. Its objective value had been already put in question by the variation 3. ....B—B 4 ; 4. B—Q 3, P—K 3 ! introduced by me at San Remo, 1930, against the same player and adopted since, for instance, by Dr. Euwe against me in a match game, 1935. The defence chosen

here by Flohr allows White to fulfil his plan of development.

3.	P—K 3
4. B—Q 3	P—B 4
5. P—B 3	Kt—B 3
6. Q Kt—Q 2	Q—B 2
7. Castles	B—K 2
8. Q—K 2	Castles
9. P—K 4	......

As I found out afterwards, this rather natural move had not been tried before. By adopting the usual 9. P × P, B × P ; 10. P—K 4, I would have been put in the not altogether pleasant position of having to fight against another innovation of mine (game against Gilg, Kecskemet, 1927)—namely, 10.....B—Q3!; 11. R—K 1, Kt—K Kt 5 ! etc., with about even prospects.

| 9. ...... | P × K P |

Unsatisfactory would be 9. .... P × Q P because of 10. P—K 5 !, Kt—Q 2 (or Kt—K R 4 ; 11. Kt—Kt 3 threatening P—Kt 4) ; 11. P × P, Kt—Q Kt 5 ; 12. B—Kt 5 !, P—Q R 3 ; 13. B—R 4±.

| 10. Kt × P | P × P |
| 11. Kt × P | ...... |

Not 11. P × P, as it is in White's interest to exchange the maximum of pieces able to attack his isolated Pawn.

| 11. ...... | Q Kt × Kt |
| 12. P × Kt | Kt × Kt |

Instead 12. ....Kt—Q 4 ; 13. Q—B 3 ! etc., would have led to a more complicated middle-game position. However, the text-move should have been sufficient for equality.

| 13. B × Kt | P—B 4 |

But from now on Flohr decidedly over-estimates his position, which he very seldom does. After the simple 12. ....B—Q 2 ; 13. Q—B 3, B—Q B 3, the natural outcome would have been a draw.

14. B—B 3   B—B 3

This move and the next one are the logical consequences of the unfortunate attempt to exploit the "weakness" at Q 4. Comparatively better was still 14. ....B—Q 2.

15. R—Q 1   R—Q 1
16. B—K 3   P—B 5 ?

Suicidal. But also after the comparatively better 16. ....P—K Kt 4 ; 17. P—K R 3, Q—Kt 2 ; 18. Q R—B 1, it would soon become evident that White's Q's Pawn could be captured only at the price of a further decisive compromising of Black's position.

17. Q R—B 1   Q—Q 3
18. B—Q 2   B × P

This Pawn is poisoned, as the answer shows. But also 18. .... R—Kt 1 ; 19. P—Q R 3 ! threatening 20. B—Q Kt 4, etc., was already practically hopeless.

19. B—Q R 5 !   R—Q 2

If the Rook leaves the Q's file, then 20. Q—B 4 ! wins immediately.

Position after Black's 19th move.

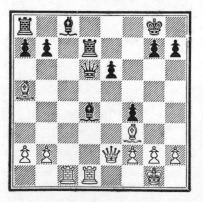

20. R × B !   ......

The convincing refutation of Black's ultra-materialistic tendencies in this game.

20. ......   Q × R
21. Q × P ch   R—B 2

After 21. ....K—B 1 ; 22. R—K 1, P—K Kt 3 ; 23. B—B 3 Black would lose the Queen.

22. R × B ch   R × R
23. Q × Q R ch   R—B 1
24. Q × P   R—K 1
25. P—K R 3   ......

But not 25. B—B 3 ? because of 25. ....Q × B !

25. ......   Q—B 4
26. B—B 3   Q—K 2
27. B—Q 5 ch   K—R 1
28. Q × Q   Resigns.

GAME 56

RUY LOPEZ

Pasadena Tournament, August, 1932.

Black : H. Steiner

1. P—K 4   P—K 4
2. Kt—K B 3   Kt—Q B 3
3. B—Kt 5   P—Q R 3
4. B—R 4   Kt—B 3
5. Castles   B—B 4

Having been for a period rather partial towards this move (cf. "My Best Games" 1908–1923), I must, to my regret, now admit that it is not quite sufficient against accurate play. And as 5. ....P—Q 3 has been recently also somewhat discredited, Black has been practically brought back to the old choice between the speculative 5. .... Kt × P and the cautious 5. ....B—K 2.

6. P—B 3	Kt×P
7. P—Q 4	B—R 2
8. Q—K 2	......

I decided to follow here the line of play adopted against me by Yates at Hastings, 1922; although White obtained in that game only a draw I hoped to find over the board some better moves than those made by Yates—but there actually happened to be none. Much better than the Queen's move is 8. R—K 1 (which is also more logical, as it brings a new piece into action), and if 8. ....P—B 4, then 9. Q Kt—Q 2, Castles; 10. Kt×Kt, P×Kt; 11. B—K Kt 5, followed by 12. R×P with a clear advantage.

8.	P—B 4
9. P×P	Castles
10. B—Kt 3 ch	K—R 1
11. Q Kt—Q 2	Q—K 1

An interesting idea à la Marshall: Black sacrifices 1—2 Pawns for a rapid development, after which White's position will, for a while, look somewhat critical. However, the attempt can, and will, be refuted; much to be preferred was therefore (as happened in the Hastings game mentioned) 11. .... P—Q 4; 12. P×P (e.p.) Kt×Q P; 13. Kt—B 4, P—B 5!; 14. Q Kt—K 5 (or 14. Kt×Kt, P×Kt!; 15. R—Q 1, B—Kt 5), Kt×Kt; 15. Kt×Kt, Q—Kt 4, etc., with fairly good prospects for Black.

12. Kt×Kt	P×Kt
13. Q×K P	P—Q 4!

The point of the first sacrifice—Black will develop his Q's Bishop with tempo.

| 14. B×P | ...... |

Better than 14. Q×P, B—Kt 5; 15. Kt—Kt 5, Kt×P, etc., with unpleasant threats.

14.	B—K B 4
15. Q—K R 4	Kt×P
16. B×P!	......

The only way to meet successfully Black's attack against K B 2. Unsatisfactory would be, instead, 16. Kt×Kt, Q×Kt; 17. B×P, because of 17. ....B—Q 6!; 18. B×R, B×P ch!; 19. K—R 1, Q—K 1! (stronger than 19. .... B×R; 20. Q—K 4!), etc., with a strong pressure of Black.

16.	R—Q Kt 1
17. Kt×Kt	R×B

If now 17. ....Q×Kt, then 18. B×P! parrying Black's main threat ....B—Q 6. This was the point of White's 16th move.

| 18. R—K 1! | ...... |

Black has no means of profiting by this momentary weakening of White's K B 2.

18.	R—Kt 4
19. Kt—B 3	Q—B 1
20. P—B 4	R—Kt 2
21. P—Q Kt 3	......

In connection with the next move a much more rapid solution than the passive 21. P—K R 3.

21.	B—Kt 5
22. B—R 3!	......

Practically forcing the reply which makes an end to Black's hopes on his diagonal Q R 2—K Kt 8.

22.	P—B 4

Of course not 22. ....R—B 3 because of 23. Q×B.

| 23. Kt—K 5 | ...... |

From now on White has an easy job.

23. .....   B—B 4
24. P—K Kt 4 !   ......

In order to force the Black Bishop to abandon the defence of White's K Kt 6.

24. ......   P—Kt 4

Despair.

25. B—Kt 2   ......

A spectacular move (25. ....P × Q ; 26. Kt—B 7 double ch, K—Kt 1; 27. Kt—R 6 mate)—but the simpler 25. Q—R 5 was also good enough. Not so convincing, on the contrary, would have been 25. Q × P, R—Kt 2 ; 26. B—Kt 2, K—Kt 1 ! etc.

25. ......   K—Kt 1

Hoping after 26. Q × Kt P ch, R—Kt 2, etc., to enter the last variation mentioned.

26. Q—R 5 !   B—K 3

Position after Black's 26th move.

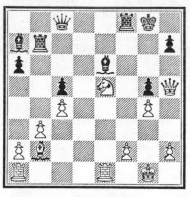

27. Kt—Q 7 !   ......

A kind of "pendant" to the final move of the Borochow-game (No. 117). In case of 27. ....Q × Kt,White forces the win like this : 28. Q × Kt P ch, K—B 2 ; 29. Q—B 6 ch,

K—Kt 1 ; 30. Q—R 8 ch !, K—B 2 ; 31. Q × P ch, K—K 1 ; 32. Q—Kt 6 ch, K—K 2 ; 33. Q R—Q 1 !, Q—B 3 ; 34. Q—Kt 5 ch, K—B 2 ; 35. Q—B 6 ch and mate in two.

Resigns.

GAME 57

KING'S FIANCHETTO

Folkestone Team Tournament, July, 1933.

Black : V. Mikenas

1. P—K 4   P—K Kt 3

This move is rightly considered as inferior, as it concedes White the full control of the central squares. It is, however, not quite easy for the first player to transform this advantage in space into a decisive one.

2. P—Q 4   B—Kt 2
3. Kt—Q B 3   P—Q 3
4. Kt—B 3   Kt—Q 2
5. B—Q B 4   P—K 3

By choosing this Pawn-structure, Black, strategically, prevents in this stage of the game a further advance of White's central Pawns, as both P—K 5, P—Q 4 or P—Q 5, P—K 4, would allow the second player to obtain later an initiative in the centre by means of ....P—Q B 4 or ....P—K B 4. White's strategy in the next stage of the game will consist, therefore, in restricting more and more—by leaving the central position intact—the already limited field of action of the enemy's pieces.

6. Castles   Kt—K 2
7. P—Q R 4 !   ......

A very important move in this kind of position, worthy to be noticed by the student. Its aim is either to prevent the fianchetto of Black's Queen's Bishop (P—Q Kt 3, P—Q R 5±) or induce Black to weaken — by answering ....P—Q R 4—his Q Kt 4.

7. ......   Castles
8. B—K 3   P—K R 3

Preventing 9. Q—Q 2, followed by B—K R 6, which would eliminate the only more or less active Black piece.

9. Q—Q 2   K—R 2
10. P—R 3   ......

In order not to count any more with the possibility ....Kt—B 3 and if P—K 5, then ....Kt—Kt 5, etc.

10. ......   P—Q B 3

This, obviously, weakens his square Q 3—a circumstance which, however, should not have had a decisive character. Besides, it is already extremely difficult to indicate a suitable plan of further development for Black.

11. B—D 4   P—Q 4

Also unsatisfactory was 11. .... P—K 4 ; 12. P×P, P×P (in case of retaking with pieces on K 4, Black would, after the exchange of Queens, finally lose his K B's Pawn). 13. B—K 3±. But by playing 11. ....Kt—Kt 3 ; 12. B—Q 3, P—Q R 4, Black could obtain a comparatively steadier position than after the compromising Pawn move in the text.

12. B—Q 3   P—R 3 ?

Black does not realise that his square Q 3 has to be protected at all costs. From now on, the dominating position of White's Q's Bishop will alone prove sufficient to decide the battle. Necessary was,

therefore, 12. ....Kt—B 3 (—K 1) with a playable game, although White would still find it easy to increase his pressure—for instance, by means of 13. P—R 5, etc.

13. B—Q 6   P—K B 4

Or 13. ....Kt—B 3 ; 14. P—K 5, Kt—K 1 ; 15. B—R 3, followed by P—R 4, etc., with an easy King's attack.

14. P—K 5   R—K Kt 1

Position after Black's 14th move.

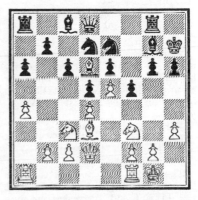

15. P—R 4   ......

White's overwhelming positional advantage allows him quietly to select the method he prefers for entering the enemy's not too well protected fortress. Besides the text-move, which inaugurates an irresistible plan (*status quo* on the King's side ; opening of a file on the other wing), he could also start a King's attack with the spectacular coup 15. Q—Kt 5, which, however, would not give any immediate results after the right answer 15. ....B—B 1, and if 16. Kt—K 2 (or 16. Q—R 4, P—K Kt 4; 17. Q—R 5, Kt—K Kt 3) then 16. .... R—Kt 2 with at least a temporarily sufficient defence.

15. ......   P—Kt 3 !

Preparing ....Kt—B 1, which here would be a mistake, because of 16. Q—Kt 5 ! etc. But from now on this Queen's move can be met by ....R—R 2 !

16. Kt—K 2   Kt—B 1
17. P—Q R 5   ......

Before breaking in, White weakens to a maximum the dark-coloured squares of Black's position ; the final section of the game will illustrate the usefulness of this procedure.

17. ......   P—Q Kt 4
18. P—K Kt 3 !   ......

In connection with the next two moves, a prophylactic manœuvre, by which White prevents once for all any serious attempt by Black to obtain an attack against his King.

18. ......   R—R 1
19. K—Kt 2   K—Kt 1
20. R—R 1   K—B 2

The King is no better here than at K R 2. But as Black is not yet in a mood to resign he has willy-nilly to move something . . .

21. Kt—B 4   R—K Kt 1
22. P—Kt 3   ......

After this, White's strategical scheme becomes quite obvious— there is no more defence against P—Q B 4 in connection with the opening of the Q Kt's or Q B's file.

22. ......   Kt—R 2
23. P—B 4   B—Q 2
24. Q R—Q B 1   B—K B 1
25. B—K 2 !   ......

Freeing the square Q 3 for the Knight, and at the same time preventing the advance of Black's K Kt's Pawn—for instance, 25.

....P—Kt 4 ? ; 26. R P×P, Kt× P ; 27. Kt×Kt ch, P×Kt (or R× Kt ; 28. Kt—R 3 followed by B— R 5 ch and wins) ; 28. B—R 5 ch, K—Kt 2 ; 29. Kt×P ch, B×Kt ; 30. Q×P ch, followed by mate.

25. ......   Kt—B 1
26. P×Q P   ......

It does not happen often that a game is strategically decided much before the first capture, which here signifies not the beginning, but practically the end of the fight.

26. ......   B P×P

Or 26. ....Kt×B ; 27. P×P ch, B×P ; 28. Kt×B, K×Kt ; 29. R× P and wins.

27. B×B   ......

The Bishop has done more than his duty and can now quietly disappear.

27. ......   Kt×B
28. R—B 5   Kt—Q R 2
29. Kt—Q 3   K—Kt 2

As a consequence of White's 18th-20th moves, the rejoinder ....P— Kt 4 would obviously be entirely in his favour.

30. K R—Q B 1   R—B 1
31. R×R   B×R
32. Q—B 3   ......

All the dark squares in Black's camp are as many open wounds. No wonder that he decides to try the following desperate diversion.

32. ......   K—R 2
33. Q—B 5   R—Kt 2
34. Q—Kt 6 !   ......

All very simple, but with deadly effect. The Knight, after having been brought to Q B 5, will undertake the execution.

34. ......   Q—K 2
35. Kt—B 5   P—Kt 4

At last ! But as the following convincingly proves, this attempt is now perfectly harmless.

36. P×P   P×P
37. Kt—K 1 !   ......

In order to meet 37. ....P—B 5 by 08. B—Kt 4 ! and 37. .... P—K Kt 5 by 38. Kt (K 1)—Q 3 followed by Kt—B 4.

37. ......   Kt—Kt 3
38. Kt (K 1)—Q 3 P—B 5
39. R—R 1 ch   K—Kt 1
40. B—Kt 4   P×P
41. P×P   ......

The agglomeration of forces on the K Kt's file is rather picturesque. Instead of the following "sacrifice," Black could as well resign.

41. ......   Kt—R 5 ch
42. P×Kt   P×P
43. Kt—B 2   R—B 2
44. Kt×K P   K—R 2
45. Q—Q 6   Resigns.

A strangulation game à la Rubinstein or Dr. Tarrasch of the early days.

GAME 58

RUY LOPEZ

Folkestone Team Tournament, July, 1933.

White : L. STEINER

1. P—K 4   P—K 4
2. Kt—K B 3   Kt—Q B 3
3. B—Kt 5   P—Q R 3
4. B—R 4   P—Q 3
5. P—B 3   B—Q 2
6. P—Q 4   Kt—B 3
7. Q—K 2   B—K 2
8. Castles   Castles

Threatening now 9. ....Kt×Q P.

9. B—Kt 3   Q—K 1

Right or wrong, this move is my invention, one of the ideas of which is to exert a frontal pressure on the K's file after ....B—Q 1. Before it gets called by the name of a particularly hospitable city or of a particularly generous patron of chess (as happened, for instance, with the "Kecskemet" move ....B—K 1) I suggest calling it the "Timbuktu" variation. At least this will be the author's choice.

10. Q Kt—Q 2   K—R 1 !

Black does not play yet 10. .... B—Q 1, as there is still a hope of utilising this piece in a more active way. With the move in the text he prepares eventually ....Kt—K Kt 1, followed by ....B—K B 3 or ....P—K B 3, etc.

11. P×P   ......

Not 11. Kt—B 4, because of 11. ....P×P; 12. P×P, P—Q 4, etc. But comparatively better is the simplifying variation 11. R—K 1, aiming at Kt—B 1—Kt 3, etc.

11. ......   P×P
12. Kt—B 4   B—Q B 4
13. P—Q R 4   ......

Interesting enough, this normal-looking move creates—as will be shown in the course of the game—a slight weakness at Q Kt 3. Preferable was 13. B—B 2 (threatening to gain space by means of 14. P—Q Kt 4, etc.), P—Q R 4 ; 14. B—K 3, etc., with about even prospects.

13. ......   P—Q R 4

Prophylactic. White's B—B 2 must not be accompanied by the expansion threat P—Q Kt 4 !

14. B—Kt 5 ......

A rather superficial developing move. Instead, 14. B—K 3 was still preferable.

14. ......   Kt—R 4 !

With this energetic reply (instead of the tame 14. ....Kt—K Kt 1, probably expected by White), Black obtains a solid initiative. White's comparatively best reply was now 15. K Kt × P, after which an endgame would be reached with better prospects for Black :—15. ....Kt × Kt ; 16. Q × Kt (not 16. Kt × Kt because of 16. ....Q × Kt followed by 17. ....P—K B 3, with the win of a piece), Kt × Kt ; 17. B × Kt— and now *not* 17. ....Q × P (as suggested by the annotators), but 17. ....P—K B 3 !; 18. Q × Q, K R × Q ; 19. B—K 3, B × B ; 20. P × B, R × P—with unpleasantness for White ; if, for instance, 21. B— Q 5, then R × K P ; 22. B × P, R—Q Kt 1 ; 23. K R—Q 1, B—K 1 etc., with a clear advantage. In view of these rather sad prospects, it is not altogether surprising that Steiner chose a risky counter-demonstration, the consequences of which were by no means easy to calculate.

15. Kt—R 4   Kt—B 5
16. Q—B 3   ......

If 16. B × Kt, P × B ; 17. Q—R 5, Black would have had the good reply 17. ....P—B 4 !

16. ......   P—B 3 !

This is the move which probably was underestimated by White ; after the following forced exchange, the Knight at R 4 will be exposed to attacks and the domination by Black of his K 4 will soon prove decisive.

17. B × Kt   P × B
18. Kt—B 5   P—K Kt 3 !

Wins an important *tempo* in

comparison with the immediate 18. ....P—K Kt 4.

19. Kt—R 6   P—K Kt 4
20. P—Kt 4   ......

Black threatened 20. ....Q— Kt 3 ; 21. Kt—Kt 4, P—R 4 and also—as it happens in the game— 20. ....B—K 3, etc.

20. ......   B—K 3

Planning 21. ....B × Kt ; 22. B × B, Kt—K 4 ; 23. Q—K 2, P—B 6.

21. Kt—Q 2   Kt—K 4
22. Q—R 3   R—Q 1
23. B × B   ......

If this Bishop could have been protected by the Q R's Pawn (compare the note to the 13th move of White), White would still have temporary defence in 23. Q R—Q 1. But now this move would simply be answered by 23. ....R × Kt, etc.

23. ......   Q × B
24. Kt—Kt 1   ......

If 24. Q R—Q 1, then 24. .... R—Q 6, followed by 25. ....K R— Q 1 would win a piece.

24. ......   R—Q 6
25. Q—R 5   ......

Position after White's 25th move.

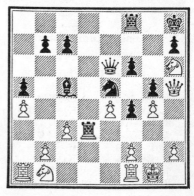

It is almost unbelievable that a position like this could occur in a modern master-game after 25 moves of a Ruy Lopez !

25. ......   Kt—B 6 ch

If now 26. K—R 1, then 26. .... Q×K P ; 27. Kt—B 7 ch, R×Kt ; 28. Q×R, Kt—R 5 disc. ch ; 29. P—K B 3 ; 30. Q×P ch, followed by mate in two.
Resigns.

GAME 59

QUEEN'S GAMBIT DECLINED (ORTHODOX DEFENCE)

Paris, October, 1933.

Black : J. CUKIERMANN

1. P—Q 4	P—Q 4
2. P—Q B 4	P—K 3
3. Kt—Q B 3	Kt—K B 3
4. B—Kt 5	B—K 2
5. P—K 3	Q Kt—Q 2

Nowadays (1939) 5. ....P—K R 3 is the fashion.

6. Kt B 0	Castles
7. R—B 1	P—Q Kt 3

This old-fashioned fianchetto defence cannot be considered quite satisfactory as Black will not be able to avoid some Pawn weaknesses in the centre.

8. P×P	P×P
9. B—Kt 5	......

The most logical way to exploit the slight weakness of Black's Queen's side. Instead, a "play for the attack" by posting this Bishop on the diagonal Q Kt 1—K R 7, would be quite out of place as Black's King position is for the moment perfectly safe.

9.	B—Kt 2
10. Castles	P—Q R 3
11. B—Q R 4	P—B 4 ?

This at first sight logical move finds here a decisive refutation. But also after the more cautious 11. ....R—B 1 and 12. B—Kt 3 ! etc., Black's position would remain unsatisfactory.

12. K B×Kt !   ......

Much more exact than 12. P×P, Kt×P, etc., with a playable game for Black, as it happened in a game Capablanca-Teichmann in 1913. If now 12. ....Q×B, then 13. P×P, P×P ; 14. Kt—Q R 4 ! with a decisive position advantage.

12.	Kt×B
13. B×B	Q×B
14. P×P	Q×B P

In order not to lose a Pawn immediately, Black is forced to expose his Queen dangerously—and this circumstance, added to the most unfortunate position of his Bishop, will enable White to discover without much difficulty the winning procedure.

15. Kt—Q 4   ......

Threatening 16. Q Kt—Kt 5, followed by 17. R—B 7, etc.

15.	Q R—B 1
16. Kt—B 5	K—R 1 !

A defence against the threat 17. Kt×Q P and at the same time a pitfall : namely, if 17. Kt×Kt P—hoping to win a Pawn after 17. .... K×Kt ; 18. Q—Kt 4 ch, etc.—then, 17. ....P—Q 5 ! ; 18. P×P, Q—K Kt 4, or 18. Q×P, Q×Q ; 19. P×Q, R—K Kt 1, etc., to Black's advantage.

17. Kt—K 2 !   ......

In order to force the exchange of Queens at Q 4 without alteration of the Pawn constellation. It is noteworthy how helpless Black's position will be in the following end-game !

17. ......   Q—Kt 5
18. Q—Q 4   Q × Q
19. Kt (K 2) × Q   R × R

Or 19. ....Kt—B 4; 20. Kt— Q 6, R—Q Kt 1; 21. P—Q Kt 4, etc. ±

20. R × R   Kt—B 4

Instead 20. ....R—B 1 ?; 21. R × R ch followed by 22. Kt—Q 6 would have lost a piece immediately.

21. Kt—Q 6   B—R 1

Again forced, as can easily be seen.

22. P—Q Kt 4   Kt—Q 6
23. R—B 7   ......

Of course not 23. Kt × P ch, K—Kt 1, etc. ∓

23. ......   K—Kt 1

Position after Black's 23rd move.

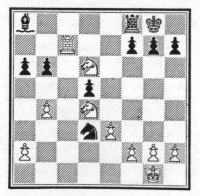

24. Kt—B 8 !   ......

After 24. P—Q R 3, Black could easily have saved his Bishop by playing 24. ....Kt—K 4 followed by ....Kt—B 5 after which a long resistance would be possible. With the text-move, White starts an attack against the unfortunate Bishop which is obviously unable to escape from its fate.

24. ......   Kt × Kt P
25. Kt × P   ......

Threatening 25. R—R 7, etc.

25. ......   R—Kt 1
26. Kt—Q 7   ......

But not 26. R—R 7, B—Kt 2 ; 27. Kt—Q 7, R—Q B 1 followed by 28. ....B—B 3 saving the piece.

26. ......   R—Q 1
27. P—Q R 3   Kt—Q 6
28. R—R 7   R—Q B 1
29. K—B 1   ......

After this 30. Kt—Kt 6 etc., is unavoidable.

Resigns.

GAME 60

RUY LOPEZ

Paris Tournament, October, 1933.

White : E. Znosko-Borovsky

1. P—K 4   P—K 4
2. Kt—K B 3   Kt—Q B 3
3. B—Kt 5   P—Q R 3
4. B—R 4   Kt—B 3
5. Castles   P—Q 3

Safer is first 5. ....B—K 2, as after the text-move White, according to the latest investigation, can obtain an advantage by continuing 6. B × Kt ch, P × B ; 7. P— Q 4, Kt × P ; 8. R—K 1, P—

K B 4 ; 9. P×P, P—Q 4 ; 10. Kt—
Q 4, P—B 4 ; 11. Kt—K 2 followed
by Kt—B 4, etc.

6. P—B 3	B—Q 2
7. R—K 1	B—K 2
8. P—Q 4	Castles
9. Q Kt—Q 2	B—K 1

This original move (the idea of
which is to keep the central position
intact by means of ....Kt—Q 2
and utilise—after P—K B 3—the
Q's Bishop on diagonal K 1—K R 4)
was introduced by me (after the
moves 9. ....K—R 1 ; 10. P—
K R 3) in my game against L.
Steiner in Kecskemet, 1927.

Afterwards it was baptised (not
by me) the Kecskemet Variation.
This denomination is illogical, inasmuch as ....B—K 1 is the key-
move not of a "variation" but of a
system !

The present game presents some
theoretical interest as it shows that
White, even if he is playing only for
a draw, cannot obtain an absolute
equality by liquidating the tension
in the centre after the move in text.

10. B×Kt	B×B
11. P×P	P×P
12. Kt×P	R×P
13. Kt×B	Q×Q !

A mistake would be 13. ....Kt×
Kt, because of 14. Kt—Q 7 ! etc.

14. Kt×Kt ch   ......

After 14. R×Q, Kt×Kt, there
would be still enough material left
for complicating the fight. After
the exchange of the Knights White
expect to reach a "dead draw"
position (14. ....B×Kt ; 15. R×
Q, B×Kt ; 16. B—K 3, etc.).
But ...

14. ......   P×Kt !

The only way—and an absolutely
safe one—to play "for the win."

15. R×Q   P×Kt

Position after Black's 15th move.

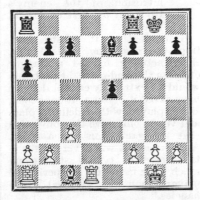

The end-game position thus
reached is by no means as easy to
conduct—especially for the first
player—as it looks. Black's plan
of campaign—which will prove a
complete success—is divided into
the following parts :—

(1) Exchange of one pair of
rooks.

(2) Bringing the King to K 8
where he will be protected
from a frontal attack by the
King's Pawn and be used to
prevent the entrance of the
remaining White Rook at
Black's Q 2.

(3) By operating with the Rook
on the open K Kt's file and
advancing the K R's Pawn,
force the opening of the
K R's file.

(4) After this the White King—
and eventually also the
Bishop—will be kept busy
in order to prevent the
intrusion of the Black Rook
at White's K R 1 or 2.

(5) In the meantime Black, by
advancing his Q R's and
Q Kt's Pawns will sooner or
later succeed in opening one
file on the Queen's side. And

(6) as at that moment the White
King will still be on the

other wing, the first player will not dispose of sufficient forces to prevent the final intrusion of the enemy's Rook on his first or second rank.

Granted that if White had, from the beginning, realised that there actually existed a danger of losing this end-game, he probably would by extremely careful defence have saved it. But as it happened, Black played with a definite plan, and White only with the conviction that the game must be a draw. And the result was a very instructive series of typical stratagems much more useful for inexperienced players than the so-called "brilliancies."

16. B—R 6   ......

Certainly not an error but a proof that White has not grasped as yet the spirit of the position. Otherwise he would not have been anxious to "force" the exchange of one pair of Rooks which, as mentioned, is quite welcome to the opponent.

| 16. ...... | K R—Q 1 |
| 17. K—B 1 | ...... |

A more aggressive line starting by 17. P—K Kt 4 would perhaps be advisable. But Black would also in this case maintain opportunities for complicating matters after 17. ....P—K B 3, followed by K—B 2 —K 3, etc.

17.	P—K B 4
18. R × R ch	R × R
19. P—K Kt 3	......

19. ....P—B 5 was a serious threat.

19.	K—B 2
20. B—K 3	P—K R 4
21. K—K 2	K—K 3
22. R—Q 1	R—K Kt 1

If now 23. P—K R 4, then 23. ....R—Kt 5 with the strong threat 24. P—B 5. White is therefore practically forced to allow the opening of the K R file.

23. P—B 3	P—R 5
24. B—B 2	P × P
25. P × P	R—K R 1
26. B—Kt 1	B—Q 3
27. K—B 1	......

In order to meet 27. ....P—K 5 by 28. P × P, P × P ; 29. K—Kt 2, etc.

| 27. ...... | R—K Kt 1 |
| 28. B—B 2 | P—Kt 4 ! |

Now Black shows his cards. In the event of White leaving his Pawn position on the Queen's side intact, the attacking plan would be .... P—Q B 4—B 5 followed by P—R 4 and P—Kt 5; his next Pawn move shortens the procedure.

29. P—Kt 3 ?	P—R 4
30. K—Kt 2	P—R 5
31. R—Q 2	......

In case of 31. P—Q Kt 4, the intention was 31. ....R—Q B 1 ; 32. B—B 5, R—Q R 1 ! followed by R—R 3,—B 3, etc.∓

| 31. ...... | P × P |
| 32. P × P | R—Q R 1 |

Thus Black has reached the position he aimed at when starting this end-game. His positional advantage from now on will prove sufficient for the victory, especially as he always can succeed in forcing the advance of his King by pinning the White Rook through the defence of one of the weak Pawns.

33. P—Q B 4   ......

Practically the only attempt, as 33. P—Q Kt 4, for instance, would

prove immediately fatal after 33.
....R—R 8 ; 34. R—Q 3, R—R 6,
etc.

33. ......   R—R 6 !

The winning course.

34. P—B 5   B—K 2
35. R—Kt 2   P—Kt 5
36. P—Kt 4   ......

One of the last resources: he tries
to create a passed Pawn which *may*
become a force in case of the exchange of the Bishops. But Black
does not need to hurry with that
exchange.

36. ......   P—B 5
37. K—B 1   R—R 8 ch
38. K—K 2   R—Q B 8

With the main object 39. ....
R—B 6 definitely pinning all
enemy's pieces. White's next
Rook's expedition is therefore
merely desperation.

39. R—R 2   R—B 6
40. R—R 7   K—Q 2
41. R—Kt 7   R × Kt P
42. R—Kt 8   R—Kt 7 ch
43. K—B 1   P—Kt 6
44. K—Kt 1   K—B 3
45. K—B 1   K—Q 4

Of course not 45. .... B × P ? ;
46. B × B, K × B ; 47. P—Kt 5,
etc., with drawing chances. But a
slightly quicker procedure was 45.
....P—K 5 ! ; 46. P × P, P—B 6,
etc.

46. R—Kt 7   P—K 5 !
47. P × P ch   K × P
48. R × B P   K—B 6
49. R × B   R × B ch
50. K—K 1   P—Kt 7
51. R—Q Kt 7   R—B 7
52. P—B 6 !   ......

A nice final joke : 52. ....R—
B 8 ch ; 53. K—Q 2, P—Kt 8
(Queen) ; 54. R × Q, R × R ; 55.

P—B 7, etc. But Black had exactly
calculated that his other passed
Pawn would force the win !

52. ......   K—Kt 6 !
53. P—B 7   P—B 6
54. K—Q 1   R × P
55. R × P   P—B 7
Resigns.

GAME 61

QUEEN'S GAMBIT DECLINED
(SLAV DEFENCE)

Second Match - Game, Baden-
Baden, April, 1934.

Black : E. BOGOLJUBOW

1. P—Q 4   Kt—K B 3
2. P—Q B 4   P—D 3
3. Kt—Q B 3   P—Q 4
4. P—K 3   P—K 3
5. B—Q 3   Q Kt—Q 2
6. Kt—B 3   P × P
7. B × B P   P—Q Kt 4
8. B—Q 3   P—Q R 3
9. Castles   ......

Nowadays the leading masters
consider that 9. P—K 4, P—B 4 ;
10. P—K 5, P × P ; 11. Kt × Kt P,
Kt × P ; 12. Kt × Kt, P × Kt ; 13.
Q—B 3 !, etc., is decidedly advantageous for White. But in 1934 the
13th move of White in this variation
had not yet been sufficiently considered and the Meran variations
shares stood pretty high. Therefore
the quiet move in text.

9. ......   P—B 4
10. P—Q R 4   ......

10. Q—K 2 played experimen-
tally instead of this in the games
Sämisch-Capablanca (Moscow,1925)
and Dr. Vidmar-Bogoljubow (Bled,
1931) brought to the first players—
at least in the opening stages—only
disappointment.

10.	P—Kt 5
11. Kt—K 4	B—Kt 2
12. Q Kt—Q 2	......

After his tame 9th move White has hardly any other way to complicate matters without disadvantage than this attempt to blockade the opponent's Q s side.

| 12. ...... | B—K 2 |

Black does not need to prevent the opponent's next move as he is sufficiently developed to start almost immediately a counter-action in the centre.

13. P—R 5	Castles
14. Kt—B 4	Q—B 2
15. Q—K 2	Kt—Kt 5

Black has obtained a fairly good position, but from now on begins to over-estimate his chances. Instead of the adventurous text-move, which finally leads to the win of a Pawn but allows the intrusion of the White Knight at Kt 6, with a powerful effect, he would have done better to simplify matters—for instance, by means of 15. .... B—K 5.

| 16. P—K 4 ! | ...... |

A surprise for Black who most likely expected only the half-suicidal 16. P—K Kt 3....

| 16. ...... | P×P |
| 17. P—R 3 | K Kt—K 4 |

To 17. ....K Kt—B 3 White would have answered 18. B—Kt 5, Kt—B 4 ; 19. Kt—Kt 6, Q R—Q 1 ; 20. Q R—B 1, Q—Kt 1 (these moves are recommended by Bogoljubow in the match book as the best ones for Black) and now not 21. P—K 5 ? (Bogoljubow) but 21. B×Kt !, P×B ; 22. R—B 4, P—K 4 ; 23. Kt—K R 4, etc., with an ample positional compensation for the minus Pawn.

18. K Kt×Kt	Kt×Kt
19. B—B 4	B—Q 3
20. B×Kt	B×B
21. Kt—Kt 6	......

The point of the sacrificial combination initiated by the 16th move. From now on the Knight will paralyse the whole Black's Queen's side.

| 21. ...... | R—R 2 |

In case of 21. ....Q R—Q 1 White would not have taken the Q R's Pawn at once, but would have first prevented the eventual advance of the Q's Pawn by playing 22. K R—Q 1 ! with a distinct positional advantage.

| 22. Q R—B 1 | Q—Q 3 |

Or 22. ....Q—Q 1 ; 23. Q—Q 2 !, B—Q 3 ; 24. P—B 4, etc. ±

| 23. R—B 4 | P—B 4 ? |

The opening of the K's file leads, owing to Black's multiple Pawn weaknesses, to a rapid catastrophe. But also the quieter 23. ....B—B 5 recommended by Bogoljubow is not satisfactory, as after 24. R—Q 1, P—K 4 ; 25. Q—K 1, etc., White would have regained the Pawn, still maintaining a strong pressure.

| 24. P×P | P×P |
| 25. R—K 1 ! | ...... |

The threat to change Queens at K 6 with an easily-won end-game now makes Black desperate, and he tries to elaborate a complicated attacking combination, which, however, is bound to fail because of the uselessness of his Q's Rook.

| 25. ...... | Q—Kt 3 |
| 26. P—B 3 | ...... |

Position after White's 26th move.

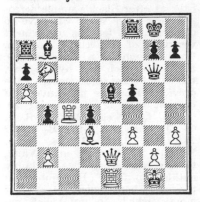

26. ......   R—K 1

In the event of Bishop's moves Bogoljubow gives the following variations :

I. 26. ....B—Kt 6; 27. Q—K 6 ch, K—R 1; 28. Q×Q, P×Q; 29. R—K 6, R—Q 1; 30. R×Kt P, P—B 5; 31. R—K 6.

II. 26. ....B—B 5; 27. R×Q P, Q—Kt 6; 28. B—B 4 ch, K—R 1; 29. Q—K 7—with a win for White in both eventualities.

27. P—B 4   Q—Kt 6
28. P×B   R×P
29. R—B 8 ch !   ......

The refutation.

29. ......   K—B 2
30. Q—R 5 ch   ......

The alternative 30. R—B 7 ch was not quite as elegant, but slightly more rapid; for instance, 30. .... K—Kt 3; 31. R×P ch ! or 30. ....K—Kt 1; 31. B—B 4 ch, K—R 1; 32. R—B 8 ch, followed by 33. Q×R,

30. ......etc.   P—Kt 3
31. Q×R P ch   K—B 3
32. R—B 8 ch   K—Kt 4
33. P—R 4 ch   K—B 5
34. Q—R 6 ch   P—Kt 4

35. R×P ch !   R×R
36. Q—Q 6 ch   K—Kt 5
37. B×R ch and mate in three.

GAME 62

QUEEN'S GAMBIT DECLINED (SLAV DEFENCE)

Fourth Match-Game, Villingen, April, 1934.

Black : E. BOGOLJUBOW

1. P—Q 4   P—Q 4
2. P—Q B 4   P—Q B 3
3. Kt—Q B 3   Kt—B 3
4. P—K 3   P—K 3
5. B—Q 3   Q Kt—Q 2
6. P—B 4   ......

Not a happy opening idea, as it enables Black to undertake quickly a successful action in the centre. Still, as the game actually developed, White had at one moment the opportunity to equalise without much difficulty.

6. ......   P×P

This, in connection with the next four moves, is a natural and good method of development.

7. B×B P   P—Q Kt 4
8. B—Q 3   B—Kt 2
9. Kt—B 3   P—Q R 3
10. P—Q R 4   ......

The idea of advancing this Pawn to Q R 5—analogous to the previous game—is, in this position, much too elaborate. The logical course was 10. Castles, P—B 4; 11. P—B 5, etc.

10. ......   P—Kt 5
11. Kt—K 2   P—B 4
12. Castles   B—K 2
13. P—R 5 ?   ......

And even now 13. P—B 5, K P × P; 14. B × B P, Castles ; 15. Kt—Kt 3 would have led to a colourful game with chances for both sides. After the move made, White can only hope, by careful play, to equalise.

13. ...... Castles
14. Kt—Kt 3 P—Kt 3 !

It was now vital to prevent 15. P—B 5.

15. Q—K 2 P × P
16. P × P ......

The isolation of the central Pawn is certainly a bold decision, but—as the course of the game shows—more apt to equalise the chances than the alternative 16. Kt × P, Kt—B 4, etc.

16. ...... Kt—Kt 1

Threatening to win a Pawn with impunity by 17. ....Kt—B 3.

17. Kt—K 5 ! ......

If 17. P—B 5 !? Black would hardly accept the piece sacrifice, as after 17. ....K P × P ; 18. B × B P, P × B ; 19. Kt × P White's threats would become too strong ; but by answering 17. ....B × Kt ; 18. Q × B, Q × P ch ; 19. K—R 1, Q Kt—Q 2 with the threat 20. .... Kt—K 4 Black would obtain the upper hand. After the text-move he would, on the contrary, get in great trouble by playing 17. .... Q × P ch ; 18. B—K 3 followed by 19. Kt—B 4 or K R—Q 1, etc. ±

17. ...... Kt—B 3 !

Doubtless the right answer, which definitely annihilates White's attacking hopes. The following exchange is practically forced.

18. Kt × Kt B × Kt
19. B—B 4 ? ......

But this is decidedly too optimistic, as after Black's simple defensive next move White will have no compensation for the permanent weakness of his central position. Good enough for a draw was 19. B × R P—which was, by the way, the only logical consequence of the previous Knight's manœuvre. If in that case 19. ....R × B ; 20. Q × R, Q × P ch ; 21. K—R 1, Q—Q 4, then 22. Q—K 2, B—Kt 4 ; 23. Q—B 3, B × R ; 24. Q × Q, Kt × Q ; 25. Kt × B ; and White, to say the least, has certainly nothing to fear. Bogoljubow in the match-book indicates two other moves, which, in my belief, are equally harmless. They are (a) 19. ....R—R 2, which can be answered by 20. R—Q 1, Q—R 1 ; 21. B—Kt 5 ; (b) 19. ....Kt—Kt 5, after which White would even obtain a sort of counter-attack by means of 20. Q × Kt, R × B (or Q × P ch ; 21. K—R 1, R × B ; 22. Q—K 2, followed by 23. B—K 3, etc.) ; 21. P—B 5 ! etc.

19. ...... B—Kt 2
20. B—K 3 Q—Q 3

Dr. Lasker, in his excellent booklet about this match, claims (in my opinion quite correctly) that Black has already a strategically won position ; besides he also tries to prove that *a forced win* could be obtained here by means of 20. .....Kt—Q 4, and gives with that line of play variations going as far as the 35th move ! But, strangely enough, in doing so he does not take in consideration the simple move that I would certainly have made in answer to 20. ....Kt—Q 4. This move is 21. Kt—K 4, eventually followed by Kt—B 5, etc. And it is more than probable that Bogoljubow did not select the otherwise natural 20. .... Kt—Q 4 because he did not want to permit the unhappily placed White Knight to take an active part in the battle.

21. Q R—Q 1	K R—K 1
22. P—Kt 3	......

As both White's Q's Bishop and Knight have no future, he wants at least to strengthen the position of his other Bishop ; moreover, the text-move, as will be seen, facilitates the protection of the Q R's Pawn.

22.	B—K B 1
23. R—Q 3	......

Owing to his numerous weaknesses White is reduced to a complete passivity. Luckily for him, Black does not prove to be equal to the situation either strategically or tactically.

23.	Q—B 2
24. Q—R 2	B—Q 3
25. B—Q 2	Q—B 3

The pressure against White's K Kt 2 is extremely painful for the first player—and would become even more so if Black had not deliberately removed his Queen from this dominating position (see 29th move)....

26. B—K 1	Q R—Q 1
27. R—Q 2	R—K 2

A strange move. Why not the obvious 27. ....B—Kt 1 followed by 28. ....B—R 2 ?

28. Q—Kt 2	R—Q 2
29. R—Q B 2	......

"A tactical mistake," says Dr. Lasker. But in this desperate position I would be curious to see the move which by subsequent analysis would not appear a "tactical mistake" ! In other words, White was lost whatever he played.

29.	Q—Q 3 ?

As White was not threatening anything there was no reason to delay matters. 29. ....Kt—Kt 5 ! would have won at least a Pawn by a still dominating position.

This game—more than any other —proves how useless from the sporting point of view was the arrangement of this second match, and at the same time explains my indifferent play on a number of occasions. I felt sure that Bogoljubow was no longer able to take advantage of the opportunities my play might present to him, and— very unfortunately for the general artistic value of the present match— the score 7 to 1 in my favour after the 22nd game, fully justified my sanguine outlook.

30. Kt—K 2	......

At last the poor Knight begins to contribute to the defence ; but White's prospects still remain pretty dark.

30.	Kt—Q 4
31. Q—B 1	B—Q 1
32. B—Kt 3	Q—K 2

Bogoljubow claims—and probably he is right—that 32. ....Q— B 3 would have led to favourable complications for Black ; but also the simple 32. ....P—B 4 was good enough. On the other hand, the Queen's manœuvre, inaugurated by the text-move, only leads to the exchange of Queens and thus relieves White from the worry about his K Kt 2. An unhappy strategy !

33. R—R 2	Q—B 3
34. Q—Q 2	Q—B 4
35. B—Q 3	Q—B 3
36. B—B 4	B—K 2
37. Q—Q 3	R—K B 1
38. B—K 1	Q—B 4
39. Q—Q 2	Q—K 5

At last deciding to simplify matters, and thus implicitly admitting that in the last 20 moves absolutely nothing has been achieved.

40. B—Q 3	Q—K 6 ch
41. B—B 2	Q × Q
42. R × Q	......

The position thus reached is naturally still in Black's favour. But to win, it would require the end-game art of a Lasker or a Capablanca of the old days, even considering the fact that the game was adjourned here. But if the game is not easy to win for Black it is difficult to imagine how he can lose it.

42.	R—B 1
43. B—B 4	K—Kt 2
44. P—Kt 3	......

The possibility of this defensive move is the result of the disappearance of the Queens, as before that a further weakening of the diagonal K R 1—Q R 8 would have proved rapidly fatal.

| 44. ...... | R (B 1)—Q 1 |
| 45. R—B 1 | P—R 3 |

The beginning of a dangerous plot—against his own position. Instead 45. ....Kt—B 6 ! would still keep the positional advantage.

| 46. B—Q 3 | P—B 4 |
| 47. R (Q 2)—B 2 | P—Kt 4 ? |

As the surprising answer shows, this advance leads at best only to equality. But 47. ....K—B 2, suggested afterwards by Bogoljubow, would not prove effective, as White could in that case play, for instance, 48. K—B 1 eventually followed by Kt—Kt 1—B 3—K 5, etc.

| 48. P—Kt 4 ! | ...... |

Black could not well accept the Pawn's sacrifice thus offered—for instance 48. ....P × Kt P ; 49. P—B 5 !, K—B 2 ; 50. P × P ch, K × P ; 51. Kt—Kt 3 followed by 52. R—K 1 ch, etc. ± But he could—and should—play 48. ....P × B P ; 49. P × P, K—B 2, etc., with about a balanced position.

| 48. ...... | Kt × P ? |

This exchange of his best-posted piece against the cripple at K R 2 definitely spoils Black's position. It is interesting to observe from now on the joyous revival of all White's pieces, which for hours were hardly able to move.

| 49. Kt × Kt | P × Kt |
| 50. P × P | P—K 4 |

In the vain hope that White will be satisfied with Bishops of different colours after 51. P × P followed by 52. P—B 6 ch, etc.

| 51. R—K 1 ! | P × P |

Not foreseeing the following pretty combination. His only chance of salvation was 51. .... B—K B 3, which White would have answered by 52. R—B 4 !, P × P ; 53. R × Kt P, etc., with much the better prospects.

Position after Black's 51st move.

52. R×B ch!   ......

The unexpected point of this at first sight harmless transaction is the inevitable promotion of the K B's Pawn. As it is easy to see, Black has from now on an absolutely fixed line of play.

52. ......   R×R
53. B—R 4   K—B 2

Otherwise 54. P—B 6 ch.

54. B×R   K×B
55. R—B 7 ch   R—Q 2
56. P—B 6 ch   K—K 1
57. B—Kt 6 ch !   ......

More exact than 57. P—B 7 ch, R×P ; 58. B—Kt 6, B—Q 4, etc.

57. ......   K—Q 1
58. P—B 7   K×R
59. P—B 8=Q   P—B 6
60. Q×Kt P   R—Q 3
61. B—Q 3   Resigns.

GAME 63

BENONI'S DEFENCE

Ninth Match-Game, Pforzheim, April, 1934.

White : E. BOGOLJUBOW

1. P—Q 4   P—Q B 4

I consider the choice of this move (which in consequence of my success in the actual game became for a time a sort of fashion) as one of my chess sins. Because if a champion, being human, cannot sometimes help adopting inferior opening moves, he must at least avoid those which he himself considers as not quite satisfactory.

2. P—Q 5   P—K 4
3. P—K 4   P—Q 3
4. P—K B 4   ......

This decidedly premature rejoinder can only be explained by the fact that Bogoljubow had again missed a win in the previous game, and was particularly anxious to make a better show in this one. A natural and good line is, instead, 4. Kt—Q B 3 and in case of 4. .... P—Q R 3 ; 5. P—Q R 4 followed by Kt—B 3—Q 2—B 4, etc., which would secure to White the initiative for a long time.

4. ......   P×P
5. B×P   Q—R 5 ch

It was hardly worth while to provoke the weakening move P—K Kt 3 at the cost of a development *tempo.* The simple 5. ....Kt—K 2 followed by ....Kt—Kt 3, etc., would keep the control on K 4, with a fairly good game.

6. P—Kt 3   ......

The Pawn's sacrifice 6. B—Kt 3 would not be correct because 6. ....Q×P ch; 7. B—K 2, R—R 4, etc.

6. ......   Q—K 2
7. Kt—Q B 3 ?   ......

It was essential to prevent Black's following move by 7. Kt—K B 3! after which 7.....Q×P ch, 8. K—B 2, etc., would be too risky ; Black would play instead 7. .... B—Kt 5 ; 8. Kt—B 3, P—Q R 3, followed by .... Kt—Q 2, etc., with about even chances.

7. ......   P—K Kt 4 !

The strong position of his K's Bishop on the long diagonal secures Black, from now on, an easy, pleasant game.

8. B—K 3   Kt—Q 2
9. Kt—B 3   P—K R 3
10. Q—Q 2   ......

Aimless would have been instead
10. Kt—Kt 5, K—Q 1 ! etc.

10. ......   K Kt—B 3
11. Castles   Kt—Kt 5
12. B—K 2   ......

Also 12. B—R 3—recommended
by Bogoljubow—Kt × B ; 13. Q ×
Kt, B—Kt 2, etc., would not have
relieved White of his troubles.

12. ......   B—Kt 2
13. K R—B 1   Kt × B

It was certainly tempting to add
the advantage of the two Bishops
to that already acquired. But as
the Knight at Kt 5 was well posted
and White's Q's Bishop for the time
being was harmless, the immediate
13. ....P—R 3 was possibly even
more consequent.

14. Q × Kt   P—R 3
15. Kt—K Kt 1   P—Kt 4
16. Q R—K 1   B—Kt 2
17. Kt—Q 1   ......

This Knight must be brought to
K B 5—the only strong point of
White's position.

17. ......   Castles (Q R)
18. B—Kt 4   ......

As the Bishop has not many
prospects its exchange against the
dangerous black Knight can hardly
be criticised.

18. ......   K—Kt 1
19. B × Kt   R × B
20. Q—Q 2   ......

Again the natural consequence of
the manœuvre started by his 17th
move.

20. ......   P—K Kt 5 !

Immobilising White's King's
Knight and thus securing the important square K 4 for the Queen.

21. Kt—K 3   Q—K 4
22. P—B 3   P—K R 4
23. Kt—B 5   B—K B 3

Position after Black's 23rd move.

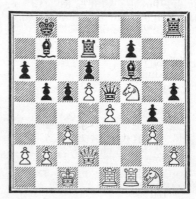

24. Q—B 4 ?   ......

The exchange of Queens transforms a difficult, but by no means
hopeless, position (White could,
for instance, try 24. K—Kt 1
as a preparation for 25. Kt—R 4)
into a lost one.

It is interesting that Bogoljubow
is rather prone to make this
mistake ; for instance, in the 11th
game of the same match, in
the position reached after Black's
34th move, namely :—

White (Bogoljubow) : *K* : K Kt 1,
Q : Q B 4, *RR* : Q 1 and Q 3,
Kt : K Kt 3, *PP* : Q R 4, K 3, K B 2,
K B 4, and K R 4. *Black* (Dr.
Alekhine) : *K* : K R 1, *Q* : K B 3,
RR : Q Kt 7 and K B 1, *B* : Q B 4,
PP : Q R 4, Q 3, K B 4, K Kt 3
and K R 4—instead of trying a
counter-attack, with an uncertain
result, by means of 35. Q—R 6,
he preferred to exchange Queens :
35. Q—B 3 ?, Q × Q ; 36. R × Q,
R—R 7 ; 37. R—B 4, R—Q Kt 1
—and had to resign after a few
more desperate moves.

About the same thing, if not in
quite such typical form, occurred in
the 5th and 22nd games of our first

match (see Part II). But also—strangely enough—my other match opponent, Dr. Euwe, has the same peculiar tendency to exchange Queens at inappropriate moments : compare, for instance, the 7th and 24th games of the 1935 match, the second match game and especially the third exhibition game of 1937.

I am mentioning these coincidences by no means in order to put undue blame on my opponents, but merely to remind the average amateur how particularly difficult the question of an opportune Queen's exchange is, and how much attention this question deserves. If even the leading exponents of our game are often inclined to fail rightly to appreciate their end-game chances, what, really, is to be expected from the "di minores" ?

| 24. ...... | Q × Q |
| 25. P × Q | R (Q 2)—Q 1 ! |

Threatening to dislodge the Knight at K B 5, whose position has been weakened through the obstruction of the K B's file by a Pawn. Besides his other advantages Black has now also got the Pawn majority on the opposite wing to the White King. The game is strategically over.

| 26. P—B 4 | ...... |

This attempt to find another safe square (Q B 4) for the Knight will be refuted by Black's 27th move. But otherwise 26. ....B—B 1, etc., would rapidly prove fatal for White.

26.	P × P
27. Kt—K 3	P—B 6 !
28. P—Kt 3	B—Q 5
29. Kt—B 4	P—B 4 !

Bringing at last the second Bishop into activity, after which White might as well resign.

| 30. P—K 5 | P × P |

31. P × P	B × Q P
32. R × P	Q R—K B 1
33. R × R ch	R × R
34. P—K 6	R—K 1
35. P—K 7	Q B × Kt
36. P × B	B × Kt
37. R × B	R × P
38. P—K R 3	P × P
39. K—B 2	P—R 7
40. R—Kt 1 ch	R—Kt 2
41. R—K R 1	R—Kt 7 ch
42. K × P	R × P
43. K—Q 3	K—B 2
44. K—K 4	K—B 3
45. K—B 5	P—R 4
46. K—Kt 5	P—Q R 5
Resigns.	

GAME 64

RUY LOPEZ

Sixteenth Match-Game, Bayreuth, May, 1934.

Black : E. BOGOLJUBOW

1. P—K 4	P—K 4
2. Kt—K B 3	Kt—Q B 3
3. B—Kt 5	P—Q R 3
4. B—R 4	Kt—B 3
5. B × Kt	Q P × B

I believe Bogoljubow is right in stating that 5. ....Kt P × B is an even more convincing answer to the rather artificial fifth move of White. As a matter of fact, I chose in this game the exchange variation of the Lopez chiefly because, although playing with the White pieces, I did not cherish any particular ambitions ; as a consequence of the match arrangements I had spent the whole previous night in travelling by car from Munich to Bayreuth and felt hardly fit for intensive mental work.

| 6. Kt—B 3 | B—Q 3 |
| 7. P—Q 3 | P—B 4 |

8. P—K R 3	B—K 3
9. B—K 3	P—R 3
10. P—Q R 4 !	......

If immediately 10. Kt—Q 2, then 10. .... P—Q Kt 4 ; 11. P—Q R 4, P—B 3, etc. But now White "threatens" to obtain an absolutely safe position by means of Kt—Q 2—B 4, etc.

10.	P—B 5 (?)

By opening the position in the centre at this particular moment Black only increases the activity of the opponent's pieces. A reasonable manœuvre, instead, would be 10. .... Kt—Q 2 followed by .... Kt—Kt 1—B 3, etc.

11. P—Q 4	P × P

If 11. .... B—Q Kt 5, then 12. P—Q 5. ±

12. B × Q P	B—Q Kt 5
13. Castles	P—B 3 (?)

A strange move which weakens his Q Kt 3 without any necessity. He should, instead, castle and would probably obtain a draw after 14. P—K 5, B × Kt ; 15. B × B, Kt —Q 4 ; 16. Q—Q 2, etc.

14. P—K 5	Kt—Q 4

Now practically forced, as 14. .... B × Kt ; 15. P × Kt !, B × B ; 16. Kt × B, Q × P ; 17. Kt × B, P × Kt ; 18. Q—R 5 ch ! followed by 19. Q—Q B 5, etc., would have been decidedly to White's advantage.

15. Kt—K 4	Kt—B 5

A lesser evil was 15 .... Castles.

16. B—B 5 !	......

The logical exploitation of the weak dark-coloured squares of Black's position.

16.	B × B
17. Q × Q ch	R × Q
18. Kt × B	P—Q Kt 3 ?

A miscalculation. Necessary was 18. .... R—Q Kt 1, although after 19. Kt × B, Kt × Kt (P × Kt is not better) ; 20. P—R 5 ! (threatening both 21. R—R 4 and 21. Kt—Q 2, etc.) his position would remain anything but pleasant.

19. Kt—Kt 7 ?	......

Black's R's Pawn was by no means poisoned and its capture would prove rapidly decisive. For instance, 19. Kt × P, B—B 1 ; 20. Kt—B 7 ch, K—Q 2 ; 21. Kt—R 8 (this is the move I overlooked in my calculations), Kt—Q 4 ; 22. P—R 5 (also 22. K R—Q 1 is good enough), P × P ; 23. R × P, B—Kt 2; 24. R—R 7, R—Q Kt 1 ; 25. R—K 1 !, P—Q B 4 ; 26. P—K 6 ch, and Black would obviously not succeed in capturing the adventurous Knight. After the timid textmove Black temporarily recovers.

19.	R—Q 2
20. Kt—Q 6 ch	K—K 2
21. Kt—Q 4	B—Q 4
22. P—K Kt 3 !	......

The value of this bold move—by making which White, after having missed the win at his 19th move, played only for a draw—has been completely misapprehended by the critics—Bogoljubow, Nimzowitsch, Dr. Lasker and others. They all claim that White, without any necessity, is taking chances and should now get into difficulties. In reality (a) *the defences of the K Kt's Pawn would prove unsatisfactory* as (I) 22. P—K B 3 would be answered by 22. .... P—Kt 3 ! threatening both 23. .... P—Q B 4 and 23. .... P—B 3 ; (II) after 22. Kt (Q 6)—B 5 ch, K—B 1 Black would again threaten 23. .... P—Q B 4, etc. ; (III) in the event of 22.

Kt (Q 4)—B 5 ch, Black would be perfectly entitled to play 22. .... K—K 3 !; 23. Kt×P ch, K× P and if 24. Kt (Q 6)—K 8 then simply 24. .... Kt × P ! etc., with advantage. (*b*) *After the acceptance of the sacrifice by the opponent, White, even by an adequate defence, would have no trouble in obtaining a draw.*

22.	Kt × P ch
23. K—R 2	Kt—Kt 4
24. P—B 4	Kt—K 5
25. Kt (Q 6)—B 5 ch	K—Q 1 ?

Playing for a counter-attack and obviously not taking into consideration the interesting 27th move of White. Necessary was 25. .... K— B 1, which would be answered by 26. Kt—K 3, K—Kt 1 ; 27. P—B 5, K—R 2 ; 28. P—K 6, etc., with an ample compensation for the minus Pawn.

| 26. Kt × Kt P | P—B 3 |
| 27. Q R—Q 1 ! | ...... |

The *tempo* thus gained (27. .... R × Kt ? ; 28. Kt—K 6 ch) secures White a net, if not yet a decisive, advantage.

| 27. ...... | K—B 1 |
| 28. Kt (Q 4)—B 5 | P × P |

The alternative 28. ....R— Kt 1 would also have left White with the better end-game chances : for instance, 29. Kt—R 5, P × P ; 30. P × P, R—K 1 ; 31. Kt—B 6 !, Kt × Kt ; 32. P × Kt, R—K 7 ch ; 33. K—R 3, and now either (A.) 33. ....B—K 3 ; 34. P—K Kt 4, B × Kt ; 35. P × B, or (B.) 33. ....B— Kt 7 ch ; 34. K—Kt 4, B × R ; 35. R × R, K × R ; 36. P—B 7, R—K 1 ; 37. P × R (Q) ch, K × Q ; 38. P— B 3 ! followed by Kt × P, etc.— both to White's advantage.

| 29. P × P | R—Kt 1 ? |

After the previous exchange this move is already a decisive mistake, instead of which 29. ....Kt—Kt 4 ; 30. R × B !, R × R (better than P × R ; 31. P—K 6 ±) ; 31. Kt—K 7 ch, K—Q 2 ; 32. Kt × R, P × Kt ; 33. R—B 6, R—K Kt 1, etc., still offered chances of salvation.

Position after Black's 29th move.

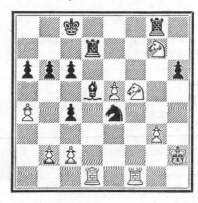

| 30. P—K 6 ! | ...... |

This short, sharp combination with a promotional point is a true pendant to the final attack of the fourth game.

30.	R (Q 2) × Kt
31. Kt × R	R × Kt
32. R × B	......

The Bishop must be eliminated as he protects Black's K B 2.

32.	P × R
33. R—B 8 ch	K—B 2
34. R—B 7 ch	K—Q 3

A sad necessity, as after 34. .... R × R ; 35. P × R, this Pawn could not be stopped.

35. R × R	K × P
36. R—Kt 6 ch	K—K 4
37. K—Kt 2	......

The black Pawns will not run away !

37.	......	P—Kt 4
38.	P—R 5	P—Q 5
39.	R×Q R P	P—Kt 5
40.	K—B 3	P—B 6
41.	P×P	Kt P×P
42.	R—K 6 ch !	K×R
43.	K×Kt	Resigns.

GAME 65

QUEEN'S GAMBIT ACCEPTED

Seventeenth Match-Game, Kissingen, May, 1934.

White : E. Bogoljubow

1.	P—Q 4	P—Q 4
2.	P—Q B 4	P×P
3.	Kt—K B 3	Kt—K B 3
4.	Kt—B 3	......

Unusual, but playable. The logical course is, however, the immediate regain of the Gambit Pawn (4. P—K 3 followed by 5. B×P).

4.	......	P—Q R 3
5.	P—K 4 ?	......

But this is merely an adventure, which could be selected only by a player who had already but little to lose (the state of the match was at that moment 5 to 1 in my favour). Necessary was 5. P—Q R 4 followed by 6. P—K 3, etc.

5.	......	P—Q Kt 4

Of course ! As Black has no really weak spots the following attacking moves of White are easy to meet.

6.	P—K 5	Kt—Q 4
7.	Kt—Kt 5	P—K 3
8.	Q—B 3	......

Also 8. Q—R 5, Q—K 2, etc., would prove harmless.

8.	......	Q—Q 2
9.	Kt×Kt	P×Kt
10.	P—Q R 3	......

It is most certainly unpleasant to be compelled to make such defensive moves while in material disadvantage ; but the threat 10. ....B—Kt 5 ch was too strong.

10.	......	Kt—B 3
11.	B—K 3	Kt—Q 1

As the following shows, this relieves the Queen of the defence of the Queen's Pawn.

12.	B—K 2	Q—B 4 !

Because if 13. Q×P ? then 13. ....B—Kt 2 wins the Queen.

13.	Q—Kt 3	P—R 3
14.	Kt—R 3	......

Or 14. Kt—B 3, Q—Kt 5, etc.

14.	......	P—Q B 3

Prepares the following successful escapade.

15.	P—B 4	Q—B 7 !
16.	Q—B 2	......

Apparently defending everything, as both 16. ....Q×P ; 17. Castles, or 16. ....P—B 6 ; 17. P—Q Kt 4 !, etc., would be dangerous for Black. But there is a big surprise coming.

Position after White's 16th move.

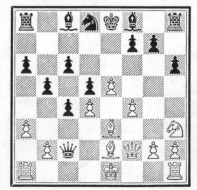

16. ......   B×P !

It becomes more and more difficult to find original combinations in chess, especially in the earlier stages of the game. This, I think, is one of them : although the Bishop's move *has* been made in analogous positions (for instance, with White's Pawn at Q R 2 and his Bishop at Q B 1) it has not, to my knowledge, ever before been combined with the idea of a Rook's capture after R × B, Q × Kt P, etc.

17. Castles   ......

There is no choice, as 17. R × B, Q × P, 18. R—R 5, Q—Kt 5 ch ; 19. B—Q 2, P—B 6, etc., would lose rapidly.

17. ......   B × P
18. Q R—K 1   B—B 4

The idea of posting this Bishop at K 5 and of castling (Q's side) afterwards is doubtless good enough. But with Black's overwhelming material advantage (three Pawns !) he had every reason to simplify matters : 18. .... B × Kt ; 19. P × B, Kt—K 3, and if 20. P—B 5, Kt—Kt 4, etc., would probably settle matters even more quickly.

19. P—Kt 4   B—K 5
20. P—B 5   Kt—Kt 2
21. Kt—B 4   ......

If 21. Q—R 4—in order to prevent Black's next move—the answer 21. .... P—B 4 ! would be very strong.

21. ......   Castles (Q R) !
22. Q—Kt 3   P—Kt 4

One of the easiest methods, as White's activity on the K B's file will be rapidly paralysed by the still threatening (and unavoidable) counter-attack .... P—Q B 4.

23. P × P (*e.p.*)   P × P
24. B—Q 1   Q—B 6
25. Kt—K 6   Q R—K 1
26. R—B 6   R—K 2
27. Q R—B 1   K R—K 1
28. Kt—B 4   ......

After 28. Kt—B 5, Kt × Kt ; 29. R × P ch, K—Kt 2 ; 30. R × Kt, the Queen's sacrifice 30. .... Q × P !, etc., would make an end.

28. ......   Kt—Q 1
29. Q—B 2   ......

Or 29. Kt × Kt P, B × Kt ; 30. R × B, P—B 4 !, etc., winning easily.

29. ......   Q—R 6
30. B—B 3   B × B
31. Q × Q B   P—Kt 4
32. Kt—K 2   R—K 3
33. R—B 5   Q—Q 6
34. P—R 4   R—Kt 3
35. P—R 5   R (Kt 3)—K 3
36. Q—B 2   P—B 4 !

At last !

37. R—B 3   Q—D 7
38. Q—K 1   Kt—B 3
39. R (B 1)—B 2   Q—K 5
40. Kt—Kt 3   Q × Kt P
41. K—Kt 2   B × P
Resigns.

GAME 66

QUEEN'S GAMBIT ACCEPTED
(IN FACT)

Twenty-fifth Match-Game, Berlin, June, 1934.

White : E. BOGOLJUBOW

1. P—Q 4   P—Q 4
2. P—Q B 4   P—Q B 3
3. Kt—K B 3   P × P

An unusual line of play (instead of 3. .... Kt—B 3) which is certainly not refuted in the present game.

4. P—K 3	B—Kt 5
5. B×P	P—K 3
6. Kt—B 3	......

Bogoljubow thinks that he could here get some end-game advantage by continuing 6. Q—Kt 3, Q—Kt 3 ; 7. Kt—K 5 ; yet after 7. ....B—K B 4; 8. Kt—Q B 3, Kt—B 3; 9. P—B 3, K Kt—Q 2 !, etc., there would not have been much to expect for White.

6.	Kt—Q 2
7. P—K R 3	B—R 4
8. P—R 3	......

Very slow. But as Black does not plan any action in the centre such preventive moves cannot be criticised.

8.	K Kt—B 3
9. P—K 4	B—K 2
10. Castles	Castles
11. B—B 4	P—R 4

As White is, for the time being, stronger in the centre, Black undertakes a diversion on the Q's wing. Its result will be the exchange of a couple of pieces which will gradually relieve his somewhat cramped position.

12. B—Q R 2	Q—Kt 3
13. P—K Kt 4	B—Kt 3
14. Q—K 2	Q—R 3 !
15. Q—K 3	......

The exchange of Queens would obviously deprive him of any serious winning hopes.

| 15. ...... | P—Kt 4 |
| 16. Kt—K 5 | Kt×Kt |

Also possible was 16. ....P—Kt 5 ; 17. Kt×B, R P×Kt ; 18. Kt—K 2, P—B 4—but I was not particularly enthusiastic about the variation 19. P—K 5, Kt—Q 4 ; 20. B×Kt, P×B ; 21. B—Kt 3 followed by P—B 4, etc. ; and, besides, I believed in the future of my temporarily encaged Q's Bishop.

17. B×Kt	P—Kt 5
18. B×Kt	B×B
19. Kt—K 2	......

After this, Black definitely gets the initiative, which he will keep until the very end. But also after 19. Kt—R 4 (recommended by Nimzowitsch and Bogoljubow), P × P ; 20. P×P, P—K 4 ! ; 21. P—Q 5, B—K 2, etc., his prospects would remain satisfactory.

19.	P×P
20. P×P	P—B 4
21. Q R—B 1	P×P
22. Kt×P	B×Kt !

The exchange of the active K's Bishop looks at first sight surprising, but in reality offers the greatest possibilities of exploiting the weak spots of White's position both in the centre and on the King's wing.

| 23. Q×B | K R—Q 1 |
| 24. Q—B 4 ! | Q—Kt 2 |

The interesting variation 24. .... Q×Q ; 25. R×Q, R—Q 6 ; 26. P—B 4 !, R×Q R P ; 27. R—K B 2, R×R P ; 28. P—B 5, R—Kt 6 ch ; 29. K—R 2, R×P ; 30. P×B, R×P, etc., would have brought Black 4 Pawns for the piece, but no real winning chances.

| 25. P—B 3 | P—R 4 |

Without having a "hole" for his King Black cannot dream of launching a serious offensive. At the same time this Pawn move is the first step for the emancipation of the prisoner at K Kt 3.

| 26. Q—K 2 | R—Q 5 |
| 27. Q—K 3 | ...... |

Dr. Lasker suggests instead of this, 27. K R—Q 1, which, however, after the exchange of Rooks, would lead to about the same position as the one we reached after the 33rd move.

27. ......   R—Q 2

After 27. ....Q R—Q 1, White would have forced the exchange of Queens by playing 28. B—Q 5, Q—Kt 7 ; 29. R—Kt 1, etc.

28. P×P   ......

White hopes to obtain some counter-attack on the Q B's file and in order to win a *tempo* for doubling the Rooks, gives some fresh air to the poor Bishop.   Bogoljubow indicates as a better line 28. K R—Q 1, Q R—Q 1 ; 29. R×R, R×R ; 30. R—B 4—but after 30. ....P—Q R 5! followed by ....P—R 5 the dark-coloured squares of his position would still remain very weak.

28. ......   B×R P
29. R—B 5   B—Kt 3
30. K R—B 1   Q R—Q 1 !
31. B—B 4   ......

He cannot take the R's Pawn because of 31. ....Q—Kt 7 ! with an immediate win.

31. ......   R—Q 8 ch
32. B—B 1   R×R
33. R×R   P—R 5 !

In spite of the fact that this Pawn cannot, for the present at least, be supported by the Bishop, it is by no means weak, as Black will be perfectly able to protect it by counter-attacks.

34. R—B 4   R—Q 8
35. R—Kt 4   ......

Not 35. R×P because of 35. .... R×B ch followed by 36. ....Q—Kt 4 ch,

35. ......   Q—B 2

Threatening mate in three by 36. ....Q—Kt 6 ch, etc.

36. P—B 4   Q—Q 1 !
37. Q—B 2   ......

37. R×P would be refuted by 37. ....R×B ch and 38. ....,Q—Q 8 ch. The end is approaching.

Position after White's 37th move.

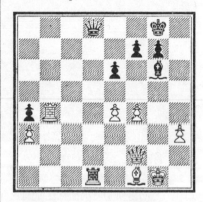

37. ......   P—B 4 !

The resurrection of the Bishop, which will not only rescue the Q R's Pawn but also contribute to an effective exploitation of White's disorganised King's position.

38. P—K 5   B—K 1
39. R—Kt 6   Q—B 1
40. R—Q 6   ......

Or 40. K—R 2, Q—B 6 ! and wins.

40. ......   R—B 8
41. Q—Q 4   ......

There is no defence left. If for instance 41. K—R 2, then 41. .... R—B 7 ; 42. R—Q 2, R×R ; 43. Q×R, Q—B 4 ! winning a Pawn and the game.

41. ......   K—R 2

In order to answer 42. R—Q 8 by
42. ....Q—R 3 ! etc.

42. K—B 2   Q—B 7 ch
43. Q—Q 2   ......

Or 43. B—K 2, B—Kt 4 ; 44.
Q—Q 2, B×B ! ; 45. Q×B, Q—B 4
ch., etc., winning.

43. ......   Q—B 4 ch

44. Q—K 3   ......

If 44. Q—Q 4 then 44. ....Q ×
R P after which White could also
quietly resign.

44. ......   R × B ch
Resigns.

This game practically finished
the Match, as it gave me 15 points
to my opponent's 10.

PART III. (1934-1937)

Tournament Games and Matches with Dr. Euwe

GAME 67

QUEEN'S PAWN OPENING

Zurich Tournament, July, 1934.

Black :
Marquis S. Rosselli del Turco

1. P—Q 4	P—Q 4
2. Kt—K B 3	Kt—K B 3
3. P—K 3	P—K 3

Not a mistake, of course, but 3. ....B—B 4 ; 4. B—Q 3, P—K 3 ! would solve without disadvantage the otherwise rather tiresome problem of the Queen's Bishop's development.

4. B—Q 3	P—B 4
5. P—Q Kt 3	......

An old—and rather harmless—method of mobilisation instead of which the modern Colle's System starting by 5. P—B 3 offers more attacking possibilities. It succeeds here, however, because Black answers it by an unjustified clearing of the situation in the middle.

5.	P×P ?

Oddly enough, this exchange—which opens for White the central file without compensation (as there is nothing for Black to do with the Q B's file)—is not made infrequently even by very experienced players. The course of the present game illustrates the faultiness of this strategy in a typical way.

6. P×P	B—Q 3
7. Castles	Castles

8. B—Kt 2	Kt—B 3
9. P—Q R 3	......

More exact than immediately 9. Q Kt—Q 2, as after 9. ....Q—B 2 ! Black would threaten both 10. ....Kt—Q Kt 5 and 10. .... P—K 4.

9.	P—Q Kt 3
10. Q Kt—Q 2	B—Kt 2
11. Q—K 2	Q—B 2
12. Kt—K 5	Kt—K 2
13. P—K B 4	Q R—B 1
14. Q R—B 1	......

In order to add to the already existing advantages (greater space in the centre and chances on the King's side) another trump—the dynamization of the Q B's Pawn. However, the general situation after the erroneous exchange at the 5th move is so favourable for White that a King's attack could be carried through *even without using that trump*. A characteristic example of such an attack is my game (given below) with Asgeirson (Black) from the Folkestone Team Tournament, 1933, which, with a slight inversion of moves, soon reached the same type of position as the present game: 1. P—Q 4, Kt—K B 3 ; 2. Kt—K B 3, P—K 3 ; 3. P—K 3, P—B 4 ; 4. B—Q 3, Kt—B 3 ; 5. P—Q R 3, P×P ? ; 6. P×P, P—Q 4 ; 7. Castles, B—Q 2 ; 8. P—Q Kt 3, B—Q 3 ; 9. R—K 1, R—Q B 1 ; 10. B—Kt 2, Castles ; 11. Kt—K 5, B—Kt 1 ; 12. Kt—Q 2, P—K Kt 3 ; 13. Q—B 3, Kt—K R 4 ; 14. Q—K 3, Kt—Kt 2 ; 15. Q—R 6, Kt—K 2 ; 16. P—K Kt 4 !, K—R 1 ; 17. Q Kt—B 3, Kt—Kt 1 ; 18. Q—R 3, B—K 1 ; 19. B—Q B 1,

B—Q 3 ; 20. Kt—Kt 5, P—K R 4 ;
21. P × P, Kt × P (or 21. .... P × P ;
22. Kt—R 7 !, winning the exchange) ; 22. Kt (Kt 5) × P ch !,
B × Kt ; 23. B × P, B × B ; 24. Kt ×
B ch, K—Kt 2 ; 25. Kt × R, Q × Kt;
26. Q—Kt 4 ch ! Resigns.

| 14. ...... | P—Kt 3 |

This, in connection with the two
next moves, does not prove sufficient to meet the threatening advance of White's K Kt's Pawn. But
equally an attempt by Black to post
his Knight at K 5 would not
succeed—for instance, 14. .... Q—
Kt 1 ; 15. R—B 2 !, Q—R 1 ; 16.
R—K 1, followed by P—K Kt 4,
etc. ±.

| 15. P—K Kt 4 | P—K R 4 |
| 16. P—R 3 | K—Kt 2 |

As will be seen, this only facilitates the advance of White's Q B's
Pawn.

| 17. P—B 4 | Q—Q 1 |

Position after Black's 17th move.

| 18. P—Q B 5 ! | ...... |

This is the strategical decision, as
White forces herewith a protected
passed Pawn on the Q's side without
weakening his pressure on the other
wing. Black, obviously, cannot
now play 18. .... P × B P ; 19. P ×
B P, B × P ch because of 20. R × B !

followed by 21. P—Kt 5, etc.,
winning.

18.	B × Kt
19. B P × B	Kt—Q 2
20. P—Kt 4	R P × P
21. R P × P	R—K R 1

The occupation of this file is
without importance, as the light
pieces cannot co-operate.

22. Kt—B 3	P × P
23. Kt P × P	Kt—Q B 3
24. Q—K 3 !	......

Threatening 25. Kt—Kt 5.

| 24. ...... | Q—K 2 |
| 25. K—Kt 2 | ...... |

Threatening now 26. R—K R 1 !
followed by Q R—B 1 and B—B 1,
etc., and thus inducing Black to
take desperate action in the centre.

25.	P—B 4
26. P × P ch (*e.p.*)	Kt × P
27. Q—Kt 5	R—R 3
28. R—K R 1	Q R—K R 1
29. R × R	R × R
30. R—K 1 !	......

Even stronger than 30. R—K R 1
which would win only a Pawn.

| 30. ...... | Kt—Q 1 |
| 31. Kt—K 5 | Kt—Kt 1 |

Or 31. .... Kt—B 2 ; 32. Kt × Kt
followed by 33. Q—K 5, etc., with
an easy win.

| 32. B—Q B 1 ! | ...... |

One of the points of 30. R—K 1.

32.	Q—K 1
33. R—B 1	B—B 3
34. R—B 6 !	Kt × R
35. Q × R ch	K—Kt 1
36. B—K Kt 5	......

Wins about two minor pieces.

Resigns.

GAME 68

RUY LOPEZ

Zurich Tournament, July, 1934.

Black : H. JOHNER

1.	P—K 4	P—K 4
2.	Kt—K B 3	Kt—Q B 3
3.	B—Kt 5	P—Q R 3
4.	B—R 4	Kt—B 3
5.	Castles	P—Q 3

This permits White to start an immediate action in the centre without being obliged to protect first the K P by R—K 1 or Q—K 2, which would be the case after 5. ....B—K 2.

6.	P—B 3	D—Q 2
7.	P—Q 4	B—K 2
8.	P—Q 5	......

This blockade manœuvre was introduced by Bogoljubow in a Match-game against me (Rotterdam 1929). Its peculiarity is to lead generally to slow positional battles of heavy calibre.

8.	......	Kt—Q Kt 1
9.	B—B 2	B—Kt 5

Keres tried against me in the Team Tournament at Warsaw 1935 a more aggressive line of play involving the renunciation of castling and starting with 9. ....P—R 3. The continuation, 10. P—B 4, Q—B 1 ; 11. Kt—K 1, P—K Kt 4 ; 12. Kt—Q B 3, Kt—R 4 ; 13. Kt—K 2 ! (of course not 13. Q × Kt, B—Kt 5), Kt—B 5 ; 14. Kt—Kt 3, P—Q B 3 ; 15. Kt—B 5, P × P ; 16. B × Kt, Kt P × B ; 17. B P × P, B × Kt ; 18. P × B—proved, however, favourable to the first player who, by taking advantage of the open Q B file, succeeded in forcing resignation by the 37th move. For ....P—Q R 4 ! in conjunction with Kt—

Q R 3—Q B 4, see my consultation game against Kashdan (No. 119).

10.	P—B 4	Q Kt—Q 2
11.	P—K R 3 !	......

In the above-mentioned game, Bogoljubow played here 11. Kt—B 3, and after 11. ....Kt—B 1 ; 12. P—K R 3 ?—this is now out of place since the Bishop can simply remove to Q 2—Black was able to start a King's attack by the pawn-sacrifice, ...P—K Kt 4 ! and to obtain soon a won position.

11.	......	B—R 4
12.	Kt—B 3	Castles
13.	P—K Kt 4	B—Kt 3
14.	Q—K 2	......

Preparing for Kt—K R 4, which, played immediately, would have been met by 14. ....B × P, etc.

14.	......	Kt—K 1
15.	B—Q 2	P—R 3

The seemingly more aggressive 15. ....P—K R 4 would be favourably answered by the manœuvre Kt—Q 1—K 3—K B 5.

16.	K—Kt 2	B—R 2
17.	R—R 1	P—K Kt 4 !

By constructing this pawn-barricade, Black at least eliminates the immediate danger that threatens his King.

18.	P—K R 4	P—K B 3
19.	Kt—Q 1	R—B 2
20.	Kt—K 3	......

This Knight must be exchanged at K B 5 before Black finds time to bring a Knight to his K B 5 via K Kt 3.

20.	......	Kt—B 1
21.	Kt—B 5	B × Kt
22.	Kt P × B	R—R 2

One must admit that Black defends his position logically. He now succeeds in still bringing a Knight to K B 5 by another route (K Kt 2 —K R 4), but it's his bad luck that his other pieces are too poorly placed to permit a really effective resistance !

23. Q R—K Kt 1	Kt—Kt 2
24. K—B 1	Q—K 1
25. Kt—R 2	Kt—R 4
26. Kt—Kt 4	Kt—B 5
27. Q—B 3 !	......

Threatening 28. B × Kt, K P × B; 29. Q × P !, Kt P × Q ; 30. Kt × R P doub. ch. followed by mate.

| 27. ...... | K—Kt 2 ! |

The only parry ; for 27. ....K—R 1 would soon lose after 28. Kt × R P !, R × Kt ; 29. P × P, etc.

28. P × P	R P × P
29. R × R ch	Kt × R
30. R—R 1	K—R 1
31. R—R 6	Q—B 2
32. B—Q 1	R—K Kt 1
33. Q—Q Kt 3 !	......

As all Black's pieces are more or less engaged on the King's side, the Queen undertakes a little promenade on the other wing—not for sight-seeing, but in order to grab anything insufficiently protected. This material win, by no means accidental, is the logical consequence of a persistent initiative, which prevented Black from protecting at the same time all his vulnerable spots.

| 33. ...... | P—Kt 3 |
| 34. Q—R 4 | B—B 1 |

If 34. ....P—R 4, then 35. Q—Q 7, etc., winning rapidly.

35. Q × P	B × R
36. Kt × B	Q—Kt 2
37. Kt × R	K × Kt

38. Q—B 8 ch	Kt—B 1
39. B × Kt	K P × B
40. Q—K 8	......

After gaining a material advantage, the attack, as so often, vanishes, and White must now be particularly careful against a possible counter-attack ; for instance, Black's strong threat was 40. .... Q—K 2 and ....Q—K 4.

40.	P—Kt 5
41. Q—R 5	P—B 6
42. B—R 4	Kt—R 2
43. B—B 2	......

The necessary preparation for the surprising assault in the middle.

| 43. ...... | Kt—B 1 |

If 43. ....Kt—Kt 4, White would win through 44. Q × P, Q—R 3 ; 45. K—Kt 1 !—for instance, I. 45. ....K—B 1 ; 46. B—Q 1, Kt—R 6 ch ; 47. K—B 1, Q—Q 7 ; 48. Q × P. II. 45. ....Q—Kt 2; 46. Q—Kt 3 with an easy technical work in both cases.

Position after Black's 43rd move.

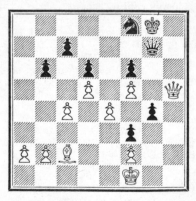

| 44. P—K 5 ! ! | ...... |

The sealed move at the adjournment, which transforms a complicated technical problem into a sharp, short, winning procedure.

44. ......   Q P×P

Or 44. ....B P×P ; 45. P—B 6 !,
Q×P ; 46. Q×P ch followed by 47.
B—K 4, etc., with no more fight
left.

45. P—Q 6 !   P—B 4

After 45. ....P×P, the third
point, 46. P—B 5 ! threatening 47.
B—Kt 3 ch, etc., would successfully
finish the work.

46. B—K 4   Q—Q 2
47. Q—R 6 !   ......

More exact than 47. Q×P ch.
Resigns.

GAME 69

DENONI'S DEFENCE

Zurich Tournament, July, 1934.

White : F. GYGLI

1. P—Q 4   P—Q B 4
2. P—Q 5   P—K 4
3. P—K 4   P—Q 3
4. P—K Kt 3   ......

An elaborate method of development which does not cause Black
much trouble.   White should, in
my opinion, try in this opening to
combine the two following strategical ideas : (1) Occupation of the
square Q B 4 by a Knight and the
strengthening of that position, and
(2) preparation of the advance P—
K B 4 *which has, however, to be
executed only as an immediate re-
action to Black's P—K B* 4.   In the
latter case the opening of the position in the middle should always
end to the advantage of the party
who has already a superiority in
space.

4. ......   P—B 4

5. Kt—Q B 3   Kt—K B 3
6. B—Kt 2   B—K 2

Also the immediate 6. ....P—
Q Kt 4 (7. Kt×P, Kt×K P, etc.)
came into consideration.   As Black
does not take advantage of that
possibility, White would have done
better to prevent it now by playing
7. P—Q R 4.

7. K Kt—K 2   P—Q Kt 4 !

The tactical consequences of this,
positionally, quite justified advance
had to be carefully examined, as
the following proves.

8. P×P   P—Kt 5
9. Kt—K 4   B×P
10. Kt×P   ......

A tempting, but unsatisfactory,
transaction, as it only helps the
deployment of Black's forces.   Still,
a tame alternative would only
underline the inefficiency of the
first opening moves.

10. ......   P×Kt
11. P—Q 6   P—K 5 !

And not 11. ....B—K 5 ; 12.
B×B, Kt×B ; 13. Q—Q 5±.

12. P×B   Q×Q ch
13. K×Q   K×P
14. B—K 3   Q Kt—Q 2

The middle-game without Queens,
resulting from the exchanges in the
centre, is in Black's favour—chiefly
because of the uncomfortable position of White's King, preventing
the combined action of the Rooks.

15. P—K R 3   P—K R 4
16. P—R 3   P—R 4
17. P×P   R P×P
18. K—Q 2   K—B 2 !

An important move, whose object
is to prevent the capture of the

Q B's Pawn *with check* in case of ....Kt—K 4.

19. Kt—B 4 ?   ......

This proves an important, if not decisive, loss of time, and was obviously based on a tactical miscalculation. By playing 19. P—Kt 3 White would still keep a playable—although inferior—game.

19. ......   P—Kt 4
20. Kt—K 2   ......

White probably intended to play 20. R×R, R×R ; 21. Kt×P— and found out now that this would have led to a hopeless position after 21......Kt×Kt ; 22. P—Kt 4, Kt—B 5 ; 23. B×Kt, P×B ; 24. P×B, P—B 6 ; 25. B—B 1, K—B 3, etc. But what will happen after the retreat in the text is not very much better for him either.

20. ......   Kt—K 4 !

With the threats ....Kt—B 5 ch and ....Kt—B 6 ch, both of which cannot be parried.

21. R×R   R×R
22. R—Q 1   Kt—B 6 ch

Even more convincing than 22. ....Kt—B 5 ch ; 23. K—K 1, Kt×P; 24. R—Kt 1, etc.

23. B×Kt   P×B
24. Kt—B 1   P—B 5 !

Puts the White Knight in a stalemate position in which it will remain until the very end.

25. K—K 1   P—Kt 5

There is no hurry to take the Q B's Pawn as White's answer is compulsory : if 26. P×P ? then 26. ....P×P followed by 27. ....R—R 1 and ....Kt—K 5 with a mating attack.

26. P—R 4   B×P
27. R—Q 4   ......

Position after White's 27th move.

27. ......   P—B 6 !

Forcing a powerful passed Pawn and, at the same time, finishing the encircling of the enemy's King. White cannot play now 28. R×Q Kt P because of 28. ....R—Q 1 ; 29. B—Q 4, R×B !; 30. R×R, P×P and wins.

28. P×P   P×P
29. R—K B 4   K—K 3
30. R—B 4   Kt—Q 4
31. B—Kt 5   K—Q 3
32. B—R 6   ......

White has still fewer and fewer moves at his disposal.

32. ......   R—K 1 ch
33. K—B 1   B—Q 8 !
34. R—Q 4   B—K 7 ch
35. K—K 1   ......

Or 35. K—Kt 1, B—Kt 4 ! followed by ....R—K 8 ch, B—B 8, B—Kt 7 and R—R 8 mate.

35. ......   K—B 3
36. B—Kt 5   B—B 5 disc ch
37. K—Q 1   K—B 4 !

Capturing the Rook, in the very middle of the board !

38. R × Kt ch	K × R
39. K—B 2	R—K 7 ch !
40. K × P	R × P

Resigns.

GAME 70

QUEEN'S GAMBIT DECLINED (ORTHODOX DEFENCE)

Zurich Tournament ,July, 1934.

Black : DR. EM. LASKER

1. P—Q 4	P—Q 4
2. P—Q B 4	P—K 3
3. Kt—Q B 3	Kt—K B 3
4. Kt—B 3	B—K 2
5. B—Kt 5	Q Kt—Q 2
6. P—K 3	Castles
7. R—B 1	P—B 3
8. B—Q 3	P × P

As mentioned elsewhere, this exchange gives Black more defensive resources if preceded by ....P—K R 3 ; B—R 4.

9. B × P	Kt—Q 4
10. B × B	Q × B
11. Kt—K 4	......

This move, "my patent," is as good as the more usual 11. Castles, but probably not better. In both cases White usually gets an advantage in space and has not to worry about a possible loss.

| 11. ...... | K Kt—B 3 |
| 12. Kt—Kt 3 | P—K 4 |

An interesting attempt by Lasker to solve swiftly the problem of the Queen's Bishop. Capablanca regularly played here in our Match-games 12. ....Q—Kt 5 ch, and, after the exchange of Queens, suc-

ceeded in drawing, but not without difficulties.

| 13. Castles | P × P |
| 14. Kt—B 5 | ...... |

This sharp-looking move is in reality less aggressive than the straightforward 14. P × P, which, on account of the open K's file, would cause Black real development trouble—for instance, 14. ....Kt—Kt 3 ; 15. R—K 1, Q—Q 3 ; 16. B—Kt 3, and, if 16. ....B—Kt 5, then 17. P—K R 3, B × Kt ; 18. Q × B, etc., offering the Queen's Pawn for a strong attack. After the text move, White will be practically forced to take at Q 4 with a piece and to allow, as a consequence, an unwelcome simplification.

| 14. ...... | Q—Q 1 |
| 15. K Kt × P | ...... |

If 15. Q (or P) × P, then .... Kt—Kt 3.

15.	Kt—K 4
16. B—Kt 3	B × Kt
17. Kt × B	Q—Kt 3 ?

Underestimating, or overlooking, the answer, which gives White a strong and hardly resistible attack. The right move, sufficient for equality, is 17. ....P—K Kt 3, played by Flohr against Euwe at Nottingham, 1936. Neither 18. Q—Q 6 (R—K 1 !), nor 18. Kt—Q 6 (Q—K 2) would then prove successful.

18. Q—Q 6 !   Q Kt—Q 2

Also 18. ....Kt—Kt 3 ; 19. Kt—R 6 ch, P × Kt ; 20. Q × Kt, Q—Q 1; 21. Q—Q B 3, would be bad enough.

19. K R—Q 1	Q R—Q 1
20. Q—Kt 3	P—Kt 3
21. Q—Kt 5 !	......

With the main threat 22. R—Q 6, Black has already no real defence.

21.	K—R 1
22. Kt—Q 6	K—Kt 2
23. P—K 4 !	......

Not only in order to use this Pawn as an attacking factor, but also, as will be seen, to free the third rank for the Rooks.

| 23. ...... | Kt—K Kt 1 |
| 24. R—Q 3 | P—B 3 |

24. ....P—K R 3 would have led to a pendant-variation, viz., 25. Kt—B 5 ch, K—R 2 ; 26. Kt × P !, P—B 3 ; 27. Kt—B 5 !, P × Q ; 28. R—R 3 ch and mate follows.

25. Kt—B 5 ch   K—R 1

Position after Black's 25th move.

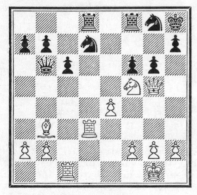

26. Q × P !

The spectacular final coup of an attack that could hardly have been conducted in a more effective manner after Black's superficial 17th move.   Resigns

GAME 71

QUEEN'S GAMBIT DECLINED (ORTHODOX DEFENCE)

Orebro Tournament, May, 1935.

Black : E. LUNDIN

1. P—Q 4	P—Q 4
2. P—Q B 4	P—K 3
3. Kt—Q B 3	Kt—K B 3
4. B—Kt 5	Q Kt—Q 2
5. Kt—B 3	P—B 3
6. P—K 4	......

This old move—a radical method of avoiding the Cambridge Springs' Defence—has been adopted by me twice with success in the 1929 Match against Bogoljubow and also on a few occasions later. Its advantage is to gain at once some space in the centre, its defect—to allow early exchanges of minor pieces, which facilitates the mobilisation of Black's pieces.

| 6. ...... | P × K P |
| 7. Kt × P | B—K 2 |

Besides this simple developing move, Black has at his disposal at least three other continuations, each involving a different plan of development :

I. 7. ....Q—Kt 3. This counter-attack aims at an immediate material win at the cost of time and, eventually, space—a dangerous and to my mind, unchessy idea, which, however, in this particular case is by no means easy to refute. In the eleventh match-game against Bogoljubow, I adopted the ultra-cautious 8. Kt × Kt ch, P × Kt ; 9. B—B 1— and soon obtained a winning attack, but only because my opponent, with his typical over-estimation of his resources, replied with 9. .... P—K 4 ? instead of 9. ....Q—B 2, thus opening the position before having finished development. The continuation was : 10. B—Q 3, P × P ; 11. Castles, B—K 2 ; 12. R—K 1, Kt—B 1 ; 13. Kt—R 4 !, B—K 3 ; 14. Kt—B 5, B—Kt 5 ; 15. Kt—Kt 7 ch, K—Q 2 ; 16. R— K 4 !, R—K Kt 1—after which White could have made a rapid end by playing 17. Kt—B 5 ! with the threat R × P ch, etc.

Also successful, but not quite convincing, was another attempt of mine against Colle at Bled, 1931, where I played—after 7. ....Q—Kt 3 ; 8. B—Q 3. My opponent decided to accept the pawn-offer, but did it in not the most secure way : instead of 8. ....Kt×Kt ; 9. B×Kt, Q—Kt 5 ch !—introduced with success by Dr. Euwe in a consultation-game against Flohr—he played immediately 8. ....Q×Kt P, allowing White to bring his King into safety. The attack that developed afterwards—on the basis, first of a space advantage and, later, of the two Bishops supremacy—was both typical and instructive. The game went on as follows : 9. Castles, Kt×Kt ; 10. B×Kt, Kt—B 3 ; 11. B—Q 3, Q—Kt 3 ; 12. R—K 1, B—K 2 13. Q—B 2, P—K R 3 ; 14. B—Q 2, P—B 4 ; 15. B—B 3, P×P ; 16. Kt×P, Castles ; 17. Kt—B 5 !, Q—Q 1 ; 18. Kt×B ch, Q×Kt ; 19. Q R—Kt 1, R—Q 1; 20. R—K 3, P—Q Kt 3 ; 21. Q—K 2 !, B—Kt 2 ; 22. K R—Kt 3, Kt—K 1 ; 23. R—K 1, K—B 1 ; 24. Q—Kt 2, P—B 3 ; 25. B—Kt 4, Kt—Q 3 ; 26. K R—K 3, K—B 2 ; 27. P—D 4 !, Q—Q 2 ; 28. Q—K 2, R—K 1 ; 29. Q—R 5 ch, K—Kt 1 ; 30. Q—Kt 6, P—B 4 ; 31. B×Kt, Q×B ; 32. B×P, Q×P ; 33. Q—R 7 ch, K—B 1 ; 34. B—Kt 6, Q—Q 5 ; 35. B×R, R×B ; 36. K—R 1, Q—B 3 ; 37. Q—R 8 ch, K—B 2 ; 38. Q×R ch ! Resigns.

As neither attempt can be considered satisfactory from the theoretical point of view, White must, after 7. ....Q—Kt 3, complete his development in a way that will not permit an unwelcome reduction of the fighting units. With this idea, I would recommend a continuation that has been tried but once by Marshall against Tchigorin in Hannover, 1902, and completely forgotten since, viz. : 8. P—B 5 !, Q×Kt P—and only now 9. B—Q 3 followed by 10. Castles, with ample positional compensation for the Pawn.

II. 7. ....B—Kt 5 ch, with the object of exploiting the temporary weakness of the diagonal K 1—Q R 5 and, at the same time, of preparing a break-through in the centre by ....P—K 4. The idea is, however, too artificial and too time-wasting to become a success. The following game, played by me in the Warsaw Team Tournament, 1935, illustrates in a drastic way White's possibilities in this variation : Black, Silbermann (Roumania). 8. Kt—B 3, Q—R 4 ; 9. B—Q 2, Q—B 2 ; 10. B—Q 3, P—K 4 ; 11. P×P, Kt×P ; 12. Q—K 2, Kt—Q 2 ; 13. Castles (K R), Castles; 14. Kt—Q 5 (a rather original combination by which White finally wins the exchange for a Pawn), P×Kt ; 15. B×B, Kt×B ; 16. Q×Kt, P×P ; 17. Q—K 3 !, Q—Kt 3 (if ....R—Q 1, then 18. Q—K 7 with a winning position) ; 18. B×R, Q×Q ; 19. P×Q (the following end-game is harder to win than one would think, especially as Black defends himself with great determination), K×B ; 20. Q R—Q 1, K—K 2 ; 21. R—Q 5, P—B 3 ; 22. K R—Q 1, P—Q Kt 3 ; 23. R—Q 6, Kt—B 4 ; 24. R—Q 8, B—Kt 2 ; 25. R×R, B×R ; 26. Kt—Q 4, B—K 5 ; 27. R—Q B 1, B—Q 4 ; 28. Kt—B 5 ch, K—K 3 ; 29. Kt×P ch, K—K 4 ; 30. Kt—R 5 !, B—B 2 ; 31. Kt—B 4, Kt—K 5 ; 32. P—Q R 3, P—Kt 4 ; 33. R—Q 1, Kt—B 4 ; 34. R—Q 8, P—Q R 3 ; 35. K—B 2, Kt—R 5 ; 36. R—Q 7, B—Kt 3 ; 37. R—Q 5 ch, K—K 5 ; 38. R—Q 2, B—B 4 ; 39. P—R 3, P—B 6 (this tempting advance is met by a mating threat, which decides the game at once. Compare with the same end-game stratagem in the games against Tartakover from San Remo and the 24th of the 2nd match with Euwe) ; 40. R—Q 4 ch, K—K 4 ; 41. K—B 3 !, Kt—Kt 3 ; 42. P×P, B—Q 2 ; 43. Kt—Q 3 ch, K—B 4 ; 44. R—Q 6. Resigns.

III. 7. ....P—K R 3 !, practically forcing the exchange of White's Q's Bishop. Although, after

8. B×Kt, Kt×B; 9. Kt—B 3,
P—Q Kt 3 followed by ....B—Kt 2
etc., White would still enjoy more
freedom, at least temporarily,
Black's chances for the future,
because of the two Bishops, would
be quite satisfactory, and that is
why I have recently given up the
otherwise playable 6. P—K 4.

8. Kt—B 3   Castles
9. Q—B 2   ......

This move in connection with
Castles (Q R) had, I believe, never
been made before my 1929 Match
with Bogoljubow. On a previous
occasion, Gilg played against Spielmann 9. B—Q 3 and Castles (K side),
after which Black can easily
equalise with ....P—B 4.

9. ......   P—K 4 !

A new and interesting attempt
to liberate the Q's Bishop, and
which forces White to play very
carefully in order to maintain advantage in space. Decidedly too
passive is, instead, 9. ....P—
Q Kt 3; 10. Castles, as, for instance,
my two following games rather
convincingly show :

I.   *Black, Bogoljubow; 19th
Match Game*, 1929. 10. ....B—
Kt 2; 11. P—K R 4, Q—B 2; 12.
B—Q 3, K R—K 1; 13. K—Kt 1,
Kt—B 1; 14. B×Kt !, B×B; 15.
Kt—K 4, P—B 4; 16. Kt×B ch,
P×Kt; 17. Q—Q 2, Kt—Kt 3; 18.
P—R 5, Kt—B 5; 19. R—R 4,
B×Kt; 20. P×B, P—K 4; 21.
P—Q 5, Q—Q 3; 22. P—R 6!,
K—R 1; 23. Q—B 2, Kt×B; 24.
Q×Kt, R—K Kt 1; 25. P—B 4!,
R—Kt 3; 26. Q—B 5, P—R 3; 27.
R—K 1, P×P; 28. R×P ! (by
giving up the K R P White gets
the full control of the central file
and, gradually, an irresistible King's
attack), R×P; 29. R (B 4)—K 4,
R—K Kt 1; 30. R—K 7, R—K B 1;
31. P—R 4 !, R—R 5; 32. R—K 8,
R×R; 33. R×R ch, K—Kt 2;

34. Q—B 8, K—R 3; 35. R—Kt 8 !,
Q—K 2; 36. K—R 2, P—Kt 4;
37. R—Kt 3 !, P—B 4; 38. Q×
K B P, P—B 3; 39. R—K 3, Q—
K B 2. Here I played 40. R—K 6
and eventually won in 77 moves;
but 40. Q—K 6 ! would have forced
an almost immediate resignation.

II.   *Black, J. Vasquez, Mexico
City Tournament*, Sept., 1932. 10.
....P—B 4; 11. P—K R 4, Q—
B 2; 12. P—Q 5, P×P; 13. P×P,
P—Q R 3; 14. B—Q 3, P—R 3; 15.
B—R 7 ch, K—R 1; 16. Kt—K 4 !,
B—Q 3; 17. B—B 5, Kt×Kt; 18.
Q×Kt, Kt—K 4; 19. Kt×Kt,
B×Kt; 20. P—Q 6 !, B×P; 21.
Q×R, B×B; 22. Q—B 3, B—Kt 3;
23. P—R 5, B—R 2; 24. B×P !,
B—K 4; 25. B—Kt 5, P—B 4;
26. P—R 6, P—K B 5; 27. Q—
Q 5 !, P—B 6; 28. P×P ch, Q×P;
29. R×B ch !, K×R; 30. R—R 1
ch, K—Kt 3; 31. B—R 6, B—B 5
ch; 32. B×B, R×B; 33. P×P,
Q—Q 5; 34. Q—Kt 8 ch, K—B 3;
35. R—R 6 ch, K—K 2; 36. R—
K 6 ch. Resigns.

10. Castles   ......

The acceptance of the offer would
be favourable to Black, for instance:
10. P×P, Kt—Kt 5; 11. B—B 4,
B—B 4; 12. Kt—K 4, B—Kt 5 ch,
or, 10. Kt×P, Kt×Kt; 11. P×Kt,
Kt—Q 2; 12. B×B, Q×B; 13.
P—B 4, P—B 3, etc.—in both cases
with enough compensation for the
Pawn.

10. ......   P×P
11. Kt×P   Q—R 4
12. P—K R 4   ......

As the reader may see from the
games above, this move is an important link in the plan inaugurated
by 9. Q—B 2.

12. ......   Kt—B 4
13. K—Kt 1   R—Q 1

If 13. ....B—K 3, White would
not exchange this Bishop at once,

but first finish his development as in the actual game—B—K 2—B 3, etc.

| 14. B—K 2 | Q—B 2 |
| 15. B—B 3 ! | ...... |

Judiciously resisting the temptation to dislodge the Knight by 15. P—Q Kt 4, since, after 15. .... Kt—K 3; 16. P—R 3, P—B 4 !, Black would obtain a counter-attack he cannot count upon after the positional text-move.

| 15. ...... | P—Q R 4 |
| 16. K R—K 1 | ...... |

At this particular moment the Rook is more useful in the centre, especially as the King's attack is very slow to develop owing to Black's well-timed preventative manœuvres.

| 16. ...... | P—K Kt 3 |

Almost necessary if he wants to dislodge White's central Knight by ....Kt—K 3. Besides, the move also involves the direct threat 17. ....R × Kt, followed by 18. .... B—B 4.

17. P—K Kt 4	Kt—K 3
18. Kt × Kt	B × Kt
19. P—R 5 !	......

Threatening 20. P × P, R P × P; 21. R × B ! etc., and not worrying about the Q B P, since 19. .... B × P is met by 20. R × B !, Q × R ; 21. Kt—K 4, R × R ch ; 22. Q × R, etc., with a winning advantage.

| 19. ...... | R × R ch |
| 20. Kt × R | Kt—K 1 |

In order to prevent the sacrifice of the exchange at his K 3.

| 21. B—R 6 | B—B 3 |
| 22. P × P | R P × P |

Position after Black's 22nd move.

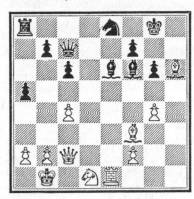

23. Kt—B 3 !   ......

I count this Pawn sacrifice amongst my most difficult combinations, since it was extremely hard to calculate that the little material left in the main variation would prove sufficient to increase the pressure in a definite way. And a win *was* necessary, for both my opponent and myself had 7½ out of 8 and this was the last round !

23. ......   B × B P

Otherwise, after 24. Kt—K 4, White would have an easy attacking game.

24. Kt—K 4   Q—K 4

This counter-attack will be refuted by White's next two moves. The main variation mentioned arises from 24. ....B—Q 4, and its real difficulty lay in finding, after 25. Kt × B ch, Kt × Kt ; 26. Q—B 3, Q—Q 3 ; 27. B × B, P × B, the two quiet moves 28. *R—R 1*, Q—K 3 (if ....P—Q 5, then 29. Q—K R 3, etc.) ; 29. *P—B 3 !*, with the chief threat Q—Q 2— R 2, after which the open K R-file would sooner or later triumph.

25. P—Kt 5 !   ......

The Bishop thus attacked cannot be moved because of 26. Kt—B 6 ch.

25. ......   Q—Kt 4

This was obviously the point of the previous move : the piece is temporarily saved, but Black now loses because of the weakness of his K Kt 2.

26.	Kt×B ch	Kt×Kt
27.	Q—B 3 !	R—K 1
28.	R—Q B 1	......

And not 28. P×Kt, Q—B 4 ch ; 29. K—R 1, R×R ch followed by 30. ....Q×B.

28.	......	Q—B 4 ch
29.	K—R 1	K—R 2
30.	Q×B	Resigns.

GAME 72

QUEEN'S GAMBIT DECLINED (SLAV DEFENCE)

First Match-game, Amsterdam, October, 1935.

Black : DR. M. EUWE

1.	P—Q 4	P—Q 4
2.	P—Q B 4	P—Q B 3
3.	Kt—K B 3	Kt—B 3
4.	Kt—B 3	P×P
5.	P—Q R 4	B—B 4
6.	Kt—K 5	......

It has been proved in our second match that this aggressive move, which has been fashionable for about ten years, is decidedly less promising than the natural 6. P—K 3. Black's best answer to the text-move is, however, not 6. ....Q Kt—Q 2 but 6. ....P—K 3, and, if 7. B—Kt 5, B—Q Kt 5 ; 8. P—K B 3, then 8. ....P—K R 3 ! etc. (11th Match-game, 1937).

6.	......	Q Kt—Q 2
7.	Kt×P (B 4)	Q—B 2
8.	P—K Kt 3	P—K 4
9.	P×P	Kt×P
10.	B—B 4	K Kt—Q 2
11.	B—Kt 2	B—K 3

Black does not need to cede to the white Queen the square Q B 2 ; but—as the first Match-game, 1937, convincingly showed—even by the best continuation, 11. ....P—B 3 ; 12. Castles, R—Q 1 ; 13. Q—B 1, B—K 3 White obtains a clear positional advantage by continuing 14. Kt—K 4 !

| 12. | Kt×Kt | Kt×Kt |
| 13. | Castles | B—K 2 |

Black tries in the following to avoid the weakening of his K 3 through ....P—K B 3 and gradually gets into great difficulty because of the insufficient protection of his Knight.

14. Q—B 2   ......

Threatening either Kt—Q 5 or Kt—Kt 5—Q 4, etc. Black can hardly succeed in keeping his pair of Bishops much longer.

14. ......   R—Q 1

Also 14. ....Q—R 4 ; 15. Kt—Kt 5 ! etc., would be advantageous for White.

| 15. | K R—Q 1 | Castles |
| 16. | Kt—Kt 5 | R×R ch |

If immediately 16. ....Q—R 4, then 17. R×R, R×R ; 18. B×Kt, P×Kt ; 19. B×Q Kt P, R—Q 7 ; 20. Q—B 6, etc. ±.

| 17. | R×R | Q—R 4 |
| 18. | Kt—Q 4 | B—B 1 |

Position after Black's 18th move.

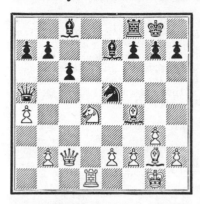

19. P—Q Kt 4 !   ......

The spectacular beginning of a "minority" attack whose immediate result will be the obtaining of the extremely important square Q 5. The tactical justification of the text-move is shown by the following variation : 19. ....B × P ; 20. Kt—Kt 3, Q—B 2 ; 21. Q—K 4, B—B 6 (or B—Q 3 ; 22. Q—Q 4 and wins) ; 22. R—Q B 1, B—Kt 7 (or P—K B 4 ; 23. Q—B 2, etc.) ; 23. R—B 2, P—K B 4 ; 24. Q—Kt 4 ! etc., with a winning position.

19. ......   Q—B 2
20. P—Kt 5   P—Q B 4
21. Kt—B 5   P—B 3

After this the weakness of the light-coloured squares will soon prove fatal. But also after 21. ....B—B 3 ; 22. Kt—Q 6, R—Q 1 ; 23. Kt—B 4 !, etc., the realisation of White's positional advantage would have been merely a matter of time.

22. Kt—K 3   B—K 3
23. B—Q 5 !   ......

Even more effective than 23. Kt —Q 5.

23. ......   B × B
24. R × B   Q—R 4

There is no longer a defence left. If, for instance, 24. ....R—Q 1, then simply 25. B × Kt, P × B ; 26. Q—B 5, etc., winning easily.

25. Kt—B 5   Q—K 8 ch
26. K—Kt 2   B—Q 1
27. B × Kt   P × B
28. R—Q 7 !   ......

Finishing the game by a mating attack.

28. ......   B—B 3
29. Kt—R 6 ch.   K—R 1
30. Q × P   ......

If now 30. ....R—K 1 then 31. Q—Q 5 !, P × Kt ; 32. Q—B 7, B— K 2 ; 33. R × B followed by mate.

Resigns.

GAME 73

FRENCH DEFENCE

Third Match-Game, Amsterdam, October, 1935.

Black : Dr. M. Euwe

1. P—K 4   P—K 3
2. P—Q 4   P—Q 4
3. Kt—Q B 3   B—Kt 5
4. P—Q R 3   ......

This seldom-played move is certainly better than its reputation and has not been even nearly refuted either by the actual game or by the subsequent analysis. Less recommendable is, in spite of its practical success, another attempt made by me in the ninth game of the same match, which continuation was : 4. Q—Kt 4 (too risky because of the yet unsettled situation on the Q's side), Kt—K B 3 ; 5. Q × P, R—Kt 1 ; 6. Q—R 6, R—Kt 3 ; 7. Q—K 3, Kt × P ? (by playing 7. ....P—B 4 ! Black would have obtained a sound initiative) ; 8. B—Q 3 !, P—K B 4 ; 9. Kt—K 2,

P—B 4 ; 10. B×Kt, B P×B ; 11. Q—R 3 !, Kt—B 3 ; 12. Q×P, Q—B 3 ; 13. Kt—B 4 !, P×P ; 14. Kt×R, P×Kt ; 15. P—Q Kt 3, Kt—K 2 ; 16. Kt×Kt, B×Kt ; 17. P—K R 4, Q—B 2 ; 18. Q—R 8 ch, Q—B 1 ; 19. Q×Q ch, K×Q ; 20. B—Kt 5, P—K 4 ; 21. P—B 3 !, P×P ; 22. P×P ? (After 22. B×B ch, K×B ; 23. P×P, etc., White would have but little trouble to force the win ; the less exact text-move leads to an interesting end-game with Bishops of different colours), B—Q R 6 ! ; 23. P—B 4 !, B—K B 4 ; 24. P×P, B×P ; 25. Castles ch, K—Kt 1 ; 26. Q R—B 1 !, B×R ; 27. R×B, B—B 4 ; 28. R×P, R—Q B 1 ; 29. R—B 3, R—B 1 ; 30. B—B 6, B—K 5 ; 31. R—Kt 3 ch, K—B 2 ; 32. P—R 5 !, R—B 1 ; 33. R—Kt 7 ch, K—K 3 ; 34. P—R 6 !, P—Q 5 ; 35. P—R 7, R—B 8 ch ; 36. K—B 2, R—B 7 ch; 37. K—Kt 3, B×P ; 38. R×B, R×P ; 39. K—B 4, P—Kt 4 ; 40. K—K 4, R—K 7 ch ; 41. K×P, Resigns.

4.	B×Kt ch
5. P×B	P×P
6. Q—Kt 4	Kt—K B 3

A safer alternative was 6. .... K—B 1 ; 7. Q×P at K 4, Kt—Q 2 followed by Q Kt—B 3, etc. After the text-move the dark-coloured squares of Black's position become decidedly weak.

7. Q×Kt P	R—Kt 1
8. Q—R 6	P—B 4
9. Kt—K 2	Q Kt—Q 2

In order to relieve the Queen from the protection of the other Knight. If 9. .... Kt—B 3 White's simplest answer would be 10. P×P !, but also 10. B—Kt 5 as played by Romanovski against Botvinnik in the half-final of the Soviet Championship, 1938, would be sufficient for equalising, for White lost that game only because he was outclassed in the later stages.

| 10. Kt—Kt 3 | R—Kt 3 ? |

After this loss of time Black's game becomes very difficult. Comparatively better was to play for further complications by 10. .... Q—R 4, although White's prospects would remain more favourable even in that case after 11. B—Q 2, Q—R 5 ; 12. P×P ! etc.

| 11. Q—K 3 | Kt—Q 4 |

He must already look for a compensation for his Pawn at K 5 which is now bound to be lost.

| 12. Q×P | Kt×P |
| 13. Q—Q 3 | Kt—Q 4 |

Also 13. ....P×P ; 14. Q×P, Q—B 3 ; 15. Q×Q, Kt×Q ; 16. B—Q 3, R—Kt 2 ; 17. B—Q 2, etc. would not be satisfactory. As a matter of fact Black's game after his inconsiderate tenth move was hardly to be saved.

14. B—K 2	Q—B 3
15. P—Q B 3	P×P
16. P×P	Kt (Q 2)—Kt 3

The exchange of Black's best posted piece by 16. ....Kt—B 5 ; 17. B×Kt, Q×B ; 18. Castles, etc., would only have made matters easier for White.

Position after Black's 16th move.

17. B—R 5 !   ......

This Bishop-manœuvre, consisting of four consecutive moves, forces a practically decisive weakening of Black's Pawn position. The following play on both wings is very instructive and, I believe, typical of my style.

| 17. ...... | R—Kt 2 |
| 18. B—B 3 | ...... |

Threatening 19. Kt—R 5.

18.	Q—Kt 3
19. B—K 4 !	P—B 4
20. B—B 3	K—B 1
21. P—Q R 4 !	......

The diagonal Q R 3—K B 8 is here the best field of activity for the Bishop.

21.	R—Q B 2
22. Castles	B—Q 2
23. B—R 3 ch	K—Kt 1
24. P—R 5	R—B 6

This leads to the loss of a Pawn without any improvement of Black's position ; but also the apparently better move 24. .... Kt—B 5 would not have saved the day. The continuation would be 25. B—B 5 ! (stronger than 25. Kt × P, K—R 1 ! etc.), Kt—K 4 ; 26. P × Kt, R × B ; 27. K R—B 1, Q R —Q B 1 ; 28. R × R, R × R ; 29. Q—Q 4 ! winning at least the Q R P in an overwhelming position. The remaining part is—in spite of Black's desperate efforts to 'swindle' —easy enough.

25. Q—Kt 1 !	Kt—R 5
26. B × Kt	P × B
27. Q × Kt P	Q—Q B 3
28. P—R 6 !	......

If now 28. .... Q × Q ; 29. P × Q, R—Kt 1, then 30. K R—Kt 1, Kt— Kt 3 ; 31. B—Kt 4 followed by R × P and wins.

28.	Kt—Kt 3
29. B—B 5	P—B 5
30. Kt—B 5 !	......

More exact than 30. Kt—K 2 which would also be sufficient.

30.	K—R 1
31. Kt—K 7	Q—K 3
32. B × Kt	B—B 3

Mere desperation.

33. Kt × B   R—K Kt 1

Threatening perpetual check by 34. .... R × P ch, etc.

| 34. Kt—K 5 ! | R—Kt 2 |
| 35. Q—Kt 8 ch ? | ...... |

As in so many games of that unfortunate match, I played, after the decision was practically reached, too rapidly—without, however, in this particular case, affecting the ultimate result. Instead, 35. B × P ! would force Black to resign immediately.

35.	R—B 1
36. Kt—Kt 6 ch	R × Kt
37. Q × B P	Q × B
38. Q—K 5 ch	R—Kt 2
39. Q × P	R—Q 1
40. Q—K 5	Q × Q P
41. Q × Q	Resigns.

GAME 74

KING'S INDIAN DEFENCE

Fourth Match-Game, The Hague, October, 1935.

White : Dr. M. Euwe

1. P—Q 4	Kt—K B 3
2. P—Q B 4	P—K Kt 3
3. Kt—Q B 3	P—Q 4
4. Q—Kt 3	......

The praxis of the last two to three years has proved that this Queen's move is less effective than 4. B—B 4, B—Kt 2 ; 5. P—K 3, Castles ; 6. Q—Kt 3, P—B 3 ; 7. Kt—B 3 etc., with an unquestionable advantage in space.

4. ......   P×P
5. Q×B P   B—Kt 2

Also playable is 5. ....B—K 3 ; 6. Q—Kt 5 ch, Kt—B 3 ; 7. Kt—B 3, but now *not* 7. ....R—Q Kt 1 (as in the second match game, 1935) but 7. ....Kt—Q 4 ! etc., with fairly good counter-chances.

6. B—B 4   P—B 3
7. R—Q 1 ?   ......

An artificial and unnecessary move, instead of which 7. Kt—B 3, Castles ; 8. P—K 4, etc., was indicated. Black can now obtain at least an even game.

7. ......   Q—R 4

Threatening 8. ....B—K 3.

8. B—Q 2   P—Q Kt 4 ?

There are some moves of mine in the first Euwe match which I actually simply cannot understand. Neither before nor since have I played such decidedly unsound Chess, especially in the openings ! Here, for instance, the spoiling of the Pawn-skeleton on the Queen's side cannot even be excused by the lack of other promising continuations; for the simple 8. ....Q—Kt 3 ; 9. B—B 1, B—B 4 followed by .... Castles would have secured Black a distinct advantage in development. I am adding, however, the present game to this collection in spite of the poor opening strategy of both sides—because of the particularly interesting tactical complications of the well-played middle-game.

9. Q—Kt 3   P—Kt 5

Has the advantage of being at least consistent ; Black prevents P—K 4 —but at what a price !

10. Kt—R 4   Kt—R 3
11. P—K 3   B—K 3

Black could also play immediately 11. .... Castles since 12. B×Kt, B×B ; 13. Q×P, Q—Q 4 or 13. B×P, Q—Q Kt 4, etc., would be in his favour. But he would not like in that case the answer 12. B—B 4.

12. Q—B 2   Castles (K R)
13. P—Q Kt 3   ......

If instead 13. Q×B P then 13. ....Kt—B 2 with the threats 14. ....B—Q 2 or 14. ....B×P.

13. ......   Q R—Kt 1
14. B—Q 3   ....

Because of his slightly belated development White decides not to take the Q B's Pawn—and rightly so ; after 14. Q×B P, B—B 1 ! the open Q B's file would become a dangerous weapon in Black's hands —for instance, 15. Kt—K B 3, B—Kt 2 ; 16. Q—B 2, K R—B 1 ; 17. Q—Kt 1, Kt—K 5, eventually followed by ....Kt—B 6, etc.

14. ......   K R—B 1
15. Kt—K 2   ......

Obviously underestimating the value of the following Pawn offer; otherwise he would have continued with 15. B×Kt, Q×B ; 16. Kt—B 5, Q—Kt 4 ; 17. Kt—B 3 ! (but not 17. Kt×B, P×Kt followed by ....P—K 4, etc., with a good game for Black), Kt—Q 2 ; 18. R—Q B 1, etc., with the better endgame prospects. This possibility clearly proves the unsoundness of Black's 8th and 10th moves.

15. ...... P—B 4 !

An absolutely correct combination which would have given—against White's best defence—easy equality. But as a matter of fact my opponent, fortunately for me, underestimated the danger.

16. B × Kt   Q × B
17. Kt × P   Q—Kt 4
18. Kt—B 4 ?   ......

Permitting Black to open the centre and thus put the opponent's house in flames. The correct defence consisted in 18. P—K 4 !, Kt—Q 2 ; 19. B—K 3, B × Q P ; 20. Kt × K B, Q × Kt ; 21. Q × Q, Kt × Q, etc., with a probable draw as a result.

18. ......   B—Kt 5 !
19. P—B 3   ......

If 19. R—Q D 1 the answer 19. ....P—K 4 would also have been strong.

19. ......   P—K 4 !
20. Kt (B 4)—Q 3 ......

Equally unsatisfactory was 20 P × B, P × Kt, etc. ∓

Position after White's 20th move.

20. ......   P × P !

A pretty and exactly calculated

piece offer, which White is practically forced to accept, since both 21. P × P, Kt—Q 4 ! and 21. P—K 4, Kt—Q 2 would have left him even fewer chances of salvation.

21. P × B   P × P
22. B × K P   ......

A comparatively more difficult variation for Black was 22. B × Kt P, Kt—Q 4 ; 23. P—Q R 3, P—Q R 4 ; 24. Q—B 4 !, P × B ! ; 25. Q × Kt, P × P ; 26. R—K B 1 (or 26. P—Kt 4, B—B 6 followed by ....B × P), P—R 7 ! ; 27. R × P, B—B 6 ch ; 28. K any, R × Kt and wins.

22. ......   Kt × P
23. B—B 4   ......

Anything else was equally unsatisfactory—for instance : I. 23. B—Kt 1, B—B 6 ch ; 24. K—B 1, R—Kt 3, etc. II. 23. B—B 2, B—B 6 ch ; 24. K—B 1, R—B 3 ! ; 25. K—Kt 1, Kt × B ; 26. Q × Kt, R—Q 1, etc., with a winning position.

23. ......   B—B 6 ch
24. R—Q 2   ......

Obviously forced.

24. ......   R × Kt !
25. Kt × R   ......

If 25. B × R then 25. ....Q—K 1 ch ! wins immediately.

25. ......   Q × Kt

Black has at last enough from all the complications and selects the clearest variation, which secures him a slight material advantage (Queen and Pawn against two Rooks) by persisting attack. A shorter way to victory was, however, 25. ....R—K 1 ch ! with the following main variation : 26. Kt—K 4, P—B 4 ; 27. K—Q 1, R × Kt ; 28. R—Q 8 ch, K—B 2 ; 29. B—

Kt 5, P—B 5 ! ; 30. K—B 1, R—
K 7 ; 31. Q—Q 3, Q×B ! and wins.

26. B×R	Q—K 2 ch
27. K—Q 1	Kt—K 6 ch
28. K—B 1	Kt×Q
29. R×Kt	P—K R 4 !

A necessary preparation for
B—Kt 2.

| 30. R—Q 1 | B—Kt 2 |
| 31. P—K R 3 | P—R 4 |

Black's chief trumps—which by
right use must guarantee the win—
are (1) the permanent insecurity of
White's King ; (2) the unprotected
position of the Bishop, whose efforts
to find a safe square are bound to
fail. The game remains lively and
instructive until the very end.

32. B—B 4	Q—K 5
33. B—B 7	Q—K 6 ch
34. K—Kt 1	P—Q R 5 !

By this break-up, which could not
in the long run be prevented, Black
wins perforce at least the exchange.

35. P×P	P—Kt 6
36. P×P	Q×P ch
37. K—B 1	B—R 3 ch
38. K R—Q 2	Q×Q R P
39. B—K 5	......

Instead, 39. K—Q 1 would have
slightly prolonged the game, as
Black would be compelled first to
force the white King back on the
Q's side by means of 39. .....B×R ;
40. K×B, Q—K 5 !; 41. K—B 1,
Q—K 8 ch, etc.—and only after
that decide the game· on the other
wing through a gradual advance of
his Pawns supported by the King.

| 39. ...... | K—R 2 |
| 40. B—B 3 | Q—Kt 4 ! |

Preventing 41. K—Q 1.

| 41. B—Q 4 | .... |

White no longer has satisfactory
moves left. If, for instance, 41.
B—R 1, then 41. ....Q—B 8 ch,
followed by ....B—Kt 2 ch, etc.

41.	Q—K 7 !
42. P—Kt 4	Q—K 8 ch
43. K—Kt 2	B×R
44. R—B 8	B—B 8 ch !
Resigns.	

GAME 75

FRENCH DEFENCE

Seventh Match-Game, Utrecht,
October, 1935.

Black : Dr. M. Euwe

1. P—K 4	P—K 3
2. P—Q 4	P—Q 4
3. Kt—Q B 3	B—Kt 5
4. Kt—K 2	P×P
5. P—Q R 3	B—K 2

Even more convincing is 5. ....
B×Kt ch ; 6. Kt×B, Kt—Q B 3
with at least an even game.
This possibility practically refutes
White's fourth move.

| 6. Kt×P | Kt—Q B 3 |

Also here the Knight's move is
good enough. In the fifth game of
this match I tried here 7. B—K 3
(if 7. P—Q B 3 then 7. ....
P—K 4), but did not obtain after
7. ....Kt—B 3 ; 8. K Kt—B 3,
Castles (threatening already Kt×
Kt followed by P—K B 4) more
than equality. Therefore I decided
to try in the present game the
following paradoxical-looking Pawn
move, the obvious idea being to
combine the fianchetto development
of the King's Bishop with a possible
Pawn attack on the King's side.

| 7. P—K Kt 4 !? P—Q Kt 3 |

This is not even an attempt at a
refutation and White soon obtains
the kind of position he was aiming

at. True enough, the most natural answer 7. ....P—K 4 would also not be convincing, because of 8. P—Q 5, Kt—Q 5 ; 9. K Kt—B 3 (but not 9. Kt×Kt, Q×P!∓)— and if 9. ....P—K B 4 then 10. P×P, B×B P; 11. B—K 3, etc., with fair fighting chances for White ; but 7. ....Kt—B 3 ! ; 8. Kt×Kt ch, B×Kt ; 9. B—K 3, Q—Q 4, etc., would have secured for Black a comfortable development of all his forces and thus prove the inefficiency of White's seventh move.

   8. B—Kt 2   B—Kt 2
   9. P—Q B 3   Kt—B 3
  10. K Kt—Kt 3   Castles ?

Even if it could be proved that Black can find an adequate defence against the following King's side attack, the text-move should still be condemned as bringing Black's game into danger without any profit or necessity. After the simple 10. ....Q—Q 2 followed by .... Castles (Q R) White would remain with an unimportant advantage in space but without any real attacking prospects.

  11. P—Kt 5   Kt×Kt
  12. Kt×Kt   K—R 1

Preparing for ....P—K B 4 which White prevents by his following strong move.

  13. Q—R 5 !   ......

If now 13. ....P—B 4 then of course 14. P—Kt 6 with deadly effect.

  13. ......   Q—K 1

Threatening again ....P—B 4 but allowing the following promising combination. Safer was, anyhow, 13. ....Kt—R 4, as the variation 14. P—Kt 4, Kt—Kt 6 ; 15. Kt—B 6, P×Kt ; 16. B×B,

P—K B 4 ! etc., would not be dangerous for Black. In that case White would improve his pressure by finishing his development—14. B —B 4 eventually followed by Castles (Q R), etc. ±

Position after Black's 13th move.

  14. Kt—B 6 !   ......

A correct Pawn-offer securing White a strong and most likely irresistible offensive.

  14. ......   B×Kt

The alternative was 14. ....P× Kt ; 15. P×P, Kt—R 4 (If 15. .... B×B P ? then 16. B—K 4 followed by mate) ; 16. P×B, Q×P ; 17. B×B, Kt×B ; 18. B—Kt 5, P— K B 3 ; 19. B—R 6, R—K Kt 1 ; 20. Castles (Q R), Kt—Q 3 ; 21. K R—K 1, etc., with a clear advantage for White.

  15. P×B   P×P
  16. Q—R 4   Q—Q 1

Forced, since 16. ....Q—K 2 would lose a piece after 17. B—K 4 ! etc.

  17. B—B 4 !   ......

This continuation of the attack— which point consists in the Bishop's retreat on the next move—was by no means easy to find. Black's comparatively best chance was now to give back his extra-Pawn by playing 17. ....P—B 4—although after 18. Q×Q, Q R×Q ; 19. B×P, R—Q 2 ; 20. B—B 4, Kt—R 4 ; 21. R—K Kt 1 ! etc., White's end-game advantage would be quite evident.

17. ......   P—K 4
18. B—Kt 3 !   P—B 4

There is hardly anything better now. If, for instance, 18. ....P×P then 19. Castles (Q R) !, etc., with an easy attacking play.

19. P×P   ......

Also here 19. Castles (Q R) was strong. But the simple recuperation of the material sacrificed is, considering White's powerful attacking possibilities, convincing enough.

19. ......   R—K Kt 1
20. B—B 3 ?   ......

But this inexact move permits Black to inaugurate a saving counter-attack. Practically decisive was instead 20. Q—R 3 ! after which 20. ....Q—Q 6 would have been refuted by 21. B—R 4 ! and 20. .... R—Kt 5 by 21. Castles ! threatening P—K B 3 with a win of material by persisting attack.

20. ......   Q—Q 6 !

An ingenious resource ; but, as the following shows, Black, in adopting it, did not actually realise how many interesting possibilities it opened to him.

21. B—K 2   ......

White has nothing better, since 21. B × Kt ? would be fatal, because of 21. ....B—R 3 ! ; 22. Q—R 5, R—Kt 5 ! etc.

Position after White's 21st move.

21. ......   Q—K 5 ?

Leading to a lost end-game. From an objective point of view it is certainly a pity that Black avoids the fantastical complications deriving from 21. ....Q—B 7 !—a move which by right continuation would have secured him a draw.   Here follows the main variation as well as some minor possibilities :

22. Q—B 6 ch, R—Kt 2 ; 23. R—K Kt 1 ! (a) Q×P ; 24. P—K 6 ! !, Q×R ch ; 25. B—Q 1, Kt—Q 5 ! ! ; (b) 26. Q×R ch ! (c) K×Q ; 27. B—R 4 dis. ch, K—R 3 ! (d) 28. B—Kt 5 ch, K any ; 29. B—R 4 dis. ch, etc. Draw by perpetual check.

(a) Not good is the plausible 23. P—K 6 because of 23. ....R—K 1! ; 24. K R—Kt 1 !, B—R 3 ! ! (.... R × P ; 25. B—K 5 ! and wins) ; 25. B × B, R × P ch ; 26. B—K 5, Q—K 5 ch ; 27. K—B 1, Q×B, etc., with advantage for Black.

(b) But not 25. ....R—Q 1 nor 25. ....Q—Kt 8 because of the answer 26. B—Q 6 ! ! with a win for White.

(c) There are no winning chances for White by the continuation 26. Q×Kt, P—K B 3 ! ; 27. Q×B P, B—B 6 ; 28. K—Q 2, Q—R 7 ch ; 29. B—B 2, B—K 5 etc.

(d) Instead 27. ....K—B 1 loses : 28. P—K 7 ch, K—K 1 ; 29.

R—Kt 8 ch, K—Q 2 ; 30. R—Q 8
ch and wins.

| 22. | Q×Q | P×Q |
| 23. | B—R 4 ! | ...... |

The winning move, probably
overlooked by Black when he
played 21. ....Q—K 5. After 23.
Castles (Q R) he would have obtained excellent drawing chances by
continuing 23. ....R×B ! ; 24.
R P×R, Kt×P etc.

23.	......	P—K R 3
24.	Castles	Q R—K 1
25.	B—B 6 ch	K—R 2
26.	P—K B 4 !	P×P e.p.
27.	B×P	......

Of course much stronger than
winning the exchange for a Pawn
by 27. B—Q 3 ch, etc. The White
Bishops are now dominating the
board and Black is unable to prevent the intrusion of the hostile
Rook on his second rank.

| 27. | ...... | Kt—R 4 |

The exchange of Bishops, which
possibly would have saved the
battle in the early middle game,
does not bring any relief at this
stage.

| 28. | B×B | Kt×B |
| 29. | R—Q 7 | ...... |

The beginning of the execution.

29.	......	Kt—B 4
30.	R×P ch	K—Kt 3
31.	R×P	Kt—Q 6 ch
32.	K—Kt 1	......

Also the simple 32. K—B 2 was
good enough.

32.	......	K—B 4
33.	R—Q 1	Kt×K P
34.	R—B 1 ch	K—K 5
35.	R×P	Kt—B 5

Or 35. ....Kt—B 6 ; 36. R—
R 4 ch, K—K 6 ; 37. B—Q 4 ch,
etc. Black's game is quite hopeless.

36.	R—Q 7	K—K 6
37.	R—K 1 ch	K—B 6
38.	R×R	R×R
39.	R—Q.4	Kt—K 6
40.	R—K R 4	Kt—B 4
41.	R—Q Kt 4	Resigns

GAME 76

VIENNA OPENING

Twenty-seventh Match - Game,
The Hague, December, 1935.

Black : Dr. M. Euwe

1.	P—K 4	P—K 4
2.	Kt—Q B 3	Kt—K B 3
3.	B—B 4	Kt×P
4.	Q—R 5	Kt—Q 3
5.	B—Kt 3	......

Instead, 5. Q×K P ch, Q—K 2,
etc., leads to a perfectly even game.
Being compelled to play for a win
at any price, I decided to allow my
opponent to make the offer of an
exchange which for about 30 years
has been known to give him excellent attacking chances. It is : 5.
....Kt—Q B 3 (!) ; 6. Kt—Kt 5.
P—K Kt 3 ; 7. Q—B 3, P—B 4 ; 8,
Q—Q 5, Q—B 3 ; 9. Kt×P ch,
K—Q 1 ; 10. Kt×R, P—Kt 3 (or
Q Kt 4) followed by ....B—Q Kt 2
after which White would have to
suffer—for a while, at least. It is,
however, psychologically easy to
understand that with two points
ahead Euwe did not want to take
such chances.

| 5. | ...... | B—K 2 |
| 6. | Kt—B 3 | Kt—B 3 |

Instead, 6. ....Castles would be
slightly premature because of the
possibility 7. P—K R 4.

7. Kt × P   Kt × Kt ?

An instructive opening mistake.
Black underestimated the potential
power of the opponent's K's Bishops
which could be eliminated after 7.
....Castles ; 8. Kt—Q 5, Kt—Q 5 !;
9. Castles, Kt × B ; 10. R P × Kt,
Kt—K 1, etc., with about even
prospects. After the text-move
White succeeds in preventing for
rather a long time the normal development of Black's Q's side and
maintains a gradually increasing
pressure.

8. Q × Kt   Castles
9. Kt—Q 5 !   ......

It was important to prevent 9.
....B—B 3.

9. ......   R—K 1
10. Castles   B—B 1
11. Q—B 4   P—Q B 3

As Black will not succeed in
playing ....P—Q 4, this move does
not make matters easier for him.
Worth considering was, instead, 11.
....P—Q Kt 3, since 12. Kt × P
(Q × Kt ? ; 13. B × P ch ±) would
be erroneous because of 12. ....
R—K 5 !

12. Kt—K 3   Q—R 4
13. P—Q 4   ......

Chiefly in order to prevent 13.
....Q—K 4. That Black has temporarily the control upon his K 5 is
comparatively unimportant.

13. ......   Q—R 4

Of course not 13. ....R—K 5
because of 14. B × P ch, etc.

14. P—Q B 3   Kt—K 5

If 14. ....Kt—Kt 4, then 15.
P—Q R 4, B—Q 3 ; 16. Q × P ch,
Q × Q ; 17. B × Q ch followed by P ×
Kt, etc., to White's advantage.

Position after Black's 14th move.

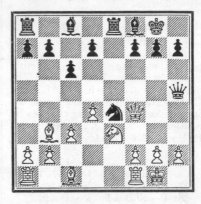

15. P—B 3 !   ......

By this important intermediate
move White practically forces the
isolation of Black's Q P and thus
obtains an appreciable end-game
advantage.

15. ......   Kt—Kt 4

There is nothing better. If, for
instance, 15. ....B—Q 3, then 16.
Q × P ch ! etc., finally winning a
Pawn, and if 15. ....Kt—B 3 then
16. Kt—Kt 4 ! etc., also with a
strong advantage.

16. P—Q 5 !   ......

Threatening, of course, 17. P—
K R 4.

16. ......   P × P
17. Kt × P   Kt—K 3
18. Q—K Kt 4   ......

The seemingly more energetic 18.
Q—Kt 3, Q—Kt 3 ; 19. P—K B 4
would, in fact, not be so clear
because of 19. ....B—B 4 ch ; 20.
K—R 1, Q × Q ; 21. P × Q, R—
Kt 1 ; 22. P—B 5, Kt—B 1, etc.

18. ......   Q—Kt 3
19. B—K 3   P—Kt 3
20. Q R—Q 1   B—Kt 2

21. Q × Q   ......

After all White's forces have been mobilised there is time for transforming the battle into an end-game in which Black's Pawn weaknesses will become even more apparent than they are at the moment.

21. ......   R P × Q
22. K R—K 1   Q R—B 1
23. K—B 2   B—B 4

What else ? If, for instance, 23. ....Kt—B 4, then 24. B—B 2 followed by the doubling of Rooks against Black's weakness at Q 2.

24. B × B   B × Kt

If 24. ....P × B then 25. Kt—K 3 followed by Kt—D 4 Q 6, etc., with a big advantage. But 24. ....R × B would possibly have allowed a more stubborn resistance.

25. B × R   Kt × B
26. R × R ch   R × R
27. P—Q Kt 4 ! ......

The point of the previous exchanges. White—rightly—considers that in the following Rook end-game his Pawn majority on the Q's side, *supported by the King and strengthened by the fact that the enemy's King is completely out of play*, will become decisive. Black, obviously, cannot avoid the exchange of minor pieces as 27. .... Kt—R 5 ; 28. B—Kt 3 followed by R × P, etc., would be hopeless.

27. ......   Kt—K 3
28. B × Kt   Q P × B
29. R—Q 7   ......

After 29. P—Q B 4, R—Q B 1 ; 30. R—Q B 1, K—B 1, etc., White's advantage would not be decisive.

29. ......   R—Q B 1
30. R × R P   R × P
31. R—R 8 ch   K—R 2

Position after Black's 31st move.

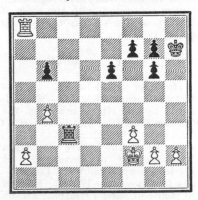

32. P—Q R 4 ?   ......

This rather obvious mistake in a technically won position has not —to my knowledge—been noticed by any of the eminent critics who have devoted many pages to the analysis of the possibilities offered by this end-game. The main disadvantage of the text-move is that it leaves the squares Q R 3 and Q Kt 3 free for the Black Rook, which therefore from now on can be dislodged from the third rank only at cost of valuable time. Correct—and simple enough—was 32. K—K 2 ! after which the black Rook would be (1) either dragged into a purely passive position—as in the actual game—after 33. K—Q 2, etc.; (2) or forced to undertake immediately the counter-attack 32. .... R—B 7 ch with the result 33. K—Q 3, R × Kt P ; 34. K—B 4 !—and one would not need to count *tempi* in order to realise that White's passed Pawn, supported, if necessary, by the King, will be by far the quickest. The fact that I missed this simple win after having deserved it by the previous difficult positional play, proves once more the poor form I was in in 1935. In the second match I—fortunately—took advantage of such opportunities regularly and without hesitation (compare, for instance, the analogous King's manœuvre connected with the offer of the whole Q's side in the second game, 1937, No. 97) !

32. ......   R—Kt 6

Hopeless would be 32. ....R—B 7 ch because of 33. K—K 3 followed by the King's march to the Q's side ; but after 32. ....P—K 4 ! (certainly a difficult move to find in a practical game) there would not be—according to several Soviet Masters, supported by Dr. Lasker—any forced win for White. Even if so (some of their variations are by no means convincing), this would only prove that White's previous move was an even bigger omission than it actually seemed to be ; but for the general appreciation of the *character* of the Rook ending reached after Black's 28th move all that analysing has no importance whatsoever.

33. P—Kt 5   P—Kt 4
34. K—K 2   ......

Because of Black's loss of time at his 32nd move this King's trip will be successful even now.

34. ......   P—K 4
35. K—Q 2   P—B 3
36. K—B 2   R—Kt 5
37. K—B 3   R—Q 5

Black has succeeded in preventing the formation of *two* passed Pawns, but, to his bad luck, *one* Pawn, supported by the King, is amply sufficient !

38. R—R 6   K—Kt 3
39. R × P   R × P
40. R—R 6   R—Q 5
41. P—Kt 6   Resigns

GAME 77

QUEEN'S GAMBIT ACCEPTED

Bad Nauheim Tournament, May, 1936.

White : K. AHUES

1. P—Q 4   P—Q 4
2. P—Q B 4   P × P
3. Kt—K B 3   P—Q R 3

This move, in connection with the next, was introduced by me in the third game of the 1934 Match with Bogoljubow. Even if it can be convincingly proved (which has not been done) that the Bishop's development at K Kt 5 is not good for Black, the text-move will still be used by those who prefer to avoid the variations starting with White's Q—R 4 ch.

4. P—Q R 4   ......

White has no reason for preventing ....P—Q Kt 4, since the variation 4. P—K 3, P—Q Kt 4 ; 5. P—Q R 4, B—Kt 2 ; 6. P × P, P × P ; 7. R × R, B × R ; 8. P—Q Kt 3, etc., is to his advantage. The text-move, besides losing time, weakens also White's Q Kt 4 and, therefore, has to be decidedly condemned. The two following positional fights may give an idea as to Black's possibilities after 4. P—K 3, B—Kt 5. The character of the ensuing conflict depends on whether White leaves the pawn-structure intact in the centre (as in I), or tries to solve the centre-problem in a dynamic way (as in II).

I. *White : E. Zinner, Podebrad,* 1936. 4. *P—K 3, B—Kt 5 ; 5. B × P, P—K 3 ; 6. P—K R 3— B—R 4 ; 7. Q—Kt 3, R—R 2 (or ....B × Kt ; 8. P × B, P—Q Kt 4) ; 8.* P—Q R 4, Kt—Q B 3 ; 9. B—Q 2, Kt—B 3 ; 10. B—B 3, Kt—Q 4 ; 11. Q Kt—Q 2, Kt × B ; 12. P × Kt. Kt—R 4 ; 13. Q—R 2, Kt × B ; 14,

Q×Kt, B—Q 3 ; 15. R—Q Kt 1,
O—O ; 16. O—O, B—Kt 3 ; 17.
R—Kt 2, P—Q B 3 ; 18. Q—Kt 3,
P—Kt 4 ; 19. P—B 4, R—Kt 2 ;
20. R—R 1, R—Kt 1 ; 21. K R—
R 2, B—B 2 ; 22. Q—Q 1, B—Q 6 ! ;
23. B P×P, B P×P ; 24. Kt—K 1,
B—K Kt 3 ; 25. Q—K 2, Q—Q 3 ;
26. Q Kt—B 3, P—Kt 5 ! ; 27.
Kt—Q 3, B—K 5 ; 28. Kt—B 5,
B—Q 4 ; 29. Kt—Kt 3, K R—B 1 ;
30. R—R 1, P—Q R 4 ; 31. R—
Q B 1, B—Kt 3 ; 32. Q R—B 2,
R×R ; 33. Q×R, Q—Q 2 ! ; 34.
P—K 4, B×Kt ; 35. Q×B, R—
Q B 1 ; 36. R—B 4, R×R ; 37.
Q×R, P—R 3 ; 38. P—Q 5, Q×
R P ; 39. Q—B 8 ch, K—R 2 ; 40.
Q—Kt 7, B—Q 1 ! ; 41. Q×B P,
Q—R 8 ch ; 42. K—R 2, Q—B 3 ;
43. Q—Q 7, P—Kt 6 ; 44. P—R 4,
P—Kt 7 ; 45. Q—Kt 5, P×P ; 46.
Resigns.

II.   *White : Axelsson, Orebro,*
1935. (The six first moves as in
the previous game.) 7. O—O, Kt—
K B 3 ; 8. Kt—B 3, Kt—B 3 ; 9. B—
K 2, B—Q 3 ; 10. P—Q Kt 3 (better
than P—R 3 played in an anal-
ogous position by Bogoljubow in the
game mentioned above), O—O ; 11.
B—Kt 2, Q—K 2 ; 12. *P—K 4*, B×
Kt ; 13. B×B, Q R—Q 1 ; 14. Kt—
K 2, B—B 4 ; 15. R—B 1, B—Kt 3 ;
16. Q—B 2, P—K 4 ; 17. P—Q 5,
Kt—Q Kt 5 ; 18. B—R 3 ! , P—
Q R 4 ; 19. Q—B 4, Kt—K 1 ; 20.
K R—Q 1, Q—R 5 ! ; 21. B×Kt,
Q×P ch ; 22. K—R 2, P×B ; 23.
Q×Kt P, Kt—Q 3 ; 24. P—Q R 4,
R—R 1 ; 25. R—B 1, Q—R 5 ;
26. Q—Q 2, P—Kt 3 ! ; 27. P—Kt 3,
Q—K 2 ; 28. Kt—B 3, P—K B 4 ;
29. P×P, P×P ; 30. Q R—K 1,
Q—Kt 2 ; 31. P—Q Kt 4, P—K 5 ;
32. B—Q 1, Kt—B 5 ; 33. Q—B 1,
Kt—K 4 ; 34. B—K 2, P—B 3 ! ;
35. P×P, P×P ; 36. R—Q 1, K—
R 1 ; 37. P—R 5, R—K Kt 1 ; 38.
Q—B 4, B—B 2 ; 39. Q—B 2, Kt—
Q 6 ! ; 40. Resigns.

| 4. | ...... | Kt—K B 3 |
| 5. | P—K 3 | B—Kt 5 |

| 6. | B×P | P—K 3 |
| 7. | Kt—B 3 | Kt—B 3 |

As one may see from the prefixed
games, this Knight's development
belongs to the system inaugurated
by ....B—K Kt 5. In this particular position it is more appropriate than ever, Black having at
his disposal, if needed, the square
Q Kt 5.

8.	B—K 2	B—Kt 5
9.	Castles	Castles
10.	Kt—Q 2	......

White is over-anxious to simplify
and allows, to his disadvantage,
the following advance of Black's
K P. The quieter 10. B—Q 2 would
probably leave him more equalising
chances.

| 10. | ...... | B×B |
| 11. | Kt×B | P—K 4 ! |

As the opening of the central files
through P×K P would be here, or
on the following moves, obviously
to the benefit of the better developed party, White will practically be compelled to allow a
further advance of this Pawn, after
which the activity of his Bishop
will be limited to a minimum.

| 12. | Kt—K B 3 | R—K 1 |
| 13. | B—Q 2 | B—Q 3 |

The exchange of the opponent's
poorest piece would be, of course,
a grave strategical error.

| 14. | Kt—Kt 3 | P—K 5 |
| 15. | Kt—K 1 | B×Kt ! |

After this exchange, the im-
mobilised Pawn mass on the King's
side will be unable to prevent in the
long run the attacking formation
....Kt—K Kt 5 and ....Q—K B 4

(or K R 4). The little counter-demonstration that White will now undertake on the open Q B-file can be parried without effort or loss of time.

16. R P × B   Kt—K 2

The full control upon Black's Q 4 is the key of the situation.

17. P—Q Kt 4   Q—Q 2
18. Kt—B 2   Q Kt—Q 4
19. Kt—R 3   P—Q Kt 4 !

Confining the mobility of the hostile Knight.

20. P × P   P × P
21. Q—K 2   P—B 3

This Pawn could eventually become weak—had not Black already prepared a plan for an irresistible mating attack !

22. Kt—B 2   Q—B 4

White cannot even answer this move by P—B 3—his Knight being unprotected—and he has nothing better than to prepare a desperate King's flight.

23. K R—Q B 1 P—R 3

A useful precaution—especially as White has left such small choice of moves.

24. R—R 5   Q R—B 1
25. Kt—R 1   ......

The Knight dreams of at last reaching a more suitable square (Q B 5), but it is much, much too late !

25. ......   Kt—Kt 5

With the strong threat 26. .... Q—R 4

26. K—B 1   ......

Position after White's 26th move.

26. ......   R—K 3 !

A similar stratagem to that in the Dresden game against Bogoljubow (No. 79) : Black gives up a useless unit in order to gain the K B P and thus denude the enemy's King.

27. R × Kt P   R—B 3
28. Q R—B 5   Kt × B P
29. K—K 1   ......

Or, 29. K—Kt 1, Kt—Kt 5 followed by ....Q—R 4 and mate.

29. ......   Kt—Q 6 ch
30. K—Q 1   Q—B 8 ch
31. B—K 1   R—B 7 !

Expecting 32. Q × Q, after which I would have the pleasant choice between the Knight-mate at Q Kt 7 and K 6.

White resigns.

GAME 78

QUEEN'S GAMBIT DECLINED (CAMBRIDGE SPRINGS DEFENCE)

Bad Nauheim Tournament, May, 1936.

Black : E. BOGOLJUBOW

1.	P—Q 4	P—Q 4
2.	P—Q B 4	P—K 3
3.	Kt—Q B 3	Kt—K B 3
4.	B—Kt 5	Q Kt—Q 2
5.	P—K 3	P—B 3
6.	Kt—B 3	Q—R 4
7.	Kt—Q 2	......

The most logical reply to Black's 6th move, for it reduces his possibilities on the diagonal Q R 4—K 8 to a minimum.

7.	......	B—Kt 5
8.	Q—B 2	P×P

Obtaining the pair of Bishops, which, however, is hardly sufficient compensation for the abandonment of the centre. The older 8. .... Castles together with ....Kt—K 5 is comparatively more promising.

9.	B×Kt	Kt×B
10.	Kt×P	Q—B 2
11.	P—K Kt 3	Castles

Useless would be 11. .....P—B 4, because of 12. B—Kt 2, after which 12. ....P×P would be met by 13. Q—R 4 ch.

12.	B—Kt 2	B—Q 2

Here, also, 12. ....P—B 4, would have led to nothing after 13. Castles K R, P×P; 14. Kt—Kt 5, etc. But, after the text-move, White has to count upon the possible advance of the Q B P, which explains his next two moves.

13.	P—Q R 3	B—K 2
14.	P—Q Kt 4	Kt—Q 4
15.	Castles (K side)	......

15. Kt—K 4 also came into consideration, but I estimated that White's advantage after the exchange of Knights would be convincing enough and that there was not, therefore, any necessity for trying to complicate matters by avoiding it.

15.	......	Kt×Kt
16.	Q×Kt	K R—Q 1
17.	Q R—B 1	......

The right utilisation of the pair of Rooks on the half-open files often presents a very difficult problem. Here, for instance, it was obvious enough that *one* Rook has to be posted on the Q B-file in order to make the realisation of ....P—Q B 4 even more difficult, but where develop the other—at Q Kt 1 or Q 1 ? As the reader will see, I did not select here the most effective method, thus permitting my opponent to obtain, at one moment, a fairly even game. The correct scheme was K R—Q B 1 and Q R—Kt 1.

17.	......	B—K 1
18.	K R—Q 1	Q R—B 1
19.	Kt—R 5	......

Trying, through the threat P—Q Kt 5, to provoke Black's next move. But far more important was still 19. R—Kt 1 !, P—Q Kt 3 ; 20. K R—Q B 1, preventing the freeing ....P—Q B 4.

19.	......	P—Q R 3
20.	Kt—B 4	P—Q Kt 3 !
21.	R—Kt 1	......

Too late !

21.	......	B—B 3

Black still prepares for ....P—

Q B 4, not realising that he could—and should—play it immediately. As White would not profit either from I. 22. Kt×P!?, P×Kt P!; 23. Q×Q, R×Q; 24. P×P, R—Kt 1; 25. Kt—R 8, R—R 2, or from II. 22. Kt P×P, P×P; 23. R—Kt 7, P×P; 24. R×P, R×R; 25. R×Q, R—Q 8 ch, followed by R×R∓, he would have had nothing better than 22. Kt P×P, P×P; 23. P—Q 5!, P×P; 24. B×P, B—Q R 5; 25. R—Q 3, B—K B 3; 26. Q—Q 2, B—Q Kt 4, etc., with a draw in prospect owing to the unavoidable "different coloured" Bishops. Now White succeeds in taking full advantage of his opportunity.

22. K R—Q B 1   ......

Protects the Knight once more in order to make possible, after 22. ....P—B 4?, the manœuvre 23. Kt P×P, P×P; 24. R—Kt 7, etc.

22. ......   Q—R 2
23. Q—B 2!   ......

Definitely preventing ....P—B 4 and threatening to advance the Q R P in order to gain the square Q Kt 6 for the Knight.

23. ......   R—B 2
24. P—Q R 4   B—K 2

Or 24. ....P—B 4; 25. P—R 5!, etc.

25. P—R 5   P×P
26. P×P   P—Q B 4

Now this move has no more effect, since the White pieces have in the meantime taken possession of the commanding spots. It is instructive to observe how little the famous "two Bishops" have to say here, if chiefly because of a previous inexact handling of the heavy pieces.

27. Kt—Kt 6   B—Q Kt 4
28. P—Q 5   P×P

29. B×P!   ......

Much stronger than 29. Kt×P, for the Bishop will be very useful at B 4 for blocking the passed Pawn.

29. ......   B—B 1
30. R—Q 1   R—Q 3
31. B—B 4   ......

At the same time, White gets control of the open file, his powerful Knight preventing the free manœuvring of Black's Queen and Rook. The second player deservedly pays the penalty for his short-sighted 21st move.

31. ......   R×R ch
32. R×R   Q—Kt 1
33. Q—Q 3   Q—K 1
34. Q—Q 8   ......

From now on simplicity is trumps!

34. ......   R—K 2
35. Q×Q   B×Q

After 35. ....R×Q, there would have been a short, sharp win: 36. B×B, P×B; 37. P—R 6, P—B 5; 38. P—R 7, P—B 6; 39. R—Q 7!, B—B 4; 40. P—R 8 (Q), R×Q; 41. Kt×R followed by 42. R—Q 8 ch and 43. R—B 8.

36. R—Q 8   B—B 3

Position after Black's 36th move.

37. B × P   ......

This first material win is absolutely decisive, since Black cannot even try to obtain compensation by 37. ....R—R 2 because of 38. Kt—B 8 ! etc. In spite of White's inexactitude on the 17th and 19th moves, the game is a fairly good illustration of the Cambridge Springs Defence with White's 7. Kt—Q 2.

37.	P—Kt 3
38. B—B 4	R—Kt 2
39. K—B 1	K—Kt 2
40. K—K 2	B—K 2
41. R—Q B 8	B—Kt 7
42. P—B 3	P—R 4
43. P—K 4	B—R 6
44. R—K 8	B—K B 1
45. P—R 6	R—B 2
40. P—K 5 !	,,....

Preventing ....B—Q 3 and threatening now 47. R—Kt 8 followed by R—Kt 7 etc.

46.	B—Q 2
47. Kt × B	R × Kt
48. R—Kt 8	Resigns.

GAME 79

THREE KNIGHTS' GAME

Dresden Tournament, May, 1936.

Black: E. Bogoljubow

1. P—K 4	P—K 4
2. Kt—K B 3	Kt—Q B 3
8. Kt—B 3	P—K Kt 3

Playing at his best Bogoljubow would hardly have selected such an obviously inferior defence—since he knows very well how to play the Four Knights' game with Black (see, for instance, his game against Maroczy, London, 1922).

4. P—Q 4	P × P
5. Kt—Q 5 !	B—Kt 2
6. B—K Kt 5	Q Kt—K 2

This unnatural looking move is already the only one, since after 6. ....P—B 3 ; 7. B—K B 4, P—Q 3, the diagonal K Kt 1—Q R 7 would become fatally weak.

7. P—K 5   ......

White has the choice between this only seemingly more aggressive move—which in fact is leading to a favourable end-game—and the simple 7. Kt × P, with excellent middle-game prospects after 7. ....P—Q B 3 ; 8. Kt × Kt, Kt × Kt ; 9. Q—Q 2 followed by Castles, etc. Possibly this way was the more logical one.

7. ......   P—K R 3 !

Otherwise 8. Kt—B 6 ch. would be too strong.

8. B × Kt   ......

The sacrifice of a pawn by 8. B—B 6, B × B ; 9. Kt × B ch, Kt × Kt ; 10. P × Kt, Kt—Kt 1 followed by ....Q × P would not have paid.

8.	Kt × B
9. Q × P	Kt × Kt
10. Q × Kt	......

White's advantage in space begins to become alarming, so Black must try to exchange Queens as quickly as possible in order to avoid an unanswerable King's side attack.

10. ......   P—Q B 3

If 10. ....P—Q 3 then 11. Castles, B—K 3 ; 12. Q—Kt 5 ch ! etc. ±

11. Q—Q 6	B—B 1
12. Q—Q 4	Q—Kt 3
13. Castles !	......

By offering his K B P, White wins an important developing *tempo*. Black rightly refuses this offer, for, after 13. ....B—B 4 ; 14. Q—B 3, B×P ; 15. Kt—Q 4 !, his position would have rapidly gone to pieces.

| 13. ...... | Q×Q |
| 14. Kt×Q | ...... |

An interesting and difficult moment. White decides not to prevent the opening of the centre followed by the emancipation of the Bishop, for he is entitled to expect appreciable profits from the two central files dominated by his Rooks. The consequences of the alternative 14. R×Q, B—Kt 2 ; 15. R—K 4, P—Q Kt 4, followed by ....B—Kt 2 and .... Castles (Q R) were, to say the least, not evident, especially as it would be Black who would have the initiative for opening the position.

| 14. ...... | P—Q 4 |

Almost forced, because White, in addition to all the other unpleasant-nesses, threatened P—K B 4—B 5.

15. P×P *e.p.*	B×P
16. B—B 4	Castles
17. K R—K 1	......

The White pieces are beautifully placed while Black's Q B is still looking for a suitable square. Its next sally is the best proof of the difficulties he has to deal with.

17.	B—K Kt 5
18. P—K B 3	B—B 1
19. P—K Kt 3	......

Holding the square K B 4 and now threatening 20. Kt×P.

| 19. ...... | B—Q B 4 |
| 20. Kt—Kt 3 | ...... |

The beginning of an interesting

Knight's manœuvre for the strength-ening of the pressure against Black's K B 2. Also good was 20. P—K Kt 4 followed by P—K R 4-5, etc.

| 20. ...... | B—Kt 3 |
| 21. Kt—Q 2 | ...... |

If 21. R—K 7, then 21. ....K—Kt 2 and eventually ....K—B 3.

| 21. ...... | B—R 6 |
| 22. Kt—K 4 | B—R 4 |

In order to save the Q Kt P by ....P—Q Kt 4.

| 23. P—B 3 | Q R—Q 1 |
| 24. Kt—Q 6 | ...... |

If 24. R×R the answer would not be 24. ....R×R ; 25. Kt—B 2 ! followed by 26. R—K 7 ± but 24. ....B×R ; 25. Kt—Q 6, P—Q Kt 4 ; 26. B—Kt 3, B—B 3, etc. =

| 24. ...... | P—Q Kt 4 |
| 25. B—Kt 3 | R—Q 2 |

Protects for the time being all the vulnerable points. Speaking in general, one must admit that, after his extravagant opening, Bogol-jubow has defended his position most carefully and still preserves fighting chances.

| 26. Kt—K 8 | ...... |

A sound alternative was 26. Kt—K 4, R×R ch ; 27. R×R, although Black would still have a temporary defence by 27. ....K—Kt 2, etc. The text manœuvre is linked with a temporary sacrifice of a Pawn and leads, with the best defence, at least to the capture of Black's K B P.

| 26. ...... | R×R ch |
| 27. K×R | B—Kt 7 |

This counter thrust is Black's best chance. After, for instance,

27. ....B—Q 1, White would increase the pressure without much trouble by 28. Kt—Q 6, B—B 3 ; 29. K—K 2, etc.

28. Kt—B 6 ch ......

White realises that the Black King will be at least no better at R 1 than at K Kt 1, and therefore takes the opportunity of gaining time on the clock. If Black, on his 29th move, had played .... K—Kt 1, I intended to continue as in the actual game, 30. K—B 2, B × K B P ; 31. Kt—Q 6, leading to variations examined further on.

28.	K—Kt 2
29. Kt—K 8 ch	K—R 1
30. K—B 2 !	B × K B P
31. Kt —Q 6	B—Q 4 ?

After Black's stubborn defence so far, this misappreciation of the position seems incredible, as by the further exchange, White obtains : (1) The elimination of Black's pair of Bishops ; (2) The Pawn majority on the Queen's side ; (3) The central square Q 4 for his Knight ; (4) Play against Black's isolated Q P ; (5) The possibility of penetrating with his Rook via K 7 or K 8. Any one of these considerations taken separately should have deterred Bogoljubow from selecting the text-move, and, in fact, he could have set his opponent a by no means easy task by playing 31. .... K—Kt 2. My intention was to continue with 32. R—K 7, and, if 32. .... B—Kt 3 (best), then 33. B × P, B—B 4 ; 34. B—Kt 3 dis. ch, K—R 1 ; 35. Kt—B 7 ch, K—Kt 2 (but not .... K—R 2 ; 36. Kt—Kt 5 dbl. ch, followed by mate) ; 36. R—Kt 7 !, B—K 5 ch ; 37. K—Q 1, K—B 3 ; 38. Kt × P, R—Q 1 ch ; 39. K—K 2, and Black would not have found sufficient compensation for the minus Pawn. Still, it would have been some kind of a fight, whereas what now happens merely reminds one of precisely executed butcher's work !

32. B × B	P × B
33. Kt × P	B—Kt 3
34. K—Q 3	K—Kt 2
35. P—Q Kt 4	......

White's game now plays itself.

35.	R—Q 1
36. P—Q R 4	P—R 3
37. Kt—Q 4	R—Q 3
38. R—K 8	P—K R 4

If, instead, ... R—K B 3, White would first play P—R 5.

| 39. R—Q R 8 | R—K B 3 |

A desperate trap. Needless to say, anything else would be equally hopeless.

Position after Black's 39th move.

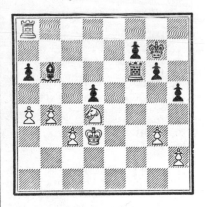

40. R × P ! ......

White walks into the trap and proves that this is the quickest way to win !

40.	B × Kt
41. R × R	B × R
42. P—R 5	......

The extra Bishop is unable to stop the two passed Pawns. If, for instance, 42. ....B—Q 1, then simply 43. K—Q 4, followed by K×P, K—B 6, etc.

| 42. ...... | B—K 4 |
| 43. P—Kt 5 ! | P—R 5 |

Or ....B—B 2 ; 44. P—Kt 6, B—Q 1 ; 45. K—Q 4, etc.

44. P—R 6   ......

Settles the matter, for 44. .... P×P would be answered by 45. P×P, and if 44. ....B×P then 45. P—R 7.

Resigns.

GAME 80

RUY LOPEZ

Podebrad Tournament, June, 1936.

Black : E. ELISKASES

1. P—K 4	P—K 4
2. Kt—K B 3	Kt—Q B 3
3. B—Kt 5	P—Q R 3
4. B—R 4	Kt—B 3
5. Castles	B—K 2
6. R—K 1	P—Q Kt 4
7. B—Kt 3	P—Q 3
8. P—B 3	Kt—Q R 4
9. B—B 2	P—B 4
10. P—Q 3	......

More usual is 10. P—Q 4, which enables White—if he wants to—to blockade the position in the centre by P—Q 5 in order to start a not very promising attack on the King's side. The text-move aims at first finishing development on the Q's side and to play P—Q 4 only afterwards—when, or if, it appears opportune.

| 10. ...... | Kt—B 3 |
| 11. Q Kt—Q 2 | Castles |

| 12. Kt—B 1 | R—K 1 |

A quite acceptable plan—if it had been conceived for defensive purposes only. Another plausible way to finish development without much inconvenience was 12. ....B—K 3 ; 13. Kt—K 3, P—R 3 followed by ....Q—B 2 and ....Q R—Q 1.

| 13. Kt—K 3 | P—Q 4 ? |

A typical mistake : Black is in a hurry to "punish" White for having delayed P—Q 4, and himself starts an operation in the centre—but, as will be promptly shown, at a very unfortunate moment. Logical was 13. ....B—B 1, especially as 14. Kt—Q 5 was not then to be feared : 14. ....Kt×Kt ; 15. P×Kt, Kt—K 2 ; 16. P—Q 4, K P×P ; 17. P×P, P—B 5 !, etc. The chances in that case would be about even.

14. P×P	Kt×P
15. Kt×Kt	Q×Kt
16. P—Q 4 !	......

The refutation : White opens the position in the centre at a moment when the opponent has not yet finished his development and thus succeeds in taking full advantage of the various insufficiently protected points (Kt at Q B 3 the first) in Black's camp.

| 16. ...... | K P×P |
| 17. B—K 4 | Q—Q 2 |

Or, 17. ....Q—Q 3 ; 18. B—B 4.

| 18. P×P | B—B 3 |

Otherwise the further advance of the centre Pawn would prove overwhelming — for instance, 18. ....B—Kt 2 ; 19. P—Q 5, Kt—Q 1 ; 20. Kt—K 5, Q—Q 3 ; 21. B—B 4, etc., with all positional trumps in the hand.

Position after Black's 18th move.

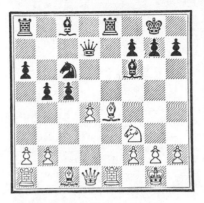

19. B—Kt 5 !   ......

The main idea of this move is shown by the following short variation : 19 . . , B × P ; 20. B—B 5 !, R × R ch ; 21. Q × R, Q—Q 3 ; 22. Q—K 8 ch, Q—B 1 ; 23. B × P ch and wins the Queen ; and since 19. ....B × B ; 20. Kt × B, P—Kt 3 ; 21. P × P etc. would have led to a hopelessly lost end-game, Black, *nolens volens*, must try the following sacrifice of the exchange.

19.	R × B !
20. R × R	B × P
21. Kt × B	Kt × Kt

If Black could have found time to finish the development of his Queen's side, White's slight material gain would have been very difficult to exploit. White, therefore, must act with extreme energy.

22. Q—R 5 !   ......

The point of this rather difficult attacking move may be seen from the continuation : 22. ....B—Kt 2 ; 23. R—R 4 !, P—R 3 ; 24. B × P, Kt—B 4 ; 25. B × P ! and Black would be mated in two if 25. .... K × B.

22. ......   B—Kt 2

Also 22. ....Q—B 3 ; 23. Q R—K 1, B—K 3 ; 24. R—R 4, B—B 4 ; 25. B—K 7 ! would not prove sufficient.

23. R—R 4   Q—B 4

Since 23. ....P—R 3 loses at once (*cf*. above note), Black has no choice.

24. B—K 3 !   ......

Another surprising point of the attacking manœuvre : White forces the exchange of Queens and at the same time dislodges the Knight from its strong central post. After the "normal" moves, 24. .... Q × Q ; 25. R × Q, Kt—B 7 ; 26. R—Q 1 !, Kt × B ; 27. P × Kt, P—B 5 ; 28. R—Q B 5 followed by 29. R—Q 7, the end game would be quite easily won.   Black's next mistake, therefore, only shortens the agony.

| 24. ...... | R—Q 1 ? |
| 25. R × Kt. | Resigns. |

GAME 81

SICILIAN DEFENCE

Podebrad Tournament, June, 1936.

Black : P. FRYDMAN

1. P—K 4	P—Q B 4
2. Kt—K B 3	Kt—Q B 3
3. P—Q 4	P × P
4. Kt × P	Kt—B 3
5. Kt—Q B 3	P—Q 3
6. B—K Kt 5	......

The idea of this move is to eliminate the possibility of .... P—K Kt 3 and ....B—Kt 2 (The Dragon Variation), and it practically forces Black to adopt the so-called Scheveningen Variation, one of the

characteristics of which is the exposed—although quite defensible—
Queen's Pawn on the open file.
White would be mistaken, however,
if he thought that from now on he
could count on a serious opening
advantage ; for my part, in spite of
a 100% success with the text-move,
I am very far from that illusion.

| 6. ...... | P—K 3 |
| 7. Kt—Kt 3 | ...... |

This harmless removal, typical
of many variations in the Sicilian,
contains—as, amongst others, the
present game shows—more venom
than one would suppose. For 7.
B—Kt 5 see my game against
Foltys at Margate (No. 92).

| 7. ...... | B—K 2 |
| 8. Q—Q 2 | ...... |

This attempt to enforce the
pressure against Q 6 should be met
by 8. ....P—K R 3 ! and—only
after 9. B—R 4—Castles, with
the threat 10. ....Kt×P, etc.,
equalising easily. White should,
therefore, play 9. B—K 3 (instead
of B—R 4), but Black, anyhow,
would not for the time being have
to worry about his Queen's Pawn.

| 8. ...... | Castles ? |

Strangely enough, this so plausible answer is already a decisive
mistake, for from now on Black
will only have the choice between
different evils.

| 9. Castles | ...... |

Threatening 10. B×Kt, B×B
(P×B would permit a winning
King's attack starting with 11. Q—
R 6) ; 11. Q×P, etc. Black has
therefore no time either for the
preventative ....P—Q R 3 or for
the simplifying ....P—K R 3.

| 9. ...... | Kt—Q R 4 |

Hoping, after 10. B×Kt, Kt×
Kt ch ; 11. R P×Kt, B×B ; 12.
Q×P, to obtain a counter-attack
through 12. ....Q—R 4 etc.; but
White's strong next move stops
this plan.

| 10. K—Kt 1 ! | Kt×Kt |
| 11. R P×Kt | ...... |

The point of the 10th move is
that Black can no longer play 11.
....Q—R 4 because of 12. Kt—Q 5,
and, likewise, 11. ....Q—Kt 3
would have led to a rapid debacle
after 12. B×Kt, B×B ; 13. Q×
P, Q×B P ; 14. P—K 5, B—Kt
4 ; 15. P—R 4 !, B—B 5 ; 16. B—
Kt 5 ! threatening 17. Q×R ch !
with mate in two. His next move is
therefore the only way, if not to
save the day, at least to prolong
the fight.

11.	Kt—K 1
12. B×B	Q×B
13. Kt—Kt 5	B—Q 2

Expecting, not without reason,
that White's doubled Pawns will
cause him some technical trouble
in finding the winning procedure.

14. Kt×Q P	Kt×Kt
15. Q×Kt	Q×Q
16. R×Q	B—B 3
17. P—K B 3	K R—Q 1
18. R×R ch	R×R
19. B—Q 3	......

The ensuing end-game is highly
instructive. In the first place, White
intends to take full advantage in
the trumps he already possesses :
the open Q R-file and especially
the dominating spot Q R 5.

| 19. ...... | P—K 4 |

Gaining some space in the centre
and intending eventually to use the
Rook on the third rank.

| 20. K—B 1 | K—B 1 |

21. K—Q 2   K—K 2
22. R—R 1   P—Q R 3
23. K—K 3   R—Q 3
24. R—R 5 !   ......

Just at the right moment, as the obligation to protect the King's Pawn will prevent Black from undertaking the intended diversion with the Rook.

24. ......   P—B 3
25. P—Q Kt 4   K—Q 2
26. P—K Kt 3 !   ......

Of course, 26. P—Kt 5, P×P ; 27. B×P would be premature because of 27. ....R—Q 8 etc. The advance in the centre, started by the text-move, will force the Black Rook to leave the open file.

26. ......   P—K Kt 4
27. P—K B 4   Kt P×P ch
28. P×P   R—K 3

After 28. ....P×P ch ; 29. K×P followed by R—R 5 etc., White's work would be easier.

29. P—B 5 !   R—K 2

If 29. ....R—Q 3, then 30. R—R 1— K Kt 1, etc., and the White Rook would have an easy play on the King's side. Now, on the other hand, the doubled Pawn can at last be dissolved.

30. P—Kt 5 !   P×P
31. B×P   R—Kt 2
32. B×B ch   K×B
33. R—R 8   R—Kt 7

This counter attempt is Black's only chance, since 33. ....R— K B 2 ; 34. R—K 8 followed by R—K 6 ch would be fatal.

34. R—B 8   R×R P
35. R×P ch   K—B 4

With the menace 36. ....R—R 6 ch followed by .... K—Q 5.

Position after Black's 35th move.

36. P—Kt 4 ! ch   ......

The first link in the final combination ; White gains the square Q 6 for his Rook.

36. ......   K—B 5 !

If 36. ....K×P, then 37. R— K 6 etc., wins easily.

37. R—Q 6   ......

Threatening 38. R—Q 5, which, however, Black tries to prevent in an ingenious manner.

37. ......   R—R 6 ch
38. K—K 2   R—R 5
39. K—B 3   P—R 4 !

Still making efforts—which are in fact crowned with a kind of " moral " success—to complicate matters. By making this move, Black suggests that White cannot win by playing the natural 40. R—Q 5—and the opponent believes him !

40. R—K 6   ......

This can hardly be called an error since it wins perforce and is coupled with another pretty point. But with 40. R—Q 5 ! White could prove to his opponent that his trap ....was not a trap at all. The continuation would be : 40. .... R—B 5 ch ; 41. K—K 3, R×P ; 42. P×R, K×R ; 43. P—B 4 ch, K—Q 3 ; 44. P—Kt 5, P—Kt 3 (or P—R 5 ; 45. K—B 3, etc.) ; 45. P—B 6, K—K 3 ; 46. P—B 5 and wins. The idea behind that Pawn end-game is that while Black's passed Pawns are separated by only two files and can therefore be stopped by the hostile King, White is able to obtain passed Pawns at a distance of three files from each other. This example is worthy of notice.

40. ......   R—B 5 ch

If 40. ....K—Q 5, then 41. P—B 3 ch (a second, deviating offer) followed by 42. R×P, etc.

41. K—K 3   P—R 5
42. R×P   P—R 6 !

Very neat—but White's material advantage assures him a safe defence against tactical tricks of this kind.

43. R—Q 5   R—R 5
44. R—Q 4 ch !   K—B 6
45. R—Q 1   P—R 7
46. R—K R 1   R—R 6 ch
47. K—B 4   R—R 5 ch
48. K—K 5   K—Q 7
49. P—B 6   K—K 6
50. K—Q 6 !   R×P
51. R×P   R—Q 5 ch
52. K—K 6   Resigns.

GAME 82

QUEEN'S GAMBIT DECLINED (ORTHODOX DEFENCE)

Podebrad Tournament, June, 1936.

Black : J. FOLTYS

1. P—Q 4   P—Q 4
2. P—Q B 4   P—K 3

3. Kt—Q B 3   Kt—K B 3
4. B—Kt 5   B—K 2
5. P—K 3   Q Kt—Q 2
6. Kt—B 3   Castles
7. Q—B 2   ......

This fashionable move—which, for reasons unknown, was disdained for about a quarter of a century—allows Black to start a counter-attack in the centre through 7. ....P—B 4 ; but, as this action cannot be supported by Rooks, the resulting opening of files should turn to White's advantage. Therefore, in my opinion, one should consider, instead of 7. .... P—Q B 4, the following system : 7. ....P—B 3 ; 8. P—Q R 3 (preventing ....Kt—K 5), P—K R 3 ; 9. B—R 4, Kt—K 1 ; 10. B×B (or 10. B—Kt 3, Kt—Q 3), Q×B, followed by ....Kt—Q 3, etc.

7. ......   P—B 4
8. R—Q 1   ......

As Black's reply proves sufficient to equalise, better would have been, as I played in two match games in Buenos Ayres—8. P×Q P, Kt× P ; 9. B×B, Q×B ; 10. Kt×Kt, P×Kt ; 11. P×P, followed by B—K 2 and Castles K R, with a secured slight end-game advantage.

8. ......   Q—R 4
9. B—Q 3   P—K R 3
10. B—R 4   Kt—Kt 3

A good move, which forces White to clear the situation in the centre before he has castled.

11. P×Q P   B P×P

Although not directly bad, this intermediate move certainly cannot be recommended, for it permits White to complicate matters without taking many chances. Incisive and good enough for equalising

was 11. ....Q Kt × P, threatening
12. ....Kt—Q Kt 5 or eventually
....P × Q P etc.

12. P—Q 6 !   ......

This should not bring much—
but, still, it was a relief for White
to be able to leave the routine,
"theoretical" path and force the
opponent to find the best answer by
himself !

12. ......   B × P

Better than 12. ....P × Kt ; 13.
P × B, P × P dis. ch ; 14. R—Q 2, R
—K 1 ; 15. B × Kt, P × B ; 16. Q ×
P, etc. ±

13. B × Kt   P × B ?

But this weakening of the King's
side was certainly unnecessary.
After 10. ....P × Kt ; 14. B × B P,
B—Kt 5 ! ; 15. B × B, Q × B ch ;
16. Q—Q 2, etc., the positional
advantage left to White would be
negligible.

14. Kt × P   B—Kt 5

The Bishop's position at Q 3 was
not safe and, besides, the following
exchange will give Black some kind
of compensation for the disorganised left wing.

15. Castles   B × Kt
16. P × B   B—Q 2
17. P—Q B 4 !   ......

This Pawn is about as weak here
as at B 3—but now, at least, it
makes the important square Q 5
inaccessible to the Black Knight.

17. ......   B—R 5
18. Kt—Kt 3   Q—Kt 5
19. Q—K 2 !   ......

Both an attacking and a defensive
move. If now 19. ....B × Kt, then
first 20. R—Kt 1.

19. ......   K R—B 1
20. R—Kt 1   Kt × P

This looks very dangerous and,
in fact, proves fatal. But, as the
Black King has been abandoned to
his fate by all his troops, it is, in
truth, already too late to prevent a
direct assault by passive tactics. If,
for instance, 20. ....B × Kt, then
21. R × B, Q—K 2 (or, ...Q—B 1 ;
22. Q—B 3, etc.) ; 22. Q—Kt 4 ch,
K—B 1 ; 23. Q—R 4, K—Kt 2 ; 24.
P—B 4 with an easy attack.

21. Kt—Q 4   Q—B 4

When taking the Pawn on the
previous move, Black probably calculated that he would have a saving
defence should White make the
natural move 22. R × P. Actually,
the position of the second player
would have been precarious enough
even so, especially in view of
White's threat 23. Kt × P, which
would win promptly, for instance,
after 22. ....R—B 2, or 22. ....
Kt—Q 3, or 22. ....B—K 1. Also
22. ....Kt—K 4 would lose rapidly
after 23. Q—R 5, Q—B 1 ; 24. P—
B 4, Kt × B ; 25. Kt × P etc.—
but 22. ....Q—Q 4, in order to
answer 23. Kt × P ? by 23. ....
Q × Kt and 23. R—Kt 4 by ....
Kt—Kt 3, etc., would still prolong
the battle. The following combination by White is, therefore, the most
convincing way to force a decisive
advantage.

Position after Black's 21st move.

22. Kt×P !   ......

Leads finally "only" to the win of a Pawn—but, by the weakening of Black's King's position, *permits White to force favourable exchanges*, which will prove amply sufficient.

22. ......   P×Kt
23. Q—Kt 4 ch   K—R 1

After 23. ....K—B 1, death would be quicker : 24. R×P, Q—K Kt 4 ; 25. Q×P, Kt—K 4 ; 26. P—B 4 !, etc.

24. R×P   ......

Threatening mates at K Kt 7 and K R 7.

24. ......   R—B 2
25. R×R   Q×R
26. B×Kt   P—K 4
27. Q—R 4   Q—K Kt 2
28. B—Q 5   ......

As Black's King is now adequately protected, White rightly decides to simplify matters.

28. ......   R—Q 1
29. Q×B   R×B
30. Q—B 6 !   ......

It was important to prevent Black's doubling the pieces on the central file.

30. ......   Q—K B 2
31. P—K R 3   ......

In order to make also the Rook active.

31. ......   K—Kt 2
32. R—Kt 1   R—Q 2
33. P—Q R 4 !   ......

This Pawn now threatens to come as far as R 6, after which R—Kt 7 would be decisive. Black is therefore practically forced to offer the exchange of Queens.

33. ......   R—B 2
34. Q—Kt 5   Q—Q 2
35. Q×Q ch   R×Q
36. R—Kt 5 !   ......

The following end-game will be easily won, and chiefly because of the dominating position of the Rook.

36. ......   K—Kt 3
37. P—Kt 4   P—K R 4
38. K—Kt 2   P×P
39. P×P   R—Q 3
40. R—R 5   P—R 3
41. K—Kt 3   R—B 3
42. P—B 4 !   P×P ch
43. P×P   R—Kt 3
44. R—Q B 5 !   ......

The Rook will prove even more effective on the 7th rank than on the 5th. If now 44. ....R—Kt 5 then simply 45. R—B 6, R×R P ; 46. P—Kt 5 and wins.

44. ......   K—Kt 2
45. R—B 7 ch   K—R 3
46. R—R 7   R—Kt 6 ch
47. K—R 4   R—Kt 5

Or 47. ....R—Kt 3 ; 48. P—R 5, R—B 3 ; 49. R—K B 7 !, K—Kt 3 ; 50. R—Kt 7 followed by 51. R—Kt 6 and wins.

48. R×P   Resigns.

For if 48. ....R×B P then 49. R×P ch ! etc.

GAME 83

QUEEN'S INDIAN DEFENCE

Podebrad Tournament, June, 1936.

White : MISS V. MENCHIK

1. P—Q 4   Kt—K B 3
2. Kt—K B 3   P—Q Kt 4

At such early stages it is a sound principle not to give the opponent an objective, such as this : the enterprise may succeed, as it does here, but only if the adversary continues to develop the pieces without trying to avail oneself of the unusual situation. Instead of the fianchetto-development as selected by the Ladies' World Champion, a good method would have been, for instance, 3. B—B 4, B—Kt 2 ; 4. P—K 3, P—Q R 3 ; 5. P—Q R 4, P—Kt 5 ; 6 P—B 4, and, whether Black takes *en passant* or not, his position remains slightly inferior.

3.	P—K Kt 3	B—Kt 2
4.	B—Kt 2	P—K 3
5.	Castles	B—K 2
6.	Q Kt—Q 2	......

Owing to her pointless mobilization-plan, White has obtained no advantage from the opening. The text-move, which prepares for the exchange of Black's exposed Q Kt P is no worse than 6. P—Q R 4 (....P—Q R 3, etc.) and is certainly better than 6. P—Kt 3 (....P—Kt 5 ! etc.).

| 6. | ...... | Q—B 1 ! |

Protecting the Bishop in order to answer 7. R—K 1 by 7. ....Kt —K 5 !; and after 7. P—B 4, the Queen will obviously find a large field of action on the Queen's side.

7.	P—B 4	P×P
8.	Kt×P	Castles
9.	P—Kt 3	......

As so often in the Queen's Indian Defence, White cannot find a suitable square for the Queen's Bishop. Comparatively better than the text-move which weakens the Q's side, is 9. Kt—K 5, in order to clear as soon as possible the situation on the diagonal K R 1—Q R 8.

| 9. | ...... | P—Q R 4 ! |

Not only preventing once for all Kt—Q R 5 (which on the previous move would be met by ....B—Q 4), but also threatening eventually ....P—R5.

10. P—Q R 3 ?   ......

A decisive strategical error in an already delicate position. White should profit from the fact that the threat mentioned was not of an immediate character by proposing exchange of Bishops with 10. B—Q R 3. After 10. ....B×B ; 11. Kt×B, Kt—B 3 followed eventually by ....Kt—Q Kt 5, Black's position, although superior, would not be anything like so easy to improve decisively as after the text-move, which creates an incurable weakness on Q Kt 3.

10.	......	B—Q 4
11.	Q—B 2	Q—Kt 2
12.	B—Kt 2	......

White has only the choice between a few evils; for instance, after 12. B—Q 2, Kt—B 3, Black would already threaten 13. ....Kt×P.

12.	......	Kt—B 3
13.	Kt—K 1	Q R—Kt 1
14.	B×B	......

The only way that temporarily saves the Pawn.

14. ......   P×B !

Much stronger than 14. ....Kt× B—the point is Black's next move.

15. Kt—Q 2   ......

Position after White's 15th move.

15. ......   Kt—K 5 !

Thus Black becomes master of the central sector. The Q Kt P is not lost immediately but cannot long escape its fate. This purely positional battle is, in my opinion, noteworthy chiefly because of the methods adopted by Black in order to exploit his opening advantage : these methods, unusual at first sight, were in fact quite simple.

16. K Kt—B 3   ......

If 16. Kt × Kt, then, of course, 16. ....Q × P ! etc., winning material.

16. ......   P—B 4
17. K R—Kt 1   Q—Kt 4 !

If now 18. P—K 3 (which was comparatively the best), then 18. ....Q—K 7 ; 19. R—K B 1, P—Kt 4 ! ; 20. Q R—K 1, Q—Kt 4 ; 21. Kt × Kt, Q P × Kt ; 22. Kt—Q 2, P—Q 4 ; 23. R—B 1, R—Kt 3 and White would be finally executed on the King's flank ; but Miss Menchik prefers to succumb in open fight.

18. Kt × Kt   B P × Kt
19. Kt—K 5   Kt × Kt

Simplest. 19. ....Q × Kt P would probably have won also, but after 20. Q—B 1, more resistance would have been possible than in the end-game forced by the text-manœuvre.

20. P × Kt   Q—B 4 !

Rough, but extremely sound.

21. Q × Q   B × Q
22. P—K 3   R × Kt P
23. B—Q 4   B × B
24. P × B   K R—B 6 !

Wins perforce a second Pawn.

25. R × R   R × R
26. R—Q B 1   P—B 3
27. P—K 6   P × P

28. R × P   K—B 2
29. R—B 7 ch   K—B 3
30. P—Kt 4   P—R 3
31. P—K R 4   R × P
Resigns.

GAME 84

FRENCH DEFENCE

Nottingham Tournament, August, 1936.

Black : Dr. M. Euwe

1. P—K 4   P—K 3
2. P—Q 4   P—Q 4
3. P—K 5   ......

I adopted this favourite move of Nimzowitsch for the first time in my career only because I thought that Dr. Euwe, after his failure in the games of the 1935 Match (continued by 3. Kt—Q B 3, B—Kt 5), had in the meantime made a particularly careful study of that line of play. Although the result of the opening-play in the present game was rather in my favour, I shall hardly repeat an experiment permitting Black to assume from the very beginning a kind of initiative and to obtain (at the cost of his Pawn configuration, it is true) a free development of his pieces.

3. ......   P—Q B 4
4. Kt—K B 3   ......

In the last years of his activity Nimzowitsch preferred the peculiar move 4. Q—Kt 4, thus showing the clear design to exploit immediately the advantage of space obtained on the K's side. The idea has, however, some inconveniences, as, for instance, the following short game, in which I had to fight against it in the Montevideo Tournament, 1938 (White : J. Canepa), shows in a characteristic way : 4. ....Kt—Q B 3 ; 5. Kt—K B 3, K Kt—K 2 (if this move was not played before, this would only be a further proof of the short-sightedness of Lady Theory ; because the development-problem of this Knight, *being here the most elaborate one*, must be solved on the very first opportunity) ; 6. P—B 3, Kt—B 4 ; 7. B—Q 3, P×P ! ; 8. Castles, B—Q 2; 9. R—K 1, P×P ; 10. Kt×P, P—K Kt 3 ; 11. B—K Kt 5, B—K 2 ; 12. Q—K B 4, Q Kt—Q 5 ! ; 13. B—B 6, Kt×Kt ch ; 14. P×Kt, R—K Kt 1 ; 15. K—R 1, B—B 3 ; 16. B×Kt, Kt P×B ; 17. B×B, Q×B ; 18. Kt—K 2, P—Q 5 ! ; 19. Kt×P, Q—Kt 5 ! ; 20. R—K Kt 1, R×R ch ; 21. R×R, Castles ; 22. R—Q 1, Q×P ; 23. R—Q 2, R×Kt ! ; 24. R×R, Q×B P ; Resigns.

| 4. ...... | Kt—Q B 3 |
| 5. B—Q 3 | ...... |

The central Pawn is sacrificed only temporarily, but its recovery will cost White some valuable time. The whole plan can, therefore, hardly lead to more than a balanced position.

| 5. ...... | P×P |
| 6. Castles | P—B 3 |

If 6. ....Q—Kt 3 White could transform the game into a regular gambit by 7. P—B 3, P×P ; 8. Kt×P, etc., with some chances of success.

7. B—Q Kt 5   ......

There is nothing better than to re-establish equilibrium in material; if, for instance, 7. B—K B 4, then 7. ....P—K Kt 4 followed by .... P—Kt 5.

7.	B—Q 2
8. B×Kt	P×B
9. Q×P	P×P
10. Q×K P	......

It was by no means easy to decide which move is better—this or 10. Kt×P. My actual choice was determined by the consideration that in retaking with the Knight I would in most variations be practically obliged to exchange Black's "bad" Q's Bishop at Q 2; while I already hoped here to be able to chase his dark-coloured colleague successfully.

| 10. ...... | Kt—B 3 |
| 11. B—B 4 | ...... |

Preventing ....Q—Kt 1 and preparing the protection of the K B P by B—Kt 3.

11.	B—B 4
12. Kt—B 3	Castles
13. B—Kt 3	......

White's slight advantage (the control of his K 5) is extremely difficult to exploit—especially as Black still possesses the pair of Bishops and two open files for his Rooks. In the following section of the game, however, neither player takes the maximum advantage of his opportunities.

13. ......   Q—K 2

Here, for instance, 13. ....Q—K 1, in order to be able to answer 14. Q Kt—R 4 by 14. ....B—K 2—was decidedly more promising.

14. P—Q R 3 (?) ......

White should without lingering attack the K's Bishop by 14. Kt—Q R 4, for instance, 14. .... B—Kt 3 (14. ....B—Kt 5 ; 15. P—Q R 3, B—R 4 ; 16. P—Kt 4, B—Q 1 ; 17. Kt—B 5, etc., would be decidedly too artificial) ; 15. Kt×B, P×Kt ; 16. Q—B 7 !± The text-move allows Black to "save" his Bishop.

14. ......   P—Q R 4

15. K R—K 1   ......

I did not occupy this open file with the other Rook, in view of the possible answer 15. ....B—B 1, which, however, would not be dangerous : 15. Q R—K 1, B—B 1 ; 16. R—Q 1 ! followed by K R—K 1, etc. ±

15. ......   R—R 2 ?

Comparatively better was 15. ....B—Kt 3 in order to answer 16. Kt—Q R 4 by ....B—Q 1.

16. Kt—Q R 4   R—Kt 2

A mistake would be 16. .... Kt—K 5 because of 17. Kt × B, Kt × Kt (Q × Kt ; 18. R × Kt) ; 18. Q—Q 6 ! and wins.

17. Q—B 3   ......

Even this rather risky and complicated manœuvre finally turns to White's advantage ; but still more convincing was the simple 17. Kt × B, Q × Kt ; 18. R—K 2 followed by the exploitation of the dark-coloured squares.

17. ......   B—R 2
18. Q × R P   ......

Because of Black's counter-attack against K B 2 this win of material will have only temporary character.

18. ......   Kt—K 5
19. Q—R 6 !   ......

But for his intermediate move White would even have the worst of it, as Black threatened eventually ....R—Q R 1, etc.

19. ......   B—K 1
20. P—Kt 4   ......

Preparing the following counter-

sacrifice which makes an end of Black's immediate threats.

20. ......   P—Kt 4 ?

This move has been generally blamed, and with reason, since Black will soon have to regret the compromising of his King's position. But most of the critics were mistaken in believing that instead 20. ....P—K 4 would be not only satisfactory but even advantageous for Black. In that case I intended to sacrifice the exchange, thus obtaining fair winning prospects—for instance, 21. R × Kt !, P × R ; 22. Q—B 4 ch, B—B 2 ; 23. Q × K P, B—Q 4 ; 24. Q × P, B × Kt ; 25. Q × Q, R × Q ; 26. P × B, R × P ; 27. K—Kt 2, R—B 1 ; 28. P—Q B 4, B—Q 5 ; 29. R—Q 1, etc. ± Black's comparatively best counter-chance was therefore 20. ....B—R 4 ; 21. Kt—B 5 ! (but not 21. Q × P, B—K 1 ! ; 22. Q—R 6, B—Kt 4 ; 23. Q—R 5, Q—K 1, etc. ∓), B × K Kt ; 22. P × B, B × Kt ; 23. P × B, R × P ; 24. Q × Q P, Kt × Q B P, etc., still with fighting possibilities. It must be admitted, however, that even after the inferior text-move the second player will keep for rather a long time some practical saving chances, which he will try to exploit with the energy of despair.

21. Kt—B 5 !   ......

According to programme and very efficient, as Black's strongest Bishop will now disappear.

21. ......   B × Kt

Not 21. ....Kt × Kt ; 22. P × Kt, B × P because of 22. R × P ! etc.

22. P × B   Kt × Q B P
23. Q—K 2   Kt—K 5
24. Q—K 3   ......

White's superiority has now

become evident. His Pawns are much more soundly placed; he still has the control of K 5, typical in this variation; and, last but not least, he has a rather menacing Q R P.

24. ......   B—Kt 3

Even against the somewhat better 24. ....P—B 4 White would maintain his advantage by simply advancing his passed Pawn. But the exchange of two minor pieces, possible after the text-move, facilitates his task considerably.

25.	Kt—K 5 !	P—B 4
26.	Kt × B	P × Kt
27.	P—K B 3	Kt × B
28.	P × Kt	K—B 2
29.	P—R 4 !	......

In order to exploit Black's weaknesses in the centre and on the K-side, White makes first a demonstration on the other wing, forcing the opponent to leave some vulnerable spots uncovered.

29.	......	R—Q R 1
30.	K—B 2	......

With the sudden threat of a mating attack starting with R—R 1.

30.	......	R—Kt 7
31.	R—K 2	P—B 5

Under the circumstances the best, although not quite sufficient. As a matter of fact no human being could hope to protect at the same time: (1) The Q R-file; (2) the K R-file; (3) the Q B P; (4) the K P; (5) the K Kt P; and (6) the square K 4. It is really a little too much!

32.	R—R 1	K—Kt 1

Position after Black's 32nd move.

33. Q—K 5 !   ......

From now on both players produce —unlike the first part of the game —really first-class Chess. Particularly interesting is the method adopted by Dr. Euwe to avoid a rapid debâcle, and the chances he succeeds in finding in spite of the unavoidable loss of two Pawns.

33.	......	Q—R 2 ch
34.	K—B 1	R—Kt 8 ch
35.	R—K 1	R × R ch
36.	K × R	Q—K Kt 2 !

Of course the only move, after which White, if he wants to play for a win, will have to proceed with exceptional care.

37.	Q × P ch	K—B 1
38.	Q × Q P !	......

Instead 38. Q—Q 6 ch, Q—K 2 ch, etc., would only lead to a draw. But now the white King seems to be in even greater danger than the black one.

38. ......   Q—B 6 ch

The alternative was 38. ....R—K 1 ch; 39. K—Q 2 ! (not 39. K—B 2, Q—R 2 ch; 40. K—B 1, K—Kt 2 ! threatening Q—K 6), Q—

B 3 ; 40. R—R 7 ! after which 40.
....R—Q 1 would lose at once
because of 41. R—R 8 ch, etc.

39. K—B 2 !   R—K 1

Hopeless would be 39. ....Q×
Q B P ch; 40. K—Kt 1, Q—
Kt 8 ch ; 41. K—R 2, Q—Kt 1 ;
42. Q×B P, etc.

40. P—Kt 4 !   ......

Checks at Q 6 and then Q 7
would be useless. The Queen is
best placed in the centre.

40. ......   Q—K 6 ch
41. K—Kt 3   Q—B 5 ch
42. K—R 3   R—K 2

If 42. ....K—Kt 2, then 43.
Q—Q 7 ch.

43. Q—B 5 !   ......

The right move. After 43. P—
Kt 3, Q—K 6 ! the win would be
doubtful.

43. ......   Q—B 3
44. P—Kt 3   ......

Not 44. R—K 1, Q—R 1 ch ; 45.
K—Kt 3, Q—R 5 mate !

44. ......   Q—R 1 ch

If 44. ....Q×P then 45. R—K 1
wins.

45. K—Kt 2   Q—B 6
46. R—R 7   Q×Q B P ch
47. K—R 3   Q—K 7
48. R×R   Q×R
49. Q×B P   ......

In the following difficult Queen
end-game Black's drawing chances
are based mainly on the fact that
the White King cannot well be
brought into safety. If, however,
White's Pawn at K Kt 4 were at
K B 2 Black's game would be ripe

for resignation. But not only that:
by mere chance Black can even,
in certain circumstances (for
instance, if White's passed Pawn
is brought as far as R 7) speculate
on a stalemate by playing his King
to K R 3. No wonder that the
game lasts over thirty moves more,
and, but for the inexactitude of
Black on the 61st move, would
probably have lasted even longer !

49. ......   Q—K 8
50. Q—B 5 ch   K—B 2
51. K—Kt 2   Q—R 8
52. Q—Q B 2   K—B 3
53. Q—Kt 3   K—K 4 ?

We were both very short of time,
which explains the text-move and
the inadequate reply. The King
should, of course, return to K Kt 2.

54. K—B 2 ?   ......

The last move before time control, instead of which 54. Q—Kt 8
ch, K—Q 4 (or K—K 3 ; 55. Q—
K 8 ch) ; 55. Q—Kt 8 ch—winning
both K Kt's Pawns for the Q R P—
would finish the game rapidly.

54. ......   K—B 3
55. Q—Kt 6 ch   K—Kt 2
56. Q—Kt 4   ......

The game was adjourned here for
the second time, and White starts
on the serious final task. His plan
is (1) to play as soon as possible
P—R 5 ; (2) after that to eliminate
once for all any possibility of stalemate combinations by playing P—
B 4.

56. ......   Q—R 8
57. Q—K 1   Q—R 7 ch
58. K—K 3   K—R 2
59. P—R 5   Q—R 7
60. Q—Q 2   Q—R 8
61. K—K 2   K—R 3

The best chance of a long resistance consisted in 61. ....Q—R 8.

After the text-move White gets in P—B 4 in the most favourable circumstances, leaving him no difficulties for his final King's trip which makes his passed Pawn irresistible.

62. P—B 4 !	P × P
63. P × P	Q—R 5
64. K—B 2 !	......

In order to play P—Kt 5 at the moment when Black cannot answer with ....K—R 4.

64.	K—R 2
65. P—Kt 5	Q—R 6
66. Q—Q 7 ch	K—R 1
67. Q—B 8 ch	K—R 2
68. Q—B 7 ch	......

Thus the Queen protects both R P and B P, and the King is ready for the final walk.

68.	K—R 1
69. K—K 2	Q—R 7 ch
70. K—K 3	Q—Kt 6 ch
71. K—Q 4	Q—Kt 5 ch
72. K—Q 5	Q—Kt 4 ch
73. K—Q 4	......

The third adjournment. White could also play 73. K—K 6, and after 73. ....Q—B 4 ch ; 74. K—K 7, Q—B 1 ch ! ; 75. K—Q 7. But he did not need it.

73.	Q—R 3
74. Q—Kt 6	Q—B 1
75. Q—Q 6 !	......

The simplest scheme.

75.	Q—B 7
76. P—R 6	Q—Q 7 ch
77. K—K 5	Q—B 6 ch
78. K—K 6	Q—B 1 ch
79. K—K 7	K—R 2
80. Q—Q 7 !	Q—B 6
81. K—K 6 dis. ch	

At last forcing the exchange of Queens.

Resigns.

GAME 85

FRENCH DEFENCE (IN EFFECT)

Nottingham Tournament, August, 1936.

White : W. WINTER

1. P—Q 4	P—K 3
2. P—K 4	P—Q 4
3. P × P	......

This move is generally adopted to show that White is only playing for a draw. But, as a matter of fact, Black will at least have not fewer opportunities for complicating, if he wants to do so, than in most of the other variations of the French.

3.	P × P
4. B—Q 3	Kt—Q B 3
5. Kt—K 2	B—Q 3
6. P Q B 3	......

Giving Black the welcome chance of taking the initiative. The alternative, however, 6. Q Kt—B 3, Kt—Kt 5 would lead either to the exchange of White's K's Bishop or to its removal to ineffective squares after 7. B—Kt 5 ch, P—B 3.

| 6. ...... | Q—R 5 ! |

It was important to prevent 7. B—K B 4.

| 7. Kt—Q 2 | B—K Kt 5 ! |

A correct offer of a Pawn. After 8. Q—Kt 3, Castles ; 9. Q × P, Kt —B 3, followed by ....K R—K 1, Black would have an overwhelming advantage in development.

| 8. Q—B 2 | Castles |
| 9. Kt—B 1 | ...... |

If 9. B—B 5 ch then simply 9. .... K—Kt 1.

| 9. ...... | P—K Kt 3 |

Preparing for the exchange of White's "good" Bishop (Q 3) after which the light-coloured squares of his position will become somewhat weak.

10. B—K 3	K Kt—K 2
11. Castles	B—K B 4
12. Q Kt—Kt 3	B × B
13. Q × B	P—K R 3

To secure the position of his Queen, which might become uncomfortable after White's Q—Q 2.

14. P—K B 4 ? ......

This move, weakening without compensation important squares on the K-file, may be considered the decisive strategical mistake. Comparatively better was 14. Kt—Kt 1, followed by Kt—B 1, with a rather cramped but still defensible position.

14. ...... Q—Kt 5

Black aims—and with success—at keeping his K B 4 under control. How important this is will be evident in the second half of the game.

| 15. P—K R 3 | Q—Q 2 |
| 16. K R—B 1 | P—K R 4 ! |

If now 17. P—B 5, then 17. .... P—R 5 ; 18. P—B 6, Kt—K Kt 1 ; 19. Kt—R 1, R—K 1 and the white K B's Pawn would fall.

17. Kt—Kt 1	P—R 5
18. Q Kt—K 2	Kt—B 4
19. Kt—B 3	P—B 3

All White's minor pieces will henceforth suffer from an obvious lack of space, and he will therefore be unable to prevent an increasing pressure on his K-file.

20. Kt—R 2	Q R—K 1
21. B—Q 2	R—K 3
22. Kt—Kt 4	K R—K 1

23. Q R—K 1	K R—K 2
24. K—Q 1	Q—K 1
25. Q—B 3	......

In order to move the Kt from K 2 which was at present impossible because of 25. ....R × R ch followed by ....B × P.

25. ...... Kt—R 4 !

By this manœuvre Black quickly obtains decisive material superiority. White cannot now play 26. Q × P because of 26. ....R × Kt ; 27. R × R, R × R ; 28. Q × Q Kt, Kt—Kt 6 ; 29. R—B 3, Q—K 5 ! and wins.

26. P—Q Kt 3 ......

Position after White's 26th move.

26. ...... Kt—B 5 !

A forceful finish. If 27. P × Kt, then 27. ....Q—R 5 ch ; 28. K—B 1, B—R 6 ch ; 29. K—Kt 1, R—Kt 3 ch ; 30. K—R 1, Q—B 7 and mates in two.

27. B—B 1	Kt(B5)—K6ch
28. B × Kt	Kt × B ch
29. Kt × Kt	R × Kt
30. Q—B 2	Q—Kt 4 !

Threatening 31. ....Q—Q 6 ch ;

32. K—B 1, B—R 6 mate. White is thus forced to give up a Pawn.

31. Kt—B 1	R × B P
32. R × R	B × R
33. Q—K 1	K—Q 2

If Q × R, now or next move, Black replies with Q × R ch followed by Q × B P or Kt P and wins.

34. P—B 5	R—K 6 !
35. Q—B 2	P—Kt 4
36. R—K 1	R—K 5
37. R × R	......

This exchange, giving Black a strong passed Pawn, shortens matters. But White was helpless in any case.

| 37. ...... | P × R |
| 38. K—Q 2 | B—Q 3 |

Threatening 30. ....P—K 6 ch !

| 39. K—B 2 | B—B 5 |
| Resigns. | |

GAME 86

QUEEN'S INDIAN DEFENCE

Nottingham Tournament, August, 1936.

Black : C. H. O'D. ALEXANDER

Brilliancy Prize

1. P—Q 4	Kt—K B 3
2. P—Q B 4	P—K 3
3. Kt—K B 3	B—Kt 5 ch
4. Q Kt—Q 2	......

The usual move is 4. B—Q 2 in order, after the exchange of Bishops, to develop the Knight on the more natural square Q B 3. By avoiding the exchange White tries to complicate matters without actually taking too many chances.

4.	P—Q Kt 3
5. P—K Kt 3	B—Kt 2
6. B—Kt 2	Castles
7. Castles	B × Q Kt ?

Instead of this exchange, which yields White the advantage of the pair of Bishops without necessity, Black could play either 7. ....P—Q 4 (Rubinstein–Alekhine, Semmering, 1926) or even 7 .....B—K 2 followed by ....P—Q 3, ...Q Kt—Q 2, etc. In both cases he would have better equalising prospects than in the actual game.

| 8. Q × B | ...... |

The correct recapture, as the Q's Bishop is wanted on the long diagonal.

8.	P—Q 3
9. P—Kt 3	Q Kt—Q 2
10. B—Kt 2	R—Kt 1

Black shows his hand decidedly too early. The obvious object of the text-move is to play Kt—K 5, followed by ....P—K B 4, for which purpose the Bishop must be protected, to avoid the possible answer Kt—Kt 5. But the same idea could have been combined with a mobilisation of forces, by 10. .... Q—K 2 ; 11. ....Q R—Q 1 and eventually B—R 1.

| 11. Q R—Q 1 ! | ...... |

An interesting and effective method of meeting Black's plan. The white Q's Bishop is to play in the following development a most important and practically decisive part.

| 11. ...... | Kt—K 5 |

If 11. ....Q—K 2, then 12. Q—K 3 (Kt—K 5 ; 13. P—Q 5).

| 12. Q—K 3 | P—K B 4 |
| 13. P—Q 5 ! | ...... |

This Pawn will only apparently be weak as White can easily protect it by counter-attacks.

13. ......   P×P

13. ....P—K 4 instead would lose a Pawn by 14. Kt—R 4 ! etc.

14. P×P   Q Kt—B 3
15. Kt—R 4   Q—Q 2

If 15. ....Q Kt×P then 16. R × Kt !, B×R ; 17. Q—Q 4 wins a piece.

16. B—K R 3   ......

Again preventing ....Q Kt×P, this time because of 17. Q×Kt.

16. ......   P—Kt 3
17. P—B 3   Kt—B 4
18. Q—Kt 5   ......

Threatening not only 19. B×Kt, but also 19. B (or Kt)×P ; and if 18. ....Kt×Q P, then 19. Kt× Kt P and wins. Black's reply is therefore forced.

18. ......   Q—Kt 2
19. P—Q Kt 4   Kt (B 4)—Q 2

Equally hopeless would be 19. ....Kt—R 5 ; 20. B—R 1, etc.

20. P—K 4 !   ......

The initial move of the decisive sacrificial combination.

20. ......   Kt×K P

Black clearly based his last hopes on this ingenious stroke. If now 21. B×Q, Kt×Q ; 22. B×R, then 22. ....Kt×B ch ; 23. K—Kt 2, R×B ; 24. K×Kt, Kt—B 3 followed by Kt×P with good fighting chances.

21. Q—B 1 !   ......

Much more effective than 21. P× Kt, Q×B ; 22. P×P, Q—B 3, etc., yielding White only a possible win after a laborious end-game.

21. ......   Kt (K 5)—B 3

Position after Black's 21st move.

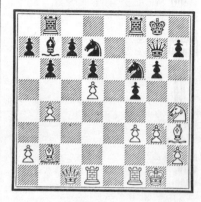

22. B×P !   ......

The surprising sequel of 20. P— K 4. After 22. ....P×B ; 23. Kt× P Black would either lose his Queen or be mated (23. ....Q—R 1 ; 24. Kt—R 6 ch, K—Kt 2 ; 25. Q—Kt 5 mate).

22. ......   K—R 1
23. B—K 6   ......

At last the Q P is definitely safe.

23. ......   B—R 3
24. K R—K 1   Kt—K 4
25. P—B 4 !   ......

The simplest way to force resignation.

25. ......   Kt—Q 6
26. R×Kt   B×R
27. P—Kt 4   ......

There is no remedy against P— K Kt 5.

Resigns.

GAME 87

QUEEN'S GAMBIT DECLINED
(SLAV DEFENCE)

Nottingham Tournament, August, 1930.

Black : E. BOGOLJUBOW

1. P—Q 4	P—Q 4
2. P—Q B 4	P—Q B 3
3. Kt—K B 3	Kt—B 3
4. Kt—B 3	P × P
5. P—Q R 4	P—K 3 ?

This was the third time within a year that I had the pleasure of meeting the indifferent text-move —and of taking advantage of it. Much better is, of course, 5. .... B—B 4.

6. P—K 4	B—Kt 5

Comparatively better, although not quite sufficient for equalising, is 6. .... P—B 4.

7. P—K 5	......

Very promising is also 7. Q—B 2, P—Q Kt 4 ; 8. B—K 2, and 9. Castles with a more than sufficient positional compensation for the Pawn.

7.	Kt—K 5

For 7. .... Kt—Q 4 see Game No. 26.

8. Q—B 2	Q—Q 4
9. B—K 2	P—Q B 4

The game with Helling, Dresden 1936, continued as follows : 9.

.... Castles ; 10. Castles, Kt × Kt ; 11. P × Kt, B—K 2 ; 12. Kt—Q 2, P—Q B 4 ; 13. B × P, Q—Q 1 ; 14. Q—K 4, P × P ; 15. P × P, B—Q 2 ; 16. B—Q 3, P—K Kt 3 ; 17. B—R 3, B—Q B 3 ; 18. Q—Kt 4, R—K 1 ; 19. Kt—B 4, P—K R 4 ; 20. Q—B 4, B—K Kt 4 ; 21. Q—Kt 3, B—R 5 ; 22. Q—K 3, Q—Q 4 ; 23. P—B 3, B—Q 1 ; 24. Kt—Q 6, R—K 2 ; 25. B—Q B 5 !—and Black, whose Queen is imprisoned in quite a spectacular way, resigned after a very few moves.

10. Castles	Kt × Kt
11. P × Kt	P × P
12. Kt × P	......

The 19th Euwe Match-game 1935 continued as follows : 12. P × P, P—B 6 ; 13. B—Q 2 !, Q—R 4 ; 14. B × P !, B × B ; 15. Kt—R 3, Kt—D 3 (if B—Q 2 then 16. R × B, B × P ; 17. B—Kt 5 ch !! and wins) ; 16. R × B, B—Q 2 ; 17. R—Kt 1, Castles K R ; 18. R—B 5, Q—Q 1 ; 19. R × P, B—B 1 ; 20. R—Kt 1, Kt × QP ; 21. Kt × Kt, Q × Kt ; 22. B—B 3 and with the exchange up White had a technically easy win.

By recapturing here with the Knight, I wanted to satisfy myself whether it is stronger than the line adopted by me previously. As this game proves, White also wins back the Pawn sacrificed, while keeping excellent attacking chances; the question which of the two moves gives him the greater advantage is, therefore, rather academic.

12.	B—B 4
13. Kt—B 3 !	Kt—Q 2
14. R—Q 1	Q—B 3
15. B × P	Castles

The King must fly, because after 15. .... B × P ch ; 16. Q × B and 17. B—R 3 Black would rapidly succumb.

16. Kt—Kt 5 . . . . . .

Forcing the weakening of Black's King-side position.

16.	P—K Kt 3
17. B—Kt 5	Q—B 2
18. Kt—K 4	B—K 2

Of course not 18. . . . . Kt × P because of 19. Kt × B followed by B—R 3, etc.

19. P—K B 4 . . . . . .

This is not the strongest continuation of the attack. The right idea of exploiting Black's cramped position consisted in forcing the exchange of his K's Bishop by means of 19. B—K R 6, R—Q 1 ; 20. P—K B 4, followed by B—K Kt 5, etc., after which the weakness of the dark coloured squares would rapidly become fatal to the second player. The text-move was based on a slight over-estimation of White's attacking possibilities in the position which actually occurred after Black's 21st move.

19.	Kt—B 4
20. Kt—B 6 ch	. . . . . .

Under the circumstances more promising than 20. Kt—Q 6, which however, was quite playable.

20.	B × Kt
21. P × B	B—Q 2
22. B—K 3 ?	. . . . . .

I made this move instantly, having calculated the whole variation on the 19th move. Instead 22. B—R 3 !, K R—Q 1 ; 23. R—Q 4, etc., would maintain the advantage of space without any offers.

22.	B × B
23. P × B	Kt—Q 2 !
24. P—Kt 3	. . . . . .

Comparatively best as 24. B—Q 4, Q × K B P ; 25. R—K B 1, Q—Kt 4 would give Black in addition to his material gain some attacking prospects (. . . . P—K 4).

24.	Kt × P
25. B—Q 4	. . . . . .

Realising that 25. R × P—planned already a few moves before—would be answered not by 25. . . . . R × R ; 26. P—Kt 6, etc. ±, but by 25. . . . . Kt—Q 4 ! ; 26. R × R, Kt × B ; 27. R × R ch, K × R ; 28. Q—Q 3, Kt × R ; 29. Q × Kt, Q—B 4 ch, etc, with a better Queen-ending for Black. After the text-move White obtains sufficient compensation for the Pawn, because of his powerful Bishop—but that is about all. By the following moves Black could force simplification which most probably would lead to a draw.

25.	Kt—Q 2
26. Q—B 2	P—Kt 3
27. R—K 1	. . . . . .

Preventing 27. . . . . P—B 3 followed by . . . . P—K 4.

27.	Q—B 5
28. Q R—Kt 1	Q R—B 1
29. Q—K 3	K R—K 1
30. Q—B 3	P—B 3

Black begins to play with fire. Here, or even at the next move, he should offer the exchange of Queens by . . . . Q—Q 4, since he would still be able to protect his backward Q R P. The variation 30. . . . . Q—Q 4 ; 31. Q × Q, P × Q ; 32. R × R ch, R × R ; 33. R—R 1, R—R 1 should, as mentioned, probably result in a peaceful draw. After the text-move and the next one White succeeds in building up a formidable K.-side attack.

31. R—Kt 4   Q—B 2 ?
32. R—Kt 2 !   ......

Now Black's K P becomes weak.

32. ......   R—K 2
33. Q R—K 2   K—B 2
34. P—Kt 4   Q R—K 1
35. P—Kt 5 !   ......

With a hidden purpose which Black entirely overlooks.

35. ......   P × P

His only chance of salvation was 35. ....P—B 4 when White would still have excellent winning prospects by continuing P—R 4—R 5, etc.

Position after Black's 35th move.

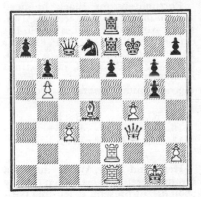

36. P—B 5 ! !   ......

A problem-like move which forces the win in all variations. Besides the continuation in the text, the following possibilities came into consideration :

I. 36. ....*K P × P* ; 37. Q—Q 5 ch, K—B 1 ; 38. B—Kt 7 ch ! and wins.

II. 36. ....*Kt P × P* ; 37. Q—R 5 ch, K—B 1 ; 38. Q—R 6 ch, K—Kt 1 ; 39. Q × Kt P ch and wins.

III. 36. ....*P—K 4* ; 37. Q—Q 5 ch, K—B 1 ; 38. Q—B 6 !, Q × Q ;

39. P × Q, P × B ; 40 R × R, R × R ; 41. R × R, K × R ; 42. P—B 7 and wins.

36. ......   Q—K B 5

Neither better nor worse than the variations just given.

37. P × K P ch   R × P
38. Q—Q 5   ......

Another winning line was 38. Q—R 3, Q—R 5 ; 39. R—B 1 ch, K—Kt 1 ; 40. R × R ! and wins.

38. ......   Kt—B 3

White threatened also 39. R—K B 1, etc.

39. B × Kt   Q—Kt 5 ch
40. R—Kt 2   Q—B 4
41. B—K 5   ......

But not 41. Q—B 4 ?, Q—B 4 ch and Black would win !

41. ......   K—Kt 1
42. R—K B 2   Q—Kt 5 ch
43. K—R 1   P—K R 4
44. R—K Kt 1   Q—K R 5
45. R—B 6   K—R 2
46. R × R   R × R
47. Q—Q 7 ch   Resigns.

GAME 88

CATALAN OPENING

Nottingham Tournament, August, 1936.

White : DR. S. TARTAKOWER

Quality Prize

1. P—Q 4   Kt—K B 3
2. P—K Kt 3   P—Q B 4

Intending, if 3. P—Q 5, to play a King's Fianchetto. But a sounder answer to White's unusual second move is 2. ....P—Q 4.

| 3. Kt—K B 3 | P—Q 4 |
| 4. B—Kt 2 | ...... |

Giving Black the predominance in the centre. A safer line was 4. P—B 3 entering into the Schlechter Variation of the Slav Defence with a *tempo* more.

| 4. ...... | P×P |
| 5. Castles | B—Kt 5 |

And not 5. ....Kt—B 3 ; 6. Kt×P, P—K 4 ; 7. Kt×Kt, P× Kt ; 8. P—Q B 4, etc., with superior fighting chances for White.

| 6. Kt×P ? | ...... |

This is completely in accordance with Black's wishes. Instead 6. Kt—K 5 ! would have kept the balance of the position, since after 6. ....B—R 4 ; 7. Q×P the win of a Pawn by 7. ....B×P would prove decidedly too risky after 8. R—K 1, B—R 4 (or R 3) ; 9. P— Q B 4, etc. ±

6.	P—K 4
7. Kt—K B 3	Kt—B 3
8. P—K R 3	B—K B 4

Even more exact was 8. ....B— Q 2 (but not 8. ....B—K 3 ; 9. Kt—Kt 5) after which 9. P—B 4 could be simply answered by 9. .... P×P.∓ But the text-move is, after all, also good enough.

| 9. P—B 4 ! | P—Q 5 |
| 10. Q—Kt 3 | Q—B 2 (?) |

But after this White gets the opportunity of equalising chances. The more natural 10. ....Q—Q 2 (not ....Q—B 1 because of 11. Kt×K P ! followed by 12. B× P±) would also be the best ; if

11. P—K 3, then 11. ....B—K 2 ; 12. P×P, P×P followed by .... Castles (K R) etc., with a clear advantage.

| 11. P—K 3 | B—K 2 |

Black must now get his King into safety as rapidly as possible.

| 12. P×P | P×P |
| 13. B—B 4 | ...... |

This most important win of a *tempo* is a direct consequence of Black's inaccurate 10th move.

| 13. ...... | Q—B 1 |
| 14. R—Q 1 | Castles |

Fortunately for Black he need not trouble about his centre Pawn, for he will find compensation in the capture of White's K R P. If now 15. P—Kt 4, then B—K 5 ! ; 16. Q Kt—Q 2, B—Kt 3, etc., with a complicated but not disadvantageous middle-game position.

15. Kt×P	B×P
16. Kt×Kt	P×Kt
17. B×B ?	......

Here, and later, White makes a few indifferent moves, which rapidly spoil his, at present, defensible position. It was obviously inadvisable to bring the black Queen through this exchange to a strong attacking post. He should first and foremost finish his development with 17. Kt —B 3.

17.	Q×B
18. Q—K B 3	Kt—Kt 5
19. Kt—B 3	......

Again underestimating Black's attacking chances. Better was 19. Kt—Q 2 and if 19. ....P—K B 4 then 20. Kt—B 1.

19. ......   P—K B 4 !

With the powerful threat 20. ....
B—B 4, at present premature on
account of 20. Kt—K 4. From now
on Black's conduct of the King's
attack is irreproachable and explains the distinction given to this
interesting game.

20. Q—Kt 2   Q—R 4
21. R—K 1   ......

Equally unsatisfactory was 21.
B—Q 6, B×B ; 22. R×B, P—B 5,
etc. ∓

21. ......   B—B 4
22. Kt—Q 1   P—Kt 4
23. B—K 5   ......

23. B—K 3, B×B ; 24. Kt×B,
Kt—K 4 followed by P—B 5 would
give Black an equally easy attack.

23. ......   Q R—Q 1

After this there is no defence
against ....R×Kt, etc.

24. B—B 3   R×Kt !

Not only winning a Pawn, but
completely demolishing the remains
of White's fortress.

25. Q R×R   B×P ch
26. K—B 1   B×R

Tempting, but less convincing
was 26. ....B—K 6 because of the
answer 27. K—K 2 !

27. R×B   P—B 5
28. P×P   ......

The desperate resource 28. R—
K 7 would prove insufficient on
account of 28. ....Kt—K 6 ch ;
29. K—Kt 1, Q—Q 8 ch ; 30. K—
R 2, P×P ch, etc.

28. ......   R×P ch
29. K—Kt 1   ......

Position after White's 29th move.

29. ......   Kt—R 7 !

The deadly stroke. If 30. Q×
Kt, then 30. ....R—Kt 5 ch ; 31.
K—R 1, R—R 5, etc. White chooses
another method of giving up his
Queen, but he is soon persuaded
that further resistance is quite
hopeless.

30. R—K 3   R—B 8 ch
31. Q×R   Kt×Q
32. K×Kt   Q—B 2 ch
33. K—Kt 2   Q×P
34. R—K 7   Q—Q 4 ch
35. K—R 3   P—K R 4
Resigns.

GAME 89

QUEEN'S GAMBIT DECLINED
(ORTHODOX DEFENCE)

Hastings Tournament, December,
1936.

Black : Dr. M. Vidmar

1. P—Q 4   P—Q 4
2. P—Q B 4   P—K 3
3. Kt—Q B 3   Kt—K B 3
4. B—Kt 5   Q Kt—Q 2
5. P—K 3   B—K 2
6. Kt—B 3   Castles
7. R—B 1   P—B 3

8. Q—B 2   ......

Nowadays this Rubinstein move is considered rather harmless because of the reply 8. ....Kt—K 5 !; but as Dr. Vidmar had had an unpleasant experience with that move (in a quite analogous position) in our game at Bled (see No. 44), he decided to adopt the older and more complicated defensive method.

8. ......   P—Q R 3
9. P×P   ......

Seldom played at this particular moment, but quite in accordance with modern tendencies : against the most natural answer 9. .... K P×P, White plans a minority attack on the Queen's side.

9. ......   Kt×P

And after this the position will bear the characteristics of the so-called Capablanca Defence, but with the important difference, in White's favour, that Black has difficulties in freeing his game with ....P—K 4.

10. B×B   Q×B
11. B—B 4   ......

Of course not 11. B—Q 3 because of ....Kt—Kt 5; but 11. P—Q R 3 also came into consideration.

11. ......   Kt×Kt
12. Q×Kt   P—Q B 4

As 12. .... R—K 1 (aiming at ....P—K 4) would be efficiently answered by 13. R—Q 1 !, Black decides to start operations on the Queen's wing. After the text-move he threatens, of course, 13. .... P—Q Kt 4, etc., with a quite satisfactory game.

13. P×P   ......

A move difficult in its simplicity : White temporarily sacrifices space in order to regain it with some additional advantages. Not quite so convincing would be 13. B—K 2, P×P ; 14. Kt×P, Kt—B 3 or 14. Q×P, P—K 4, etc., with more chances for Black to equalise than in the actual game.

13. ......   Q×P

As Black intends to avoid the exchange of Queens, more logical was 13. ....Kt×P ; 14. B—K 2, Kt—K 5 ; 15. Q—Q 4, Kt—B 3 ; 16. Castles, etc., with only a slight superiority for White.

14. B—Kt 3 !   P—Q Kt 3

Certainly the end-game after 14. ....Q×Q ; 15. R×Q would have offered but slight chances of salvation because of the possible intrusion of the White Rook on to the 7th rank and the position of his King in the middle ; but now the Black Queen will be pursued until White obtains material advantage.

15. Q—Q 2   Q—K R 4

15. ....Q—K 2 ; 16. R—B 7, etc., was even less satisfactory.

Position after Black's 15th move.

16. B—Q 1 !   ......

This modest-looking retreat practically decides the game. White not
only threatens 17. R × B followed
by 18. Q × Kt—which at this moment would be wrong because of
....K R—Q 1 ; 19. Q—K 7, R—
B 8 ch ; 20. K—K 2, Q—Kt 4 ch and
mate next move—but he also eventually intends to dislodge the Black
Queen by means of 18. Kt—Q 4 and
to occupy after that the long
diagonal by B—B 3, etc., with
deadly effect.   Black is therefore
forced to the following time-wasting
Knight's tour, which, as a direct
consequence, will lead to the loss of
a Pawn.

16.	Kt—B 4
17. P—Q Kt 4 !	......

But not 17. Kt—Q 4, because of
17. ....Q—Kt 3, threatening 18.
....Kt—Q 6 ch.

17.	Kt—K 5
18. Q—Q 4	B—Kt 2

Dr. Vidmar tries, as he usually
does in compromised positions, to
complicate matters. If White takes
the Pawn immediately, Black might
get some sort of counter attack
after (19. Q × Kt P), B—Q 4 ; 20.
P—Q R 3, Q—Kt 3 ! (21. Castles ?
Kt—Q 7) etc. But a twenty-five
years' old experience with the Yugo-
Slavian Grand-Master (see, for instance, my game with him at
Carlsbad, 1911, in *My Best Games,
1908-1923*) had taught me to be
extra careful after having strategically outplayed him.   In fact, my
next simple move left him with no
hopes of further "swindles."

19. Castles	P—Q Kt 4

Instead, 19. ....B—Q 4 would
be hopeless : 20. Kt—Q 2, Q—Kt 3 ;
21. B—B 2, P—B 4 ; 22. Kt × Kt,
P × Kt ; 23. P—B 3 ! etc.

20. Kt—K 5	Q—R 3
21. Kt—B 6	......

Forcing the following exchange,
after which the Bishop will prove
much more powerful than the
Knight in both the middle- and
end-game.

21.	B × Kt
22. R × B	Kt—B 3
23. B—B 3	......

This is the type of position I
aimed at when playing 16. B—Q 1 !
It becomes quite obvious that the
decentralised black Queen is unable
to co-operate in the protection of
the menaced Queen's flank.

23.	Q R—Q 1
24. R—Q 6	......

White is in the agreeable position
of being able to use the simplest
methods—a reward of the adoption
of the right strategical plan.

24.	R × R
25. Q × R	Q—R 5
26. P—Q R 3	......

Black's Pawn is now bound to
fall, and, in order to prevent further
damage, he has to permit the exchange of Queens.   The ensuing
end-game, though theoretically won
for White, still remains highly instructive, especially as Dr. Vidmar
defends it with extreme care and
resourcefulness.

26.	Q—Q B 5
27. Q × R P	Kt—Q 4
28. P—Q R 4 !	Kt—B 2

After 28. .... Q × P ; 29. B
× Kt, P × B ; 30. Q × P, etc., White
would win rapidly.

29. Q—B 6	Q × Q
30. B × Q	P × P
31. R—R 1	R—Kt 1
32. R × P	K—B 1

33. P—Kt 4   ......

The following winning plan is easy to explain, but technically rather hard to execute. White profits by the fact that the Black pieces are busy on the Queen's side with the passed Pawn, *to create*—by gradual advance or eventual exchanges of Pawns—*permanently vulnerable points in the centre and on the King's side of Black's camp;* and only after this preliminary work is achieved can the final assault begin.

33. ......   K—K 2
34. P—Q Kt 5 !   ......

Obviously the last opportunity to secure a steady position for this Pawn.

34. ......   P—K 4

Of course not 34. ....Kt × P ? ; 35. R—Kt 4.

35. P—B 4 !   ......

Black is faced with two evils: either to give up control of White's Q 4 or, as in the game, to allow the isolation of his K P.

35. ......   P—B 3
36. P × P   P × P
37. R—R 2   ......

Frustrating 37. ....K—Q 3 because of 38. R—Q 2 ch, etc.

37. ......   R—Kt 3
38. R—Q Kt 2   P—R 3
39. K—B 2   K—K 3
40. K—B 3   Kt—Q 4
41. P—R 4   ......

The exchange of minor pieces, here or on the 42nd and 43rd moves, would naturally have considerably increased Black's drawing chances.

41. ......   Kt—K 2
42. B—K 4   Kt—Q 4
43. R—Kt 3   K—Q 3

44. P—Kt 5 !   ......

Prevents ....Kt—B 3 and diminishes the mobility of Black's K Kt P. The end-game crisis approaches.

44. ......   P × P
45. P × P   K—K 3
46. B—Q 3   ......

The Rook will gradually recover its freedom of movement.

46. ......   K—Q 3
47. R—R 3   Kt—B 2
48. R—R 7   R—Kt 1
49. K—K 4   ......

Threatening 50. K—B 5 and this practically forces the following weakening Pawn-move.

49. ......   P—Kt 3
50. R—R 3 !   ......

The time has come to dislodge the King from Q 3.

50. ......   R—Kt 3
51. B—B 4   R—Kt 1
52. R—Q 3 ch   K—B 4

Position after Black's 52nd move.

53. R—Q 7 !   ......

After about twenty preparatory

moves, the Rook enters into the enemy's formation with decisive effect. Black's following desperate fight is as good as useless, for he will no longer be able to offer the exchange of minor pieces without losing both his remaining Pawns.

53.	Kt—K 1
54. B—B 7	Kt—Q 3 ch
55. K×P	R—Kt 3
56. P—K 4	......

Of course, not 56. B×P ?—.... Kt—B 5 ch ; 57. K—B 5, Kt×P ch, etc.

56.	Kt×Kt P

This Pawn is now of no importance, for the fight is to be decided on the other side. The rest is agony.

57. R—Q 5 ch !	K—Kt 5
58. R—Q 8	Kt—R 2
59. R—Q 6	Kt—B 3 ch
60. K—Q 5	Kt—K 2 ch
61. K—K 6	Kt—B 3
62. K—B 6	K—B 4
63. R—Q 5 ch	K—Kt 5
64. P—K 5 !	K—B 5
65. R—Q 1 dis ch	K B 4
66. R—B 1 ch	K—Q 5
67. P—K 6	K—K 6
68. B×P	Kt—Q 5
69. B—B 7	Kt—K 7
70. R—K 1	K—B 7
71. R×Kt ch	Resigns.

GAME 90

RUY LOPEZ

Hastings Tournament, January, 1937.

Black : R. FINE

1. P—K 4	P—K 4
2. Kt—K B 3	Kt—Q B 3
3. B—Kt 5	P—Q B 3
4. B—R 4	Kt—B 3
5. Castles	B—K 2

6. R—K 1	P—Q Kt 4
7. B—Kt 3	P—Q 3
8. P—B 3	Kt—Q R 4
9. B—B 2	P—B 4
10. P—Q 4	Q—B 2
11. Q Kt—Q 2	Castles

So far everything is conventional, but here the generally adopted move is 11. ....Kt—B 3, trying to force White to a decision in the centre. The most promising continuation for White is then, 12. P—Q R 4, R—Kt 1 ; 13. P×Kt P, P×Kt P ; 14. P×B P, Q P×P ; 15. Kt—B 1 followed by Kt—K 3, etc.

12. Kt—B 1	B—Kt 5

The continuation of this game proves convincingly that the early exchange of this Bishop gives White promising attacking opportunities on the King's side but a fully satisfactory plan is not easy to find. The comparatively most logical method seems 12. ....B—Q 2 followed by ....K R—B 1 and ....B—K B 1.

13. Kt—K 3 !	......

The most forcible reply, which does not even oblige White to sacrifice anything on the next moves if he does not want to.

13.	B×Kt
14. Q×B !	......

After the simple 14. P×B, White would have the pair of Bishops and some attacking chances on the basis of the open K Kt-file ; but the text-move, by which he preserves his Pawn-structure intact, is more precise and stronger.

14.	B P×P
15. Kt—B 5 ?	......

But this risky offer—mainly explained by my being a half-point behind Fine and having to win at all costs in order to be first—cannot be recommended objectively, although after it White keeps the initiative for a quite long time. The right move was 15. P × P ! since, after 15. ....P × P ; 16. Kt—B 5, Q × B ; 17. Kt × B ch, K—R 1 ; 18. Kt—B 5 ! (threatening 19. Kt × Kt P !, K × Kt ; 20. B—R 6 ch, etc.), White would have obtained a decisive advantage. Also 15. ....Kt—B 3 (the answer I actually expected to 15. P × P) ; 16. P—Q 5 !, Kt—Q 5 ; 17. Q—Q 1, Kt × B ; 18. Kt × Kt (threatening 19. Kt—Kt 4, etc.), P—Q R 4 ; 19. B—Q 2 followed by R—Q B 1, etc., would have been in White's favour. The following few defensive moves of Fine are not only good but the only ones.

15. ......   P × P
16. Q × P !   K R—B 1 !

Protecting the Knight at R 4 by an attack against White's King's Bishop.

17. Q—K Kt 3   B—B 1
18. B—Q 3   ......

If, instead, 18. B—Kt 5, then simply 18. ....Q × B ; 19. B × Kt, P—Kt 3, etc.

18. ......   Kt—B 3
19. B—Kt 5   Kt—K 1
20. Q R—B 1 (?) ......

As an eventual exchange of Rooks would be entirely to Black's advantage, there was no need for White to play his Rook on to the open file. Indicated was at once 20. Q R—Q 1 (see 24th move) followed by P—Q R 3 and B—Kt 1—R 2, etc. The extra *tempo* would probably have been of great importance. From now on, on the contrary, Black has a comparatively easy defensive play.

20. ......   Q—Kt 2

21. P—Q R 3   ......

The manœuvre intended here, B—Kt 1—R 2—Q 5 induces Black to start a counter demonstration on the Queen's side, and, in order to do so, he must first force the exchange of the White Knight.

21. ......   P—Kt 3
22. Kt—R 6 ch   B × Kt
23. B × B   ......

Black's dark squares are somewhat weak now—but his Knight at K 1 is a stout defender.

23. ......   Kt—Q 5
24. Q R—Q 1   P—Kt 5
25. P—B 4 !   ......

The opening of this file offers fair equalising prospects—but with right answers hardly more.

25. ......   P × B P

The defence of K 4 by 25. .... P—B 3 would be advantageously met by 26. P—B 5 ! etc.

26. Q × P   P × P
27. P × P   R—B 6 !

An ingenious drawing combination : if, namely, 28. P—K 5, then 28. ....R × B ! ; 29. R × R, Kt—K 7 ch ; 30. R × Kt, Q—Kt 8 ch ; 31. K—B 2, Q × R ; 32. P—K 6 !, Q—B 4 ; 33. Q × Q, P × Q ; 34. P—K 7, P—B 3 ; 35. K—K 3 ! and the presence of White's King on the Queen's side would eliminate the danger of his losing. But as a draw meant as much as a loss to me, I did not even take this variation into serious consideration.

28. Q—B 2   Kt—K 3 ?

From now on, Fine's resistance begins gradually to weaken. The game has not developed quite according to his expectations (i.e.—the frustrated chance of simplifying by means of 28. ....R×B, etc.). After the natural 28. .... Kt—Q B 3 ; 29. B—Q B 1 !, Kt—K 4 ; 30. B—B 1 (Kt—Kt 5 ; 31. Q—Q 4), he would have slight winning chances, although the White Bishops would have *almost* counterbalanced the not over-important extra Pawn.

29. P—Q R 4 ......

This insignificant-looking Pawn will henceforth support White's threats in a very efficient way.

29. ...... **Q R—B 1**

Again out of place, since it will immediately become evident that his Q R P needs more protection. The other Rook should have returned to B 1.

30. R—K B 1 ......

Threatening 31. B×P, etc.

30.	K R—B 2
31. R—Kt 1	Q—D 3
32. P—R 5 !	......

Incredible but true—White has suddenly obtained a strong pressure on the Queen's side. A rather confusing result of Black's manœuvres on that sector of the board !

32. ...... **Kt—B 4 ?**

The evolutions of this Knight have been decidedly unlucky, and after this last one there will be no salvation. Comparatively best was 32. ....R—R 1, after which White would have increased his positional advantage with 33. Q R—B 1 followed by 34. B—Q B 4, etc.+

33. B—Q B 4 ......

If now 33. ....Kt×P, then 34. B×P ch, K—R 1 ; 35. Q—Q 4 ch and wins. Black's answer is therefore forced.

33. ...... **Q—Q 2**

Position after Black's 33rd move.

34. Q—R 2 ! ......

It is odd how sometimes exactly the same attacking ideas repeat themselves within a short period of time ! One may compare the text-move, for instance, with 37. Q—Q 2 in my game against Tylor (No. 91) where the transposition of a vertical attack by the Queen into a diagonal one brought an equally rapid decision.

34. ...... **Kt×P**

Or 34. ....Kt—K 3 ; 35. B×Kt etc.

35. R×P	Q×R
36. B×Q ch	R×B
37. Q—K 6 !	Resigns.

An interesting fight—but certainly influenced by the exceptional importance of the result.

GAME 91

RUY LOPEZ

Margate Tournament, April, 1937.

Black : T. H. TYLOR

1. P—K 4	P—K 4
2. Kt—K B 3	Kt—Q B 3
3. B—Kt 5	P—Q R 3
4. B—R 4	Kt—B 3
5. Castles	B—K 2
6. Q—K 2	Castles ?

A rather common error : White does not threaten anything at this moment (for instance, 7. B × Kt, Q P × B ; 8. Kt × P, Q—Q 5 ; 9. Kt—K B 3, Q × K P, etc., equalising easily) so Black thinks he has time to castle—and forgets that precisely after this move White can win a Pawn, the Bishop at K 2 being no longer protected by the King ! The correct move is, of course, 6. ....P—Q 3.

7. P—B 3 ?   ......

An exaggerated faith in the knowledge of my opponents was always the vulnerable point of my opening play ; for instance, at San Remo, 1930, I did not take a Pawn on the tenth move which my opponent, Rubinstein, left *en prise* in an even more obvious way than in this game ! It is quite obvious that 7. B × Kt, Q P × B ; 8. Kt × P could and should have been played, since 8. ....Q—Q 5 ; 9. Kt—K B 3. Q × K P ? costs a piece after 10. Q × Q followed by 11. R—K 1. The slight advantage in development that Black would have obtained after, for instance, 8. ....R—K 1 ; 9. P—Q 3, B—Q B 4 ; 10. Kt—K B 3, B—K Kt 5, would by no means compensate for the material loss. After the tame text-move well known positions will be reached.

7. ......   P—Q 3

8. P—Q 4	B—Q 2
9. P—Q 5	Kt—Kt 1
10. B—B 2	Kt—K 1

The manœuvre 10. ....P—Q R 4 followed by Kt—R 3—B 4, played by me in a consultation game against Kashdan (see No. 119), proved quite successful. But also the text-move, aiming at a rapid counter-attack in the centre, can hardly be criticised.

11. P—B 4   P—K B 4

But here he should prepare for this advance by 11. ....P—K Kt 3 followed eventually by ....Kt—Kt 2, in order not to give up completely the control upon White's K 4. From now on White obtains a clear positional advantage, which he exploits in an impeccable manner until an advanced stage of the middle-game.

12. P × P	B × P
13. B × B	R × B
14. Kt—B 3	Kt—Q 2
15. Kt—K 4	Kt—B 1 !

Tylor henceforth defends his difficult position extremely well until the fateful 32nd move. White would gain no advantage by playing now 16. P—K Kt 4, R—B 2 ; 17. K Kt —Kt 5, B × Kt ; 18. Kt × B, R— K 2 ; or 18. B × B, Q—Q 2, etc.

16. B—K 3	Kt—Kt 3
17. P—K Kt 3	P—R 3

In order to be able to move the King's Knight or the Queen without allowing White's Kt—Kt 5.

18. K Kt—Q 2   ......

Threatening 19. Q—Kt 4.

18.	K—R 2
19. Q—Q 3	Q—Q 2

Preparing an eventual demonstration on the King's side starting with ....R—R 4 and Q—R 6. White has therefore no time for the logical advance P—Q Kt 4, P—B 5, etc.

20. P—B 4 ......

White rightly calculated that hereby he will gain the square K 6 for his Knight and that the possible sortie of the black Queen against his King will not much improve the opponent's chances.

20. ...... K—R 1

White's threat was 21. P×P, Kt×P; 22. Kt—Kt 5 ch, etc.

21. Kt—K B 3! ......

An important intermediate move that permits the relaxation of the tension in the centre without ceding the important square K 5 to the black Knight.

21. ...... P×P
22. Kt—Q 4 R—B 2

Quite useless would be 22. .... Kt—K 4 ; 23. Q—R 2, etc.

23. B×P (?) ......

A slight strategical error that prevents White from taking full advantage of his strong position. The two following important considerations spoke in favour of retaking with the Pawn : (1) As Black's position is somewhat cramped, White should avoid any further exchange. (2) The white Bishop was particularly useful for the protection of the dark-coloured squares. As a matter of fact, the whole next section (up to the 32nd move) is influenced by the potential power of the black Bishop, liberated from his chief antagonist.

23. ...... Kt×B
24. P×Kt ......

It was difficult to decide whether it was advisable to provoke the exchange of one pair of Rooks by 24. R×Kt : Black's Rook at K B 2 has appreciable defensive power—but, on the other hand, the prospects of play with both Rooks on the open files were also tempting.

24. ...... Q—Kt 5 ch
25. K—R 1 ! ......

White had already calculated this Pawn-offer when playing 20. P—B 4. Of course the simple 25. Q—Kt 3 was also playable and would secure a comfortable end-game.

25. ...... Kt—B 3 !

Quite rightly refusing the Danälan Gift, since 25. ....R×P ; 26. R×R, Q×R ; 27. R—K B 1 would have catastrophic consequences for Black : I. 27. ....Q—K 4 ; 28. R—B 5. II. 27. ....Q—R 5 ; 28. Kt—B 5. III. 27. ....Q—Kt 5 ; 28. R—B 7 !, Q—R 5 ; 29. Kt—K B 3 —with an easy win in all cases.

26. Kt—K B 2 ......

An artificial - looking retreat, which, in fact, should have led only to an equal game. Appropriate was 26. Q R—K 1 or immediately 26. Kt—K 6 ; in the latter case the following curious variation would be possible : 26. ....Q—B 4 ; 27. Q R—K 1, P—B 3 ; 28. R—K Kt 1 !, P×P ; 29. Kt×Q P !, Q×Q ; 30. Kt×R ch and mate next move.

26. ...... Q—R 4

White's previous move would have proved strong only after 26. ....Q×P ; 27. Kt—K 6, Q—R 5 ; 28. Kt—R 3 ! threatening Kt—B 4 —Kt 6 etc. ±.

27. R—K Kt 1   ......

Now 27. Kt—K 6 is ineffective
because of the simple 27. ....P—
B 3 etc.

27. ......   Kt—Q 2 !

Again a very good manœuvre,
which practically forces the desirable exchange of Knights.

28. Kt—K 6   Kt—B 4
29. Q—K 3   ......

Instead, 29. Q—K Kt 3 would
prevent the immediate exchange at
K 6 but, on the other hand, would
permit 29. ....B—B 3.

29. ......   Kt × Kt
30. P × Kt   ......

White's still existing advantage
in space is herewith compensated for
by the attack that this Pawn can
be subjected to, while its neighbour
at K B 4 will need permanent
defence. The chances are now about
even.

30. ......   R—B 3
31. Q R—K 1   Q R—K B 1

This Rook was needed for a guard
to his K Kt P and should have been
moved to K Kt 1 at once. Still,
the text-move does not spoil anything yet.

32. Q—K Kt 3   P—K Kt 4 ?

An error, but an excusable one,
for the following tactical attack by
White was indeed very difficult to
foresee. Correct was 32. ....R—
K Kt 1 ; 33. R—K 4, Q—K B 4 ;
34. Q—K 3 followed by Kt—Q 3,
etc., with an open fight going on.

33. Kt—R 3   ......

Although there is no direct threat
in this move (34. P × P ?, R—B 6,
etc.), Black's game now becomes
most troublesome : he even can no
longer dream of a successful attack
against White's K P.

33. ......   R—B 4

34. Q—Kt 2 !   ......

A fine preparatory move to the
ensuing Rooks' manœuvre, against
which Black will be unable to find
an adequate defence.

34. ......   P—B 3
35. R—K 3 !   ......

Only after this move does White
begin to threaten. Black must now
find something against 36. Kt × P !,
B × Kt ; 37. R—K R 3 ! followed by
38. P × B, etc.

35. ......   K—Kt 2 !

A paradoxical-looking, but, for
the moment, sufficient defence.

36. R—K Kt 3   ......

Taken separately, this move—as
most of its immediate predecessors
—looks rather harmless. In fact,
after 37. P × P, P × P ; 38. Kt × P,
B × Kt ; 39. R × B ch, R × R ; 40.
Q × R ch, Q × Q ; 41. R × Q ch, K—
B 3, etc., the game would end in a
draw; and only the next quiet move
gives to the whole attacking scheme
its real significance.

36. ......   P—Q 4
37. Q—Q 2 !   B—Q 3

After 37. ....B—B 4 ; 38. R—
K 1 (simplest), White's win would
be easy.

Position after Black's 37th move.

38. Kt×P ! ......

The immediate object of this pseudo-sacrifice is quite obvious— Black cannot take the Knight without losing his Queen ; but the consequences of Black's rejoinder were misleading, as often happens when there are several possibilities from discovered checks.

38. ...... **B×P !**
39. Q—B 3 ch ! ......

The first point—White delays the "discovery" and rejects the tempting 39. P—K 7 which would prove a pure hallucination after 39. .... B×Q; 40. Kt—K 6 dis. ch, K—R 1! etc.

39. ...... **R (1)—B 3**

If 39. .... B—K 4, then 40. Kt— B 3 dis. ch, etc.

40. Kt—K 4 dis. ch ! B)(R
41. R×B ch **K—R 1**

Or 41. .... K—B 1 ; 42. Q—Kt 4 ch ! and mate in a few moves.

42. Q×R ch ! ......

The final point, reminiscent of some compositions by Greco and Stamma.

42. ...... **R×Q**
43. R—Kt 8 ch ! ......

After 43. .... K×R ; 44. Kt×R ch, K—B 1 ; 45. Kt×Q, P×P ; 46. K—Kt 2, White would not even need his extra Knight to stop the Pawns on the Queen's side; there- fore—

Resigns.

GAME 92

SICILIAN DEFENCE

Margate Tournament, April, 1937.

Black : J. FOLTYS

1. P—K 4 **P—Q B 4**

2. Kt—K B 3 **Kt—Q B 3**

If one wants to play the "Dragon" Variation (the flank development of the King's Bishop), one had better start by 2. .... P—Q 3 since White will not then have an opportunity of playing B—K Kt 5 before .... P—K Kt 3—for instance, 3. P— Q 4, P×P ; 4. Kt×P, Kt—K B 3 ; 5. Kt—Q B 3, P—K Kt 3, etc. Still, if no improvement can be found for Black in the variation of my Nottingham game against Botvinnik (6. B—K 2, B—Kt 2 ; 7. B— K 3, Kt—B 3 ; 8. Kt—Kt 3, B— K 3 ; 9. P—B 4, Castles ; 10. P— Kt 4, P—Q 4 !; 11. P—B 5, B—B 1 ; 12. P×Q P, Kt—Kt 5 ; 13. P—Q 6 !, Q×P ; 14. B—B 5, Q— B 5 ! ; 15. R—K B 1, Q×R P ! ; 16. B×Kt, Kt×P ; 17. B×Kt, Q— Kt 6 ch ; 18. R—B 2, Q—Kt 8 ch, etc. — drawn) — it hardly seems tempting for him to adopt that line of play—providing, of course, he plays for a win.

3. P—Q 4 **P×P**
4. Kt×P **Kt—B 3**
5. Kt—Q B 3 **P—Q 3**

Inadvisable is here 5. .... P— K Kt 3, because of 6. Kt×Kt followed by P—K 5.

6. B—K Kt 5 **P—K 3**

Black can also delay this move by playing, for instance, 6. .... B—Q 2, since 7. B×Kt, Kt P×B, etc., would have both advantages and disadvantages—but this delay would be useless for .... P—K 3 is still unavoidable. My game with Silva-Rocha (Black) (Montevideo, March, 1938) continued as follows : 6. .... B—Q 2 ; 7. B—K 2, P— Q R 3 ; 8. Castles, P—K 3 (What else ?) ; 9. Kt—Kt 3, P—Q Kt 4 ; 10. P—Q R 3, Kt—R 4 ; 11. Kt× Kt, Q×Kt ; 12. Q—Q 4 !, B—K 2 ; 13. K R—Q 1, Q—B 2 ; 14. P— Q R 4 !, P—Kt 5 ; 15. B×Kt, P×B ;

16. Q × Kt P with a decisive advantage for White.

7. B—Kt 5 ......

In order to induce Black to put his Queen's Bishop at Q 2 and thus eliminate the possibility of a fianchetto-development. This system is at least as worth considering as 7. Kt—Kt 3 in conjunction with Q—Q 2 (see my game against P. Frydman, No. 81).

7. ...... B—Q 2
8. Castles P—K R 3
9. B—K R 4 ......

The present game shows that this seemingly logical retreat is not without danger. Since the main object of 6. B—K Kt 5—the prevention of the "Dragon" Variation —has been achieved, 9. B—K 3 was good enough.

9. ...... P—Q R 3
10. B—K 2 B—K 2
11. Kt—Kt 3 ......

Trying to exploit the weakness at Q 6 in a similar manner as in the Frydman game; but the Czechoslovakian master, having played in Podebrad, knew that game also and had profited by its lesson.

11. ...... Q—B 2
12. P—B 4 ......

Further pressure against the Q P would prove ineffective—for instance, 12. Q—Q 2, Q R—Q 1 ! (not Castles ; 13. Q R—Q 1, Kt × K P ; 14. Kt × Kt, B × B ; 15. Q × Q P, etc. ±) ; 13. Q R—Q 1 ; B—B 1, etc., with a solid position. Therefore White decides to prepare a King's attack, counting chiefly on 12. .... Castles ; 13. Q—K 1 !, P—Q Kt 4 ; 14. B—K B 3 and eventually P— K Kt 4±. But Black's next move gives the battle quite another aspect.

12. ...... P—K Kt 4 !

Bold and effective, for Black secures herewith, and one may say until the end of the game, the powerful central square K 4 for his Knight. It is interesting to note that this move—solely because Black actually lost—has been completely misjudged by the critics. For instance, one of the most famous modern annotators writes the following : "This move has chiefly a psychological value, because, as it is known that Alekhine does not like defensive positions, there was but little chance that he would choose the variation 13. P × P, P × P ; 14. B × P, P—Q 4 !; 15. P—K R 3, etc." I confess that I did not accept the Pawn-offer quite independently of a would-be distaste for defensive play, but because *I actually do not like to be mated*—and this unpleasantness would most likely occur after 15. ....R × R P ! etc. . . . An ungrateful thing, these excursions into another master's psychology !

13. B—Kt 3 ! ......

The only way to keep the balance of position, for White now obtains some pressure on the K B-file in compensation for Black's strong square for his Knight.

13. ...... P × P
14. R × P Kt—K 4
15. Q—K B 1 Kt—R 2
16. R—B 2 ! ......

Threatening 17. B × Kt followed by R × P, and thus as good as forcing ....Castles, after which the presence of his King will prevent Black from increasing his initiative on that side.

16. ...... Castles (K R)
17. B—R 5 P—B 3

Also almost forced, but not too disadvantageous, since in exchange for the weakening of K 3 Black has added strength for his Knight's position.

18. B—B 4   K—Kt 2
19. Q R—K 1   ......

Dreaming of seriously bothering the black King after 20. R—K 3 and R—Kt 3 ch; but the opponent prevents this in a simple and effective manner.

19. ......   Q—B 5 !

Threatening to exchange Queens, thus obtaining a good end-game because of his well-protected centre. Safest for White would be to repeat moves by 20. B—K 2, Q—B 2 ; 21. B—R 5, etc., but he prefers to risk the ensuing complicated middle-game, relying less on the strength of his position than on his greater experience.

20. Q R—K 2   B—K 1
21. B × B   Q R × B
22. Q—B 1   Kt—Kt 4
23. P—K R 3   K—R 2
24. K—R 1   R—K Kt 1

Black's King is now completely safe, the open K Kt-file is a factor in his favour, and even on the Queen's side he has some prospects of initiative owing to the Q B-file. Foltys has so far conducted the game very well and certainly should not have lost by right play.

25. Q—K 3   R—Kt 2
26. Kt—Q 4   Q R—K Kt 1 ?

But this little carelessness permits White to obtain a serious initiative. Black obviously only saw that P—Q Kt 3 was not a direct menace—for the Queen would protect the K P from Q B 1—and underestimated the importance of 28. Kt—R 4 ! If he had played instead 26. ....P—Kt 4 !, the chances would have remained about even.

27. P—Q Kt 3   Q—B 1

Otherwise 28. B × Kt (Kt 5) and 29. Kt × P.

28. Kt—R 4 !   ......

With the strong threat 29. B × Kt (Kt 5) followed by 30. Kt—Kt 6 and 31. Kt × P.

28. ......   B—Q 1
29. P—B 4   ......

Now White has succeeded in gaining considerable space in the centre and threatens to improve his position further by 30. R—B 2 followed by P—B 5, etc. Black's next move facilitates the realisation of that plan.

29. ......   Q—Q 2
30. P—B 5 !   ......

If now 30. ....P × P, then 31. Kt × B P, Q—K 2 ; 32. B × Kt (Kt 5) followed by 33. Kt × K P or 33. B × R P etc.

30. ......   P—Q 4
31. B × Kt (Kt 5)   R × B

Position after Black's 31st move.

32. P—B 6 !   ......

Permitting the Knights to enter menacingly into the enemy's fortress. Besides its actual strategical value, the whole manœuvre has also a strong psychological (since "psychology" seems to be the fashion in Chess nowadays) effect : baffled by the complete change of situation, Black undoubtedly does not offer the most effective resistance in the very last stages.

32.	......	P×B P
33.	Kt—Q B 5	Q—Q 3
34.	Q Kt×K P	R—Kt 6

Permitting the following transaction, after which the white Knights, "doubled" in an original manner on the 6th rank, will speedily make any further resistance useless. Also after the better 34. ....K R—Kt 3 (35. P×P, P×P ; 36. Kt×B, R×Kt ; 37. R—B 2, R—K 1 ; 38. Q—B 4, etc.), White would win owing to the numerous weaknesses in the opponent's position.

35. Q×P ch !   ......

It is much less this Pawn that is of importance than the possibility of an intrusion of the second Knight.

35.	......	K×Q
36.	Kt—B 5 ch	K—R 2
37.	Kt×Q	Kt—Q 6
38.	R—B 1	P×P

The loss of a second Pawn is unavoidable.

| 39. | Kt×P | K R—Kt 3 |
| 40. | Kt×B | Resigns. |

GAME 93

ALEKHINE'S DEFENCE

Kemeri Tournament, June, 1937.

Black : S. RESHEVSKY

1.	P—K 4	Kt—K B 3
2.	P—K 5	Kt—Q 4
3.	Kt—K B 3	P—Q 3
4.	P—Q 4	B—Kt 5
5.	P—B 4	......

There is no hurry to dislodge the Knight. The immediate 5. B—K 2 allows White, if ....P×P, to retake with the Knight without being forced to sacrifice a Pawn.

5.	......	Kt—Kt 3
6.	B—K 2	P×P
7.	Kt×P	......

This was my intention when adopting 5. P—B 4 ; but—although actually White will obtain *some* compensation for the Pawn sacrifice —it was hardly advisable to make a considerable effort in order to obtain most likely only equality. In the 29th game of my first match with Dr. Euwe I played here 7. P—B 5 and obtained an opening advantage, but only because my opponent after 7. ....P—K 5 ; 8. P×Kt, P×Kt ; 9. B×P, B×B ; 10. Q×B instead of 10. ....Kt—B 3 ! selected the tame move 10. .... R P×P.

7.	......	B×B
8.	Q×B	Q×P
9.	Castles	......

Permitting the exchange of the central Knight and thus facilitating Black's defence. More to the point was 9. Kt—R 3 !, Q Kt—Q 2 ; 10. Kt—B 3, or 9. ....P—K 3 ; 10. Kt—B 2 preserving in both cases three minor pieces for attacking purposes.

9. ......   Q Kt—Q 2
10. Kt × Kt   ......

The sacrifice of the Q B P by 10. Kt—B 3 would be aimless.

10. ......   Kt × Kt ?

Strangely enough, Reshevsky decided to make this inferior move after a particularly close examination of the situation. One would think that 10. .... Q × Kt could be automatically selected because of the general consideration that otherwise the exposed Queen in the centre will permit White to win further *tempi* and thus obtain a real compensation for the Pawn. If Black had retaken with the Queen my intention was to continue with 11. P—Q R 4 !, Q—B 3 (not Kt × R P; 12. Q—B 3 !); 12. Kt—R 3, P—K 3; 13. P—R 5, Kt—Q 2; 14. Kt Kt 5 after which Black's defensive problem would still remain by no means an easy one. The text-move brings his game in danger and only the greatest circumspection saves him from a rapid debacle.

11. Kt—B 3   P—Q B 3

The threat 12. Kt—Kt 5 was too strong.

12. B—K 3   Q—K 4
13. Q R—Q 1   P—K 3
14. Q—B 3 !   ......

An important move which practically forces Black to return his extra-Pawn since his King had to be removed from the centre under all circumstances. Insufficient would be, for instance, 14. .... B—Q 3; 15. P—K Kt 3 or 14. .... B—K 2; 15. R × Kt ! followed by 16. Q × K B P or 14. .... Kt—B 3; 15. Kt—Kt 5 ! etc., with a winning attack.

14. ......   Castles !

15. B × P   ......

A grave error would be instead 15. Q × B P because of 15. .... B—Q 3 followed by .... R—B 1 winning; but now White, after having equalised forces, maintains a clear positional advantage, Black's King's position being anything but safe.

15. ......   Q—Q R 4
16. B—Q 4   ......

Prevents 16. .... Kt—K 4.

16. ......   Q—K B 4

Trying to make the best of it. The end-game after the exchange of Queens certainly looks bad enough, but is not *quite* hopeless.

17. Q—Kt 3   ......

An ex-champion's decision . . . Before 1935—and now—I would doubtless have adopted the simple line starting by 17. Q × Q which would secure me virtually an extra-Pawn on the Queen's side and eliminate any shadow of danger. But during the whole period preceding the return match I simply could not rely on my patience and nerves—which certainly would have been required for winning the end-game in question.

17. ......   P—K 4
18. B—K 3   B—Kt 5
19. Kt—R 4   ......

White's best attacking chance, since from this square the Knight will "observe" both Q Kt 6 and Q B 5. But Black's next manœuvre gives his King—at least temporarily—sufficient protection and, in fact, nearly equalises the chances.

19. ......   B—R 4 !
20. P—B 4 !   ......

Otherwise Black would even have obtained the initiative after 20. .... B—B 2 and ....P—K 5.

| 20. ...... | B—B 2 |
| 21. P—Kt 3 | ...... |

It was important to prevent Black from playing ....Q—B 7 *with tempo*.

| 21. ...... | P—B 3 |
| 22. P×P | Q—K 3 |

Of course not 22. ....Q×P ; 23. B—B 4 and wins.

23. P—K R 3 !   ......

A good positional move which, however, is neither particularly deep nor difficult to find. Its main object is to prevent the possibility ....Q—Kt 5 after 23. ....Kt× P ; 24. Kt—B 5, and also in some other variations the protection of White's K Kt 4 was essential. I was not a little surprised to read all the compliments addressed by the critics to the modest text-move, and also to be questioned—in all seriousness—after the game was over, whether by 23. P—K R 3 I already planned to play my Queen to K R 2 on the 33rd move . . .

23. ......   K R—Kt 1

At this particular moment the K Kt P was not yet in danger—but after the exchange of one pair of Rooks on the Q's file it eventually could be taken.

24. B—Q 4   ......

With the clear purpose of lessening the tension in the centre by 25. Q—K 3 or Q B 3.

24. ......   Kt×P

This looks rather promising, as

25. Kt—B 5 can be met by 25. .... Q—K 2 and 25. Kt—Kt 6 ch, K—Kt 1 ; 26. Q—Q B 3 ?—by 26. .... P—Q B 4, etc.—with advantage ; but a slight transposition of moves entirely changes the situation in White's favour. Comparatively better was therefore 24. ....P×P ; 25. Q—K 3, P—K 5 ; 26. P—B 5, Q R—K 1 after which Black's passed Pawn would in some way counter-balance White's threats on the Q's side.

25. Q—Q B 3 !   ......

Threatening both 26. Kt—B 5 and 26. Kt—Kt 6 ch. Black's reply is practically forced, since after 25. ....K—Kt 1 ; 26. Kt—B 5, Q—Q 3 ; 27. Q—Kt 4 ! etc., White's threats would prove the stronger.

| 25. ...... | Kt—Q 2 |
| 26. P—B 5 ! | ...... |

This Pawn will fulfil in the following part of the game several functions of the Bishop, which from now on will merely supervise the development of events.

| 26. ...... | K R—K 1 |
| 27. P—Q Kt 4 ! | ...... |

A Pawn-offer, the idea of which is (27. ....Q×Q R P) 28. R—R 1, Q—K 3 (or Q—Q 4 ; 29. K R—Q 1) ; 29. P—Kt 5 ! threatening 30. Kt—Kt 6 ch, etc., with a very strong attack.

27. ......   Kt—Kt 1

Also after this retreat White obtains a won game—but not so much because of his direct attack as through the fact that after the following forced exchange his Bishop will become considerably stronger than the black Knight. A satisfactory defence was, however, not visible. Black's decisive—

although by no means obvious—error was most likely 24. .... Kt×P.

28. Kt—Kt 6 ch   B×Kt
29. P×B   Q×Q R P

After his counter-chances on the diagonal Q Kt 1—K R 7 have vanished, Black rightly estimates that his only slight chance of salvation consists in extreme recklessness. As a matter of fact I confess that at this moment I even did not consider the possibility of the capture in the text. . . .

30. Q—K Kt 3 ! ......

More exact than 30. R—R 1, Q—Q 4.

30. ......   R—Q 2

Or 30. ....Q—B 2; 31. R—R 1 !, R×B, 32. R—R 8, R—K 4; 33. Q×R and wins.

31. B—B 5   ......

Good enough, but 31. B×P ! was simpler : if 31. ....P×B then 32. R×R, K×R; 33. Q—B 7 ch, K—K 3; 34. R—K 1 ch and wins.

31. ......   Q—B 2
32. R—R 1   Q—Kt 3
33. Q—R 2 !   ......

After this Black can no longer prevent the unwelcome Rook's visit to Q R 8.

33. ......   R—K 4

Or I. 33. ....Q—Kt 4; 34. R—R 8, Q—K 4; 35. B—B 2 !, Q×Q ch; 36. K×Q and after B—Kt 3 Black would lose the exchange with a hopeless position. II. 33. ....Kt—R 3; 34. P—Kt 5 !, Q—Kt 4; 35. K R—B 1 ! and wins.

34. R—R 8   R—Q 7

Black overlooks the main threat. But after a defensive move like 34. ....Q—K 1 White would also have won very rapidly by 35. Q—Kt 3 followed by 36. Q—R 3, etc.

Position after Black's 34th move.

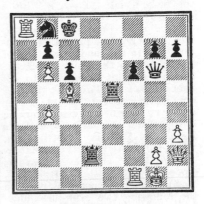

35. R×Kt ch !   K×R
36. Q×R ch ! and mate in three moves

Although in all objectivity I had to blame my 17th move (which by the way is accompanied in the Tournament Book by an !) I must admit that the final attack of this game gave me (and I hope will give the readers) much more pleasure than a scientifically correct, but purely technical exploitation of a Pawn majority on the Queen's side would do. After all, Chess is *not only* knowledge and logic !

GAME 94

QUEEN'S GAMBIT ACCEPTED

Kemeri Tournament, June, 1937.

Black : R. FINE

1. P—Q 4   P—Q 4
2. P—Q B 4   P×P
3. Kt—K B 3   Kt—K B 3

4. Q—R 4 ch ......

This Queen's manœuvre is more effective here than in the Catalan system (after P—K Kt 3) since White may in some variations wish to develop his Bishop on the diagonal K B 1—Q R 6. But also after the more usual 4. P—K 3 White's prospects are actually considered by far the more promising, and this fact is due not to a particular variation, but to the modern method of treating, with the white pieces, the Queen's Gambit Accepted : to advance the centre Pawns at the first opportunity, eventually at a cost of heavy sacrifices. Characteristic in that order of ideas are the games Reshevsky–Vidmar (Nottingham, 1936), Euwe–Alekhine (Fifth Match-game, 1937), and, even earlier, Opocensky–Rubinstein (Marienbad, 1925). In my own recent practice the following two examples, illustrating this new tendency of White, are, I believe, noteworthy :

I. Black : R. Letelier, Montevideo, 1938. 4. P—K 3, P—K 3 ; 5. B×P, P—B 4 ; 6. Castles, P—Q R 3 ; 7. Q—K 2, P—Q Kt 4 ; 8. B—Kt 3, B—Kt 2 ; 9. *Kt—B 3, Q Kt—Q 2* ; 10. R—Q 1, B—K 2 ; 11. P—K 4 !, P—Kt 5 ; 12. P—K 5, P×Kt ; 13. P×Kt, Kt×P ; 14. B—R 4 ch, K—B 1 ; 15. Q P×P, Q—R 4 ; 16. P—B 6, Q×B ; 17. P×B, R—Q Kt 1 ; 18. P×P, R×P ; 19. Kt—K 5, Q—K 5 ; 20. Q×P, R—B 2 ; 21. B—R 3 !, P—Kt 3 ; 22. B×B ch, R×B ; 23. Q—Q 6, K—Kt 2 ; 24. Q×R, Q×Kt ; 25. Q—Kt 4, Resigns.

II. Black : E. Böök, Margate, 1938. 4. P—K 3, P—K 3 ; 5. B×P, P—B 4 ; 6. Castles, *Kt—B 3* ; 7. Q—K 2, P—Q R 3 ; 8. *Kt—B 3*, P—Q Kt 4 ; 9. B—Kt 3, P—Kt 5 (in the Euwe-Alekhine game above mentioned the continuation was 9. ....B—K 2 ; 10. P×P, B×P ; 11. P—K 4 ! etc., to White's advantage) ; 10. *P—Q 5 !*, Kt—Q R 4 ; 11. B—R 4 ch, B—Q 2 ; 12. P×P, P×

P ; 13. R—Q 1 !, P×Kt ; 14. R×B !, Kt×R ; 15. Kt—K 5, R—R 2 ; 16. P×P, K—K 2 ; 17. P—K 4 !, Kt—K B 3 ; 18. B—K Kt 5, Q—B 2 ; 19. B—B 4, Q—Kt 3 (or Q—Kt 2 ; 21. Q—K 3 !, K—Q 1 ; 22. Q—Q 3 ch, K—B1 ; 23. R—Kt 1, Q×P ; 24. Kt—B 7 ! ! and wins) ; 20. R—Q 1, P—Kt 3 ; 21. B—K Kt 5, B—Kt 2 ; 22. Kt—Q 7 !, R×Kt ; 23. R×R ch, K—B 1 ; 24. B×Kt, B×B ; 25. P—K 5 !, Resigns.

4. ......   Q—Q 2

As the white Queen will not be particularly dangerous on Q B 4 there is no reason to make such an effort to force her exchange. A sound line is, instead, 4. ....P—B 3 ; 5. Q×P at B 4, B—B 4, etc.

5. Q×B P   Q—B 3
6. Kt—R 3   ......

There is but little difference between this move and 6. Q Kt—Q 2 since Black has nothing better, in order to justify this previous manœuvre, than to exchange Queens in both cases.

6. ......   Q×Q
7. Kt×Q   P—K 3
8. P—Q R 3   ......

It was very important to prevent ....B—Kt 5 ch.

8. ......   P—B 4 ?

A dogmatic move after which White succeeds in obtaining clear positional advantage. In his haste to counter-attack in the centre, Black for a moment forgets the importance of his Q 3. A bold, but by no means antipositional scheme was instead 8. ....P—Q R 4 (preventing P—Q Kt 4), and if 9. B—B 4 then P—Q Kt 4 followed by ....B—Q 3. At least White would not in that case obtain so easily the advantage of the pair of Bishops.

9. B—B 4   Kt—B 3

Slightly better was 9. . . . . Q Kt—Q 2 ; 10. Kt—Q 6 ch, B×Kt ; 11. B×B, Kt—K 5 ; 12. B—B 7, P—Q Kt 3, followed by . . . . B—Kt 2, etc. ; but the weakness of the dark-coloured squares would remain in any case.

10.	P×P	B×P
11.	P—Q Kt 4	B—K 2
12.	P—Kt 5	Kt—Q Kt 1
13.	Kt—Q 6 ch	B×Kt
14.	B×B	Kt—K 5
15.	B—B 7 !	. . . . . .

This Bishop is practically White's only winning chance at this stage, and he must play extremely carefully in order to prevent its exchange. Inadvisable would be instead 15. B—Kt 4, P—Q R 4 ! ; 16. P×P *e.p.*, Kt×R P, etc. ; or 15. B—B 4, P—B 3 ! followed by P—K 4, etc., with about equal prospects in both cases.

| 15. | . . . . . . | Kt—Q 2 |
| 16. | Kt—Q 4 ! | . . . . . . |

Again an important move, the idea of which is to build up the Pawn chain K 4, K B 3, K Kt 2. It was not quite easy to find, mainly because the two alternatives 16. P—K 3 and 16. P—K Kt 3 also offered some interesting possibilities.

16.	. . . . . .	Kt—Kt 3
17.	P—B 3	Kt—Q 4
18.	B—R 5	Kt(K5)—B 3

Another important variation was 18. . . . . Kt—Q 3 ; 19. P—K 4 (not 19. Kt—B 2, Kt—Q B 5, etc.), Kt—K 6 ; 20. B—Kt 4 !, P—K 4 ; 21. B×Kt, P×Kt ; 22. B—Q 3 !, Kt× P ch ; 23. K—B 2, Kt—K 6 ; 24. B—K 5, etc. ±.

19. Kt—B 2 !   . . . . . .

The actual point of the manœuvre inaugurated by 16. Kt—Q 4 : Black's Knight is prevented from intruding at K 6 and will be forced to play from now on a purely passive role. The chasing of the Bishop by the two Knights has thus proved a complete failure.

| 19. | . . . . . . | B—Q 2 |
| 20. | P—K 4 | R—Q B 1 |

Also this intermediate move is perfectly harmless, as the white King at Q 2 cannot be seriously bothered by the half-lamed black forces.

| 21. | K—Q 2 ! | Kt—Kt 3 |
| 22. | Kt—K 3 | Castles |

All Black's moves after 18. . . . . Kt—B 3 are virtually forced.

23. P—Q R 4 !   . . . . . .

Much stronger than the conventional 23. B—Q 3 which would permit the freeing manœuvre . . . . Kt—Q R 5—Q B 4, etc.

| 23. | . . . . . . | K R—Q 1 |
| 24. | B—Q 3 | P—K 4 |

After this weakening of the squares Q 4 and K B 4 the game can hardly be saved. The only slight chance consisted in 24. . . . . B—K 1 eventually followed by . . . . K Kt—Q 2. White's tactics in that case would have remained about the same—exchange of one pair of Rooks, removal of the R 5 Bishop and dislodging of the black Knight from Q Kt 3.

25.	K R—Q B 1	B—K 3
26.	R×R	R×R
27.	B—Kt 4	. . . . . .

Preventing also the approach of Black's King to the centre and threatening eventually B—Q 6.

27. ......   Kt—K 1
28. P—R 5   Kt—Q 2
29. Kt—Q 5 !   ......

This had to be exactly calculated since the passed Pawn resulting from the exchange will be slightly exposed. Because of the formidable threat 30. Kt—K 7 ch Black must now take the Knight.

29. ......   B × Kt
30. P × B   Kt—B 4

The "little combination" thus started finds a convincing refutation in White's 32nd move. But what could he actually do ? The recommendation of the Tournament Book, 30. ....P—K Kt 3 would in the long run be perfectly hopeless after 31. P—Q 6, P—B 4 ; 32. B—Kt 1 !, K—Kt 2 ; 33. B—R 2, K—B 3 (or Kt (K 1)—B 3 ; 34. R—K 1); 34. B—Q 5, etc.

31. B—B 5 !   R—Q 1

Or 31. ....Kt—Kt 6 ch ; 32. K—Q 3, Kt—B 8 ch ; 33. K—K 3, R—B 5 ; 34. P—Q 6 and wins.

Position after Black's 31st move.

32. K—B 3 !   ......

This pretty move eliminates both threats 32. ....Kt—Kt 6 ch and

32. ....R × P ch, the last one because of the answer 33. K—B 4 ! winning a piece. White's overwhelming advantage in space now decides the battle in a few moves.

32. ......   P—Q Kt 3

Or 32. ....Kt—Q 2 ; 33. B—K 7 and wins.

33. P × P   P × P
34. B × Kt !   ......

The Bishop has done in this game more than his duty and may now retire, for the passed Q Kt's Pawn can be only stopped at a heavy loss.

34. ......   P × B
35. P—Kt 6   Kt—Q 3
36. B—Q 7 !   R × B

Instead of resigning.

37. R—R 8 ch and mate in two.

This game is probably my best purely positional achievement of the last few years.

GAME 95

QUEEN'S GAMBIT DECLINED (ORTHODOX DEFENCE)

Quadrangular Tournament, Bad Nauheim, July, 1937.

Black : E. Bogoljubow

1. P—Q 4   P—Q 4
2. P—Q B 4   P—K 3
3. Kt—Q B 3   Kt—K B 3
4. B—Kt 5   B—K 2
5. Kt—B 3   P—K R 3
6. B—R 4   Castles
7. P—K 3   P—Q Kt 3

In conjunction with ....P—K R 3, this flank development has been rather often and successfully adopted by Dr. Tartakower. The first player has several plausible ways of meeting it, not one being an actually convincing refutation. In the present game, I decided to allow Black to fulfil his plan of mobilisation or—to be more exact—the first part of it consisting in .... B—Kt 2, ...Q Kt—Q 2, ... P—Q B 4—and to try to take advantage only from one detail of the position, namely, the fact that the black Queen is deprived of the diagonal Q 1—R 4 and will not easily find a suitable square. The course of the game will show to what extent the idea proved successful. It lacks tactical points, is emotionless—but by no means dull —and is of use to the student.

| 8. R—B 1 | B—Kt 2 |
| 9. B—K 2 | ...... |

Inducing Black to win a *tempo* by the following Pawn exchange.

9.	P × P
10. B × P	P—B 4
11. Castles	Q Kt—Q 2

If 11. ....Kt—B 3, then 12. P × P, Q × Q; 13. K R × Q and Black would get into trouble because of the possible entry of the Rook on to the seventh rank.

| 12. Q—K 2 | Kt—K 5 |

I suppose many masters would have made this move, since, by forcing the exchange of two minor pieces, it frees Black's game and, in particular, provides a safe spot for the Queen. Yet it is questionable whether the more complicated 12. ....P—R 3; 13. K R—Q 1, P—Q Kt 4 would not have offered more equalising prospects. After the exchange of Black's Queen's Bishop, the light-coloured squares on the Q-side become suddenly weak.

| 13. Kt × Kt | B × B |

Or 13. ....B × Kt ; 14. B—K Kt 3 ! etc. ±

14. Kt—B 3 !   ......

This simple retreat is more effective than 14. Kt—Q 6, B × Kt ; 15. Q × B, B—K 2, etc., forcing White to waste more time—or 14. B—Q 3, B—K B 3, after which Black would avoid the exchange of his Q B.

| 14. ...... | B—K B 3 |
| 15. K R—Q 1 | Q—K 2 |

At last the inter-communication between the Rooks is established, but now comes the actual point of White's last manœuvres.

16. B—R 6	Q R—Kt 1
17. B × B	R × B
18. Kt—K 4 !	......

In order to obtain full control along the Q B-file, White allows the isolation of his Q P, which, as the continuation will clearly show, is by no means weak.

| 18. ...... | P × P |
| 19. P × P | ...... |

Instead, 19. Kt × P, B × Kt ; 20. R × B, Kt—B 3, etc., would be just good enough for a comfortable draw.

| 19. ...... | R—Q 1 |

His position has become difficult. By playing 19. ....Kt—Kt 1 ; 20. Kt—K 5 !, etc., he could at least temporarily avoid the compromising of the Pawn skeleton on the King's side—but a further suitable plan of defence would be as difficult to find as after the move selected.

| 20. Q—R 6 ! | Kt—Kt 1 |

After 20. ....K R—Kt 1 ; 21. R—B 8 ch would be strong—and 20. ....Kt—B 1 ; 21. Kt × B ch, etc., would leave square Q B 3 defenceless.

21. Kt×B ch   P×Kt
22. Q—K 2   ......

White has now two important trumps—the open file and Black's weak King's side. By rational exploitation this will suffice.

22. ......   Q R—Q 2
23. R—Q 3   R—Q 4
24. K R—B 3   ......

As the weak Pawn requires only one protector, the Rooks can—and must—be used for exerting strong pressure on the Q B-file.

24. ......   K—R 2
25. P—K R 3   P—Q R 4

Weakens the Q Kt P—but otherwise the Q R P would need lasting defence. Already Black has only a choice between evils.

26. P—R 3   ......

As the opponent has no useful moves at his disposal, White can quietly correct the small defects in his Pawn structure.

26. ......   R—Kt 1
27. R—B 7   Kt—Q 2
28. R (1)—B 6   Q—B 1
29. Q—B 2 ch !   ......

More exact than 29. R—B 8, Q—Kt 2 ! ; 30. Q—B 2 ch, after which Black would have the answer 30. ....Q—Kt 3.

29. ......   P—B 4

Otherwise 30. R—B 8 would be even more effective.

30. R—B 8   Q—K 2
31. R × R   ......

The black Rook had to be ex-

changed, for it prevented the possible activity of the Queen on the King's side.

31. ......   K × R
32. Q—B 1   K—Kt 2
33. Q—K B 4   ......

Threatening 34. Q—Kt 3 ch, followed by R—B 8.

33. ......   Q—Q 1
34. P—Q R 4 !   ......

Preventing for once and for all ....R—Kt 4 and putting Black into a kind of *zugzwang* position.

34. ......   P—Kt 4

This natural-looking answer loses rapidly. Comparatively the best was 34. ....K—R 2, after which White finally forces the issue by playing the Queen over to the Queen's side—Q—B 1—B 4— Q R 6.

35. Q—Kt 3 ch   K—B 1

Position after Black's 35th move.

36. R—Q 6 !   ......

This wins at least a Pawn by

practically forcing the exchange of Queens. The resulting end-game will not present much difficulty, since there will be still more weaknesses to take advantage of—for instance, Black's K R 3.

| 36. | ...... | Q—R 1 |

Equally hopeless would be 36. ....P×P, e.g. 37. R×R, P×R ; 38. Q—Q 6 ch, Q—K 2 ; 39. Q×P etc.

37.	P×P	Q—Kt 2
38.	R×R	Q×R
39.	P—Kt 6 !	Q—B 3
40.	Q—B 7	Q×Q
41.	P×Q	Kt—Kt 3
42.	Kt—K 5	K—K 2
43.	Kt—B 4	......

After this the passed Q Kt P will force the presence of at least one black piece on the Queen's side and the white King will in the meantime become master of the other side of the board.

43.	......	Kt—B 1
44.	Kt×P	K—Q 2
45.	K—R 2	K×P
46.	K—Kt 3	K—Q 3
47.	K—R 4	K—Q 4
48.	K—R 5	K×P
49.	K×P	P—K 4
50.	K—Kt 5	P—B 5
51.	P—R 4	P—B 3 ch

A last "try" which White meets in the simplest manner.

| 52. | K×P | P—K 5 |
| 53. | Kt—Kt 3 ch ! | K—Q 4 |

Or 53. ....K—Q 6 (B 5) ; 54. Kt—B 5 (Q 2) ch, followed by 55. Kt×P and P—R 5, winning.

54.	P—R 5	P—K 6
55.	P×P	P×P
56.	Kt—B 1	Resigns.

GAME 96

RUY LOPEZ

Quadrangular Tournament, Bad Nauheim, July, 1937.

Black : F. SAEMISCH

1.	P—K 4	P—K 4
2.	Kt—K B 3	Kt—Q B 3
3.	B—Kt 5	P—Q R 3
4.	B—R 4	Kt—B 3
5.	Castles	B—K 2
6.	Q—K 2	P—Q Kt 4
7.	B—Kt 3	P—Q 3
8.	P—B 3	Castles

A safer course is 8. ....Kt—Q R 4 ; 9. B—B 2, P—B 4, etc., similar to the variation starting with 6. R—K 1.

| 9. P—Q R 4 ! | B—Kt 5 |

This is comparatively better than 9. ....P—Kt 5 ; 10. P—R 5, or 9. ....R—Kt 1 ; 10. P×P, P×P ; 11. P—Q 4, etc.±—but, still, has the disadvantage of bringing the Bishop out of play if White, as in the actual game, does not accept the Pawn offer.

| 10. P—R 3 | ...... |

More usual is R—Q 1 followed by P—Q 4. The text-move is the beginning of a quite different plan, which aims at limiting the activity of Black's Q B to a minimum. Inadvisable would be, instead, 10. P×P, P×P ; 11. R×R, Q×R ; 12. Q×P, Kt—R 2 !, after which Black would regain the Pawn with a good position.

| 10. | ...... | B—R 4 |
| 11. | P—Kt 4 | ...... |

The main objections against this advance in this type of position are generally : (1) A possibility of the Knight's sacrifice at K Kt 4. (2)

A disturbance of White's Pawn structure by means of ....P—K R 4. As neither of these eventualities is to be feared here (for instance, 11. ....Kt×Kt P; 12. P×Kt, B×P; 13. Q—K 3—or 11. ....B—Kt 3; 12. P—Q 3, P—K R 4; 13. Kt—R 4±)—there was no reason for postponing the imprisonment of the Bishop.

11.	B—Kt 3
12. P—Q 3	Kt—Q R 4
13. B—B 2	Kt—Q 2 ?

The full value of the system adopted by White could only be estimated if Black had built up the classical defensive position by playing 13. ....P—B 4 followed by ....Q—B 2. The inconsequential text-move—probably dictated by an exaggerated fear of White's Kt—R 4—leaves White a free hand both in the centre and on the Queen's side. The first victim of this strategy will be the Queen's Knight, which will be at once removed to a purely passive square and become in the following part of the game merely an object for White's combinative play.

14. P—Kt 4	Kt—Kt 2
15. Kt—R 3	P—Q B 3
16. B—Kt 3	Kt—Kt 3

White threatened eventually P—Q B 4, which would force Black to exchange his Q Kt P, thus weakening still further the general situation on the Queen's side. The move in the text, which prevents that danger at the cost of a *tempo*, is therefore not to be blamed.

| 17. P—R 5 | Kt—Q 2 |
| 18. B—K 3 | ...... |

In making this last preparative move to the intended Pawn advance on the Queen's side, White had to take into account the counter-attack 18. ....P—Q 4 ! ?; 19. P×

P, P—Q B 4, which he intended to meet by 20. P—Q 6 !, B×P (Q 3); 21. B—Q 5, or 20. ....Kt×P(Q3); 21. P×P, etc.; in both cases with advantage.

18. ......   K—R 1

Sooner or later compulsory in order to bring the Queen's Bishop to life.

19. P—B 4 !   ......

As will be seen, White's following tactics are based on the weakness of the Knight at Q Kt 2.

19. ......   Kt—B 3

Initiating an ingenious, although not quite sufficient, counter-attack. Indeed, he already had desperately little choice.

20. P×P   R P×P

Position after Black's 20th move.

21. Kt×Kt P !   ......

A purely positional offer or, better say, exchanging combination, which in the main variation would develop as follows : 21. ....P×Kt; 22. P—R 6, Q—Q 2; 23. P×Kt, Q×P; 24. P—Kt 5 !, R×R; 25. R×R, Kt—Q 2 (otherwise 26. R—R 7 wins) ; 26. Kt—R 4, R—R 1 ; 27. R—R 5, and Black would finally perish principally because of his helpless Q's Bishop. No wonder, therefore, that Sämisch prefers to carry on with the exploitation of White's slightly exposed King's wing and to win an important tempo by leaving the hostile Knight *en prise.*

21.	Q—Q 2 !
22. P—R 6	Kt—Q 1
23. Kt—B 3	Kt × Kt P !

The interesting point of Black's active defence, which, however, proves comparatively harmless, since White can simply continue his "work" on the other side.

| 24. P—Kt 5 ! | ...... |

Instead, 24. P × Kt, Q × P ch ; 25. K—R 1, R—R 4 ! etc., would have assured Black of at least a draw. But now matters become very difficult for him because of the formidable threat P—Kt 6 and the possibility of B—Q 5 in case of ....P × P.

| 24. ...... | Kt × B |
| 25. P × Kt | ...... |

After this forced exchange, the King's position is again quite safe.

| 25. ...... | P × P |
| 26. B—Q 5 | Kt—K 3 |

To give up a Pawn by 26. .... Kt—B 3 ; 27. Kt × Kt P would certainly not be a better alternative, while 26. ....R—R 2 ; 27. K R—Kt 1, Q—B 1 ; 28. Kt × Kt P, R × P; 29. Kt—R 7 ! would have lost the exchange just the same.

27. B × R	R × B
28. Q—Q Kt 2	Kt—B 2
29. K—Kt 2	P—B 3

The exchange of the Q Kt P against White's Q R P—here or on the next move—would mean certain death after rather long agony.

| 30. Q—Kt 3 ! | ...... |

Taking control of Q 5 and preventing at the same time ....B—B 2.

30.	B—K 1
31. P—R 7	P—Kt 3
32. R—R 5	K—Kt 2
33. K R—Q R 1	B—B 2
34. Kt—Q 5 !	......

Otherwise Black would obtain some counter chances after .... P—Q 4 ; but now he is almost forced to exchange at Q 5, since 34. ....Q—B 3 would be answered by 35. Kt × B and 34. ....B—Q 1 by 35. Kt—Kt 6 !, Q—R 3 ; 36. Kt × R ! etc.

34.	Kt × Kt
35. P × Kt	B—K 1
36. P—K 4	P—B 4

These last anæmic efforts will be rapidly stopped by an energetic final combination.

| 37. R—R 6 | P—Kt 4 |
| 38. Q—B 3 ! | P—K Kt 5 |

This would at last look like something but for the following drastic stroke.

Position after Black's 38th move.

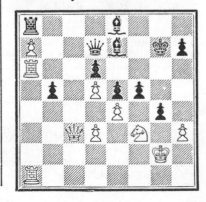

39. Kt×P ! ......

The Knights have certainly performed their best in this fight : the first one contributed in smashing to pieces Black's Queen side and his colleague can die happy after cleaving open the way to the heart of the enemy's fortress. The rest is easy.

39.	P×Kt
40. Q×P ch	K—Kt 1
41. P—Q 6 !	......

Threatening also 42. Q—Q 5 ch.

41.	Q—B 1
42. P×B	Q—B 7 ch
43. K—R 1	Q—B 7
44. Q×B P	Resigns.

GAME 97

QUEEN'S GAMBIT DECLINED (SLAV DEFENCE)

Second Match-Game, Rotterdam, October, 1937.

Black : DR. M. EUWE

1. P—Q 4	P—Q 4
2. P—Q B 4	P—Q B 3
3. Kt—K B 3	Kt—B 3
4. Kt—B 3	P×P
5. P—Q R 4	B—B 4
6. Kt—K 5	......

The discovery that the text-move is not sufficient to secure White an opening advantage was one of the assets of the present match.

6. ...... P—K 3

Played twice by Bogoljubow against me in the 1929 Match. As the experiment did not succeed (he only managed to draw one game with great difficulty and lost the other) the move 6. ....P—K 3

disappeared from master practice. But, as was proved especially by the eleventh game of this match, it is, in fact, much safer than the fashionable Kmoch Variation (6. ....Q Kt—Q 2 in conjunction with Q—B 2 and P—K 4).

7. B—Kt 5 ......

As, after 7. P—B 3, B—Q Kt 5, the move 8. P—K 4? would provoke the absolutely sound sacrifice 8. ....Kt×P ! (first played by Chéron against Przepiorka in The Hague, 1928),White must not hurry to form a Pawn centre. Still, after the following answer, he had no better move than 8. P—B 3.

7. ...... B—Q Kt 5

Much more logical than 7. .... B—K 2 as played by Bogoljubow in our Fifth Match-game, 1929 (see No. 27).

8. Kt×P (B 4) ......

Very harmless, since Black, instead of the complicated variation, actually selected, could simply play here 8. ....P—K R 3, and if 9. B—R 4 then 9. ....P—K Kt 4 ; 10. B—Kt 3, Kt—K 5 ; 11. R—B 1 (or Q—Kt 3, Kt—R 3), P—B 4, etc. with at least even prospects.

8. ...... Q—Q 4

Also a good move which leads after a short, sharp intermezzo to an equally balanced position.

9. B×Kt ......

The alternative 9. Kt—K 3, Q—R 4 ; 10. Kt×B, Q×Kt, etc., was even less promising. And if 9. Q—Kt 3, then 9. ....Kt—R 3∓.

9. ...... Q×Kt

Better than 9. ....P×B ; 10.

Kt—K 3, Q—R 4 ; 11. Q—Kt 3
with slightly better prospects for
White.

10. Q—Q 2   ......

The only move, for 10. R—B 1 ?
would have been refuted by 10. ....
P × B ; 11. P—K 4, Q—R 7 ! etc.

10. ......   P × B

More promising was 10. ....Q
—Kt 6 ! ; 11. B × P, R—Kt 1 ;
12. B—R 6, Kt—Q 2, etc., with a
strong initiative for the Pawn.

11. P—K 4   Q—Kt 6
12. P × B   Kt—Q 2
13. P × P   P × P
14. B—K 2   Castles (Q R)
15. Castles   ......

The last few moves were practically forced and the position thus
reached offers about equal attacking possibilities for both sides.

15. ......   P—K 4

This logical move—which brings
the Knight into a strong position
and opens the Queen's file to Black's
advantage—has been, in my opinion, unduly criticised. In any case,
15. ....Kt—Kt 3, which was
recommended instead, would expose
Black to dangerous threats after
16. P—R 5, Kt—R 5 ; 17. Q—K 3,
Kt × P ; 18. K R—B 1—and this
without offering him any real
winning prospects.

16. P × P   Kt × P
17. Q—B 1   B × Kt

As 18. Kt—K 4 was not really a
strong threat, this exchange should
have been postponed till a more
appropriate moment. Black should
have played 17. ....K R—Kt 1 ;
for if 18. Kt—K 4 (18. Q—K 3, Q ×
Kt P), then 18. ....Kt—B 6 ch ;
19. B × Kt, Q × B ; 20. Kt—Kt 3,

Q—Kt 5, etc., with a quite satisfactory position. After the move in
the text White obtains the better
chances because his Bishop will
prove superior to the Knight as
soon as the black piece is dislodged
from K 4.

18. P × B   K R—Kt 1
19. Q—K 3   K—Kt 1

Not absolutely necessary, since
he could indirectly protect his
Q R P by playing 19. ....Q—Q 4 ;
20. P—Kt 3, Q—Q 7 ; but after 21.
Q × Q, R × Q ; 22. K R—K 1 (Kt—
Q 6 ; 23. Q R—Q 1 !) White's end-
game chances would still be the
better.

20. P—Kt 3   ......

As this defensive move is unavoidable anyhow, it is better to
play it immediately.

20. ......   R—Q 2
21. Q R—Kt 1   Q—B 7
22. K R—K 1 !   ......

The most subtle move of the
game ! With this, White prepares
for the important P—K B 4. The
immediate advance of that Pawn
would be refuted by 22. ....R—
Q 7 ! ; 23. K R—K 1, Kt—Q 6, etc.

22. ......   Q—Q 7
23. Q × Q   R × Q
24. P—K B 4   Kt—Kt 3
25. B—B 4   K R—Q 1

Or 25. ....R—Kt 2 ; 26. R—
K 8 ch, K—B 2 ; 27. K—R 1 ! with
advantage for White.

26. R—K 6 !   ......

In order to exchange one pair of
Rooks. It must be noted that
Black cannot play 26. ....R—
Q B 7 because of 27. B—R 6, P—
Kt 3 ; 28. R × Q B P.

26.	K R—Q 3
27. Q R—K 1	K—B 2
28. R × R	R × R

If 28. ....K × R then 29. B—Kt 8 threatening both B × P and R—K 6 ch.

| 29. P—R 4 | ...... |

In order to play the King to B 2 without being disturbed by the Rook check on the second rank.

29.	K—Q 2
30. K—B 2	Kt—K 2
31. K—B 3	Kt—Q 4 ?

Allowing the white King to attack successfully the K R P. It is, however, more than doubtful whether 31. ....P—K B 4 (which was comparatively the best) would have saved the game. White would then play *not* 32. P—Kt 4 because of 32. ....P × P ch ; 33. K × P, R—Kt 3 ch followed by 34. ....Kt—B 4 with sufficient counter-chances —but first 32. P—K R 5 ! and, only after that preparation, P—Kt 4, freeing his K B P with disastrous effect for Black.

Position after Black's 31st move.

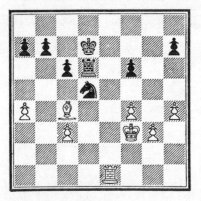

32. B—Q 3 !   ......

The decisive manœuvre forcing a further weakening of Black's Pawn position on the K-side. Eventual Pawn losses on the other wing do not matter any more because the passive position of Black's pieces prevents him from undertaking any serious counter-demonstration.

32.	P—K R 3
33. B—B 5 ch	K—Q 1
34. K—Kt 4 !	......

If now 34. ....Kt × Q B P then 35. K—R 5, Kt × P ; 36. K × P, etc., would win easily.

| 34. ...... | Kt—K 2 |
| 35. B—Kt 1 | K—K 1 |

Or 35. ....R—Q 4 ; 36. P—B 5, etc.

36. K—R 5	K—B 2
37. B—R 2 ch	K—B 1
38. K × P	R—Q 7

The main variation was 38. ....Kt—B 4 ch ; 39. K—Kt 6, Kt × Kt P ; 40. P—B 5 followed by the advance of the K R's Pawn.

39. B—K 6	R—Q 6
40. P—Kt 4	R × P
41. P—Kt 5	......

Even simpler than 41. R—Q 1, Kt—Q 4. If now 41. ....P × P then 42. B P × P, etc., winning.

Resigns.

GAME 98

QUEEN'S GAMBIT DECLINED (SLAV DEFENCE)

Sixth Match-Game, Haarlem, October, 1937.

Black : Dr. M. Euwe

| 1. P—Q 4 | P—Q 4 |
| 2. P—Q B 4 | P—Q B 3 |

3. Kt—Q B 3   ......

In my opinion this move gives White more chances of obtaining an opening advantage, and this for the following reasons : (1) The dangers of the continuation 3. ....,
P×P *in conjunction with* 4. ....
P—K 4 are clearly shown in the present game ; (2) the Winawer Counter-attack P—K 4 can be met in a simple and effective manner by 4. P×Q P, B P×P ; 5. *P—K 4 !* and if 5. ....P×K P ; 6. B—Kt 5 ch+ ; (3) in answer to 3. ....Kt—B 3 ; 4. P—K 3, P—K Kt 3 I suggest 5. *P—B* 3, which after 5. ....B—Kt 2 ; 6. P—K 4, P×K P ; 7. P×P, P—K 4 ! ; 8. P—Q 5, Castles ; 9. Kt—B 3 leads to a rather complicated position, still positionally favourable to White.

3. ......   P×P
4. P—K 4 !   ......

It is almost incredible that this quite natural move has not been considered by the so-called theoreticians. White obtains now an appreciable advantage in development, no matter what Black replies.

4. ......   P—K 4

The alternative is 4. ....P—Q Kt 4 ; 5. P—Q R 4, P—K 4 (or ....P—Kt 5 ; 6. Kt—R 2, Kt—B 3 ; 7. P—K 5, Kt—Q 4 ; 8. B× P±) ; 6. P×Kt P, P×Q P ; 7. B× P!, B—Q Kt 5! ; 8. R—R 4, P—Q R 4 ; 9. P×P *e.p.*, and White will emerge with a Pawn to the good.

5. B×P   ......

This sacrificial combination is certainly very tempting and, especially over the board, extremely difficult to refute ; but it is by no means the necessary consequence of White's previous move which has a value absolutely independent of the correctness of the piece sacrifice.

The *positional* exploitation of White's advantage in space consists in 5. Kt—B 3 !, P×P ; 6. Q×P, Q×Q ; 7. Kt×Q, after which Black would only get into further trouble by trying to protect the gambit-pawn—for instance, 7. ....P—Q Kt 4 ; 8. P—Q R 4, P—Kt 5 ; 9. Kt—Q 1, B—R 3 ; 10. B—K 3, Kt—Q 3 ; 11. P—B 3 followed by R—B 1 and B×P with a clear positional advantage.

5. ......   P×P

Fatal would be 5. ....Q×P ; 6. Q—Kt 3, Q—Q 2 ; 7. B—K Kt 5 ! with a winning attack.

6. Kt—B 3   ......

Putting before Black a most difficult practical problem . . .

6. ......   P—Q Kt 4 ?

Which he not only fails to solve but even selects a move that brings him immediately a decisive disadvantage. As a matter of fact the offer *could* be accepted since Black would have at his disposal a more effective line than the one I had analysed when proposing it. My "chief" variation was the following ; 6. ....P×Kt ; 7. B×P ch, K—K 2 ; 8. Q—Kt 3, *Kt—B 3* ; 9. P—K 5, Kt—K 5 ; 10. Castles !, Q—Kt 3 (or Kt—R 3 ; 11. Q—B 4 !, Q Kt—B 4 ; 12. B—Kt 5 ch !, Kt×B ; 13. Kt×Kt with a winning attack) ; 11. Q—B 4 !, P×P ; 12. B×P, Q×B ; 13. Q×Kt, K×B ; 14. Kt—Kt 5 ch, K—K 1 ; 15. Q—Q B 4, B—K 2 ; 16. Q—B 7 ch, K—Q 1 ; 17. Q R—Q 1 ch, B—Q 2 ; 18. Kt—K 6 ch, K—B 1 ; 19. Q×B, Q×K P ; 20. K R—K 1, Q—B 3 ; 21. R×B, Q×Q (Kt×R ; 22. Q—Q 6 winning) ; 22. R×Q with a won position. But, instead of 8. .... Kt—B 3 Black could play 8. .... *P×P !* ; 9. B×P, *Q—Kt 3 !* ; 10. *B×Kt, R×B* ; 11. *Q×R* (or 11

B—R 3 ch, P—B 4), *Q—Kt 5 ch* ;
12. *Kt—Q 2, Q × B*, after which his
middle game chances, in spite of
the approximate equality of forces,
should be estimated decidedly
higher than White's remaining possibilities of a direct attack. Consequently, unless an improvement
can be found in this last line of play,
White's Knight's offer will hardly
be repeated, at least in serious
practice.

7. Kt × Kt P !   ......

Dr. Euwe admits simply having
overlooked this reply. *This time*
the Knight obviously cannot be
taken because of 8. B—Q 5, etc.

7. ......   B—R 3
8. Q—Kt 3 !   ......

An important move with a triple
object : (a) to protect the King's
Bishop ; (b) to prevent the check
at Black's Q Kt 5 ; (c) to strengthen
the pressure against Black's K B 2.

8. ......   Q—K 2

If 8. .... B × Kt then 9. B × P ch,
K—Q 2 ; 10. Kt × P ! (not 10. B ×
Kt ?, R × B) etc., with an easy win.

9. Castles   B × Kt
10. B × B   Kt—B 3

Of course not 10. .... P × B
because of 11. Q—Q 5.

11. B—Q B 4   Q Kt—Q 2
12. Kt × P   ......

Another winning method was 12.
P—K 5, Kt × P (if .... Kt—K 5 ;
13. Q—Kt 7) 13. Kt × Kt, Q × Kt ;
14. Q—Kt 7, R—Q Kt 1 ; 15. Q ×
K B P ch, K—Q 1 ; 16. Q × R P ; but
after 16. .... B—Q 3 Black would
be able to put at least as much
further resistance as after the
simple text-move.

12. ......   R—Q Kt 1
13. Q—B 2   Q—B 4

Hereafter, White, in order to win,
has only to avoid a few little traps.

14. Kt—B 5   ......

Here, for instance, 14. Kt × P
would be wrong because of 14. ....
R—B 1 !

14. ......   Kt—K 4
15. B—B 4 !   ......

And now, after the tempting 15.
Kt × P ch, K—Q 1 ! (B × Kt ? ; 16.
B × P ch) ; 16. R—Q 1 ch, K—B 2
two white pieces would be *en prise*.

15. ......   Kt—R 4

Position after Black's 15th move.

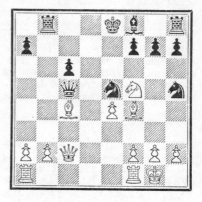

16. B × P ch !   ......

A very profitable simplification.
Less convincing would be instead
16. B × Kt, Q × B (K 4) ; 17. B—
K 2, Q—B 4 ; 18. Q × Q, B × Q ;
19. B × Kt, P—Kt 3, etc.

16. ......   K × B
17. Q × Q   B × Q
18. B × Kt   R—Kt 4
19. B—Q 6   ......

Threatening 20. P—Q R 4.

| 19. ...... | B—Kt 3 |
| 20. P—Q Kt 4 ! | ...... |

And now the Rook is in danger. Black cannot avoid further loss of material.

20.	R—Q 1
21. Q R—Q 1	P—B 4
22. P × P	B × P
23. R—Q 5 !	......

Winning at least the exchange.

Resigns.

GAME 99

NIMZOWITSCH DEFENCE

Eighth Match-Game, Leyden, October, 1937.

Black : DR. M. EUWE

1. P—Q 4	Kt—K B 3
2. P—Q B 4	P—K 3
3. Kt—Q B 3	B—Kt 5
4. Q—B 2	......

I believe that this move is the most logical of the many moves possible (4. Q—Kt 3, 4. P—Q R 3, 4. B—Q 2, 4. B—Kt 5, 4. P—K 3, 4. Kt—B 3, 4. P—K Kt 3 or even 4. B—B 4), as it achieves two important objects : it keeps control over K 4 and it prevents, temporarily at least, the doubling of the Pawns on the Queen's Bishop's file.

| 4. ...... | P—Q 4 |
| 5. P × P | ...... |

If 5. P—Q R 3, B × Kt ch; 6. Q × B, Kt—K 5 ; 7. Q—B 2, P—Q B 4 ; 8. P × B P, Kt—Q B 3 ; 9. P—K 3, Black obtains an equal game by continuing 9. ....Q—R 4 ch ; 10. B—Q 2, Kt × B ; 11. Q × Kt, P × P ! and if 12. Q × Q, Kt × Q ; 13. R—B 1, then 13. ....P—Q Kt 4 ! ; 14. P × P *e.p.*, B—Kt 2 !

| 5. ...... | Q × P |
| 6. P—K 3 | ...... |

If 6. Kt—B 3, then, for instance, 6. ....P—B 4 ; 7. B—Q 2, B × Kt ; 8. B × B, P × P ; 9. Kt × P, P—K 4 ! (Loevenfish - Botvinnik, seventh Match-game, 1937).

6.	P—B 4
7. P—Q R 3	B × Kt ch
8. P × B	Q Kt—Q 2

There is no hurry about this Knight development. More appropriate for equalising seems to be 8. ....Castles ; 9. Kt—B 3, P—Q Kt 3 !—and if 10. B—K 2, then 10. ....P × P ; 11. B P × P, B—R 3 ! as, for instance, I played (with Black) against Grau in Montevideo, 1938.

| 9. P—B 3 | ...... |

A sound strategical scheme : White intends to meet the eventual ....P—K 4 by the counter-advance P—K 4. Still more exact would be, however, *first* 9. Kt—K 2, since then 0. ....P × P ; 10. B P × P, Kt—Kt 3 would not be satisfactory because of 11. Kt—B 3.

9.	P × P
10. B P × P	Kt—Kt 3
11. Kt—K 2	B—Q 2
12. Kt—B 4	......

Played in order to obtain a slightly superior end-game after 12. ....Q—B 3 ; 13. Q × Q, etc. If, instead, 12. Kt—B 3, then 12. .... Q—B 3 with a quite satisfactory game.

12.	Q—Q 3
13. B—Q 2	R—Q B 1
14. Q—Kt 2	K Kt—Q 4

Doubtless the best move, eliminating any immediate danger in the centre.

15. Kt×Kt   P×Kt
16. B—Kt 4   Q—K 3

If 16. .... Q—Kt 3 then 17. R—B 1.

17. K—B 2   ......

The first move of the "Indian" Castling (see my game with Sultan Khan, No. 53). Actually, the King, in this position, is quite comfortable at K B 2.

17. ......   Kt—R 5

The first deviation from the logical path. By far the best drawing chance consisted in 17. .... Kt—B 5 (but not 17. .... P—B 4 ; 18. B—B 5 ! ±) ; 18. B×Kt, R×B, thus obtaining Bishops of different colours ; if, for instance, 19. Q R—Q B 1, then 19. .... R×R ; 20. R×R, B—B 3 ; 21. Q—B 3, P—B 3 ; 22. Q—B 5, P—Q R 3 ; 23. Q—Kt 6, Q—Q 2, with an adequate defence.

18. Q—Q 2   P—Q Kt 3 ?

A fatal mistake, allowing White to win by force. Necessary was 18. .... P—B 4, although White's advantage after 19. B—Q 3 followed by K R—K 1 and eventually P—K 4 would already be evident.

19. B—R 6 !   R—Q Kt 1

As the sequel shows, the threat to imprison the Bishop by .... P—Q Kt 4 is by no means an effective one. But 19. .... R—B 2 ; 20. Q R—Q B 1 would be equally hopeless.

20. P—K 4   ......

This simple opening up of the centre leaves Black without the slightest saving resource.

20. ......   P—Q Kt 4

If 20. .... P—B 3, then 21. P×P, Q×P ; 22. Q—K 2 ch !, Q—K 3 ; 23. K R—K 1, Q×Q ch ; 24. R×Q ch, K—Q 1 ; 25. B—K 7 ch, K—B 2 ; 26. R—B 1 ch and wins.

Position after Black's 20th move.

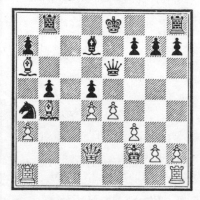

21. Q—B 4 !   ......

This powerful intermediate move destroys Black's last hopes of catching the opponent's K's Bishop. If now 21. .... R—Q 1, then 22. P×P, Q×P ; 23. K R—K 1 ch, B—K 3 ; 24. R—K 5, Q×Q P ch ; 25. Q×Q, R×Q ; 26. B×P ch and wins.

21. ......   R—Kt 3
22. P×P   ......

More precise than 22. K R—K 1 which could be answered by 22. .... Kt—Kt 7 !

22. ......   Q×P
23. K R—K 1 ch   B—K 3
24. Q R—B 1   ......

With the terrible threat 25. R—B 8 ch.

24. ......   P—B 3
25. R—B 7 !   ......

More convincing than the win of the exchange by 25. R—B 8 ch.

25. ......   K—Q 1
26. R×R P   ......

After this mate in a few moves is unavoidable.

Resigns.

GAME 100

CATALAN OPENING

Fourteenth Match-Game, Zwolle, November, 1937.

Black : Dr. M. Euwe

1. P—Q 4   Kt—K B 3
2. P—Q B 4   P—K 3
3. P—K Kt 3   P—Q 4

The Soviet grand master, Loevenfish, played in a tournament game at Tbilisi, 1937, 3. ....B—Kt 5 ch ; 4. B Q 2, B×B ch ; 5. Q×B, Kt—K 5 ; 6. Q—B 2, P Q 4 ; 7. B—Kt 2, Q—K 2 ; 8. P—Q R 3, P—K B 4—and obtained a quite satisfactory position. The text-move in conjunction with the next one leads to a modern variation of the Queen's Gambit Accepted which is slightly in White's favour.

4. Kt—K B 3   ......

White need not avoid the exchange of Queens by playing 4. B—Kt 2 since after 4. ...:P×P ; 5. Q—R 4 ch, Q—Q 2 ; 6. Q×B P, Q—B 3 ; 7. Q Kt—Q 2, etc., he would obtain an advantage both in space and development.

4. ......   P×P
5. Q—R 4 ch   Q Kt—Q 2
6. Q×B P   ......

There is no advantage to be obtained by delaying this capture, for instance, 6. B—Kt 2, P—Q R 3 ; 7. Kt—B 3—then 7. ....R—Q Kt 1 ! ; 8. Q×B P, P—Q Kt 4, etc., at least equalising.

6. ......   P—B 4

If now 6. ....P—Q R 3, then 7. Q—B 2 ! in order to answer 7. ....P—Q Kt 4 by 8. P—Q R 4. The same manœuvre would apply if Black were to play P—Q R 3 on his seventh move.

7. B—Kt 2   Kt—Kt 3

This method of playing has the disadvantage of not solving the problem of the development of the Queen's Bishop. More advisable would be first 7. ....P×P, and if 8. Kt×P, Kt—Kt 3 followed by 9. ....B—Kt 5 ch ; and if 8. Q×P, then 8. ....B—B 4, 9. Q—K R 4, B—K 2, etc., still harassing the adventurous white Queen.

8. Q—Q 3   P×P
9. Castles !   ......

In order to prevent 9. ....B—Kt 5 ch, possible, for instance, after 9. Kt×P. Black's extra-Pawn cannot be protected because of (9. ....B—B 4) ; 10. P—Q Kt 4 !

9. ......   B—K 2
10. Kt×P   Castles

Of course not 10. ....P—K 4 because of 11. Q—Kt 5 ch, K Kt—Q 2 ; 12. Kt—B 5, etc., with clear advantage.

11. Kt—Q B 3   P—K 4

The following double exchange is rather risky for the slight disturbance of White's Pawn position on the Queen's side will be more than compensated by the advantage of the two Bishops. An interesting attempt would be 11. ....Q—Q 2 aiming both at 12. ....P—K 4 and 12. ....R—Q 1.

12. Kt—B 5   B—Kt 5
13. Q—B 2 !   B×Q Kt
14. P×B   B×Kt ?

This exchange was necessary sooner or later, it is true—but why the haste ? As Black intended to play Q—B 2 he would have been better advised to do this at once, thereby giving White not so much choice of attacking moves.

15. Q×B   Q—B 2
16. B—R 6   ......

The main object of this rather difficult move is to prevent a Knight move to Q 4, possible, for instance, after 16. B—Kt 5 ; for if *now* 16. ....K Kt—Q 4, then 17. B—K 4 !, P—Kt 3 ; 18. Q—B 3, K R—Q 1 ; 19. K R—Q 1, etc., to White's advantage.

16. ......   Q Kt—Q 2
17. Q—Kt 5 (?)   ......

But by leaving his Bishop so dangerously placed, White certainly complicates matters without necessity. Simple and strong was 17. B—K 3, and if 17. ....P—K Kt 3 then 18. Q—Kt 5, etc., with a considerable positional advantage.

17. ......   Kt—K 1
18. Q R—Kt 1   ......

Also possible was 18. B—R 3— a move which I intended to play later as answer, for example, to 18. ....R—Kt 1

18. ......   Kt—B 4

The tempting 18. ....Kt—Kt 3 would have been answered by 19. P—Q R 4 !, and if 19. ....P—B 3, then 20. Q—B 5 !, P×B ; 21. P— R 5, Q—Q 2 ; 22. Q—R 5—and Black would get into serious trouble if he tried to keep the extra-piece much longer.

19. Q—Kt 4   R—Q 1

It would be hardly a wise policy to force the exchange of Queens by playing 19. ....Q—B 1 since after 20. Q×Q, R×Q ; 21. B—Kt 5, P—B 3 ; 22. B—Q 5 ch followed by 23. B—K 3 the Bishops would certainly play a vital part in the end-game.

20. B—Kt 5   R—Q 3
21. Q—Q B 4   ......

Preparing the advance of the K B P, which at this moment would have been premature—for instance, 21. P—K B 4, P—K R 3 ; 22. P×P ?, R—K Kt 3∓.

21. ......   P—Q Kt 3

White threatened also 22. B× P.

22. P—B 4   R—Kt 3 !

With this and the few following strong moves Black eliminates any immediate danger.

23. Q R—Q 1   ......

Threatening 24. B—Q 8 followed by P—B 5.

23. ......   P—K 5

Preventing the above threat since 24. B—Q 8, Kt—Q 3 ! ; 25. B×Q, Kt×Q, etc., would now be to Black's advantage.

24. B—R 4 !   ......

After this well-timed retreat Black's position begins to look very precarious, since, for instance, 24. ....Kt—Q 3 ; 25. Q—Q 5, Kt— Kt 4 ; 26. R—B 1, R—Q 3 ; 27. Q—B 4 would be in White's favour. By the following interesting Pawn's offer Black succeeds in removing the white Queen to a less active square—but at the heavy price of a serious weakening of the position of his Knight at Q B 4.

| 24. ...... | P—Kt 4 ! ? |
| 25. Q—Kt 4 ! | ...... |

The only correct answer, for 25. Q × Kt P would permit Black to place a Knight on K B 4 via Q 3 after which the threats .... Kt × B, or .... Kt—K 6 would secure him a promising initiative.

| 25. ...... | P—Q R 4 |
| 26. Q—R 3 | ...... |

And not 26. Q—Kt 2, or Kt 1 because of 26. .... Kt—R 5.

| 26. ...... | P—B 4 ? |

The wish to prevent P—B 5 and at the same time to secure the K's Pawn is quite understandable ; but the move has the grave inconvenience of making Black's position in the centre even more shaky than it was before. A perfectly satisfactory line was, however, hardly to be found. If, for instance, 26. .... R—Q 3 (recommended by the great theoretician, Prof. Becker, as even giving Black an advantage !) then 27. B—K 7 !, R × R (or Q × R ; 28. Q × Kt±) ; 28. B × Kt !, R × R ch ; 29. K × R after which Black would have to suffer further material loss. Also after the comparatively better 26. .... Kt—Q 3 White would secure a definite positional advantage by the important intermediate move 27. R—Q 5 ! Black had therefore only the choice between unpleasant alternatives.

| 27. B—Q 8 ! | ...... |

A most unpleasant shock : White gets his threat in first and thus prevents the harmonious co-operation of Black's forces.

27.	Q—R 2
28. K—R 1	R—Q R 3
29. R—Q 5	......

The simple domination of the central file by the Rooks will soon prove decisive owing to the numerous weaknesses created by the 23.-26. Pawn moves of Black.

| 29. ...... | Kt—K 3 |
| 30. K R—Q 1 | Kt × B |

If, instead, 30. .... Q—K 6, then simply 31. Q—Kt 2 and the threats would remain.

| 31. R × Kt | Q—K B 2 |
| 32. K R—Q 5 | ...... |

More effective than 32. K R—Q 7, Q—B 5.

| 32. ...... | R—Q B 3 |
| 33. R × Kt P | Q—B 5 |

Position after Black's 33rd move.

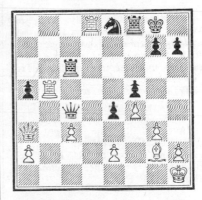

| 34. R × B P ! | ...... |

Conclusive, as 34. .... R × R ; 35. R × Kt ch, K—B 2 ; 36. Q—K 7 ch, K—Kt 3 ; 37. B × P, etc., would be absolutely hopeless for Black.

34.	Q R—B 3
35. R × R	P × R
36. R—Q 4 (?)	......

A typical "short-of-time" calculation. I was glad to find a practically forced sequence of moves that would bring me without damage over the ominous 40th move—and did not pay attention to the simple 36. Q—Kt 3, forcing an end-game with two extra-Pawns and most probably immediate resignation !

36.	......	Q×K P
37.	Q—Kt 3 ch	K—R 1
38.	R×P	Q—Q 7
39.	Q—Kt 1 !	......

Technically easier than 39. P—K R 3, Kt—Q 3 with slight fighting possibilities for Black.

| 39. | ...... | Q×Q B P |
| 40. | Q—K 1 | Q×Q ch |

Or 40. ....Q—B 1 ; 41. Q×P.

41. R×Q   ......

The ending is easily won, for White, besides his extra-Pawn, has a very strong Bishop against a Knight completely lacking safe squares in the centre of the board.

| 41. | ...... | Kt—Q 3 |
| 42. | B—B 6 ! | ...... |

Immobilizing the Knight (because of the eventual threat to exchange Rooks by R—K 8) and preventing a further advance of Black's Q R P.

42. ......   R—Q Kt 1

Or 42. ....R—Q B 1 ; 43. B—R 4.

43.	R—K 6	R—Kt 8 ch
44.	K—Kt 2	R—Kt 7 ch
45.	K—R 3	Kt—B 4
46.	R×P	Kt—K 2
47.	B—K 4	K—Kt 2
48.	R—K 6	K—B 2
49.	R—K R 6	R×P
50.	R×P ch	K—B 3
51.	R—R 6 ch	K—B 2
52.	R—R 6	Resigns.

GAME 101

QUEEN'S INDIAN DEFENCE

Twenty - first Match - Game, Amsterdam, November, 1937.

White : DR. M. EUWE

1.	P—Q 4	Kt—K B 3
2.	P—Q B 4	P—K 3
3.	Kt—K B 3	P—Q Kt 3
4.	P—K Kt 3	B—Kt 2
5.	B—Kt 2	B—Kt 5 ch
6.	B—Q 2	B—K 2

To the best of my knowledge this move has not been played before ; but an analogous idea in the Dutch Defence has been experimented with —first by Soviet players and subsequently by myself, mostly with satisfactory results as far as the opening was concerned. The idea of the Bishop's retreat is to take advantage of the somewhat unusual position of White's Queen's Bishop. Still, after this game I came to the conclusion that the old 5. ....B—K 2 (instead of 5. ....B—Kt 5 ch), which I adopted in the 23rd Match-game, is at least as good as the text-manœuvre.

7. Kt—B 3   Kt—K 5

Allowing White to obtain a slight advantage in space. Safer was 7. ....Castles ; 8. Castles, P—Q 4 and if 9. Kt—K 5, then Q—B 1 with an approximately even game.

8. Castles   ......

He could also have played P—Q 5 at once.

8.	......	Castles
9.	P—Q 5 !	Kt×B
10.	Q×Kt	......

10. Kt×Kt also would be good, since it would have left Black with hardly anything better than 10.

....Q—B 1, parrying the threat 11.
P—Q 6 !

| 10. ...... | B—K B 3 |
| 11. Q R—Q 1 | ...... |

Wasting valuable time. After 11.
Kt—Q 4 White's game would remain definitely preferable.

| 11. ...... | P—Q 8 |
| 12. P×P | ...... |

If now 12. Kt—Q 4, then 12. ....
B×Kt followed by ....P—K 4 with
a satisfactory game for Black. The
exchange in the text also leads only
to equality as Black can easily
protect his K 3.

12.	P×P
13. Kt—Q 4	B×B
14. K×B	......

Of course not 14. Kt×P ?
because of 14. ....Q—K 2 ; 15.
Kt×R, B×Kt ; 16. P×B (Q×B,
B×R), B—Kt 2 ! remaining with
two minor pieces for the Rook.

| 14. ...... | Q—B 1 |

Intending in some variations to
make use of the square Q Kt 2—
for instance, 15. P—B 4, Kt—B 3 ! ;
16. Kt×Kt, Q—Kt 2, etc., to
Black's advantage.

15. Q—K 3	B×Kt
16. R×B	Kt—B 3
17. R—K 4	......

The beginning of an entirely mistaken plan which speedily transforms a playable position into a lost
one. A solid move was 17. R—Q 2,
but even simpler was 17. R—B 4 ;
then after the exchange of Rooks
Black's attacking chances would be
reduced to a minimum.

| 17. ...... | R—B 3 |
| 18. P—B 4 ? | ...... |

Leaving the Rook in a stalemate
position. 18. R—B 4 was still the
right move.

| 18. ...... | Q—Q 2 |
| 19. P—K Kt 4 | ...... |

Weakening the K B P and thereby
adding to all his other troubles.
Instead, 19. R—Q 1 would have
given him some chances of salvation.

| 19. ...... | Q R—K B 1 |
| 20. P—Kt 5 | ...... |

Useless, as the answer demon-
strates ; but his game was already
strategically lost.

| 20. ...... | R—B 4 ! |

Black does not need to protect
his King's Pawn, since after 21.
R×P the answer 21. ....Kt—K 4
would win the exchange.

| 21. P—K R 4 | Q—B 2 |
| 22. R—B 3 | K—R 1 ! |

An important preparation for the
following advance in the centre,
instead of which the immediate 22.
....P—Q 4 would be slightly premature because of 23. R×P, P—
Q 5 ; 24. Q—K 4, P×Kt ; 25. P×
P !, Kt—Q 1 ; 26. R—K 7, etc.,
with some fighting chances for
White. And as 22. ....P—K 4
would also be unconvincing because
of 23. Kt—Q 5, Kt—Q 5 ; 24. Kt—
K 7 ch !, Q×Kt ; 25. R×Kt, etc.—
I decided to restrain the advance of
my central Pawns until such an advance would be absolutely decisive.

| 23. Q—Q 3 | P—Q 4 ! |

Now the time has come, since 24.
P×P, P×P ; 25. R—R 4, P—Q 5
would be quite hopeless for White.

| 24. R×P | Kt—Kt 5 ! |

Obviously stronger than 24. ....
Q×R.

25. Q—K 3   Kt—B 7

Instead, 25. ....P—Q 5 ; 26. Q—
K 4, P×Kt ; 27. P×P, etc., would
have allowed a longer resistance.

26. Q—Q 2   Q×R
27. P×P   Q—B 2

Position after Black's 27th move.

28. Q×Kt   ......

After this Black wins easily by a
direct attack. I expected, instead,
the subtler 28. K—Kt 3 (threatening
also 29. P—K 4) after which
the following striking variation
would occur : 28. ....Kt—K 8 ! ;
29. R—B 2, Kt—Kt 7 ! ; 30. P—K 3
(still fighting for the K B P), Kt×
R P ; 31. K×Kt, P—K R 3 !, etc.,
with decisive threats.

28. ......   R×B P
29. Q—Q 3   Q—R 4
30. R×R   R×R
31. Q—R 3   R—Kt 5 ch
32. K—B 2   P—K R 3 !

If now 33. P×P, then 33. ....
Q—B 4 ch, after which a Rook's
check would win the Queen.

Resigns.

GAME 102

RETI'S OPENING

Twenty - second Match - Game,
Delft, November, 1937.

Black : DR. M. EUWE

1. Kt—K B 3   P—Q 4
2. P—B 4   P—Q 5
3. P—K 3   ......

After 3. P—Q Kt 4 Black could
play 3. ....P—K B 3 followed by
....P—K 4 with good prospects.
The move selected prevents this
possibility, since after 3. ....P—
Q B 4 ; 4. P—Q Kt 4, P—B 3,
White can play—*not* 5. P×B P, P—
K 4 ! with about even chances—but
5. *P×Q P, P×P ;* 6. *P—B 5 !* (this
last move, which appears very effective, was discovered by myself
when preparing for the match)—
after which the weakness of the
diagonal K Kt 1—Q R 7 would
cause Black considerable trouble.
If 6. ....P—K 4, then 7. B—B 4 ;
if 6. ....Q—Q 4, then 7. Q—B 2± ;
if 6. ....P—Q R 4, then 7. Q—
R 4 ch, B—Q 2 ; 8. P—Kt 5, P—
K 4; 9. B—B 4 and Black cannot
play 9. ....B×B P because of 10.
B×Kt followed by 11. Q—B 4.
In other words, the consequences of
3. ....P—Q B 4 seem to be decidedly in White's favour.

3. ......   Kt—Q B 3

On the contrary, after this move
White will find it very difficult (if
indeed possible) to obtain any
opening advantage.

4. P×P   Kt×P
5. Kt×Kt   Q×Kt
6. Kt—B 3   Kt—B 3

Even simpler is immediately 6.
....P—K 4, but as Black could
effect that advance by his next

move, the text-continuation does not yet spoil anything.

7. P—Q 3   ......

Useless would be 7. Kt—Kt 5, Q—Kt 3 ; 8. P—Q 4, P—K 4 ! ; 9. P—B 5, Q—B 3 ; 10. Kt—B 3, P—Q R 3.

7. ......   P—B 3 ?

A serious loss of time, instead of which 7. ....P—K 4 was quite sufficient. If then 8. B—K 3, simply 8. ....Q—Q 1 ; 9. P—Q 4, Kt—Kt 5 ; or if 9. B—K 2, then 9. .... P—B 4 (or even, more solid, 9. .... B—K 2)—with an approximately equal game.

8. B—K 3   Q—Q 2

With the intention of developing the Bishops on the long diagonals. But White's advantage in space becomes evident in a very few moves.

9. P—Q 4   P—K Kt 3
10. D—K 2   B—Kt 2

Threatening ....Kt—Kt 5 which would have been useless immediately because of 11. B—B 4, followed by P—K R 3.

11. P—K R 3   Castles
12. Castles   P—Kt 3
13. B—B 3   B—Kt 2
14. P—Q R 4 !   ......

In order to make a break in the centre more effective White tries first to weaken Black's Q Kt 3. The sequel will prove the soundness of this scheme.

14. ......   Q R—Q 1

In connexion with his eighteenth move this looks like a loss of time, but in reality it is almost a sad necessity since after P—Q R 5

Black will have to deal with the threat P—R 6 ; while, on the other hand, after the exchange on his Q Kt 3 he will be obliged to offer the exchange of at least one pair of Rooks.

15. P—R 5   Q—B 2

This and the next move are necessary in order to give sufficient protection to the weak square Q Kt 3.

16. Q—Kt 3   Kt—Q 2
17. P × P   P × P
18. R—R 7   R—R 1

White's main threat was 19. P—Q 5.

19. K R—R 1   P—K 3

Otherwise the imminent P—Q 5 would be even more unpleasant than it proved to be in the actual game.

20. R × R   B × R

This move has been unduly criticised. After 20. ....R × R ; 21. R × R ch, B × R ; 22. Q—R 3, B—Kt 2 ; 23. P—Q Kt 4, White would have to face a technically easier problem than in the actual game.

21. P—Q 5 !   ......

By no means an easy decision to make, as I was fully aware that the resulting exchanges would cede to Black important squares in the centre. Still, it was necessary to undertake something definite at this particular moment since (1) White has no means of improving the excellent position of his pieces ; (2) Black, on the contrary, could eventually try to form an attack against the Queen's Pawn, starting by R—Q 1 ; and (3) this is the only possibility of taking advantage of the weakness of Black's Q Kt 3, created by the advance of White's Q R P.

| 21. ...... | B P×P |
| 22. P×P | Kt—B 4 |

The tactical justification of the move 21. P—Q 5 resides in the variation 22. ....B×Kt ; 23. P—Q 6 !, Q×P ; 24. Q×B, B×B ; 25. B—R 6 ! winning the exchange. And if 22. ....Kt—K 4, then 23. B—K 4 still threatening P—Q 6.

| 23. Q—B 4 | ...... |

If 23. B×Kt, Q×B ; 24. P×P, then 24. ....B×B ; 25. P×P ch, R×P ; 26. P×B, B×Kt ; 27. R—R 7, Q—Kt 4 ch with perpetual check.

23.	P×P
24. B×P	B×B
25. Kt×B	Q—K 4

Black selects the most aggressive line, which is certainly more promising than the purely passive 25. ....Q—Kt 2 ; 26. R—Kt 1, Kt—Q 2 ; 27. Q—Kt 5 ! with a clear advantage in space for White.

| 26. R—Kt 1 | Kt—R 5 ! |

An ingenious way of keeping the sick Pawn, at least temporarily. The next moves on both sides had to be most exactly calculated.

| 27. P—Q Kt 3 | Kt—Kt 7 |
| 28. Q—B 6 | P—Q Kt 4 ! |

The point of the previous Knight's manœuvre as this Pawn cannot be taken because of the answer 29. ....R—Q 1.

| 29. B—B 4 ! | Q—K 3 |

After this, White, as the succeeding moves show, can take the Pawn. The only adequate defence consisted in 29. ....Q—K 7 ! which

would be answered by 30. R—K B 1 ! still leaving Black with the following weak spots : (a) the Q Kt P ; (b) the square K B 3 ; (c) last but not least, the insecure position of the Knight at Kt 7.

Position after Black's 29th move.

| 30. Q×P ! | ...... |

This seemingly very risky capture secures White a material advantage which he will succeed in keeping until the end. If now 30. ....R—Q 1, then 31. R—Q B 1 !, R×Kt ; 32. Q—Kt 8 ch (this is why 29. B—B 4 was necessary), B—B 1 ; 33. B—R 6, Q—Q 3 (or Q—K 2 ; 34. R—B 8) ; 34. Q×Q, R×Q ; 35. R—B 8 and wins.

| 30. ...... | Q—K 5 |
| 31. R—Q B 1 | Kt—Q 6 |

Or 31. ....R—Q 1 ; 32. B—Kt 5 with variations similar to those mentioned above.

| 32. Q—B 4 ! | ...... |

Again the only move, but amply sufficient to maintain the advantage.

| 32. ...... | Q—K 7 |

A grave mistake would be 32.

....B—Q 5 because of 33. Kt—B 6 ch.

33. R—B 1   Kt × B

Black has practically no choice, for 33. ....R—K 1 (threatening 34. ....Q × R ch) would be easily met by 34. B—K 3.

34. Q × Kt   ......

And not 34. Kt × Kt, Q × Q ; 35. P × Q, R—B 1 ; 36. R—B 1, B—R 3 etc.—with a probable draw.

34. ......   Q—Kt 4
85. Q—B 3 !   ......

White has still to be careful. Here, for instance, the more "natural" move 35. Q—B 4 would lead to a speedy draw after 35. .... R—Kt 1.

85. ......   R—Kt 1
36. R—Kt 1   Q—R 3
37. R—Q 1   ......

This attempt to repeat moves, due to a slight shortage of time, leads to extremely interesting complications. After the simple 37. P—Q Kt 4 White would not have much trouble in taking advantage from the possession of a passed Pawn. A plausible variation would be, for instance, 37. ....Q—B 5 ; 38. Kt—K 7 ch, K—B 1 ; 39. Kt—B 6, R—Kt 3 ; 40. P—Kt 5 !, R × P; 41. Q—R 3 ch and wins.

37. ......   Q—R 6
38. R—Kt 1   Q—R 7
39. Q—Q 3   B—Q 5

This counter-attack only compromises Black's King's position. But it is difficult to suggest a satisfactory line of play, for White is threatening simply to advance his passed Pawn.

40. R—K B 1   Q—Kt 7

The alternative 40. ....Q—R 2 would also be unsatisfactory because of 41. P—Q Kt 4, etc.

41. Kt—K 7 ch ! ......

This sealed move initiates the final attack which, after a dozen moves, leads practically by force to the win of the Queen for two pieces.

41. ......   K—B 1

The only move. Hopeless would be 41. ....K—Kt 2 ; 42. Kt—B 5 ch !, P × Kt ; 43. Q—Kt 3 ch and Q × R—or 41. ....K—R 1 ; 42. Kt—B 6, B × P ch ; 43. R × B, Q—B 8 ch ; 44. K—R 2, Q × Kt ; 45. R × P, etc.

42. Kt—B 6   B × P ch
43. K—R 2 !   ......

The idea of this Pawn sacrifice (instead of 43. R × B, Q—B 8 ch ; 44. Q—B 1, Q × Kt ; 45. R × P ch, K—Kt 1 ; 46. R—B 3 with very problematical winning chances) will become apparent only after the 48th move. The ensuing Knight manœuvre is very spectacular.

43. ......   R—K 1

If 43. ....R—Kt 2, then 44. Q—K B 3, B—Kt 3 (or B—B 4 ; 45. Q—Q 5) ; 45. Kt—Q 8 ! winning at least the exchange.

44. Q—K B 3   R—K 7

Again the only move, as is also the following. But had the White King gone to R 1 on the 43rd move, then 44. ....R—K 8 would have saved Black.

45. Kt—Q 4 !   R—Q 7
46. Kt—K 6 ch   K—K 2
47. Kt—B 4   ......

Threatening 48. Kt—Q 3.

47. ......   Q—Q 5

Or 47. .... Q—B 7 ; 48. R—Q R 1 and the exposed King would succumb to the combined attack of the three White pieces.

Position after Black's 47th move.

48. K—R 1 !   ......

Only this "quiet" move, which had to be calculated a long time before, justifies the attack started by 43. K—R 2. White now threatens 49. Kt—K 2, and if Black tries to prevent this by 48. .... B—R 5 he loses as follows : 49. Q—Kt 7 ch, Q—Q 2 ; 50. Q—Kt 4 ch, K—K 1 ; 51. Kt—K 6 ! (stronger than 51. Kt×P, R P×Kt ; 52. Q×B, R—Q 8 !, etc.), B—K 2 ; 52. Q—Kt 8 ch, B—Q 1 ; 53. Kt×B, Q×Kt ; 54. Q—K 5 ch, Q—K 2 ; 55. Q—R 8 ch, K—Q 2 ; 56. Q×P, R—K B 7 ; 57. R—Q 1 ch, K—B 2 ; 58. Q—R 8 etc.

48. ......   R—R 7

Or 48. .... P—R 4 ; 49. Kt—K 2, R—Q 8, etc., which would not greatly differ from the line of play actually adopted.

49. Kt—K 2   R—R 8
50. Q—Kt 7 ch   ......

Of course not 50. Kt×Q ?, R×R ch followed by .... B—Kt 8 ch winning back the Queen.

50. ......   K—B 3 ?

The game was lost, anyhow, but 50. .... K—B 1 would have prolonged the battle—for instance, 51. Kt×Q, R×R ch ; 52. K—R 2, B—Kt 8 ch ; 53. K—Kt 3, B—B 7 ch ; 54. K—B 3, B×Kt dis. ch ; 55. K—K 4, B—B 3, or 55. K—K 2, R—B 7 ch ; 56. K—K 1, K—Kt 2 ! In this variation White, in order to force resignation, would have been obliged to use his reserve trump—the passed Queen's Knight's Pawn.

51. Kt×Q   R×R ch
52. K—R 2   B—Kt 8 ch
53. K—Kt 3   B—B 7 ch
54. K—B 3   B×Kt dis. ch
55. K—K 4   R—Q 8

Now forced, as White threatened 56. Q—R 6 ch.

56. Q—Q 5 (?)   ......

There was really no need to bother about calculating the (won) Pawn end-game after 56. .... R—K 8 ch ; 57. K×B, R—Q 8 ch ; 58. K—B 5, R×Q ch ; 59. K×R, K—K 2 ; 60. K—B 6, etc., as the simple 56. Q—B 6 ch followed by 57. Q—B 2 won immediately ! This is the only (fortunately negligible) omission I committed in this unusually difficult game.

56. ......   K—K 2
57. P—K Kt 4   P—R 4

Despair.

58. P×P   P—B 4 ch
59. K—B 3   R—Q 6 ch
60. K—K 2   R—K 6 ch
61. K—Q 2   R—K 5
62. P×P   Resigns.

GAME 103

QUEEN'S GAMBIT DECLINED
(SEMI-TARRASCH'S DEFENCE)

Twenty - fourth   Match - Game,
Rotterdam, December, 1937.

Black : DR. M. EUWE

| 1. Kt—K B 3 | P—Q 4 |
| 2. P—Q B 4 | P—K 3 |

For 2. ....P—Q 5 see Game
No. 102.

3. P—Q 4	Kt—K B 3
4. Kt—Q B 3	P—B 4
5. P × Q P	Kt × P
6. P—K Kt 3	......

A harmless deviation from the
usual 6. P—K 4. In both cases
Black has very little trouble in
developing his pieces.

| 6. ...... | P × P |

Also good enough is 6. ....Kt—
Q B 3 ; 7. B—Kt 2, Kt × P ; 8.
Kt × Q Kt, Kt × Kt ; 9. P × Kt, P ×
Kt ; 10. Q × P, Q × Q ; 11. P × Q,
B—Q 3 ; 12. P—Q R 4, K—K 2
with equality, as played in the last
of the exhibition games arranged
after the Match.

7. Kt × Kt	Q × Kt
8. Q × P	Q × Q
9. Kt × Q	B—Kt 5 ch

There is nothing to be said
against this check and the following
exchange.

| 10. B—Q 2 | B × B ch |
| 11. K × B | K—K 2 ? |

But the neglect to develop the
Queen's side pieces will from now
on be the cause of all the trouble.
Indicated was 11. ....B—Q 2 ; 12.
B—Kt 2, Kt—B 3 ; 13. Kt × Kt,
B × Kt ; 14. B × B, P × B ; 15. Q R—
Q B 1, Castles ch ; 16. K—K 3, K—
B 2 with an easily defensible Rook
end-game.

| 12. B—Kt 2 | R—Q 1 |
| 13. K—K 3 | Kt—R 3 |

Practically forced, as his Q B 2
needed protection. But the Knight
at Q R 3 will be not only out of
play but also, as the sequel will
show, dangerously exposed.   The
next part of the game, which ends
with the win of a Pawn for White,
is easy to understand but still
rather instructive.

| 14. Q R—Q B 1 | R—Q Kt 1 |
| 15. P—Q R 3 | ...... |

Useless would be 15. Kt—Kt 5
because of 15. ....B—Q 2 (16.
Kt × P ?, R—Q R 1).

| 15. ...... | B—Q 2 |

Threatening now 16. ....P—K 4
which White prevents by his next
move.

| 16. P—B 4 | P—B 3 |

This move has been criticized, in
my opinion, without much reason,
since in the long run Black would
not be able to avoid material loss
anyhow. If, for instance, 16. ....
B—K 1, then 17. P—Q Kt 4, R—
Q 2 ; 18. Kt—Kt 5, R—R 1 ; 19.
R—B 3 followed by 20. K R—Q B 1
and 21. R—B 8 or 21. Kt—B 7.
As it happens in the actual game
Black, in spite of his Pawn minus,
will still keep some drawing chances.

Position after Black's 16th move.

17. B—K 4 ! ......

A typical "centralization" which the late Nimzowitsch would certainly have enjoyed. White not only attacks the K R P, but threatens in some variations B—Q 3 and (what is still more important) prevents 17. ....P—K 4 because of 18. P×P, P×P ; 19. Kt—B 3, winning a Pawn.

17. ......   B—K 1

Preventing 18. B×R P, as the answer 18. ....P—K Kt 3 with the threats (a) B—B 2 followed by .... R—K R 1, or (b) ....Q R—B 1 followed by ....Kt—B 2, would give Black sufficient resources. But with his next two moves White succeeds in taking advantage of the weakness of Black's K 3.

18. P—Q Kt 4 !   R—Q 2
19. P—B 5 !   Kt—B 2

Comparatively better than 19. ....P—K 4 ; 20. Kt—K 6, or 19. ....P×P ; 20. B×B P, R—Q 4 ; 21. B×P, etc.—in both cases with considerable advantage for White.

20. P×P   Kt×P
21. Kt×Kt   K×Kt
22. B×R P   ......

Thus White has obtained a material plus, but his positional advantage has in the meantime almost vanished, and Black will even succeed in obtaining some pressure on the King's file.

22. ......   P—B 4
23. R—B 5 !   ......

Preparing the exchange of Bishops at Q 5.

23. ......   P—K Kt 3
24. B—Kt 8 ch   K—B 3
25. K R—Q B 1   R—K 2 ch
26. K—B 2   B—B 3
27. B—Q 5   Q R—K 1
28. R—K 1 !   ......

By far the best, as 28. K R—B 2, B—R 5 ; 29. R—Q 2, P—Kt 3 ; 30. R—B 3, R—Q 1, etc., would lead to an unpleasant pin.

28. ......   B×B
29. R×B   P—K Kt 4
30. R—Q 6 ch   K—K 4 ?

After this desperate advance the game speedily becomes hopeless. The natural course was 30. .... K—B 2 ; 31. P—K R 4, P×P ; 32. P×P, R—K R 1 ; 33. R—Q 4 and White would still have some technical difficulties in order to force the win.

31. K R—Q 1   P—Kt 5

Equally hopeless would be 31. ....R—K 3 ; 32. R—Q 7, R (K 1) —K 2 ; 33. P—K R 4, etc.

32. K R—Q 5 ch   K—K 5
33. R—Q 4 ch   K—K 4
34. K—K 3   ......

Also possible was 34. P—K 4, which would lead to the win of a second Pawn, but still permit Black a longer resistance than in the actual game—for instance (34. P— K 4) R—Q B 1 ! ; 35. R (Q 6)—

Q 5 ch, K—K 3 ; 36. P×P ch, K—
B 3, etc. The way selected is
simple enough.

34. ......   R—K 3

Or 34. ....P—B 5 ch ; 35. K—
Q 3 ! still threatening mate.

35. R (Q 4)—Q 5   K—B 3
                ch   dis. ch.
36. K—B 4   K—Kt 3
37. R×R ch   R×R
38. R—K 5   R—R 3

If 38. ....R—K B 3, then 39.
P—K 4, P×P disc. ch ; 40. K×
Kt P, R—B 7 ; 41. P—K R 4,
winning rapidly.

39. R×P   R×P
40. R—Kt 5 !   ......

The immediate 40. K×P would
probably win too—but the text-
manœuvre is more exact.

40. ......   P—Kt 3
41. K×P   ......

If now 41. ....R—K 6, then 42.
R—Kt 5 ch, K—R 3 ; 43. P—Kt 5 !
(the point of the 40th move), R×P ;
44. P—R 4, after which there
would be no fighting chances for
Black.

Resigns.

GAME 104

NIMZOWITSCH DEFENCE

Twenty-fifth and last Match-
Game, The Hague, December, 1937.

White : DR. M. EUWE

1. P—Q 4   Kt—K B 3
2. P—Q B 4   P—K 3
3. Kt—Q B 3   B—Kt 5
4. P—K 3   Castles
5. Kt—K 2   ......

This is one of the less fortunate

inventions of the great openings
artist, Rubinstein. Its weak point
is that the Knight will not have
much future either on K B 4 or on
K Kt 3 and that Black, by making
the simplest moves, will obtain a
slight advantage in development.
Preferable is therefore first 5. B—
Q 3, and if 5. ....P—Q Kt 3 then
6. Kt—K 2 (or even 6. Q—B 3);
or if 5. ....P—Q 4, then 6. Kt—
B 3, etc., with fairly good prospects.

5. ......   P—Q 4
6. P—Q R 3   B—K 2
7. P×P   ......

Since White intended to play
Kt—Kt 3 he would have done
better to delay this exchange. In
fact, after 7. Kt—Kt 3, P—B 4 ;
8. P×B P, B×P ; 9. P—Q Kt 4,
the move 9. ....P—Q 5 would have
been wrong because of 10. Q Kt—
K 4, and if 10. ....B—Kt 3 then
11. P—B 5 etc. Consequently,
Black would have been obliged to
modify his plan of development.

7. ......   P×P
8. Kt—Kt 3   ......

Rubinstein used to play here 8.
Kt—B 4—obviously in order to
prevent Black's next move, after
which the second player experiences
no more difficulty in the opening.

8. ......   P—B 4
9. P×P   ......

Preparing for the mistake at the
next move. As Black's ....P—
B 5 was not to be feared, White's
logical course was 9. B—Q 3, Kt—
B 3 ; 10. P×P, B×P ; 11. Castles,
etc.

9. ......   B×P
10. P—Kt 4 ?   ......

Obviously not foreseeing the
answer, otherwise he would have
played 10. B—Q 3.

10. ......   P—Q 5 !

The point of this interesting move
is that White cannot well answer
it by 11. Kt—R 4 because of 11.
....P×P ! ; 12. Q×Q (Kt or P×
B ?, P×P ch ; 13. K—K 2, B—
Kt 5 ch and wins), P×P ch ; 13.
K—K 2, B—Kt 5 ch ! forcing the
King to move on to the Queen's file
after which the Queen will be taken
with check, thus saving the King's
Bishop.   And as 11. Q Kt—K 4,
Kt × Kt ; 12. Kt × Kt, B—Kt 3, etc.
would also have been advantageous
for Black, White's next move is
comparatively the best.

11. P×B   P×Kt
12. Q—B 2   ......

White is decidedly in too optimistic a mood and underestimates
Black's threats. Otherwise he would
have tried to simplify matters by
12. Q×Q, R×Q ; 13. Kt—K 2, Kt
—K 5 ; 14. P—B 3, Kt×P ; 15.
Kt×P, Kt—B 3 after which, however, Black, owing to his Pawn
majority on the Queen's side and
better development, would still hold
a slight advantage.

12. ......   Q—R 4
13. R—Q Kt 1   ......

Now 13. Kt—K 2 would not be
sufficient because of 13. ....Kt—
Q 4 ; 14. P—K 4, Kt—Kt 5 ! etc.,
winning the exchange.

13. ......   B—Q 2 !

The threat 14. ....B—R 5 is now
difficult to meet. If, for instance,
14. B—B 4, B—R 5 ; 15. B—Kt 3,
then 15. ....B—Kt 4, etc. ; and
if 14. R—Kt 4 (which has been
suggested by many annotators)
then 14. ....Kt—R 3 ! ; 15. B×
Kt, Q×B ; 16. P—K 4, K R—
K 1 and White can neither castle
nor take the ominous B P because
of ....Kt—Q 4. White's decision
to give up the exchange for a Pawn
in order to finish at last the development of his pieces, therefore appears
comparatively the wisest.

14. R—Kt 3   B—R 5
15. Q×P   Q—Q 1 !

The point of the thirteenth move.
In spite of his material advantage,
it will be by no means easy for
Black to force the victory. The next
part of the game is chiefly instructive from the tactical point of view.

16. B—B 4   Kt—R 3 !

Instead of 16. ....B×R ; 17.
Q×B, Kt—R 3 ; 18. Q×P, Kt×
P ; 19. Q—Kt 5 etc., which would
have allowed White to preserve the
two Bishops.

17. B×Kt   P×B

And not 17. ....B×R ; 18. B—
Q 3 ! etc., with comparatively more
counter-chances than in the actual
game.

18. Castles   B×R
19. Q×B   R—Kt 1

The Q Kt-file will soon become a
very important factor. After the
more obvious 19. ....Q—Q 4,
White, by playing 20. Q×Q, Kt×
Q ; 21. P—K 4, etc., would still
have some chances of saving the
end-game.

20. Q—B 2   Q—Q 4
21. P—K 4   Q—Kt 6
22. Q—K 2   ......

Now, on the contrary, the end-
game after 22. Q×Q, R×Q would
be quite hopeless because of the
weakness of White's Q R P.

22. ......   Q—Kt 4 !
23. Q—B 3   ......

Comparatively better than 23.
Q—K 3, Kt—Q 2. If White wants
to avoid the exchange of Queens he
must forget about his Q B P.

23. ......   Q×P
24. Kt—B 5 ?   ......

But here 24. B—B 4, in order to prevent the following pin, offered a slightly better fighting chance. The right answer for Black would be 24. ....Q R—K 1, and if 25. P—K 5 (R—B 1, Q—Q Kt 4 ! ; 26. B—Q 6, R—B 1 etc.) then 25. .... Kt—Q 2 ; 26. Kt—K 4, Q—B 7 ; 27. R—B 1, Q—Kt 7, etc., keeping the material advantage.

24. ......   R—Kt 8
25. Q—B 4   ......

Or 25. Q—K Kt 3, Kt—R 4 ; 26. Q—Kt 5, K—R 1 !, etc., with an easy defence. But now he threatens to win the Queen by playing 26. Q—Kt 5.

25. ......   Kt × P

One might suppose that after the capture of this important Pawn the fight would be very soon over. But White succeeds in finding new attacking moves again and again.

26. P—K R 4   R—K 1

Not convincing enough would be 26. ....Kt × P because of 27. K—R 2 !

27. R—K 1   Q—B 6
28. R—Q 1   ......

Threatening 29. Q × Kt.

Position after White's 28th move.

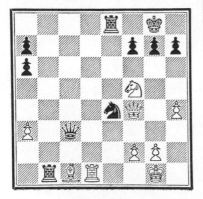

28. ......   Kt—Q 7 !

This spectacular move forces a further, most welcome, simplification, after which there will be practically no more fight left.

29. R × Kt   R × B ch

But not 29. ....Q × B ch ; 30. K—R 2, R—Kt 7 ? because of 31. Q—K 5 ! with a win for White !

30. K—R 2   Q—B 2
31. R—Q 6   R—B 4
32. P—Kt 3 !   ......

A very ingenious idea worthy of a better fate. If Black executes his threat (32. ....R × Kt) he will be obliged after 33. R—K 6 ! ! to give up his Queen for two Rooks (33. ....P × R ; 34. Q × Q, R × P ch ; 35. K—R 3, P—K 4)—after which White would be able to put up a stubborn resistance.

32. ......   R—K B 1 !

But this simple answer puts an end to the last hopes of salvation. What follows is agony.

33. P—Kt 4   ......

Instead 33. Kt × P, K × Kt ; 34. Q—B 6 ch, K—Kt 1 ; 35. R—Q 4, P—K R 4 etc., would not work.

33. ......   P—B 3
34. K—R 3   P—K R 4

The beginning of the counter-attack.

35. Q—Q 2   P × P ch
36. K × P   Q—B 2
37. P—R 5   ......

Position after White's 37th move.

37. ......   R × Kt !

At last the most hated Knight of the match can be eliminated with decisive effect, and Black, in addition to the two extra Pawns, quickly obtains a mating attack. It was an exciting struggle !

38.	K × R	Q × P ch
39.	K—B 4	Q—R 5 ch
40.	K—B 3	......

If 40. K—B 5, then mate in four : 40. ....P—Kt 3 ch ; 41. K—K 6 (41. K × P, Q—R 2 mate), Q—K 5 ch ; 42. K—Q 7, Q—Kt 2 ch ; 43. K—K 6, Q—B 2 mate.

| 40. | ...... | Q—R 6 ch |
| 41. | K—K 4 | ...... |

Or 41. K—B 4, R—K 1 with the deadly threat of 42. ....P—Kt 4 mate.

41.	......	R—K 1 ch
42.	K—Q 5	Q—Kt 6 ch
43.	K—Q 4	Q × P
Resigns		

PART IV (1924-1933)

Simultaneous and Blindfold Play: Exhibition and Consultation Games

GAME 105

QUEEN'S GAMBIT DECLINED (SEMI-TARRASCH DEFENCE)

Played in a simultaneous exhibition in New York, January, 1924.

Black : A. Kussman

1. P—Q 4	P—Q 4
2. Kt—K B 3	Kt—K B 3
3. P—B 4	P—K 3
4. Kt—B 3	P—B 4
5. B P × P	K P)(P ?

Nowadays, "theory" considers—and rightly so for once—5. .... Kt × P as the only correct reply. But when this game was played, even masters did not realise the danger of the text-move ; for instance, Dr. Vidmar played it against me in the London Tournament, 1922.

6. B—Kt 5 !	......

Much more effective here than 6. P—K Kt 3, which in the regular Tarrasch Defence (with the Black Queen's Knight at Q B 3 and the King's Knight undeveloped) would be the most promising line.

6.	B—K 3
7. B × Kt !	Q × B
8. P—K 4 !	P × K P
9. B—Kt 5 ch	B—Q 2

Or 9. ....Kt—Q 2 ; 10. Kt × P, Q—Kt 3 ; 11. B × Kt ch, B × B ; 12. Castles, etc., with advantage.

10. Kt × P	Q—Q Kt 3
11. B × B ch	Kt × B
12. Castles	P × P

Facilitating White's attack. A lesser evil would be to allow the unpleasant P—Q 5.

13. Kt × P	R—Q 1

After White's next move Black's Q 3 will need further protection.

14. Kt—K B 5 !	Kt—K 4
15. Q—K 2	P—Kt 3

Permitting an elegant finish ; but the position was, of course, lost.

Position after Black's 15th move.

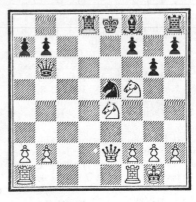

16. Q—Kt 5 ch !	Kt—Q 2

The Queen could not be taken because of 17. Kt—B 6 mate.

17. K R—K 1	......

Threatening mate again.

17.	......	B—Kt 5
18.	Kt—B 6 double ch	K—B 1
19.	Kt × Kt ch	R × Kt
20.	Q—K 5 !	

Threatening this time three different mates. That is too much !

Resigns.

GAME 106

CENTRE GAMBIT

Blindfold Record Exhibition on 26 Boards. New York, May, 1924.

Black : S. FREEMAN

1.	P—K 4	P—K 4
2.	P—Q 4	P × P
3.	P—Q B 3	P—Q 4

Doubtless the best defence, permitting Black to obtain an even game.

| 4. | K P × P | Q × P |

But here 4. ....Kt—K B 3 is even better.

5.	P × P	B—Kt 5 ch
6.	Kt—B 3	Kt—Q B 3
7.	Kt—B 3	Kt—B 3
8.	B—K 2	Castles
9.	Castles	B × Kt

So far Black has made the right moves, but this exchange is wrong as it strengthens White's centre. Correct was 9. ....Q—Q R 4.

| 10. | P × B | P—Q Kt 3 |

This, also, is not good, because the White Pawns will now advance with a win of both time and space. Better was 10. ....B—Kt 5.

| 11. | P—B 4 | Q—Q 1 |

| 12. | P—Q 5 | Kt—K 2 |
| 13. | Kt—Q 4 | ..... |

Preventing an effective development of the Black Bishop on the diagonal K R 3—Q B 8.

| 13. | ...... | B—Kt 2 |
| 14. | B—Kt 2 | ...... |

Simpler was 14. B—B 3 or 14. B—Kt 5. Still, the idea of sacrificing the central Pawn in order to increase the advantage in development was rather tempting.

14.	......	P—B 3
15.	B—K B 3 !	P × P
16.	R—K 1	R—K 1

Instead 16. ....Q—Q 2 ; 17. Kt—Kt 5 ! was certainly not better.

| 17. | Q—Q 2 | R—Kt 1 |
| 18. | Q—Kt 5 | ...... |

Threatening 19. Kt—K 6 !

| 18. | ...... | Kt—Kt 3 |
| 19. | Kt—B 5 | ...... |

After this the attack can hardly be parried. White's next threat is the simple 20. P × P.

| 19. | ...... | R × R ch |
| 20. | R × R | P × P |

If 20. ....P—K R 3 then 21. Q—Kt 3, threatening both 22. B × Kt or 22. Kt—K 7 ch, etc.

| 21. | B × B | R × B |
| 22. | B × Kt | Q × B |

Or 22. ....P × B ; 23. Q—R 6 Q—K B 1 ; 24. R—K 8, followed by mate.

Position after Black's 22nd move.

White announces mate in four moves : 23. R—K 8 ch, Kt—B 1 ; 24. Kt—R 6 ch, Q×Kt ; 25. R×Kt ch, K×R ; 26. Q—Q 8 mate.

GAME 107

ALEKHINE'S DEFENCE

Blindfold Record Exhibition on 28 Boards, Paris, February, 1925.

Black : P. POTEMKIN

1. P—K 4	Kt—K B 3
2. Kt—Q B 3	P—Q 4
3. P×P	Kt×P
4. B—B 4	Kt—Kt 3

White's treatment of the opening was by no means a refutation of the defence adopted by Black. Besides the move in text the second player could also answer simply 4. .... Kt×Kt with excellent prospects ; if in that case 5. Q—B 3, then 5. ....P—K 3 ; 6. Q×Kt, Kt—B 3 ; 7. Kt—B 3, Q—B 3 ! ; 8. Q×Q, P×Q ; 9. P—Q 4, R—K Kt 1, followed by B—Q 2 and Castles, etc.

5. B—Kt 3	P—Q B 4
6. P—Q 3	Kt—B 3
7. Kt—B 3	Kt—R 4

Black over-estimates the value of his pair of Bishops. Indicated was 7. ....P—K 3 followed by B—K 2 and Castles with a fairly good game.

8. Kt—K 5 !	Kt×B

If 8. ....P—K 3 then 9. Q—B 3 with advantage.

9. R P×Kt	Kt—Q 2

Slightly better was 9. ....B—K 3 followed by P—Kt 3, etc.

10. Kt—B 4 !	Kt—Kt 3

Equally unsatisfactory would be 10. ....P—K 3 ; 11. Kt—Kt 5 (threatening 12. B—B 4) or 10. ....P—K 4 ; 11. Q—K 2 ! But by playing 10. ....P—K Kt 3 , 11. Q—K 2 (threatening mate) B—Kt 2 ; 12. B—B 4, P—Q R 3 ; 13. Kt—Q 5, K—B 1 Black would still keep some chances of consolidating his position.

11. B—B 4	Kt—Q 4

Instead 11. ....P—Q R 3 ; 12. Castles, P—K 3 would parry the immediate threats, but the position would still remain compromised. After the move made there will be practically no salvation for Black.

12. Kt×Kt	Q×Kt
13. Castles	......

Threatening now 14. Kt—Kt 6.

13.	P—Q Kt 4
14. Kt—K 3	Q—B 3
15. P—Q 4 !	P—K 3

If instead 15. ....B—Kt 2 then simply 16. R—K 1

16. P—Q 5	P×P
17. Kt×P	......

Also 17. Q×P was extremely effective.

17. ......   B—Q 3
18. R—K 1 ch   ......

And not 18. Kt—B 6 ch, K—K 2 !

18. ......   B—K 3
19. B × B   ......

Simpler than the perhaps even more precise 19. Q—B 3 ! R—Q B 1; 20. R × P, etc.

19. ......   Q × B

Position after Black's 19th move.

20. R—R 6 !   ......

The combination initiated by this move wins more quickly than the prosaic 20. Kt—B 6 ch, K—K 2 ; 21. Q × Q ch, K × Q ; 22. Kt—K 4 ch with a win of a Pawn and a long end game to follow.

20. ......   Q—Q 1

Also after 20. ....Q—Q 2 the answer 21. K R × B ch would have won easily : for instance, 21. .... P × R ; 22. R × P ch, K—Q 1 ; 23. R—K 7, Q—Q 3 ; 24. Q—Q 2, P—Q R 4 ; 25. R × P, P—R 3 ; 26. R—Kt 6 !, Q—Q 2 ; 27. Q—B 4, etc.

21. K R × B ch   P × R
22. R × P ch   K—B 2

23. R—K 7 ch   Q × R

Or 23. ....K—Kt 1 ; 24. Q—Kt 4 winning immediately.

24. Kt × Q   K × Kt
25. Q—K 2 ch   K—B 2
26. Q—R 5 ch   ......

A little finesse : White not only wins a Pawn but also forces the King to remain in the centre.

26. ......   K—B 3
27. Q × B P   K R—Q 1
28. P—K Kt 4 ! ......

Threatening 29. Q—K B 5 ch and thus winning a third Pawn.

Resigns.

GAME 108

KING'S INDIAN DEFENCE

Blindfold exhibition in London January, 1926.

Black : N. SCHWARTZ

1. P—Q 4   Kt—K B 3
2. P—Q B 4   P—K Kt 3
3. P—K Kt 3   B—Kt 2
4. B—Kt 2   Castles
5. Kt—Q B 3   P—Q 3

If instead 5. ....P—B 3 then 6. P—Q 5.

6. Kt—B 3   Kt—B 3
7. P—Q 5   Kt—Q R 4

This Knight's position will become the cause of trouble. But 7. ....Kt—Kt 1 is also not satisfactory, as was shown by my games against Sir G. Thomas in Carlsbad, 1923 (*My Best Games of Chess 1908–23*) and against Réti, New York, 1924 (No. 1 in this collection).

8. Q—Q 3   P—Kt 3

Intending to bring the Knight as quickly as possible to Q B 4. Slightly better still was first 8. ....P—K 4, as the answer 9. P—Q Kt 4 would not be effective because of 9. .... P—K 5, etc.

9.	Kt—Q 4	Kt—Kt 2
10.	Kt—B 6	Q—Q 2
11.	Castles	P—Q R 4
12.	P—Kt 3	......

The routine method of dislodging the Knight from Q B 4.

12.	......	Kt—B 4
13.	Q—B 2	B—Kt 2
14.	P—K R 3 ..	......

Preventing Black's manœuvre Kt —Kt 5—K 4.

14.	......	Q R—K 1

Neither this move nor the next exchange was advisable. He should instead by 14. ....K Kt—K 5 ; 15. B—Kt 2, Kt × Kt, etc., try to facilitate the defence by eliminating some material.

15.	P—R 3	B × Kt
16.	P × B	Q—B 1
17.	P—Q Kt 4	P × P
18.	P × P	Kt—R3

After this the Knight will be buried alive. But also 18. .... QKt—K5 ; 19. Kt—Kt 5 ! was anything but pleasant.

19.	R—R 4 !	Kt—Kt 1

Otherwise White would force this retreat by 20. Q—R 2.

20.	P—Kt 5	P—R 3
21.	R—R 7	P—K 4
22.	K—R 2	......

In order not to have to reckon with the answer ....Kt—R 4 in case of P—B 4.

22.	......	K—R 2
23.	P—B 4	R—K 2
24.	P × P	R × P
25.	B—B 4	R (K 4)—K 1

After 25. R—R4 ; 26. Kt—Q 5, Kt × Kt ; 27. P × Kt, the Rook would be finally trapped.

26.	Kt—Q 5	Kt × Kt
27.	B × Kt	Q—Q 1
28.	P—R 4	Q—K 2
29.	P—K 3	K—R 1
30.	K—Kt 2	......

Preventing 30. ....P—Kt 4 by the eventual threat (after 31. P × P, P × P) R—R 1 ch.

30.	......	P—B 4
31.	R—K 1	K—R 2
32.	P—K 4	B—K 4
33.	P × P	P × P

Position after Black's 33rd move.

34.	P—B 5 !	......

The beginning of a ten-move combination (of which the point is 43. B—K 6 !) forcing the win of a piece.

34.	......	Kt P × P
35.	P—Kt 6	R—B 1
36.	Q—B 3 !	K R—K 1

It is obvious enough that 36..... B × Q ; 37. R × Q ch, etc., would be hopeless.

37. B×B	P×B
38. Q×K P !	......

Without this possibility the previous moves would be aimless.

38.	Q×Q
39. R×Q	R×R
40. R×P ch	R×R
41. P×R	R—K 1
42. P×Kt =Q	R×Q
43. B—K 6 !	......

Decisive.

43.	K—Kt 3
44. P—B 7	R—K B 1
45. P—B 8 =Q	R×Q
46. B×R	P—B 5
47. B—R 6	P—B 6
48. B—Q 3	K—B 3
49. K—B 3	K—K 4
50. K—K 3	P—R 4
51. B—B 2	K—B 3
52. K—B 4	K—Kt 2
53. K×P	K—R 3

Still hoping that the " blind " opponent will stalemate him by 54. K—B 5....

54. K—B 4 !	Black resigns

I consider this game to be one of my best achievements in blindfold chess.

GAME 109

NIMZOWITSCH'S DEFENCE

Second Exhibition Game, Amsterdam, December, 1926.

White : Dr. M. Euwe

1. P—Q 4	Kt—K B 3
2. P—Q B 4	P—K 3
3. Kt—Q B 3	B—Kt 5
4. Kt—B 3	P—Q Kt 3
5. P—K Kt 3	......

In the second exhibition game,

played after our match in 1937, Dr. Euwe played 5. B—Kt 5, but after the right answer (5. ....P—K R 3 and 6. B×Kt, B×Kt ch ; 7. P×B, Q×B, etc.), had to play very exactly in order to avoid being at a disadvantage. But also the fianchetto development in text is perfectly harmless.

5.	B—Kt 2
6. B—Kt 2	Castles
7. Castles	B×Kt
8. P×B	P—Q 3 (?)

After this, White profits by the fact that Black's Queen's Bishop is unprotected, and forces an advantageous transaction in the centre. Had Black made the right move (8. ....Q—B 1), he would have come out of the opening stage with the rather better prospects.

9. P—Q 5 !	P×P

Although this Pawn cannot be kept, it is nevertheless better to start an open middle-game fight than to allow, after 9. ....P—K 4, the formation 10. Kt—R 4, followed by P—K 4, P—K B 4, etc. ±

10. Kt—R 4	Kt—K 5

After 10. ....P—B 3 ; 11. P×P, Kt×P ; 12. P—Q B 4, Kt—Kt 5 ; 13. P—Q R 3, K Kt—R 3 ; 14. B—Kt 2, etc., White would dominate the board.

11. P×P	R—K 1

If 11. ....Kt×Q B P, then 12. Q—Q 3, Kt—R 5 ; 13. B—K 4 !, P—K R 3 ; 14. Q—Q 4, Kt—B 4 ; 15. Kt—B 5, P—K B 3 ; 16. B—Q 2, etc., with a decisive positional advantage.

12. B—Kt 2	......

I don't agree here with Dr. Euwe, who in the Dutch booklet devoted to these games rather severely criticises his 12th and 13th moves. In any case, the Pawn sacrifice suggested by him instead of the text-move is anything but convincing ; then after 12. Q—Q 3, Kt—B 4 ; 13. Q—B 2, P—Q Kt 4 ; 14. P—Q B 4, Black would have an adequate defence by continuing 14. ....P×P ; 15. B—Kt 2, Q Kt—Q 2 ; 16. Kt—B 5, Kt—B 3, etc.

12. ......   P—Q Kt 4

As 12. ....Q—B 3 (or—Kt 4) would be inferior, because of the answer 13. Q—R 4, Black has practically no other way to prevent P—Q B 4.

13. P—Q R 4   ......

A natural and good move. After 13. Q—Q 4, recommended by Dr. Euwe, Black would have the choice between (a) the sacrifice of a Pawn, in order to keep control over White's Q B 4 ; 13. ....P—Q B 4 ; 14. P×P (e.p.), Q Kt×P; 15. Q—Q 3, Kt—K 4 ; 16. Q×Kt P, Q—Kt 3 !; 17. P—Q R 4, B—B 3, etc. (b) the exchange of Queens, which would offer fair defensive possibilities : 13. ....Q—B 3 ; 14. P—B 3, Q×Q ; 15. P×Q, Kt—Q 7 ; 16. R—B 2, Kt—B 5 ; 17. P—K 4, Kt—Q 2, etc.

13. ......   Q—Kt 4 !

Rightly deciding to eliminate White's Pawn at the cost of a further delay in the development of the Queen's side.

14. P×P   Q×Q P
15. Q—R 4 ?   ......

But here White over-estimates his chances. He should, instead, by exchanging Queens, force a favourable end-game which, however, would have been far from

hopeless for Black. For instance, 15. Q×Q, B×Q ; 16. R—R 4 !, Kt—K B 3 ; 17. P—K 3, B×B ; 18. K×B, Q Kt—Q 2 ; 19. K R—R 1, K R—Kt 1 ; 20. P—Q B 4, R—Kt 2 ; 21. B—Q 4, Kt—Kt 3 ; 22. R—Kt 4, K Kt—Q 2 ; 23. Kt—B 5 (at last !), P—Kt 3 ; 24. Kt—K 7 ch, K—B 1 ; 25. Kt—B 6, Kt—B 4, etc., with sufficient defence. And if 15. P—Q B 4 (instead of 15. Q×Q) Black would not have taken the poisoned Pawn, but would simply have answered 15. ....Q×Q, followed by 16. ....P—Q R 3 ! with an easy defence. After the text-move, which contains only a rather obvious trap, White's advantage instantly vanishes.

15. ......   Kt—Q 2

Of course not 15. ....Q—Q 7 ? because of 16. P—Kt 6, B—B 3 ; 17. P—Kt 7 ! and wins.

16. P—Q B 4   Q—Q 7
17. Q—R 2   ......

Under the circumstances comparatively the best.

17. ......   P—Q R 3 !

Forcing a further simplification. Inferior would be 17. ....Q×P, because of 18. Kt—B 5, P—K B 3 ; 19. Kt×Kt P !, etc.

18. B—B 1   ......

Ineffective would be the Pawn's sacrifice 18. P—Kt 6, for instance, 18. ....Kt×Q Kt P ; 19. Kt—B 5, Q—Kt 4 ! ; 20. Kt×Kt P, R—K 2 ; 21. B—K R 3, B—B 1, followed by P—K B 3, etc.∓.

18. ......   Q×Q
19. R×Q   P×P
20. R—Kt 2   ......

Slightly better than 20. R×R, B×R ; 21. P×P, Kt—B 6, etc.

| 20. ...... | Q R—Kt 1 |
| 21. P × P ? | ...... |

After this, Black succeeds in emerging from the complications with a Pawn to the good. After 21. B × Kt, R × B ; 22. P × P, B—Q 4 !, etc., he would have remained only with a positional advantage.

| 21. ...... | Kt—B 6 |
| 22. B—B 6 | ...... |

Now the only way to try to keep the balance of the position.

Position after White's 22nd move.

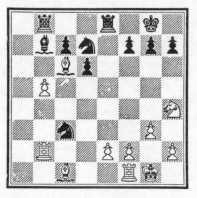

| 22. ...... | R × P ! |

An unpleasant surprise for White, justified by the variation 23. B × Kt, R × R ; 24. B × R, Kt—K 7 mate !

| 23. R—Kt 3 | ...... |

Hardly preferable would be 23. B—Q 2, Kt—R 5 ; 24. R—R 2, Kt (Q 2)—B 4, etc.

23.	B × B
24. R × Kt	B × P
25. R × P	Kt—K 4

Not the most effective way to profit by the material advantage. By 25. ....P—R 3 !, Black could prevent both 26. Kt—B 5 (because of 26. ....R—K 4, etc.) and 26. B—B 4 (because of 26. ....P—K Kt 4)—thus leaving White with practically no efficient answer.

| 26. Kt—B 5 ? | ...... |

The complications introduced by this move decidedly end in Black's favour. Necessary was 26. B—B 4 with the possible continuation 26. ....P—K.R 3 ; 27. B × Kt, R × B ; 28. R—Kt 1, R (Kt 1)—K 1 ; 29. Kt—B 3, R—Q 4, after which Black should win—but only after a long end-game.

| 26. ...... | Kt—B 6 ch |
| 27. K—Kt 2 | ...... |

Or 27. K—R 1, R—K 4, etc.

| 27. ...... | Kt—K 8 ch ! |
| 28. K—R 3 | R—K 4 |

This would also have been the answer to 28. K—Kt 1.

| 29. R—R 1 | ...... |

He could resist longer—but without any real hope—by giving up the exchange immediately : 29. R × Kt, R × R ; 30. Kt × Q P, etc.

29.	Kt—Q 6
30. Kt—K 7 ch	K—B 1
31. B—R 3	......

The last convulsions !

31.	Kt × P ch
32. K—Kt 2	Kt × R
33. B × P	R—K 3
34. B—B 5	......

Or 34. Kt—B 6 disc. ch, R × B 35. Kt × R, R—Q 8, etc. ∓.

34.	R—K 1 !
35. Kt—B 5 disc. ch.	K—Kt 1
36. Kt—K 7 ch	......

If 36. Kt—Q 6, then 36. ....B—
Q 6 ! ; 37. K×Kt, R—K 8 ch ; 38.
K—Kt 2, R (K 1)—K 7 ch ; 39. K—
R 3, P—R 3 ; 40. R×P, R—
Q B 7 ; 41. B—B 2, R—K 3 and
wins.

36.	K—R 1
37. K×Kt	B—Q 6
38. K—Kt 2	P—R 3
39. K—B 3	K—R 2
40. P—R 4	P—R 4

Resigns.

GAME 110

KING'S INDIAN DEFENCE

Third Exhibition Game, played
in Amsterdam, December, 1926.

Black : DR. M. EUWE

1. P—Q 4	Kt—K B 3
2. P—Q B 4	P—K Kt 3
3. Kt—Q B 3	B—Kt 2

At the period when this game was
played the Gruenfeld variation was
somewhat out of fashion. Nowadays
thanks to Botvinnik, Flohr, Keres
and other masters of the younger
generation it is played more often,
although without any remarkable
success.

| 4. P—K 4 | Castles |
| 5. B—K 3 | ...... |

If 5. P—B 4, P—Q 3 ; 6. Kt—
B 3—then 6. ....P—B 4 ! with a
good game for Black.

5.	P—Q 3
6. P—B 3	P—K 4
7. P—Q 5	......

Better is 7. K Kt—K 2, and only
after 7. ....Kt—B 3 (or 7. ....
B—K 3) ; 8. P—Q 5 winning tempi.
Black would in that case have
to face unpleasant development
problems.

7.	P—B 3
8. Q—Q 2	P×P
9. B P×P	Kt—K 1

Preparing the counter attack
....P—K B 4 and preventing at
the same time White's attempt to
open the K R's file (10. P—K R 4,
P—K B 4 ; 11. P—R 5, P—B 5
followed by ....P—K Kt 4, etc.).

| 10. Castles | P—B 4 |
| 11. K—Kt 1 | ...... |

It is obvious enough that the
King must be removed as soon as
possible from the open file.

| 11. ...... | Kt—Q 2 (?) |

Giving White the welcome opportunity to create—without taking
many chances—interesting complications by temporarily sacrificing
some material. By continuing 11.
....P—Q R 3 ; 12. B—Q 3, P—
Q Kt 4 ; 13. K Kt—K 2, P—B 5 ;
14. B—K B 2, Kt—Q 2 followed
by ....Kt—Kt 3 Black would have
obtained a perfectly satisfactory
position.

| 12. Kt—R 3 ! | ...... |

In order to answer both 12.
....Q Kt—B 3 or 12. ....Kt—Kt 3
by 13. Kt—K Kt 5; for instance 12.
... Kt—Kt 3 ; 13. Kt—K Kt 5, P
—B 5 ; 14. B×Kt, Q×Kt; 15. B
—B 2, B—Q 2 ; 16. R—B 1,
Kt—B 2 ; 17. P—K Kt 4 ! or 16.
....P—Q R 3 ; 17. B—Kt 6 etc.,
with excellent prospects on account
of the open Q B's file.

| 12. ...... | P—Q R 3 |

Also if Black had prevented the
following manœuvre by 12. ....
P—B 5, White's prospects would
have remained decidedly the more
favourable.

| 13. P×P | P×P |

14. P—K Kt 4 !   ......

The point of his 12th move, by
which he obtains the most important square K 4 for his pieces.

14.   ......   P×P

Comparatively better than 14.
....P—B 5; 15. B—B 2, etc.,
without any counter-chances for
Black.

15. Kt—K Kt 5   Q Kt—B 3
16. B—Q 3   Q—K 2

In case of 16. ....P×P I should
have continued the attack by 17.
Q R—K B 1 ! and if 17....P—R 3
then 18. Kt—K 6, B×Kt ; 19. P×
B, Kt—Kt 5 ; 20. Kt—Q 5 with
enough threats to frighten an
elephant to death.

17. P—K B 4   ......

Both 17. Q R—K B 1 and 17. K R
—Kt 1 were also considered. But
the prospects connected with the
move selected (the eventual opening
of the K B file or P—B 5 followed by Kt—K 6) were extremely
tempting.

17.   ......   P—K 5

By this counter sacrifice Dr. Euwe
secures the diagonal K R 1—Q R 8
for his Bishop, and at the same
time diminishes the danger threatening his King by forcing the exchange of a couple of minor pieces.
Still, even so, White's chances after
recapturing the sacrificed Pawn
remain the better ones.

18. Kt (Kt 5)×K P   ......

But this is not the most energetic
method. The Pawn should have
been taken by the other Knight,
and if in that case 18. ....Kt×Kt ;
19. B×Kt, P—R 3, then 20.
Kt—K 6± ; or 18. ....P—R 3 ;

19. Kt—K 6, B×Kt ; 20. P×B,
Q×P ; 21. Kt—Kt 3 threatening
22. P—B 5, etc. Black would
hardly have found a way to
protect his numerous weaknesses
sufficiently.

18.   ......   Kt×Kt
19. Kt×Kt   ......

Now forced as 19. B×Kt ? does
not go because of 19. ....B×Kt.

19.   ......   B—B 4
20. Kt—Kt3   ......

Blockading the K Kt's Pawn in
order to play P—K R 3 at the first
opportunity. After 20. Kt—Kt 5,
Black would protect his K 3 by
means of ....Kt—B 2.

20.   ......   B×B ch
21. Q×B   Q—B 3

A refined tactical manœuvre,
very much in Dr. Euwe's style ; he
provokes White's R—Q 2 in order
to deprive (after P—K R 3, P×P,
R×P) the first rank of its natural
protection. But by correct replies
all this refinement would prove
useless.

22. R—Q 2   Q—B 2

Because of the threat 23. Kt—
R 5.

23. P—K R 3   P×P
24. R×P   Q—Kt 3
25. P—B 5 (?)   ......

Only after this second inaccuracy
does Black suddenly get a kind of
counter-attack. Very strong here
was 25. Kt—K 4 ! and in case of
25. ....Kt—B 3 simply 26. Kt×
P, Q R—Q 1 ; 27. B—B 5 etc.; and
other replies would allow White to
strengthen his position further by
means of R—Kt 3 or R (Q 2)—
R 2, etc.

25.   ......   Q—Kt 5

26. Q R—R 2   R—B 1 !

In case of 26. .:...Kt—B 3 (which seemingly protects everything) White would play 27. B—B 1! with the strong threat 28. R—R 4. The occupation of the Q B's file gives Black some new opportunities.

Position after Black's 26th move.

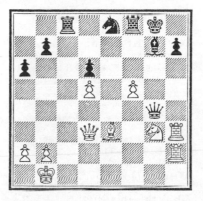

27.   P—B 6 !   ......

The main idea of this transaction is shown by the following variation : 27. .... Kt×P; 28. Kt—B 5, Q—Q B 5 !; 29. Kt—K 7 ch, K—B 2 ; 30. Q—B 5 !, K×Kt ; 31. Q—K 6 ch, K—Q 1 ; 32. B—Kt 6 ch, R—B 2 ; 33. R—Q B 3, Q—B 8 ch ; 34. K—B 2 and wins.

27.   ......   R×P !
28. Q×P ch   K—B 1
29. R—R 1   ......

This rather sad necessity is the direct consequence of Black's fine 21st move. But in spite of this partial success the position of the second player is still full of danger. If, for instance, 29. ....Q—Kt 5, then simply 30. P—R 3 and 30. ....R—K B 8 ch ? would be refuted by 31. R×R ch. And 29. ....R—K B 6 is also not satisfactory because of 30. B—R 6 ! (R×Kt ? ; 31. R× R, Q×R ; 32. Q—B 5 ch, etc.).

Consequently, Black decides to simplify matters.

29.   ......   Q—Kt 3 ch

It would have been slightly better to delay this exchange by playing first 29. ....R—Q B 2, in which case White, by continuing 30. Kt—R 5 !, Q—B 4 ch ; 31. Q× Q, R×Q ; 32. Kt—B 4, etc., would maintain a strong pressure.   After the text move he has a direct win.

30. Q×Q   R×Q
31. Kt—B 5 !   ......

Simply threatening 32. Kt×B, etc. If now 31. ....R—Q B 2 then 32. B—Q 4 !, B×B ; 33. Kt×B and Black is without resource.

31.   ......   B—K 4
32. R—B 3 !   Kt—B 3

Or 32. ....R—K B 3 ; 33. B—Kt 5, R—K B 2 ; 34. B—K 7 ch !, R×B ; 35. Kt×P dis. ch and wins.

33. R—R 8 ch   R—Kt 1
34. R×R ch   K×R
35. Kt—K 7 ch   Resigns.

GAME 111

QUEEN'S INDIAN DEFENCE

Exhibition Game, New York, June, 1929.

White : F. J. MARSHALL

1. P—Q 4   Kt—K B 3
2. P—Q B 4   P—K 3
3. Kt—K B 3   B—Kt 5 ch
4. B—Q 2   Q—K 2
5. P—K 3   ......

White can here obtain control on K 4 by playing 5. Q—B 2, but in that case Black would select another system : 5. ....B×B ch ; 6. Q Kt×

B, P—Q 3 followed by ....P—K 4,
etc.

5.	......	P—Q Kt 3
6.	B—Q 3	B—Kt 2
7.	Q—B 2	B×B ch

In order to advance a Pawn to
the centre and thus indirectly prevent White's P—K 4.

8. Q Kt×B	P—B 4

If now 9. P—K 4, then 9. ....
Kt—B 3∓.

9.	Castles (K R)	Kt—B 3
10.	P—Q R 3	Castles (K R)
11.	Q R—Q 1	P—Kt 3

Preventing P—Q 5, which, especially after White's last Rook move,
could eventually be disagreeable.

12. K R—K 1	......

A refined preparation to Kt—K 4,
which at this moment would not be
satisfactory because of 12. ....Kt
×Kt; 13. B×Kt, P—Q 4 !; 14.
P×Q P, K P×P; 15. B×Q P, Kt
×P, etc.∓

12.	......	Q R—B 1
13.	Kt—K 4	K R—Q 1

Technically simpler was 13. ....
K R—K 1, since after 14. P—Q 5,
P×P White himself would have
been obliged to change Knights.
But the move selected is at least
good enough to maintain the balance of position.

14. P—Q 5	......

Very bold—and quite in Marshall's style : he cedes Black the
Pawn majority on the Q side
without getting real compensation
elsewhere, since his pieces are not
sufficiently co-ordinated to support
an effective action in the centre.
One must admit, however, that

White's position, *owing to the elas-
ticity of Black's pawn-structure (compare the game with Miss Menchik, No.
50)*, was already slightly inferior.
Black threatened—after some further preparation, such as ....P—
Q 3—to start an action on the Q B-
file by means of ....P×P followed
by ....Kt—Q R 4.

14.	......	P×P
15.	P×P !	Kt×Kt

15. ....Kt×P would have sad
consequences, e.g., 16. B—B 4,
K Kt—Kt 5 ; 17. Q—B 3 !, Q×Kt ;
18. B×P ch, K—B 1 ; 19. P×Kt,
etc.±

16. B×Kt	Kt—R 4

Of course not ....Kt—K 4 because of 17. P—Q 6, etc.

17. Kt—Q 2	......

Black threatened 17.....P—B 4.

17.	......	P—B 5 !

Profiting by the fact that P—Q 6
is still not good. It becomes obvious that the transaction initiated
by White's 14th move was rather
favourable to his opponent.

18. B—B 3	Q—K 4

Threatening 19. ....P—B 6, etc.

19. Kt—K 4	P—Q 3

Black could also prevent the
following Rook move by playing 19.
....Kt—Kt 6 after which White
would have hardly anything better
than 20. Q—B 3 ; but he did not
think this was necessary since,
owing to his advantage in space,
the middle-game complications
should normally end to his advantage.

20. R—Q 4	......

It would not be like Marshall to exchange Queens by 20. Q—B 3 in order to obtain a distinctly inferior end-game. Looking at this Rook one cannot believe that, in the prime of its existence, it intends to commit suicide soon — and yet it is so !

20. ......   P—Q Kt 4

Now threatening 21. ....Kt—Kt 6.

21. Kt—Q 2   B—R 3

In order to leave a square for the Knight in case of Q—B 3.

22. R—K 4   Q—Kt 2
23. R—K 7   ......

The road to death.

23. ......   Kt—Kt 2 !
24. Kt—K 4   ......

Probably a difficult decision—but under the circumstances the wisest course, for the alternative 24. B—Kt 4, R—R 4 ! (not .... P—B 6 ; 25. B×R, P×Kt ; 26. R—Q 1±) ; 25. P—K 4, Q—B 3 ; 26. R—Q 7, R×R ; 27. B×R, Q—K 2 (threatening also R×P) ; 28. B—B 6, Kt—R 4, etc., would lead to material losses without any hope of a counter-attack.

24. ......   K—B 1 !

A mistake would be 24. ....Q—B 1 ; 25. Kt—B 6 ch, K—Kt 2 because of 26. Q—B 3, etc.—to White's advantage.

25. R×Kt   B×R
26. R—Q 1   ......

Although Black is now a clear exchange ahead and his Queen's side majority is as threatening as ever, the winning problem is by no means as easy or as rapid to solve

as one would imagine. White is in a position—in case of 26. ....Q—K 4, for instance—to build a good defensive position with possibilities of a Pawn counter-attack on the King's side by means of 27. Kt—B 3, P—Q R 3 ; 28. R—Q 4, etc. Still, by that line Black with further circumspection and patience would most likely have increased his advantage in a decisive way, without having to suffer from the melodramatic complications arising from his next risky move.

26. ......   P—Q R 4 ?

Preventing 27. Kt—B 3 (because of 27. ....P—Kt 5) and looking for a quick victory. From now on, Marshall takes advantage of the hidden possibilities of his position in a really remarkable fashion, reminding one of his most glorious performances.

27. B—Kt 4 !   R—B 2

Of course not 27. ....P—B 4 because of 28. Kt—Kt 5, but also not, for instance, 27. ....R—R 1, because of 28. P—Q R 4 ! etc.

28. Q—Q 2 !   ......

After this the situation begins to look even dangerous for Black, since the Q R P cannot be defended in a direct way.

28. ......   P—R 3 !

This is the temporary salvation, for by preventing Kt—Kt 5 Black threatens 29. ....P—B 4.

29. B—B 3   Q R—B 1

And after this 30. Q×P can be simply answered by 30. ....Q×P.

30. P—K R 4 !   ......

A new attacking idea, which Black tries to meet in an equally energetic way.

30. ......   Q—K 4

If instead, 30. ....P—B 4, then 31. Kt—B 3, P—Kt 5 ; 32. P × P, P × P ; 33. Kt—K 2, P—B 6 ; 34. P × P, P × P ; 35. Q—B 2 followed by the promising Knight's manœuvre Q 4 (or B 4)—K 6.

31. P—R 5 !   P × P

Also after 31. ....P—Kt 4 ; 32. P—K Kt 4 followed by Kt—Kt 3—B 5 or B—Kt 2 and P—B 4, Black's defence would remain difficult.

32. Kt—Kt 3   P—B 6
33. P × P   Q × B P

If 33. ....R × P, the answer would be 34. P—K 4 !

34. Q—K 2   P—Kt 5
35. P × P   P × P

At last Black has succeeded in obtaining the "winning" passed Pawn, but in the meantime the white forces have been concentrating against the hostile King, which can be defended only by the Queen, the other black pieces being, for the time, simply onlookers.

36. B—K 4 !   ......

Covering the diagonal Kt 1—R 7 and opening prospects to the Queen. In this second half of the game Marshall finds always the best moves, and it is a bit of hard luck that Black's resources prove in the end sufficient to meet his furious assault.

36. ......   Q—K 4 !

Hereafter begins a very difficult Queen's manœuvre whose object is to provoke white Pawn moves so as to enable at least one Rook to participate in a counter-attack.

37. P—B 4   Q—B 3

Otherwise White plays 38. Q × P with *tempo*.

38. Kt × P   Q—R 5 !

And not 38. ....Q—K 2 ; 39. Q—Kt 2 !, Q × B ; 40. Q—R 8 ch, K—K 2 ; 41. Q—B 6 ch, K—K 1 ; 42. Q—R 8 ch, K—Q 2 ; 43. Kt—B 6 ch, followed by 44. Q × R ch and Kt × Q.

39. P—Kt 3   ......

The weakening of the second rank will finally prove fatal—but if 39. B—B 3, the answer 39. ....Q—K 2 would now offer sufficient defence, since 40. Q—Kt 2 is met by 40. ....Q × P ch.

39. ......   Q—R 6 !

Possible and good because 40. B—Kt 2 can be met by 40. .... B—R 3 !

40. B—B 3 !   ......

Position after White's 40th move.

40. ......   R—B 6 !

An unexpected defence against White's two main threats—41. B—Kt 4 and 41. Q—Q Kt 2—and one that involves, in the first case, an eventual sacrifice of two exchanges : to 41. B—Kt 4 Black would reply 41. ....R×P ! ; 42. Q×R, Q×B ; 43. R—K 1, Q×Kt ! ; 44. Q—K 7 ch, K—Kt 2 ; 45. Q×R (or 45. Q×B, Q—B 6 with a winning position) Q×P and wins. With his next move the then American Champion plays out a new trump, which, however, will this time prove the last.

41. Q—Q 2 !   ......

How now to meet the threat 42. Q—Q 4 without losing the passed Pawn ? My lucky star—or Marshall's unlucky one—helped me to find the right answer—but it took no less than half an hour.

41. ......   R—K 1 !

The value of this sealed rejoinder is well illustrated by comparing its consequences with the possible results of another plausible move. 41. ....B—R 8 ; 42. Q—Q 4, R—B 7 ! ; 43. Q—R 8 ch, K—K 2 ; 44. Q—B 6 ch, K—Q 2 ; (....K—K 1 ; 45. Kt—Kt 7 ch, etc.) 45. Q×B P ch, K—B 1 ; 46. Q—K 6 *ch*, Q×Q ; 47. P×Q, P—Kt 6 ; 48. B—K 4 and, to say the least, White would not lose.

42. Q—Q 4   ......

Instead 42. Q—Q Kt 2 would not help either, because of 42.....B—R 3, etc.

42. ......   R—B 7
43. R—Q 2   ......

Simplification is nearly always sad for the materially weaker party, but there was no choice, as is shown by the variation 43. Q—R 8 ch, K—K 2 ; 44. Q—B 6 ch, K—Q 2 ; 45. B—Kt 4 ch !, Q×B ; 46. Q×B P ch, K—Q 1 ; 47. Q×R

ch, K×Q ; 48. Kt—B 6 ch, K—K 2 ; 49. Kt×Q, P—Kt 6 and wins.

43. ......   R×R
44. Q×R   B—R 3 !
45. Q—K 1   ......

Practically resignation. Almost an hour's reflection persuaded Marshall that the intended 45. Q×P leads to a forced loss as follows : 45. .... Q—B 8 ch ; 46. K—R 2, Q—B 7 ch ! (but not 46. ....Q×B ; 47. Q×P ch, K—Kt 1 ; 48. Kt—B 6 ch, K—R 1 ; 49. Q×B ! and Black would not win) ; 47. K—R 3 (or B—Kt 2, B—B 8 ; 48. Q×P ch, K—Kt 1 ; 49. Kt—B 6 ch, K—R 1 and wins), B—B 1 ch ; 48. B—Kt 4, B×B ch ; 49. K×B, Q—K 7 ch ; 50. K—R 4, Q—R 7 ch ; 51. K—Kt 4, P—B 4 ch ! and wins.

45. ......   P—Kt 6

The passed Pawn's holiday !

46. B—Q 1   P—Kt 7
47. Q—Kt 4   ......

Leads to a similar final to the one indicated.

47. ......   Q—B 8 ch
48. K—R 2   Q—B 7 ch
49. K—R 3   B—B 1 ch
50. P—B 5   B×P ch
51. B—Kt 4   B×B ch
52. K×B   Q—K 7 ch
53. K—R 4   Q—R 7 ch
54. K—Kt 4   P—B 4 ch
Resigns.

In this kind of game the loser certainly deserves as much credit as the winner.

GAME 112

RETI'S OPENING

Simultaneous Exhibition of Consultation Games, New York, March, 1929.

White :
A. KEVITZ and A. PINKUS*

1. Kt—K B 3	Kt—K B 3
2. P—B 4	P—Q Kt 3

One of the different ways of meeting adequately White's opening play. Black intends herewith to transform the game into a typical Queen's Indian Defence.

3. P—K Kt 3	B—Kt 2
4. B—Kt 2	......

Allowing Black to choose a more aggressive form of development. Instead, 4. P—Q 4, P—K 3 : 5. B—Kt 2, etc., would lead to well-known variations.

4. ......   P—K 4

This move has its advantages and defects, for the centre-pawn may become exposed. Still, the experiment was worth trying since not much risk is attached to it.

5. Kt—B 3	B—Kt 5
6. Castles	......

Decidedly too optimistic, for the doubled Pawn on the Q B-file is much more often a serious fault in the position than is generally believed and in this particular case will by no means be compensated by the pair of Bishops. Natural and good enough was 6. Q—Kt 3.

6.	B×Kt !
7. Kt P×B	......

Even less satisfactory was 7. Q P×B, P—Q 3, etc.

7. ......   P—Q 3

The black pawn-skeleton being on dark-coloured squares, there was obviously no need for Black to keep the King's Bishop.

8. P—Q 4   P—K 5

Correctly calculating that the K B-file that White will be able to open now will not compensate for a new weakness thus created on the K-file.

9. Kt—R 4	Castles
10. P—B 3	P×P

Black is already in the pleasant position of being able to proceed in the simplest manner. White's trouble now is that he cannot well retake with the Pawn because of 11. ....B—R 3 ! ; 12. P—B 4, P—B 3 followed by ....P—Q 4 with some material win. And after his next move the King's Pawn remains extremely feeble.

11. B×P	Kt—K 5
12. Q—Q 3	R—K 1
13. P—Q 5	......

The counter-attack now starting will be very short-lived. But if White had decided to restrict the action of the black Bishop on the long diagonal, he had to do it now, since, after ....Kt—Q 2, Black obviously would not be obliged to cede square K 5.

13.	Kt—B 4
14. Q—Q 4	Q Kt—Q 2
15. B—R 5	......

White hopes to provoke by one of the following moves the answer ....P—K Kt 3 which would eventually procure him some real chances on the K B-file ; but Black

---

*On the same occasion the following short game was played, which shows in a drastic way the effects of exaggerated voracity in Chess : *Black :* I. Kashdan and H. Steiner. 1. P—Q 4, P—Q 4 ; 2. P—Q B 4, P—K 3 ; 3. Kt—Q B 3, P—Q B 3 ; 4. Kt—B 3, P×P ; 5. P—Q R 4, B—Kt 5 ; 6. P—K 3, P—Q Kt 4 ; 7. B—Q 2, Q—Kt 3 ; 8. Kt—K 5, Kt—Q 2 ; 9. P×P, Kt×Kt ; 10. P×Kt, P×P ; 11. Kt—K 4, B—K 2 ; 12. Q—Kt 4, K—B 1 ; 13. Q—B 4, P—Q R 4 ; 14. B—K 2, B—Kt 2 ; 15. Castles K R, P—R 4 ; 16. Kt—K 5, B×Kt ; 17. Q×B, R—K R 3 ; 18. P—K 4 !, P—K R 5 ; 19. R×P !, P—B 3 ; 20. P×P, Kt×P ; 21. Q×Kt P !. Resigns.

resists all temptations and quietly prepares a complete blockade.

| 15. ...... | Kt—K 4 |
| 16. B—B 4 | Q—Q 2 ! |

If instead 16. ....P—Kt 3, then 17. B—B 3, P—K Kt 4 ; 18. B × Kt, P × B ; 19. Q—Kt 4, P—K R 4 ; 20. Q × P, P × Kt ; 21. B—K 4 !, Kt × B ; 22. Q × P ch, K—R 1 ; 23. Q—R 5 ch, K—Kt 1 ; 24. R—B 7 and White wins !

17. Kt—B 3	Kt—Kt 3
18. Kt—Q 2	Q—R 6 !
19. B × Kt	......

The attempt to catch the aggressive Queen—19. B—R 6, P × B ; 20. B—Kt 4—would fail lamentably because of the simple 19. ....R—K 4 !

| 19. ...... | R P × B |
| 20. P—K 4 | ...... |

The Pawn is weaker here—if possible—than on K 2, but White had already a difficult choice.

| 20. ...... | P—K B 3 |

Fixing for ever the K P and—by bringing the last Pawns on dark squares—increasing the potential range of his Bishop.

21. Q R—K 1	P—K Kt 4
22. B—K 3	R—K 2
23. K—R 1	Q R—K 1
24. B—Kt 1	B—B 1

Of course, premature would be 24. ....Kt × P ; 25. Kt × Kt, R × Kt ; 26. R × R, R × R ; 27. Q × R, Q × R ; 28. Q—K 8 ch, etc., with perpetual check. Besides, Black does not need to hurry with the liquidation at K 5 at all—*since the position must bring much more than a Pawn in the course of time.*

| 25. R—B 3 | B—Kt 5 |

| 26. K R—K 3 | ...... |

White has now weaknesses everywhere : (a) On the Queen's side—the doubled Pawn ; (b) in the middle—the backward King's Pawn ; (c) on the King's side—the weak light-coloured squares. As a direct consequence of this sad situation almost all White's pieces are stalemated and he has practically nothing better than to move his Bishop to and fro. No wonder that Black, instead of adopting the most evident plan—an attack with *five* pieces against the King's Pawn by means of ....Q—R 2 followed by .... B—R 4—Kt 3, which would finally force an end-game with an extra Pawn—prefers to prepare a decisive Pawn advance in the centre. The preliminary manœuvre takes, true enough, fifteen more moves, but the success of the scheme gives the game an artistic touch it would otherwise lack.

| 26. ...... | Q—R 4 |

Before undertaking the long King's voyage, Black reverses the places of his Queen and Bishop in order to "observe" the central weak spot with one more piece.

27. K—Kt 2	B—R 6 ch
28. K—R 1	Q—Kt 5
29. D—B 2	P—R 4
30. B—Kt 1	P—R 5

It may be of use to prevent eventually Kt—Kt 3.

31. B—B 2	R—K 4
32. B—Kt 1	R (K 1)—K 2
33. B—B 2	K—B 2

Now it is time to bring the King to his safest spot on the board—Q R 3 !

34. B—Kt 1	K—K 1
35. B—B 2	K—Q 1
36. B—Kt 1	K—B 1

37. B—B 2	K—Kt 2
38. B—Kt 1	K—R 3
39. B—B 2	Q—R 4

The final preparations : the decisive combination demands the previous configuration of Queen and Bishop !

40. B—Kt 1	B—Kt 5
41. K—Kt 2	Q—R 6 ch
42. K—R 1	P—Kt 3

At last disclosing the winning idea.

43. B—B 2   ......

Position after White's 43rd move.

43. ......   P—B 4 !

The battle must be decided not by the win of a Pawn, but by direct threats against the King. If, after 44. P × P, P × P ; again 45. B—Kt 1, then 45. ....Kt—K 5 ; 46. Kt × Kt, R × Kt inevitably followed by B—B 6 ch and wins.

44. P × P	P × P
45. R × R	P × R
46. Q—K 3	......

The main variation calculated by Black was 46. R × P, R × R ; 47. Q × R, B—B 6 ch ! ; 48. Kt × B, Q—B 8 ch ; 49. Kt—Kt 1, Kt—

Q 6 ! and wins. This possibility clearly proves the usefulness of the King's trip as far as Q R 3.

| 46. ...... | P—K 5 |
| 47. P—Q 6 ! | ...... |

Not merely in order to make a move, but with a very definite purpose.

| 47. ...... | P × P |
| 48. B—Kt 1 | ...... |

Which is seen in the following case : 48. ....B—B 6 ch ; 49. Kt × B, P × Kt ; 50. Q × B P !, R × R ; 51. Q—R 8 mate ! But Black has at his disposal a powerful intermediate move.

48. ......   P—B 5 !

If now 49. P × P, then ....B—B 6 ch, etc., wins immediately.

Resigns.

GAME 113

QUEEN'S INDIAN DEFENCE

Consultation Game, Nice, May, 1931.

White: Dr. ALEKHINE and Amateur

Black: G. STOLTZ and Amateur

1. P—Q 4	Kt—K B 3
2. P—Q B 4	P—K 3
3. Kt—K B 3	P—Q Kt 3
4. P—K Kt 3	B—Kt 2
5. B—Kt 2	B—K 2
6. Castles	Castles
7. P—Kt 3	......

Leading to more complicated— or at least less explored—positions than the usual 7. Kt—B 3, which, however, is also rather in White's favour, for instance : 7. ....Kt— K 5 ; 8. Q—B 2, Kt × Kt ; 9. Q × Kt,

P—Q B 4 ; 10. B—K 3, and in the case of further exchanges Black should always remain with some weak spots in the centre.

7. ......   Q—B 1

Against Dr. Euwe (23rd Match-game, 1937), I played here 7. .... P—Q 4 ; 8. Kt—K 5, P—B 4—and obtained a fighting game full of possibilities for both sides. Black's idea of exchanging only one Pawn in the centre gives White time to take advantage of the open Q B file without allowing any counter-play.

8. Kt—B 3   P—Q 4
9. P×P !   ......

At the right moment, since if 9. ....P×P the Q B can be developed with profit at K B 4.

9. ......   Kt×P
10. B—Kt 2   P—Q B 4

Positionally unavoidable — but from now on the Black Queen will "feel" (as the modern annotators say) uncomfortable *vis-a-vis* the White Rook.

11. R—B 1   ......

Threatening eventually Kt—Q R 4.

11. ......   Kt×Kt
12. B×Kt   R—Q 1

White intended 13. P×P, P×P ; leaving a weakling on the half-open file. The text-move parries this possibility, but only temporarily, and would therefore have been better replaced by 12. ....Q—Q 1.

13. Q—Q 2 !   ......

With the object, in case of 13. ....Kt—Q 2, for instance, of placing the Queen on the comfortable spot Q Kt 2 ; but Black's following

attempt to secure for his Queen the corresponding square brought me other, more aggressive ideas.

13. ......   B—Q 4
14. Q—B 4   Q—Kt 2 ?

In some way consistent—but neglect of development on the Q side will now prove immediately fatal. After 14. ....Kt—Q 2 ; 15. P—K 4, B—Kt 2 ; 16. P—Q 5 !, P×P ; 17. P×P, B—K B 3 (not 17. ....B×P ; 18. Kt—Kt 5 winning) he would have suffered a deal longer, but would have died just the same.

15. P×P   P×P

If 15. ....B×B P, then 16. B×P ! etc.

16. P—K 4 !   B—Q B 3

Or 16. ....B×K P ; 17. Kt—Kt 5, winning.

17. Kt—K 5   B—K 1

Position after Black's 17th move.

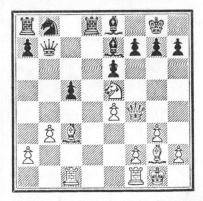

18. Kt—Kt 4 !   ......

The peculiarity of this sudden King's attack rests in the fact that it is not facilitated by any weakening pawn-move by Black on that section of the board.

18. ......   Kt—R 3

There was hopelessly little choice left, since the "natural" answer 18. ....Kt—B 3, would have led to a disaster very like the one which actually did happen:19.B × P!,K × B; 20. Q—R 6 ch, K—Kt 1 (or .... K—R 1 ; 21. Kt—B 6 and mate on the next move) ; 21. P—K 5, P—B 3 ; 22. B—K 4 !, P—B 4 ; 23. Q × K P ch, followed by Q × P, etc., winning ; and 18. ....B—Q B 3 would allow 19. B × P, K × B ; 20. Q—R 6 ch, K—Kt 1 ; 21. R × P ! etc.

19. B × P !   Black resigns.

The principal variation is now 19. ....K × B ; 20. Q—R 6 ch, K—Kt 1 ; 21. P—K 5, B—Q B 3 ; 22. Kt—B 6 ch, B × Kt ; 23. P × B, followed by mate.

GAME 114

NIMZOWITSCH'S DEFENCE

Consultation Game, Nice, April, 1931.

White:	Black :
DR. ALEKHINE	S. FLOHR
and Amateur	and Amateur

1. P—Q 4	Kt—K B 3
2. P—Q B 4	P—K 3
3. Kt—Q B 3	B—Kt 5
4. P—Q R 3	......

Nowadays this move of Sämisch is completely out of fashion—not only because it loses a *tempo* in order to force an exchange not too unwelcome for Black, but chiefly because it occupies square Q R 3, which otherwise might be useful for the Q B.

4.	B × Kt ch
5. P × B	P—B 4

6. Q—B 2   ......

To prevent an eventual ....Kt—K 5. Black could now, by playing 6. ....P—Q 4 ; 7. P × Q P, Q × P, obtain a position known from my recent title-match as satisfactory for him ; but his text-move also does not spoil anything.

6.	Kt—B 3
7. Kt—B 3	P—Q 4
8. P—K 3	Castles
9. P × Q P	K P × P

But here he misjudges the character of the position: as the following clearly shows, the isolation of the Q P is too big a price for the Bishop's diagonal Q B 1—K R 6. By retaking with the Queen, he would obtain after 10. P—B 4, Q—Q 3 ; 11. B—Kt 2, the position of my 10th game against Euwe (Hague, Oct., 1937) which some theorists (for instance, Fine) consider even advantageous for the second player. Without going so far, one must admit that this line would afford a fighting game, with possibilities for both sides.

10. P × P !   ......

Ending any possible Black hopes of blocking with an eventual .... P—B 5.

10.	Q—R 4
11. B—Q 3	Kt—K 5

After this unnecessary effort (since White's Pawn at Q B 3 in fact cannot be taken), Black's position already becomes critical. Also 11. ....B—Kt 5 would not have sufficed to re-establish the balance, since White would permit the exchange of his Knight and simply answer 12. R—Q Kt 1 or 12. P—Q R 4 ; but 11. ....Q × P (B 4) could and should be played.

12. Castles   ......

Of course the right move, since Black cannot play either 12. ....

Q×P (B 6), because of 13. B×Kt,
or 12. .... Kt×P (B 6), because of
13. B—Q 2.

    12. ......   Q×P (B 4)
    13. P—Q R 4 !   ......

At last White has the opportunity
to correct his 4th move, and thus
eliminates the only serious defect
of his position.

    13. ......   R—K 1
    14. B—R 3   Q—R 4
    15. Q R—Kt 1 !   ......

If now 15. .... P—Q R 3, then 16.
P—B 4, Kt—B 3 ; 17. Kt—Kt 5
(threatening mate in two), P—
K Kt 3 ; 18. P×P, Q×Q P ; 19.
P—B 4 ! threatening B—B 4, etc.,
with a winning attack. Black's next
step must therefore be considered
a desperate attempt to alter the
normal course of the battle.

    15. ......   Q×B P
    16. B×Kt   Q×B
    17. B×P ch   K—R 1

It is certainly surprising that this
move, which looks more natural
than .... K—B 1, loses rapidly
perforce, while after the better move
White would have satisfied himself
with a (very palpable, it is true)
positional advantage by playing 18.
B—B 5, etc.

Position after Black's 17th move.

    18. Kt—Kt 5 ! ....

As in the previous game against
Stoltz, the mating attack com-
mences quite spontaneously and
succeeds in a very few moves.
Flohr at the beginning of his career
was sometimes superficial in the
defence of his King's position—
compare, for instance, his well-
known defeat by Mikenas at
Folkestone. But, certainly, he has
now become one of the most cautious (if not *the* most) masters
living !

    18. ......   P—K Kt 3

The consequences of this were as
easy to calculate as 18. .... R—B 1
(19. B—Kt 8 !) or 18. .... Kt—Q 1
(19. B—B 5 !). The only more or
less complicated variation is after
18. .... Q—K 2 ! which would have
led to the following finish : 19. P—
D 4 !, Γ—B 3 ; 20. B—Kt 8, P—
K Kt 3 ; 21. Q×P, P×Kt ; 22.
B—B 7, B—B 4 ! ; 23. Q—R 6 ch,
B—R 2 ; 24. R×P !, Q—B 1 ; 25.
Q—B 6 ch, Q—Kt 2 ; 26. Q×Q ch,
K×Q ; 27. B×R dis. ch followed
by 28. B×Kt and wins.

    19. B×P   ......
Of course !
    19. ......   P×B
    20. Q×P   R—K 2
    21. P—K 4 !   ......

A pretty *coup de grace.* If now
21. .... P—Q 5 (there is nothing
else), then 22. R—Kt 5, B—Kt 5
(again the only move) ; 23. Q—B 6
ch, R—Kt 2 (or K—Kt 1 ; 24. Kt—
K 6 !) ; 24. R×P, Q—B 1 ; 25. R—
K B 7, etc., wins.

                          Resigns.

GAME 115

FRENCH DEFENCE

Simultaneous exhibition in Reyk-
javik, August, 1931.

Black : A. Asgeirsson

1. P—K 4	P—K 3
2. P—Q 4	P—Q 4
3. Kt—Q B 3	Kt—K B 3
4. B—Kt 5	B—K 2
5. B × Kt	......

This variation has recently been favoured by the talented German master, K. Richter—but only in conjunction with 6. P—K 5 followed by 7. Q—Kt 4. The idea here was quite a different one—to maintain the tension in the centre as long as possible, finishing first the mobilisation of forces.

5.	B × B
6. Kt—B 3	Castles
7. B—Q 3	R—K 1

A loss of time ; instead, 7. .... P—B 4 was indicated. White in that case would have hardly anything better than 8. P × B P, Q—R 4 ; 9. Q—Q 2, etc., with about even prospects.

8. P—K 5	B—K 2
9. P—K R 4 !	......

Intending, of course, to sacrifice at R 7. But is this sacrifice absolutely correct ? My opponent, the one-time champion of Iceland, hopes for the negative and starts a counter-attack. If 9. ....P— K R 3 White would have obtained also a distinct advantage by continuing 10. Kt—K 2, P—Q B 4 ; 11. P—B 3, etc.

9.	P—Q B 4
10. B × P ch	......

The soundness of this stereotyped offer is based on the possibility of White exploiting *also* the central files for attacking purposes ; only the few checks on the King's side, as is easily seen, would not produce yet a decisive effect.

10.	K × B
11. Kt—Kt 5 ch	K—Kt 1
12. Q—R 5	B × Kt
13. P × B	K—B 1

Black hoped now to come easily out of trouble after 14. Q—R 8 ch, K—K 2 ; 15. Q × P, R—Kt 1 ; 16. Q—B 6 ch, K—K 1, etc. : but White's next move showed him that the situation was much more serious than he thought.

14. P—Kt 6 !	......

This Pawn cannot be taken since after 15. Q × P there would not be any defence against 16. R—R 8 ch, etc.

14.	K—K 2
15. P × K B P	R—B 1
16. Castles (Q R)	......

By no means an automatic developing move : White threatens now 17. Kt—Kt 5, which before did not go because of 17. ....Q— R 4 ch.

16.	P—R 3
17. P × P	......

Threatening 18. Kt—K 4.

17.	Kt—Q 2

Position after Black's 18th move.

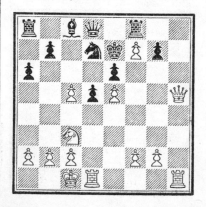

18. R×P !   ......

This secures the participation of all White's forces in the final attack. The main variation in case of the acceptance of this new offer is pretty : 18. P×R ; 19. Kt×P ch, K—K 3 ; 20. Kt—B 4 ch, K—K 2 ; 21. P—K 6, Kt—B 3 ; 22. Q—K 5 !, R×P ; 23. Kt—Kt 6 ch followed by mate in three moves.

18. ......   Q—R 4
19. Q—Kt 5 ch   ......

Preventing the escape of the black King to Q 1.

19. ......   K×P
20. R—R 7   R—K Kt 1
21. R—Q 4 !   ......

Not immediately 21. R×Kt ch, B×R ; 22. Kt—K 4 ? because of 22. ....Q—K 8 mate.

21. ......   Q×B P
22. R×Kt ch !   B×R
23. Kt—K 4   Q—Kt 5

Threatening again mate, but—

24. Kt—Q 6 ch   K—B 1
25. Q—B 6 ch !   P×Q
26. R—R 7 mate

The mating position is "pure" and, for a practical game, economical enough.

GAME 116

QUEEN'S INDIAN DEFENCE

Consultation Game played in Paris, October, 1932.

White :	Black :
DR. TARTAKOWER	DR. ALEKHINE
and Amateur	and Amateur

1. P—Q 4   Kt—K B 3
2. Kt—K B 3   P—Q Kt 3

3. P—K 3   B—Kt 2
4. B—Q 3   P—K 3
5. Q Kt—Q 2   P—B 4

Strategically important in order to counterbalance the now possible advance of White's King's Pawn.

6. Castles   Kt—B 3
7. P—B 4   ......

Instead of 7. P—B 3 or 7. P—Q R 3 eventually followed by P—Q Kt 3 and B—Kt 2 (Rubinstein), White adopts here a third plan, which has the slight disadvantage of a total absence of immediate threats in the centre—a circumstance that permits Black to finish quietly his development and to obtain an equal game.

7. ......   B—K 2
8. P—Q Kt 3   P×P

Also the simple 7. ....Castles followed by ....P—Q 3 was good enough. By the manœuvre in the text Black fixes White's Q P—which *may* become weak—but opens to the opponent the King's file and cedes him K 4.

9. P×P   P—Q 4
10. R—Kt 2   Kt—Q Kt 5

Less harmless than it looks at first sight : Black hopes to provoke sooner or later P—Q R 3 after which the manœuvre ....Kt—Q B 3—Q R 4 would become strong. Besides, White will have to count on the eventual ....Kt—K 5.

11. B—Kt 1   Castles
12. R—K 1   R—B 1
13. Kt—K 5   Kt—B 3 !

By no means a loss of time after his 10th move, since White's last two moves have entirely changed the situation : (1) Because of the Rook's position at K 1 Black's King's Bishop has got some prospects on Q Kt 5 ; (2) White's exposed central Knight may, under circumstances, be advantageously exchanged. Comparatively, the best for White was here still 14. P—Q R 3, which would be answered by 14. .... Q—B 2 followed by .... K R—Q 1.

14. Q Kt—B 3   ......

White seems to think that the preventative move 14. P—Q R 3 would in some way justify Black's last Knight's manœuvre and this is to punish the opponent for his "unscientific" play. But only a few moves will be needed to show whose appreciation of this position was the right one.

14. ......   B—Kt 5
15. R—K 3 ?   ......

Logical, but decidedly too risky. An about equal game could still be obtained by 15. Kt × Kt, B × Kt ; 16. R—K 3, Kt—K 5 ; 17. Kt—K 5, B—Kt 2, etc.

15. ......   Kt—K 2 !

This Knight is certainly trying to make himself useful : instead of being exchanged against a Knight it will now be posted on a very effective spot—K B 4—or else cost the life of the dangerous White's K's Bishop.

16. Kt—Kt 5   ......

Threatening the obvious sacrifice 17. B × P ch, Kt × B ; 18. Kt × Kt, K × Kt ; 19. Q—R 5 ch followed by 20. R—R 3—and trying at the same time to weaken the effect of Black's possible .... Kt—K 5.

16. ......   P—K R 3
17. Kt—R 3   ......

A sad necessity : a combination starting with 17. R—R 3 would

not work because of the simple reply 17. .... Kt—B 4 !

17. ......   B—Q 3

It is instructive to observe how the black pieces, after having taken advantage of the square Q Kt 5, desert it without having been forced to.

18. Q—K 2   Kt—B 4

The moment is well chosen, since the Rook cannot go back and has no safe squares on the third rank.

19. B × Kt   P × B

The pair of Bishops here are of great value because White has no permanent squares for his Knights in the centre, Black always being able to prepare and play .... P—K B 3.

20. R—Q B 1   R—B 2

With the main object of giving more room to the Queen.

21. P—B 3   Q—B 1
22. K R—B 3   R—K 1

Threatening simply Kt—Q 2 followed by .... P—B 3 and thus inducing White to simplify at positional cost.

23. P × P   Kt × P
24. R × R   B × R
25. Q—B 4   ......

Threatening eventually Kt—K B 4 ; but this threat—as a few other menaces of White in this game—is both obvious and harmless.

25. ......   Q—K 3
26. R—K 1   Q—Q 3 !

From now on the threat .... P—B 3 becomes acute.

27. Q—R 4   B—B 3
28. Q—R 3   ......

A tame attempt to save the day by exchanging Queens. Black, of course, flatly rejects this transaction.

28. ......   Kt—Kt 5 !
29. R—Q B 1   ......

There was no more adequate defence against Black's next move.

Position after White's 29th move.

29. ......   P—B 3 !

By making this move Black had to reckon with the following variations : I. 30. R × B, Kt × R ; 31. Q × Q, R × Q ; 32. Kt × Kt, R—K 8 ch ; 33. K—B 2, R—Q Kt 8 ; 34. B—B 3, R—B 8 and wins.
II. 30. Kt × B, Q × R P ch ; 31. K—B 1 (or 31. K—B 2, Kt—Q 6 ch etc.), Q—R 8 ch ; 32. Kt—Kt 1 (or 32. K—B 2, Kt—Q 6 mate), B—R 7 and wins. And also White's next desperate sacrifice permits a rapid and neat finish.

30. P—B 4   P × Kt
31. B P × P   R × P !

The prosaic 31. ....Q—K 2 ; 32. Kt—B 4, P—Q R 4, etc., would in the long run suffice, too—but the Rook sacrifice is much more forcible.

32. P × R   Q—Q 7 !
33. Kt—B 2   ......

As 33. R × B, Q—K 8 mate does not go, this is forced.

33. ......   Kt—Q 6 !
34. R—B 1   Kt × B
35. Q—K 7   Q—Q 4
36. Kt—K 4   B × P !
Resigns

GAME 117

RUY LOPEZ

Blindfold Simultaneous Exhibition in Hollywood (California), November, 1932.

Black : H. Borochow

1. P—K 4   P—K 4
2. Kt—K B 3   Kt—Q B 3
3. B—Kt 5   P—Q R 3
4. B—R 4   Kt—B 3
5. Castles   Kt × P
6. P—Q 4   P—Q Kt 4
7. B—Kt 3   P—Q 4
8. Kt × P   ......

I adopted here this old move for a particular reason : my opponent —one of the best Californian players —had defended the Ruy Lopez in exactly the same way against me in the Pasadena Masters' Tournament and reached, after the usual 8. P × P, quite a satisfactory position. Consequently, in the present blindfold game, I seized the first opportunity to leave the overexplored theoretical path. Although the text move is not the best— White's Knight having at this moment more value than Black's Knight—it is by no means a mistake.

8. ......   Kt × Kt

9. P×Kt   B—K 3

The two other playable moves
are here 9. ....B—Kt 2 and 9.
....P—Q B 3.

10. P—Q R 4   ......

This wing-diversion is too slow—
especially in view of White's insufficient development. More advisable
seems to be 10. B—K 3 followed by
P—K B 4 or Kt—Q 2.

10. ......   Kt—B 4
11. Kt—Q 2   B—K 2

Quite right, as White does not
threaten anything.

12. Q—K 2   P—Q B 3
13. P—Q B 3   Kt×B

The exchange is the consequence
of a rather instructive misappreciation of the position. Having obtained quite a satisfactory game,
Black imagines that he can already
dictate the law. He should instead
secure his King's position by
castling, or even first play 13. ....
B—B 4, with excellent fighting
chances.

14. Kt×Kt   P×P

Of course 14. ....P—Q 5 ; 15.
Kt×P, B—B 5 ; 16. Q—B 3, B×R ;
17. Q×Q B P ch, K—B 1 ; 18. K×
B, etc., would have been a very
bad speculation. After the text-
move, which is the logical consequence of the previous one, Black
expects 15. R×P, Q—Kt 3 ; 16.
Kt—Q 4, P—Q B 4; 17. Kt×B, Q
×Kt; 18. P—K B 4, P—B 4, followed
by Castles (K's side), etc., with prospects of an initiative in the centre.
But the following "intermediate"
move of White shows him that the
problem to solve will be far less
easy than he imagined.

15. Kt—Q 4 !   ......

If now 15. ....Q—B 1, then 16.
P—K B 4, P—Q B 4 ; 17. Kt×B,
P×Kt ; 18. R×P, Castles ; 19. B—
K 3, etc., with positional advantage
for White. Black's answer, although
it permits the opening of the central
file, is comparatively better.

15. ......   B—Q 2
16. P—K 6   P×P
17. R×P !   ......

A second little surprise for Black;
after 17. Kt×K P, B×Kt ; 18, Q×
B, Q—Q 2, etc., White's initiative
would vanish rapidly.

17. ......   Q—B 1

But if now 17. ....P—B4, then
18. Kt×P, B×Kt ; 19. Q×B *with
an attack against the Q R's Pawn :*
and also 17. ....Castles would, as
can easily be seen, have lost
material.

18. R—K 1   K—B 2 ?

This attempt to keep all the
earthly belongings will be refuted
in a convincing manner. The only
way of resistance consisted in 18. ....
Castles ; 19. Kt×K P, B×Kt ; 20.
Q×B ch, Q×Q ; 21. R×Q, B—
B 4 !; 22. B—B 4, R—B 3 ; 23.
R×R, P×R, after which White, in
spite of his far superior Pawn
position, would not have found it
easy to increase his advantage in a
decisive manner.

19. Kt—B 5 !   ......

Threatening not only 20. Kt×B,
but also—in many variations—20.
Kt×Kt P !, etc. And if 19. ....
Q—B 1 then 20. Kt—R 6 ch !,
K—K 1 (P × Kt ; 21. Q—R 5 ch,
etc.) ; 21. Kt—Kt 4, followed by
Kt—K 5, etc., with a winning
position.

19. ......   R—K 1

Also 19. ....P×Kt; 20. Q×B ch, followed by 21. R—K 3, etc., would be perfectly hopeless.

20. Q—R 5ch   K—Kt 1
21. Kt× P !   R—B 1

If 21. ....K×Kt, then 22. B—R 6 ch, followed by mate in three.

22. R—K Kt 4   K—R 1
23. R—K 3 !   P—K 4

This belated attempt to bring the unfortunate Q's Bishop to life again seems at first sight temporarily to protect everything (24. Q×P, B—B 3, or 24. R—R 3, B—K B 4! etc.). But the next rejoinder brings death.

Position after Black's 23rd move.

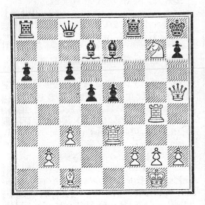

24. Kt—K 6 !   ......

Not being a problem-composer, I am not sure whether this actually *is* a "problem move." Anyhow, it is effective enough, as 24. ....B× Kt would have been followed by 25. Q×R P ch, K×Q ; 26. R—R 3 ch, B—R 5 ; 27. R×B mate.

Resigns.

GAME 118

RUY LOPEZ

Blindfold Exhibition on 15 boards, Tokyo, January, 1933.

Black : KIMURA

1. P—K 4   P—K 4
2. Kt—K B 3   Kt—Q B 3
3. B—Kt 5   P—Q R 3
4. B×Kt   Kt P×B

Although playable, this move is seldom adopted, since 4. ....Q P× B gives the second player quite a satisfactory game.

5. P—Q 4   P×P
6. Q×P   P—Q 3

More natural than 6. ....Q—B 3 tried by me against Duras in Mannheim 1014 (see, *My Best Games, 1908–1923*), which move can be advantageously answered by 7. P—K 5 !, Q—Kt 3 ; 8. Castles, etc. —for the acceptance of the Pawn sacrifice (8. ....Q×B P) would be decidedly too dangerous for Black.

7. Castles   B—K 3
8. Kt—B 3   Kt—B 3
9. B—Kt 5   ......

The positional advantage that White could obtain by playing here or on the next move P—K 5, Kt—Q 4, etc., did not look convincing enough.

9. ......   B—K 2
10. Q—R 4   B—Q 2
11. Q R—Q 1   Castles
12. P—K 5 !   ......

Now this advance secures White in one form or another a clear supremacy. The main variation I considered hereby was 12. .... Kt—Q 4 ; 13. B×B, Q×B (or 13. ....Kt×Kt ; 14. Q—R 4 !) ; 14.

Kt × Kt, P × Kt ; 15. Q—R 3 ! etc.,
bringing Black into trouble.

12.	Kt—K 1
13. B × B	Q × B
14. P × P	P × P
15. K R—K 1	Q—Q 1

A sad necessity, since after 15.
....Q—B 3 the answer 16. Kt—
K 5 ! would be practically decisive.

16. Kt—Q 4 !   ......

If now 16. ....P—Q B 4, then
17. Kt—B 6, Q—B 2 ; 18. Kt—
Q 5!, Q—Kt 2; 19. K Kt—K 7 ch,
K—R 1 ; 20. Q—R 4 (threatening
R—K 4 followed by Q × P ch!)
with a strong King's attack.

16.	Q—B 2
17. R—K 7	Kt—B 3
18. Kt—B 5 !	......

The simpler 18. Q R—K 1 would
maintain the advantage without
complications, but the line selected
was tempting—and proved correct.

18. ....   Q—Q 1

The comparatively most embar-
rassing answer for White, whose
pieces begin to "hang." The alternative 18. ....K R—K 1 would
give him an easier job : 19. Kt—
K 4 !, Kt × Kt ; 20. Q × Kt, R × R ;
21. Q × R !, R—K 1 ; 22. Q × P,
Q × Q ; 23. Kt × Q, R—K 7 ; 24.
Kt—B 4, R × Q B P ; 25. Kt—K 3
and wins.

19. R × Q P   R—K 1

Seems to force the variation 20.
R × R ch, Q × R ; 21. Kt—K 3,
after which Black, by playing, for
instance, 21. ....R—Kt 1 could
still set the "blind" opponent some
problems. All the more surprising is
the following manœuvre which in
a couple of moves deprives Black
of any fighting chances.

Position after Black's 19th move.

20. Kt—K 4 !   ......

The first point of the attack
started with 18. Kt—B 5, by which
White only seemingly allows a
desirable transaction for Black.

20. ......   R × R

Forced, as 20. ....Kt × Kt ; 21.
Q R × B, etc., would be hopeless.

21. Kt × Kt ch   K—R 1

Or 21. ....K—B 1 ; 22. Kt × P
ch, K—Kt 1 ; 23. Kt—B 6 ch, K—
B 1 ; 24. Kt × R, P × Kt ; 25. Kt ×
P, Q—K 1 ; 26. Q—Q Kt 4 !, P—R
4 ; 27. Q—B 3 and wins.

22. Kt × R   Q × Kt

Expecting not without pleasure
the variation 23. Kt—K 4, B—B 4 ;
24. R—Q 4, P—Q B 4 ; 25. R—B 4,
R—Q 1, etc., with a counter attack.

23. Q—K 4 !   ......

A most disagreeable surprise for
Black : not only the mate is protected, but White himself threatens
a mate at K R 7 and thus forces the
simplification.

23, ...   Q × Q

24. Kt×Q	B—K 3
25. P—Q Kt 3	P—Kt 3

Still hoping for 26. R×P?, B—Q 4. But after White avoids this "trap" also, Black could as well quietly resign.

26. Kt—B 5	B—B 4
27. R×B P	R—K 1

I was mistaken—there *was* still a chance to give a mate on the 8th rank . . .

28. P—K B 3	R—K 7
29. R×R P	R×P
30. Kt—K 4	B—K 3
31. P—K R 4	K—Kt 2
32. K—R 2	K—R 3
33. K—Kt 3	B—Q 2
34. P—R 4	P—B 4
35. Kt—Kt 5	R—B 6
36. R—R 7	R—Q 6
37. P—Q R 5	K—R 4
38. Kt×P	Resigns

GAME 119

RUY LOPEZ

Consultation Game, New York, September, 1933.

White :	*Black :*
I. KASHDAN	DR. ALEKHINE
and Amateur	and Amateur

1. P—K 4	P—K 4
2. Kt—K B 3	Kt—Q B 3
3. B—Kt 5	P—Q R 3
4. B—R 4	P—Q 3
5. P—B 3	B—Q 2
6. P—Q 4	Kt—B 3
7. Q—K 2	......

The protection of the King's Pawn by the Queen generally brings White more inconveniences than advantages and it would have been better therefore to substitute 7.

Castles, B—K 2 ; 8. R—K 1 etc.

7.	B—K 2
8. Castles	Castles
9. P—Q 5	......

There is hardly anything more advisable than this blocking-procedure, for Black threatens 9. .... Kt×Q P etc., and, on the other hand, 9. B—Kt 3 (or B 2) can be advantageously answered by 9. ..... P×P followed by ....Kt—Q R 4 (or Q Kt 5), etc.

9.	Kt—Kt 1
10. B—B 2	P—Q R 4 !

The idea of developing the Knight at Q B 4—analogous to many variations of the Indian Defences—is both tempting and positionally justified. A good alternative would be, however, the dynamical 10. ..... P—B 3 in order to open files on the Q's side before White has finished his mobilisation.

11. P—B 4	Kt—R 3
12. Kt—B 3	Kt—B 4
13. B—K 3	P—Q Kt 3
14. P—K R 3	P—Kt 3

Aiming at....Kt—K R 4—B 5. White's following seemingly "attacking" moves are in fact played only in order to prevent that possibility.

15. B—R 6	R—K 1
16. P—K Kt 4	B—K B 1
17. B×B	......

If 17. Q—Q 2, then 17. ....B—Kt 2 and White would eventually be forced to change in even less favourable circumstances.

17.	R×B
18. Kt—R 2	......

The move here planned P—K B 4 which will still more weaken the dark-coloured squares of White's position, must be again considered as a kind of indirect defence against Black's threatening initiative on the K R's file. White's bad luck is that he has no more time for the otherwise indicated Pawn advance of the Q's side—P—Q Kt 3 followed by P—Q R 3, P—Q Kt 4, etc.

18. ......   Q—K 2

There is no particular hurry to play ....P—R 4 since White cannot prevent it anyhow.

19. Q—K 3   P—R 4
20. P—B 4 !   ......

A purely passive defence starting with 20. P—B 3 would prove, after 20. ....K—Kt 2 followed by ..... R—R 1, etc., practically hopeless—and the Pawn sacrifice intended by the text-move is tactically justified. The only trouble is that Black need not accept it and White's K Kt P remains weak !

20. ......   P×Kt P
21. R P×P   P×P !

After 21. ....Kt×Kt P ? ; 22. Kt×Kt, B×Kt ; 23. Q—Kt 3, B—R 4 ; 24. P—B 5 White would obtain a strong attack.

22. Q×P   K—Kt 2
23. Q R—K 1   Q R—K 1
24. K—Kt 2   ......

Probably played in view of a possible exchange of Queens in case of ....Q—K 4. But Black rightly prefers first to increase his pressure by taking advantage of the open K R's file—especially as he sees that a triple attack against his Knight at K B 3 can be successfully met by a counter-attack.

24. ......   R—K R 1
25. R—K 2   R—R 5
26. Q R—B 2   Q R—K R 1
27. K—Kt 1   ......

Now it may seem for a moment that White's pressure against Black's K B 2 and K B 3 is more effective than the counter-threats on the K R's file, but the next two moves bring the situation into its true light.

27. ......   B—K 1 !

Not only defending the K B P but also giving room to the Queen's Knight.

28. Q—Kt 5   ......

The end-game after 28. Q × Kt ch etc. would be clearly to Black's advantage because of the powerful central square K 4 for his Knight.

28. ......   K—B 1 !

In its simplicity probably the most difficult move of the game : after having protected his Queen, Black threatens now 29. ....Kt× Kt P ! etc.

29. R—Kt 2   Q Kt—Q 2

Also this retreat, which permits the following seemingly dangerous rejoinder, had to be exactly calculated.

30. Kt—Kt 5   ......

Position after White's 30th move.

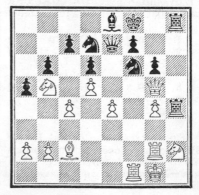

30. ......   Kt—K 4 !

The occupation of the dominating central square coincides here with the tactical decision of the game. As 31. Kt×B P would be refuted by 31. ....R×Kt ! ; 32. R×R, R×R ; 33. Kt×B, K Kt×Kt P ! ; 34. Q×Q ch, K×Q ; 35. B—R 4, R×P, etc., White has nothing better than to simplify and to hope for a miracle in the following end-game.

31. Q×K Kt   Q×Q
32. R×Q   B×Kt !

A most important "intermediate" exchange the omission of which would leave White excellent drawing chances.

33. P×B   R×Kt

In so many variations the decisive point.

34. R×R   R×R
35. R×P ch   ......

The only way temporarily to avoid material loss.

35. ......   K×R
36. K×R   Kt×P ch
37. K—Kt 3   Kt—K 4

In spite of the even material Black has quite an easy job, for besides his passed Pawn he has an obvious supremacy (two pieces against one) on the dark-coloured squares.

38. P—Kt 3   K—B 3
39. B—Q 1   Kt—Q 6
40. K—B 3   K—K 4
41. K—K 3   Kt—B 4
42. B—B 3   P—Kt 4
43. B—R 1   Kt—Q 2

Also the immediate 43. ....P—Kt 5 was good enough.

44. B—Kt 2   Kt—B 3
45. B—B 3   P—Kt 5
46. B—K 2   ......

In case of 46. B—Kt 2 Black wins easily by 46. ....Kt—R 4 followed by ....Kt—B 5 etc.

46. ......   Kt×K P
47. B×P   Kt—B 3
48. B—B 3   Kt×P ch
49. K—Q 2   K—Q 5
50. P—R 3   Kt—B 6
51. B—B 6   P—R 5 !
52. K—B 2   P—Q 4
53. P×P   K—B 5 !
Resigns

GAME 120

RUY LOPEZ

Simultaneous exhibition in Holland, October, 1933.

Black : A. van Mindeno

1. P—K 4   P—K 4
2. Kt—K B 3   Kt—Q B 3
3. B—Kt 5   P—Q 3

The Steinitz Defence, which was in fashion as late as the time of the Lasker-Capablanca match, 1921, has now completely disappeared from master practice. Actually, the modern treatment with the intermediate 3. ....P—Q R 3 (the so-called Steinitz deferred) gives Black, after 4. B—R 4, P—Q 3, considerably more choice of development plans than the self-restricting text-move.

4. P—Q 4   P×P

After 4. ....B—Q 2 the most promising line for White would be 5. Kt—B 3, Kt—B 3 ; 6. B×Kt, B×B ; 7. Q—Q 3 ! etc.

5. Q×P   ......

Of course 5. Kt × P is also good. By the text-move White plans already Castles (Q R).

5.	B—Q 2
6. B × Kt	B × B
7. Kt—B 3	Kt—B 3
8. B—Kt 5	B—K 2
9. Castles (Q R)	Castles
10. P—K R 4	......

This position has already occurred as long ago as in a tournament game of Anderssen's in Baden-Baden, 1870, in which the German champion played here 10. K R—K 1— and finally drew. In order to verify once more the value of that move I played it in Folkestone, 1933, against Anderssen's namesake, the late Danish master, E. Andersen, but although the game ended in my favour its first stage (after 10. ....Kt—Q 2; 11. B × B, Q × B; 12. R—K 3, Q—B 3; 13. Kt—Q 5, B × Kt; 14. P × B, Q × Q, etc. was not unsatisfactory for Black. The move in the text is sharper as Black must make some effort in order to dislodge White's Bishop from Kt 5.

10. ......   P—K R 3

Not to be condemned, because Black is not obliged to take the Bishop with the Pawn and he can do that only when it will be perfectly safe.

11. Kt—Q 5   ......

A correct and exactly calculated offer which Black should not accept. Still even more appropriate in order to maintain the tension was first 11. K—Kt 1.

11. ......   P × B ?

Although the final point of the sacrifice was very difficult to fore-

see, the acceptance has to be decidedly condemned : it was obvious enough that the opening of the K R-file means here a deadly danger, and, what is more, Black had here a perfectly safe (for the moment, anyhow) defence by continuing 11. ....Kt × Kt; 12. P × Kt, B—Q 2, etc.

12. Kt × B ch !   ......

Of course not 12. P × P, Kt × Kt; 13. P × Kt, B × P ch, etc., with sufficient defence.

| 12. \...... | Q × Kt |
| 13. P × P | Kt × P |

Also after other Knight's moves the doubling of Rooks on the R's file would prove decisive. And if 13. ....Q × P, then 14. P × Kt, Q × Q; 15. R × Q, B × Kt; 16. P × B, K R—K 1; 17. R—K Kt 4 !, P—K Kt 3; 18. R (4)—K R 4 followed by mate.

14. R—R 5   Q—K 3

In case of the immediate 14. .... P—B 4 White would force the win in a similar manner to the text : 15. P—Kt 6, Q—K 3; 16. Kt—K 5 !, Kt—B 3 (otherwise 16. Q R—R 1, etc.); 17. R—R 8 ch !, K × R; 18. Q—R 4 ch, K—Kt 1; 19. R—R 1, etc., with an unavoidable mate.

15. Q R—R1   P—B 4

After this Black seems to be temporarily safe since after 16. P—Kt 6, Q × Kt P; 17. Kt—K 5, he would obtain Rook and two minor pieces for the Queen by 17. .... Q × R; 18. R × Q, P × Kt, etc. But a spectacular transposition of moves ruins his hopes.

Position after Black's 15th move.

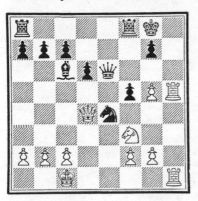

16. Kt—K 5 ! ! ......

A surprise move, whose object is

to weaken the protection of Black's Q 4.

16. ......   P × Kt

As 16. ....Q × Kt ; 17. Q × Q, P × Q ; 18. P—Kt 6 loses instantly, Black has obviously no choice.

17. P—Kt 6 ! ......

The point : if now 17. ....Q × Kt P, then 18. Q—B 4 ch followed by mate in three moves. Without the preliminary 16. Kt—K 5, P × Kt Black would still have the defence ....P—Q 4.

Resigns.

LIST OF OPENINGS

N.B. The (b) after opponent's name means Black; the (w) means White

LIST OF OPPONENTS